Borland® C++ 4.0

Object-Oriented

Programming

B O R L A N D   P R E S S

Borland® C++ 4.0 Object-Oriented Programming

Marco Cantù
Steve Tendon

RANDOM HOUSE
ELECTRONIC PUBLISHING

New York

Borland C++ 4.0 Object-Oriented Programming

Copyright ©1994 by Marco Cantù and Steve Tendon

Book composed and produced by The Coriolis Group

Published in the United States by Random House, Inc., New York, and simultaneously in Canada by Random House of Canada, Limited. Manufactured in the United States of America.

First Edition

0   9   8   7   6   5   4   3   2   1

ISBN 0-679-75154-8

New York   Toronto   London   Sydney   Auckland

Contents

PART TWO

OBJECT-ORIENTED LANGUAGE CONSTRUCTS 125

5 Abstract Data Types, Classes, and Objects 127

Acknowledgments

As is true of most books, this one owes a lot to many peaople. In particular we would like to thank Ivo Quartiroli of Apogeo for first suggesting to write it; Tamah Swenson for the initial contacts with Borland; Bruce Eckel and David Intersimone for their initial encouragement and the chats we have made from time to time (using e-mail, during our visits to the States, and theirs to Italy); Michael Hyman for his continuos explanations on Borland's long term strategies for programming languages; and Stefano Maruzzi for insightful suggestions on Windows programming.

A special thank you to Nan Borreson and Karen Giles for keeping us informed with late-breaking news and coordinating between Random House and Borland, and to Steve Guty for coordinating all efforts in producing the book, and for his valuable suggestions and endless support. Also, we don't want to forget Keith Weiskamp and the Coriolis Group for their hard work in typesetting the manuscript and correcting it on our request, and the people of Borland who read manuscripts sending us knowledgeable advice and suggestions, particularly Bob Bourbonnais and Tom Orsi.

Marco would also like to thank all of his students of C++ programming courses: discussing with them and figuring out new examples to describe the language concepts had a very positive effect on the revision of the book. The same holds for several other people and C++ programmers he has met in the last years (including representatives of Borland Italy, people on Compuserve Forums, and some friends of the San Marino Republic).

Although they were not involved the book directly, several of his friends provided support for the effort, including the girl Marco (happily) married while the book was under revision.

Foreword

One of Borland's most pivotal corporate moves has been the decision to embrace object-oriented technology as a key tool in the art of software craftsmanship. To truly realize the benefits of object orientation requires more than lip service to the idea—it requires that you re-examine the whole process of conceptualizing the task at hand.

Here at Borland, we've adopted an object-oriented approach across the board, from our development tools to the end-user application products we build with those tools. We've found that object-oriented technology has let us build better products faster, with a whole slew of very desirable side effects, ranging from the UFOs (User-Friendly Objects) that provide a consistent user interface across a range of Borland products, through the ability to integrate the activities of almost all Borland products with object-oriented tools.

We have also seen very positive benefits in other areas, such as the ability to create new international versions of our products more readily—the behavior and methods of our applications stay the same, while only the language used in messages to and from the user changes.

I think you'll find this updated book/disk edition of Steve Tendon and Marco Cantù's previous BC++ 3.1 book appealing. regardless of how much or little other exposure you're had to object-oriented programming. The authors have done an exceptional job of covering the basics in such a way that the neophyte can follow the discussion, without putting the more advanced reader to sleep. They also tie in the basics to major issues shaping the debate over future directions in object-oriented programming, providing a nice overview of trends to watch. Of course, I particularly appreciate the way they put all these concepts into play with the features of Borland C++ 4.0, including exception handling, Run-Time Type Information (RTTI), and the new features of ObjectWindows 2.0. And having all the code immediately available on disk should make it easier to focus on programming concepts instead of typing skills. If you're trying to get up to speed on C++ from a background of traditional procedural languages, this book and Borland C++ 4.0 are a winning combination.

Preface

*This book is dedicated
from Marco to Lella (now his wife)
and from Steve to Sötnosen.*

The book you're reading is the result of the investigation, experimentation, and enthusiasm of two programmers who have discovered (in different times and different ways) object-oriented programming. Now that this approach is becoming popular and widespread—also thanks to the C++ compilers from Borland International—we thought it might be useful to introduce the general ideas in a systematic and thorough way.

We hope that this book, the outcome of more than a year and a half of work, can be useful to those who would like to learn the C++ language—for those who know the C language or any other object-oriented language, as well as for those who have only a basic knowledge of programming.

The goal that has driven us in writing this text is to cover all important issues related to the C++ language, the programming methodology, the development environment, and the available libraries. Therefore, many subjects are covered: compilers, libraries, classes, objects, debuggers, polymorphism, class hierarchies, overloaded operators, Windows, inheritance, reusability, virtual functions, and so on. At the same time, different programming styles are described: object-oriented programming, evolutive programming, defensive programming, contractual programming, functional programming, and event-driven programming.

We've tried not to let ourselves be influenced by the current object-oriented craze (and everything that even smells object oriented today is extremely fashionable); we have also tried to address some subjects that have been forgotten, despite their importance. Obviously not every aspect of object-oriented programming is investigated exhaustively. We've tried, above all, to stress those C++ constructs that are useful for object-oriented programming, and in a practical manner.

The motivation behind this approach is simple: what's important today is not to become an expert in some field but to be able to face the complexity of the whole. This book is the outcome of the attempt to give a global picture of object-oriented programming in C++ for the DOS operating system and for the Windows environment. In this sense, this book is not the sum of many manuals, but a road map that C++ programmers can use to put everything in its place.

The Contents of the Book

The material in this book is presented in three parts. The first part is a general survey of Borland's development environment, object-oriented design, and the C++ language. The second part is the description of the language's instructions and constructs, with particular attention paid to object-oriented programming. The third part is about advanced tools and methods and ends by covering Windows programming.

In detail, the contents of the chapters are:

Part 1: The Basics

- Chapter 1 provides a brief introduction to C++.

- Chapter 2 describes the development environment of Borland C++ and introduces this programming language through some examples.

- Chapter 3 is a theoretical introduction to object-oriented programming and design, and includes a general description of an object-oriented design methodology and an introduction to object-oriented languages and C++.

- Chapter 4 presents the basic syntax elements of C++: simple and aggregate data types, operators, expressions, control statements, and functions. Most of these elements are common to the C language, and for this reason are only outlined here for programmers who do not already know the C language.

Part 2: Object-Oriented Language Constructs

- Chapter 5 introduces one of the fundamental elements of any object-oriented language: classes. Particular attention is paid to the topic of data abstraction.

- Chapter 6 explains the new meaning that functions take in the context of object-oriented programming; in particular, class member functions are explained, along with other advanced features like function and operator overloading.

- Chapter 7 describes a fundamental principle of object-oriented programming languages: inheritance among classes, which is explained using several examples.

- Chapter 8 covers polymorphism and dynamic binding, concepts that are peculiar to object-oriented programming.

- Chapter 9 describes hierarchies of classes with inheritance relationships, the key to good object-oriented design.

- Chapter 10 is about genericity and describes how to put into effective use one of the C++ language's most recent enhancements: templates. These are a fundamental component in writing reusable and generic code.

- Chapter 11 covers exception handling, a new feature of the C++ language which enables you to write more robust code.

Part 3: Advanced Tools and Methods

- Chapter 12 is about Run-Time Type Information (RTTI), another new mechanism of the language used to have some dynamic information on the data-type of an object.

- Chapter 13 provides some important discussions on code reusability and evolutionary development, which are made easier by object-oriented programming.

- Chapter 14 focuses on the efficiency of an object-oriented language and on the programming paradigms to avoid bugs (defensive programming vesus contractual programming and assertions) The debugger is explored, too.

- Chapter 15 describes the standard C++ libraries, such as the one defining input-output classes and Borland's Container Class Library. The importance of class libraries is emphasized, especially with regard to code-reusability issues.

- Chapter 16 explores the event-driven architecture even further by introducing Windows programming. Traditional Windows programming is then compared to the object-oriented approach made possible by Borland's ObjectWindows Library.

- Chapter 17 is entirely devoted to advanced application development techniques using the ObjectWindows Library.

The Companion Disk Samples

This text has several specific features that are worth describing. The first is the presence of a huge number of examples, with complete source code (sometimes divided in several files): all of the examples have been thoroughly tested. Sometimes the output of examples is shown in order to illustrate how they work so that you won't necessarily have to compile and run them.

All complete source code file listings that appear in the text are identified by their own *filename* at their beginning. These source files are all included in the companion disk. You have to install these samples following the simple instructions in the readme file of that disk. Installing the source code files will copy more than a hundred complete code samples, and place them in several directories. There is a main subdirectory for each chapter (numbered 02, 04, 05, and so on up to 17). The files of each chapter are further divided in subdirectories, their names referring to the name of the example itself. Usually there is one full example for each subdirectory, but sometimes related samples are place together. Each sample has a ready to use Borland C++ 4.0 project file (with the typical *.ide* extension) you can use directly. There are however a cuople of souce code files which do not have a corresponding project because they are not meant to be compiled.

To help you locate the proper disk directory, you will find in the text's margin an indication of the subdirectory the correspoding file is placed into. For example, if you see the indication of *05\date* at the side of the text, it means that you will find the source code in sudirectory *date* of directory *05*. Furthermore, all of these chapter subdirectories are placed under the default *bcppbook* directory, which is suggested by the companion disk installation program (therefore, the complete path name is *\bcppbook\05\date* plus the file name).

The Structure of the Text

The book also includes several quotations of other authors, with a bibliographic reference following each quote. The corresponding bibliography provides a complete list of references.

The introductory quotations at the beginning of each chapter refer directly to the subject of the chapter. These quotations have been chosen mainly for their contents, but also in response to the wisdom expressed by their authors.

Another aspect already mentioned is a series of exercises and questions at the end of each chapter (except Chapter 1). These are meant to involve you in some personal experiments with the chapter material. You might even change the programs or write new ones. Sometimes you are also invited to analyze and compare the ideas of object-oriented programming against your own knowledge and background.

Now—armed with the Borland C++ compiler—you are ready to delve into the rest of this book. As you read, keep in mind this phrase from Stroustrup: *"There is no substitute for thinking."* Don't be disheartened by unfamiliar language constructs: you will certainly be able to master the various syntactical idiosyncrasies of the language with time and practice, or more simply by playing around with the compiler and the examples in this book.

At the same time, though, do indeed focus on and try to fully understand and grasp the *ideas* behind these constructs. This way you will discover the real object-oriented side of C++. Enjoy the book!

Marco Cantù
Steve Tendon
Piacenza, Italy
January 31,1994

If you have any comments or questions concerning the book, feel free to use Marco's MCI or Compuserve e-mail addresses:

MCI ID: 504-6977,
CIS: 100273, 2610.

PART ONE

The Basics

1

Introduction

Programming is a constructive art. How can a constructive art be taught? One method is to crystallize elementary composable principles out of many cases and exhibit them in a systematic manner. But programming is a field of vast variety and often involves complex intellectual activity. [Wirth 76]

Who Has Never Played with Legos as a Child?

Legos are just small brightly colored plastic bricks that might seem trivial when considered one by one. However, by combining them, you could easily create models of real objects: a tree, a table, or a car. Using Legos to create these models, you were able to build, for instance, a city or a landscape.

As an older child or an adult, you might even be able to build a model of the Space Shuttle or a country house. You just need the right "bricks" along with some skill in putting them together according to some scheme.

Changes are easy to make. If you want to add a Lego tree to your Lego garden around your Lego house, you can do so within minutes: you build the tree and attach it somewhere appropriate. If you decide later to add a swimming pool, you might need to move the tree—maybe, with some wild imagination, onto the roof of the house!

Sometimes, though, things do not turn out as you have planned: that last ill-fated brick, placed incorrectly, will make the country house fall apart.

What does all this have to do with C++?

An object-oriented language is like a box of Legos. You start with many small instructions, which seem trivial when considered one by one. However, by combining these instructions, you can easily model real objects, which at first will be very simple. Later you will be able to combine these objects to describe more complex situations.

As you increase your skill in object-oriented programming, you can simulate very complex systems: you just need the right "objects" and the ability to put them together according to a design criterion.

Object-oriented programming encourages you to proceed by successive trials, and it allows a great degree of experimentation. Even errors and problems will present learning opportunities.

Essentially this book describes the Lego box (the Borland C++ compiler) and the bricks (the C++ keywords), and explains how to put them together (object-oriented programming) according to well-defined design ideas (object-oriented design) to build complex systems (Windows applications).

The Lego Box: The Borland C++ Compiler

The examples and explanations in this book apply a real-world tool: the Borland C++ compiler. We preferred not to write a generic book on C++, opting instead to give it "life" by referring to a specific environment. We'll outline the basic features of this environment and describe a variety of Borland C++ software tools (like, for instance, the debugger and the class libraries).

This is not a "user's guide" to the compiler; it is a book about object-oriented programming in C++. Although it is true that this book can stand by itself (that is, even without a compiler at hand), it is in connection with the Borland C++ compiler that the book reveals its full usefulness and potential.

Borland's integrated development environment is not described in every detail; only the essential features are outlined (as well as some of the more advanced features). For instance, when the focus is on a subject for which some tool or compiler option is available, we'll describe how to use them. We'll also explain techniques for using many of these additional tools (like the debugger) in combination with Borland's class libraries (Container Class Library, and ObjectWindows).

If you do not have a real C++ compiler at hand, it might be more difficult to read this book, and learning the language will be harder, because it is important to be able to experiment with all constructs as they are introduced. (This is why some "points to consider" will be proposed at the end of each chapter.)

The Bricks: The C++ Keywords

The focus of this book is on the C++ programming language. To learn C++ you need a basic knowledge of some other programming language (like Pascal, Basic, C, FORTRAN) and some basic practice in programming. Apart from these prerequisites, you only need a little patience—and the compiler at hand.

The book illustrates the language step by step, from the most basic elements to the most advanced. While some issues will be explained in detail, others are only sketched. We do not attempt to explain every detail of C++'s predecessor, the C language (which you're not required to know). All basic constructs and statements of the language are described, both those that are "traditional" as well as those that are specific to object-oriented programming.

The C++ language is very powerful and in some ways peculiar. According to its inventor, Bjarne Stroustrup, there are "three fundamental ways to use C++: as a better

C, [as a language] supporting data abstraction, and [as a language] supporting object-oriented programming." [Stroustrup 91B]

➤ *Note:* The phrase "data abstraction" refers basically to the ability to add (to a programming language) user-defined data types that describe abstract entities, such as a complex number, a date, a deck of cards, a group of people, an airplane, and so on.

From one point of view, "object-oriented programming" can be seen as an extension of data abstraction, because it allows you to define new abstract data types deriving properties from those data types that have already been added to the language. In this way it is possible to define "families" of related abstract data types (usually called hierarchies).

In this book, we focus on object-oriented programming. Thus C++ is described as an object-oriented programming language, and you are invited to adopt this particular programming style, although it should not be taken as absolute dogma.

In fact, it's always the language's inventor who finds fault with "people who rant and rave that you have to use C++ in a truly object-oriented way," and he holds that

you have to use C++ the appropriate way. "Appropriate" means relative to your experience, relative to your application, and relative to your hardware base. You have to think. There is no substitute for thinking. There are people who think that "object-oriented" will solve your problems for you. Rubbish! "Object-oriented" is [only] a way for you to attack your problems. It is not a magic wand that makes the problems go away without thought or effort. [Stroustrup 91B]

In this book, the language is described from a particular point of view (that of sound object-oriented programming), but provides you with alternatives and explains their pros and cons. This approach will give you the tools to decide whether you want to follow this approach to programming. In any case, it is important to know the object-oriented features of the language.

The Construction Process: Object-Oriented Programming

Stroustrup also asserts that "in the long term to get the most out of something like C++ you will need to use it in an object-oriented manner. You need to use object-oriented programming and to do object-oriented design. However, you also have to get from here to there." [Stroustrup 91B]

This last sentence concisely synthesizes the aim of this book: "to get from here to there"—that is, to switch from the concepts and methods of traditional programming to the new ones of object-oriented programming.

We've written this book with the conviction that it is simpler to make the transition from conventional programming to object-oriented programming, if you consider C++ as an object-oriented programming language. If you make this transition you will, along the way, learn to distinguish those elements of C++ that make it a better C and a C with data abstraction; these elements, though, must be clearly related to the principles of object-oriented programming.

Therefore, the approach of this book differs from those that follow a more gradual transition, where well-known concepts of the C language get enriched, then data abstraction is presented, and at last C++ is treated as an object-oriented programming language.

Once you understand the components of C++, and understand the fundamental ideas of object-oriented programming, you will certainly be more conscious of the different features and, thus, be free to decide which of the three ways is, as Stroustrup says, the one most *"appropriate"* for you, and your actual programming task.

The Architecture: Object-Oriented Design

This book explains the basic elements of object-oriented programming, and addresses design issues. What sense does this make, if you just want to learn to program in Borland C++?

If you wish to use a programming language to its full potential, you have to use it correctly. The so-called procedural languages—the traditional languages like Pascal, C, FORTRAN, and so on—have all been designed for a very particular way of programming, in which top-down functional decomposition is the most common methodology.

At the same time, to use an object-oriented programming language to its full potential (and that's how we intend to use C++) you must follow a specific methodology. This connection between programming language and design methodology is not always binding: at times you can even break the rules.

On the other hand, if the rules of the language help the programmer by providing useful constructs, and if the compiler encourages a correct usage of these constructs, then it is certainly better to use a methodology based on these rules.

In fact "the fields of software design methodology and programming language design can converge, and in some cases, they already have. The most striking example of this trend is information hiding (as a design methodology) and data abstraction (as a language design principle)." [Ghezzi 87] Object-oriented programming and object-oriented design are based on these two elements.

➤   *Note:* In short, information hiding is a design guideline for which every module of a system (such as the definition of a function or a user-defined data type) should conceal at least one implementation choice. Information hiding involves data abstraction in that the new data types hide, to the rest of the system, their "details," such as their actual internal representation and the algorithms of their access functions.

The Complex Structures: Windows Applications

The ideas we've just put forth, regarding a development methodology and the concept of using C++ as an object-oriented programming language, open the way for the building of more complex systems. An object-oriented design methodology makes it possible to subdivide complex systems into subsystems, making these more independent from one another.

Furthermore it is possible to reuse the code that describes these subsystems by means of class libraries, which are much more powerful and flexible than the function libraries offered by traditional programming languages. As you will see, it is possible to modify the abstractions described by the classes of a library without having access to their source code. In fact, object-oriented languages make it easy to effectively reuse the code that is developed by one or even more programmers.

By taking advantage of the class libraries developed by Borland, you will—by the end of this book—be able to build programs with an advanced user interface. In the same way, you will implement applications for the Microsoft Windows operating environment. Although Windows is pleasant and easy to use, programming for the Windows environment can be difficult.

A thorough reading of this book will provide you with a mastery of C++, understanding of object-oriented programming, and the ability to work with Windows applications.

2

An Introduction to the Environment and C++

In an integrated environment, the tools work well together. For example, when debugging a program, one can call the editor, fix the problem, recompile and re-link all without exiting the debugger. In the future, we can expect to see more powerful, more uniform, more integrated, and user-friendlier environments. [Ghezzi 87]

Although the goal of this book is to teach you object-oriented programming with the C++ language, it's necessary to focus on the Borland C++ compiler used to write, compile, and debug all the examples. This approach will help you to better understand the examples proposed. Although the C++ language doesn't depend on the compiler— it's almost a standard—we assume that you have the Borland compiler and will use it to try out the examples, to extend them, and to write your own programs. However, even if you have a different C++ compiler, you will probably still be able to use most of the examples unchanged with the exclusion of those involving Borland libraries.

If you are new to the Borland C++ compiler, this chapter will provide you with a simple introduction to its main properties. In the last part of the chapter, we present some C++ programs, for you to get acquainted with some elements of the C++ language and its syntax. These examples are provided as a starting point to show how to use the compiler. The constructs used in the examples will be explained more thoroughly in later chapters, with a gentler approach.

This chapter describes some general aspects of the Borland C++ package: the integrated environment, the editor, the help system, and the compilation procedure. Only the most relevant issues are described in detail, some of the issues will not be discussed until later chapters. However, this is not a guide to the environment; we assume that you have the Borland manuals and that you have experimented with the compiler (and have browsed its help system).

The Different Packages

The first problem you face is that more than one Borland C++ compiler exists. This book covers all of them, since the programming language they compile is the same.

Borland has two compiler lines: Turbo C++ and Borland C++. Turbo C++, the low end compiler line, comes in two flavors, Turbo C++ for DOS and Turbo C++ for Windows. The two products are tailored for their specific environments. Turbo C++ for DOS cannot be used to write Windows applications, and Turbo C++ for Windows cannot be used to write DOS applications. In fact, if you try to write a DOS application using Turbo C++ for Windows, it will do its best to change your application from a DOS application into a Windows application using a special library called *EasyWin*.

➤   *Note:* The *EasyWin* library is transparent when used for ordinary DOS character-based programs. All examples in the chapters can be compiled without problems. Instead of program output being sent to the full screen, it is directed to a "terminal" window that looks like an ordinary "Windows window" but behaves like a teletype.

   EasyWin can also be used to direct DOS output functions from within a "real" Windows application to the dummy terminal window. In this case, you must initialize the library with an appropriate function call (*_InitEasyWin*).

Borland C++, the professional compiler, can be used to write both DOS and Windows applications. There is a specific version of the package for the OS/2 operating system. The DOS/Windows package has a Windows-based *integrated development environment (IDE)*, but can produce DOS applications, too. Borland C++ has also a better compiler, an optimizing compiler, and comes with a number of features not found in the Turbo C++ line, including some class libraries.

Compilers and Fundamental Tools

The Borland C++ package contains both integrated and command line compilers, which come in different versions for 16 bit and 32 bit targets. These compilers can generate code for Windows, without you having to buy additional libraries or tools, and include an *integrated assembler*.

The package also contains several debuggers: an integrated debugger and the stand-alone *Turbo Debugger*. These tools verify the execution of a program and help to find programming errors. You can run a program step by step, examining the functions that are called, setting breakpoints, evaluating expressions, inspecting the value and the memory location of any variable, and so on.

The *linker* is usually executed transparently by one of the integrated environments, but it is also accessible as a stand-alone application that you can execute from the command line.

Tools for Windows Programming

The Borland's compilers include some tools to develop Windows applications, such as the *Resource Workshop*, the *resource compiler*, and the *help compiler*.

The Resource Workshop is a Windows application used to prepare the "resources" of an application: cursors, icons, bitmaps, dialog boxes, menus, and so on (more about this in Chapters 16 and 17, which are devoted entirely to Windows programming).

The professional environment also includes a *resource compiler*, a tool used to translate the resources from the textual description to a Windows format (an operation that can also be done with the Workshop), and the *help compiler*, a tool that is used to generate the help system of Windows applications.

The last Windows tools are the *WinSight* application, used to monitor Windows messages and the execution of the programs under this environment, and (starting with version 3.1 of the compiler) the *WinSpector* application, used to trap faults that force the termination of the programs.

Other Tools in the Borland C++ Package

The professional version of the Borland compilers contains a number of useful tools, which are described in the manuals included in the package and in the on-line documentation (usually placed in the BC4\DOC directory). The following list describes the most important tools:

- **MAKE** is a standalone program manager, inherited from the UNIX and C development environments. MAKE can be used to handle a project, which has several source files, and can recompile the project automatically. This important tool can be replaced by the Project facility used by Borland's IDE, which is less general but much easier to use. The Project facility can find the dependencies among the files by itself, and is fully interactive (it doesn't require a so-called *makefile*).

- **TOUCH** is a complement to MAKE. TOUCH can update the time and date stamp of a file and is used to force a complete recompilation of a project (since MAKE checks which files have been changed by looking at their time stamps).

- **TLINK** is a stand-alone linker that can be used with the command-line compiler.

- **TLIB** is the *Turbo Librarian*, a program to build and handle libraries of compiled code, which can be linked to other programs. TLIB's job is complemented by other tools: **IMPLIB**, which generates import libraries for Windows; **IMPDEF**, which creates a module definition file corresponding to an import library; and **OBJXREF**, a tool used to retrieve information from object modules and document the names they define.

- **CPP** is a preprocessor that can be used to see the effect of the compiler directives (macros, inclusions, and conditional compilation) on a source code.

- **GREP** is a utility derived from UNIX used to search a string of text in one or more files. GREP can be used to find the name of one entity (a function or a class) by looking in several files.

Most of these tools come in two flavors, a 16 bit version and a 32 bit version. Usually the latter has a "32" in the name as in TLINK32 or CPP32. But before you can even think of using any of the above mentioned tools, you must get to know the main character of this book, the Integrated Development Environment (IDE).

A Note on Installing the Borland C++ Compiler

Naturally, before you can start working with the Borland C++ Compiler, you must install it on your computer. Although the install program is quite straightforward, before doing so, it might be wise to plan ahead and decide exactly *what* you want to install and *where* you want to put it. This is almost a necessary step if your computer is not well equipped with hard disk real estate, as the complete installation will eat up as much as (approximately) 70 Mbytes!

The *Install* program's opening screen will allow you to state where you want to put the main compiler directory. As you can see in Figure 2.1, this defaults to *C:\BC4*. Furthermore, you will also be allowed to indicate if you have Windows placed somewhere other than *C:\WINDOWS*.

➤ *Note:* The project files for the examples on the diskette assume that your include and library files are in directories located under *C\:BC4*. If you have installed the compiler with a different directory, you might have to modify the default directories for all the programs.

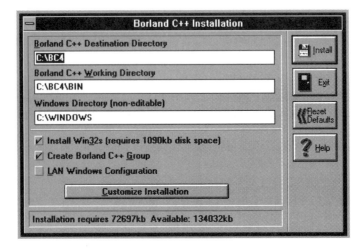

Figure 2.1 The installation program of Borland C++ 4.0

The next step is deciding which main components of the Borland C++ environment you want to install. Using the *Customize installation* button, you can see the different elements you can modify (as in Figure 2.2). Clicking on the buttons allows you to specify your choices in some dialog boxes, as in Figure 2.3.

If you (rather, your hard disk!) can afford to, you're best advised to make a full installation, and if you're new to C++, Borland C++, and/or programming in Windows, then you should really take a look at the samples that come with the package.

However, if you're short of disk space and/or need to develop for specific targets, then you might want to set up your system with only the components you really need. You can always add new components later by running the installation program again. And if you have the CD-ROM edition, you can access to the elements of a full installation without using your hard disk.

Even if you intend to use the interactive, Windows-hosted integrated development environment, consider the installation of the command line compiler as well, since it will install many utilities (such as *grep*) that you might be interested in using and calling from within the IDE. If you don't install the command line compiler, then these utilities will not be installed either.

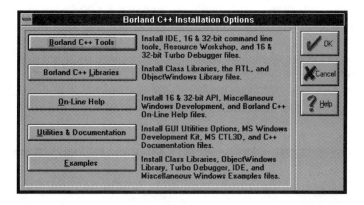

Figure 2.2 The installation program allows you to choose what to copy on the hard disk

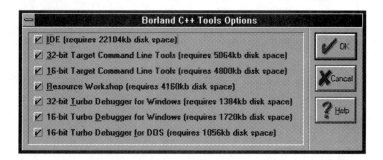

Figure 2.3 An example of the dialog boxes with installation options

If you do perform the complete installation, you will then end up with a new program group in Windows' *Program Manager*, as you can see in Figure 2.4.

The Integrated Development Environment

All the tools installed by the installation program make up a complete environment in which to develop application. The different tools included in the package are suited both for the novice programmer and for the professional. Out of the myriad program, the one that you use most in this book is the *IDE* (*integrated development environment*); it's the main program with which you can drive the entire development of a software project. The IDE includes a sophisticated text editor (with such bells-and-whistles like syntax highlighting, automatic indent, and much more), the actual C++ compiler, a very innovative and comprehensive project manager, and a full-blown Windows-hosted debugger. You can also custom tailor and reconfigure the IDE with your own set of programming tools: They will become an integral part of the development environment.

Borland has always advocated and pioneered the idea of an integrated development environment, starting way back with the very first Turbo Pascal compilers some 10 years ago. Being able to write, compile, and run a program without having to exit from the environment has been one of the most distinctive features of the Borland compilers (and one reason for Borland's success), together with their unbeatable compilation speed. Today, most of the compilers for personal computers have incorporated Borland's ideas, although Borland's commitment and extensive know-how has allowed its IDE to evolve further than most of its competitors.

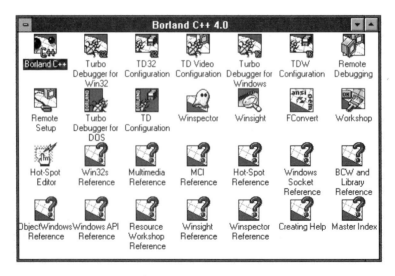

Figure 2.4 The Borland C++ 4.0 program group

Even in the user-friendly Windows environment, where "integration" of different applications is actually the point of the game, the Borland IDE gets well beyond the edge of "programmer-friendly" environments. As you might expect, the IDE allows for multiple edit windows (which can be moved, resized, scrolled, and so on); but there are also project and message windows. Most of the interaction with the system takes place through dialog boxes selected from menu items or from *local* menus (which are opened by *right*-clicking or pressing *Alt-F10* on the active screen element). Actually, the configuration of the whole system can be done this way, rather than using compiler switches. Another, innovative user interface feature is the introduction of multilevel dialog boxes, which are navigated by means of an expandable/collapsible hierarchy tree, more or less like the directory tree in Windows' *File Manager* application. Such dialogs can encompass a number of complicated, yet related, options, and allow you to get to the one you want with just a couple of mouse clicks.

Once you have installed the compiler, you can load the IDE by double-clicking on the *Borland C++* icon in the newly installed *Borland C++* group in the *Program Manager* application of Windows. The very first time you load the IDE, it will greet you with an *About* dialog box like the one shown in Figure 2.5. When you load the IDE subsequent times, it is smart enough to remember what you were doing in the foregoing session, and it will restore the exact situation that was left on exit: The same windows are open, the same parameters and options are set, and so on.

The first time you load the IDE, you can actually see what its window looks like. It is divided into three parts: a menu bar at the top, a status line at the bottom, and a large work area between the two. There is also a list of iconic buttons (called the *SpeedBar*) just beneath the menu bar; these buttons represent the most common operations you will perform in the IDE. The SpeedBar is also context sensitive, and will change its set of buttons according to the active *child* window you're working in.

The IDE is a true Windows MDI (*Multiple Document Interface*) application, so you will be able to open a number of windows inside it (as you will see shortly). The number of windows that can be opened at the same time is limited only by common sense. When there are several windows on the screen, only one is *active* (i.e., it

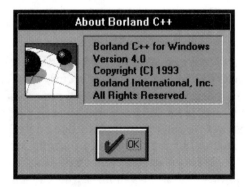

Figure 2.5 Borland C++ 4.0 "About box"

receives the keyboard input). If you get too many windows, you can move them around on the work area (the area between the SpeedBar and the status line); and if you move them "off" the IDE's main window, then scroll bars will appear in this latter window, just like in Windows' own *Program Manager* or *File Manager* applications.

First Things First

As soon as you close the initial *About* box (when you enter the environment for the very first time), a text editor window will appear. This window will be "*called*" with the name *noname00.cpp*. If you then open yet more editor windows, they will be called *noname01.cpp, noname02.cpp,* and so on, unless you save them with a specific name. As soon as you save the file (as well as when you open files that have already been saved), the title of the editor windows will contain the file's name, including its full path name.

One significant difference between version 4.0 of the Borland C++ Compiler and its earlier incarnations is the almost mandatory usage of *projects*. This is due to many reasons. First and foremost, this version of the compiler generates code targeted mainly at the Windows environment, and this implies that even the simplest program you can conceive of will be made up of several files.

In other words, while it was possible to write single source file programs with earlier versions of the compiler, with this new version it is not. So this means that before you actually can start typing C++ statements at the keyboard, you should set up a new *project* in the IDE. Note well that this does not mean that you cannot write code in a separate editor window—like *noname00.cpp*—and compile it to object code. However, if you do so, you must save the text to a file and then include that file in a project before you will be allowed to link and run it.

Another reason is that different software projects need different sets of compiler options and/or reference directories (for instance, for using existing third-party libraries): All these items can be managed easily through a project, instead of complicated command line options.

Therefore you should get into the habit of opening source files only if they belong to a well-defined *project*. Fortunately, the IDE is very well equipped for managing multifile projects.

Although the project manager is very capable and will allow you to keep track of all the files you will ever need in building your programs, another good working habit you should take up is that of setting up a separate directory for the whole project. Note that this step is not mandatory: You *can* keep several projects in the same directory, but then you will be responsible for the overall housekeeping therein.

In the following pages we will try out some features of the IDE, so we will need to set up a project, write a source file, and compile it. Even if this introductory example is very simple, we'd better stick to the mentioned rules right now, from the very beginning. So, before setting up our first project, we will make a specific directory for it. For instance, fire up the *File Manager* and create a new working directory (in the following text of this chapter, we will assume that this working directory will be *C:\BC4\TRYTHIS*, although you might prefer working somewhere else on your hard disk).

➤ *Note*: In the rest of the book, we work in the default directory made by the installation of the accompanying diskette, named *C:\BCPPBOOK*, as explained in the *Preface* and the *readme* file of the disk.

The Big Road Map: Projects

Once you have a new working directory, get back to the IDE and select the *New project...* command from the *Project* menu or use the *Create new project* button on the SpeedBar. You will immediately be presented with a *New Project* dialog box. Here you need to fill in at least the first two text boxes, and optionally specify the other items. In the first text box, *Project Path and Name*, you should type in the directory path and the file name you wish to give to the project. For instance, type in: *C:\BC4\TRYTHIS\TIME*. (You will see shortly why we call this project *time*); this will create a *time.ide* file in the specified directory, wherein *all* the compiler and project options will be retained.

Next, note that the *Target Name* text box is set automatically to *time*, the same name as the project. This will be the name of your main source file and of the resulting executable file. If you want to, you can call it something different from the project name: just type in the name you want to use in the *Target Name* text box.

Finally, from the *Target Type* list, select the kind of target code you wish to generate. For this introductory example, select *EasyWin [.exe]*. The dialog box should now look something like the one in Figure 2.6. Note that as soon as you select the *EasyWin* type

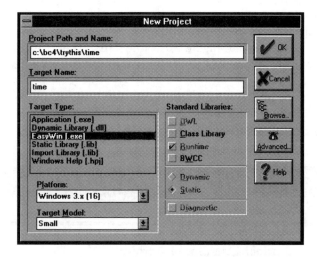

Figure 2.6 The *New Project* dialog box for the example we are building

of application, the selected *Standard Libraries* and the *Target Model* change accordingly (although we will not be concerned with these details now).

The *Target Type* list allows you to choose what kind of application you want to generate (we will get into details later). For the time being, suffice it to say that the *EasyWin* type of application will allow you to compile, link, and run in a simple "terminal type" window any "old-fashioned," character based C or C++ program. Although the resulting output capabilities might be limited and even disappointing (considering the richness of the GUI Windows environment), *EasyWin* applications will allow us to concentrate on the language features of C++ without bothering whatsoever about the many, many technicalities that you must master in order to set up a true Windows application. (You will find more information on writing Windows applications, with menus, dialogs, and all other bells and whistles you might expect, in the last chapters of the book.)

At this point we are almost ready to close the dialog. However there remains one small, but important, item to fix. The first time (during a Borland C++ session) you select an *EasyWin* application, the compiler will expect its source code to be written in the C Language, rather than in C++. Since, in this book, we are interested in discovering the features of C++, we must change this expectation to consider C++ rather than C. To do so, click on the *Advanced...* button in the *New Project* dialog. Another dialog, *New Target Options*, will appear. Here, select the *.cpp node* radio button in the *Initial Nodes* group.

The reason this dialogs refers to "nodes" will be immediately clear as soon as you close both the *New Target Options* itself and the *New Project* dialog. In the lower part of the IDE window there will appear a new *Project* window, the title of which will indicate the full path and file name you typed in the *Project Path and Name* text box of the *New Project* dialog. This window will contain a graphical representation of the dependencies among the various files that make up a project, and is the heart of the project management system of the IDE. This graphical representation takes on the form of a hierarchical tree, wherein each *node* represents a file in the project. For instance (as you can see in Figure 2.7), in this first, simple project, the file *time.exe* depends on the file *time.cpp*. In other words, the executable file depends on the source file. What a discovery!

For the time being, however, we will not be concerned with the project management capabilities of the IDE. Rather, we want to get to every programmer's meat-and-potatoes stuff: writing code.

Figure 2.7 The graphical outline of a project

The Editor and the Help System

When a source code file is listed in a project tree, it is very easy to get to it: Just double-click on its name in the project tree (or highlight it and press *Enter*). An editor window will immediately be opened on that file. For instance, if you double-click on the *time.cpp* file name in the newly created project, you will be presented with the *c:\bc4\trythis\time.cpp* editor window. Naturally, as this is a new file, there will be nothing in it. You are now ready to start typing some code.

One handy feature of the text editor is that it is well integrated with environment's help system, which is very knowledgeable about both the C++ language and its support libraries. For instance, if you type in *gettime* (the name of a function in one of the Borland C++ compiler's system libraries) and then hit the *F1* key, you will be presented with a help windows that describes that function, as you can see in Figure 2.8.

This help window is an ordinary Windows help window, so you can take advantage of all standard ways for navigating through it. For instance, you can follow the hypertext-like links to get further information on related topics, or use the help application buttons and/or menus to get around and search for specific topics. Most of the library function help windows will usually include a link to some sample code. For instance, if you follow the *Examples* link in the aforementioned help window, and then select the *gettime* link again, you will get to another help window showing how you would actually use the named function. Once you are in such a sample code help window, you can select the *Copy...* command from the *Edit* menu. Then, in the ensuing *Copy* dialog (Figure 2.9), select all source code you are interested in—for our purpose, select the whole example—and then click on the *Copy* button.

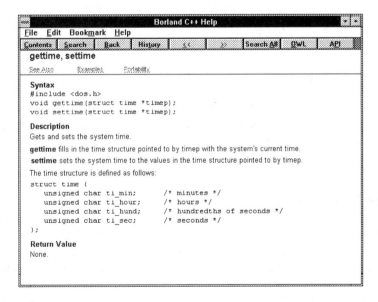

Figure 2.8 The on-line help information about the *gettime* function

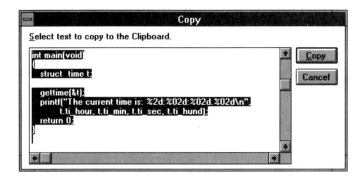

Figure 2.9   The dialog allowing you to copy an example from the on-line help

➤   *Note:* Do follow these steps. In the next few sections you will extensively modify and rewrite the example that you have just copied from the help system. The changes you will make might show off some of the constructs that are typical of C++, and that might even surprise an experienced C programmer. (We only want to make it clear that C++ is different from C. If you don't understand the meaning of the constructs shown here, don't worry; they will be explained through the book.)

Now, close the dialog and any other help windows, and get back to the original *time.cpp* editor window. Remove the *gettime* function name we used to call the help system, and select the *Paste* command from the *Edit* menu, to copy the sample code from the help system.

You will immediately notice another "programmer-friendly" feature of the IDE's text editor: syntax highlighting. The editor is smart enough to know the different "kinds of words" that can appear in source code text: comments, language keywords, constant numbers, system functions, predefined data types, strings, characters, and so on. And it will highlight each kind with a different color (you can even decide yourself what colors and/or text attributes to use for the various language elements). This is extremely useful, both when reading a program, and especially when writing it (since if you misspell a keyword, it won't change to the proper color). Another significant aid comes from colored comments, which will stand out clearly even if they span 10 or 20 lines of source code.

Compiling Your Source Code

So what have you gained from your temporarily visiting the help system: Without having written a single line of source code you now have a program ready to be compiled (although you might not fully understand its meaning, especially if you have never programmed in C before)! The first operation you should perform is to save your precious work: Select the *Save* command from the *File* menu. Since you have already given a name to the file (*time.cpp*) by setting up a project, you don't need to do so any more now. And since you selected the *cpp node* radio button in the *Initial Nodes* group of the *New Target Options* dialog, this file will be considered automatically as a C++ source code file. (Naturally *.cpp* stands for "**c-p**lus-**p**lus.")

Actually, the sample code you have copied from the help system and saved in the *time.cpp* file is a program written in the Standard C Language. At this point you could just compile and run it, and then see the result on the screen. (By the way, this would demonstrated that C can be considered as a subset of C++). These operations will be done shortly. However, before compiling the program, let's deliberately add an error to its source code so that you can get a feeling for the behavior of the integrated environment.

Compilation Errors

It's difficult—if not impossible—to write a program that runs without a glitch the first time you compile it; at least there will be some syntax errors—if not more serious functional errors. While you should have a correct program now, you can simulate the situation of an incorrect program by introducing an error intentionally.

To introduce an error, delete the first character of the *struct* keyword (on the eighth line of the program). Notice how syntax highlighting immediately signals that the general meaning of the word has changed. However, let's pretend we didn't notice this. Now that there is a spelling error in a keyword of the language, you can try to compile the program by pressing *Alt+F9* or clicking on the *Compile the file* button in the active *Edit window*'s SpeedBar.

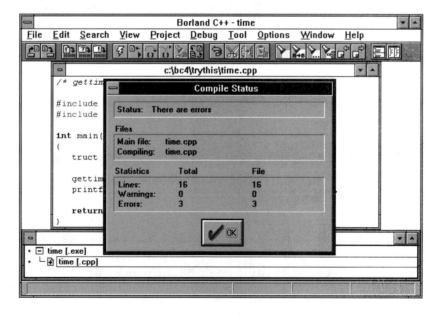

Figure 2.10 The *compilation* window after an error

A compilation window appears on the screen, describing the process as it goes on. Very shortly after, the process stops with the message dialog shown in Figure 2.10. When you click on the *OK* button, the system will show a *Message* window containing a list of error messages, as you can see in Figure 2.11.

Each message describes an error, and indicates where it occurred. In particular, the first message is highlighted:

undefined symbol 'truct'

If you move the highlight with the arrow keys, the corresponding source code window will automatically scroll to highlight and show the line containing the corresponding error. Once an error message is highlighted, you can press the *Enter* key (or double-click on an error message), and focus will immediately go to the corresponding editor window, with the cursor positioned on the line where the error occurred. You can easily move back and forth from one window to the other. You can also move from the line of an error to the following one (or the preceding one) without leaving the editor window containing the source code, by pressing the keys *Alt+F8* and *Alt+F7* (or using the corresponding SpeedBar buttons).

After identifying the error (which you should already know about, since you introduced it intentionally!), you can then close the *Message* windows (or iconize it).

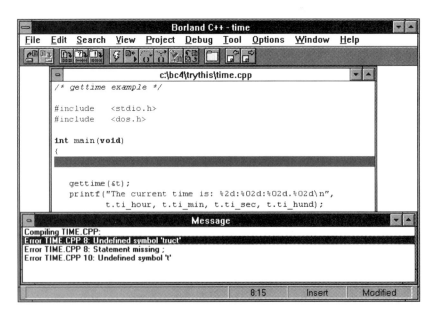

Figure 2.11 List of error messages inside the *message* window

One—No, Many Different Languages

Instead of correcting the error by rewriting the missing *s*, you can now delete the hampered *struct* keyword completely. If you now compile the program again, no error will be flagged whatsoever in the *compile status* window.

If you know the C Language, you will probably be puzzled. The program contains an error—a completely missing keyword—and the compiler didn't notice it! It did recognize the misspelled keyword, but didn't notice when it was missing. Well, maybe this happens because it is a C++ Compiler!

The only way to test it is to run the program. First, you have to close the *Compile Status* window, by clicking on the *OK* button or pressing *Enter* or *Spacebar*. Then run the program, for instance, by clicking on the *Make and run the current program* button on the SpeedBar. After a short time, during which the program is being linked, it will be executed. It will then generate an output window with the title *(Inactive: C:\BC4\TRYTHIS\TIME.CPP)* as you can see in Figure 2.12. (The actual run time of this program will be so short that it will stop almost as soon as the window is opened: that's why it is indicated as "inactive.")

➤ *Note*: This window is really generated by the *EasyWin* Library, which sends the result of the standard C output statements, like *printf*, to that window, instead of a traditional character-based screen.

As you can see, the program works flawlessly: The output shows the sentence *"The current time is:"* followed by the time when you ran it (naturally, according to your computer's system time). So this program runs even with a completely missing keyword! C++ must be powerful indeed! Really, this means that the Borland Compiler can correctly compile the program, although you know it is *not* correct C code. However, it

Figure 2.12 The output of the *time.cpp* program

is correct C++ code. As you will learn later, in C++ the identifier of a structure becomes a new (user-defined) *data type*. Later you will also discover several other differences between the two languages. For the moment, we stress only that C++ is a super-set of the C Language, which means that any working C program is a correct C++ program.

Borland C++ can optionally compile different C and C++ dialects. The choice of the specific kind of language being compiled can be set at the project level (and it can also be set individually for each file node in the project tree). Let's see how you would do this at the project level.

First, close the output window. (You will notice that the *time.cpp* node in the project tree now shows a + sign; we will get back to this + sign shortly.) Now select the *Project...* command from the *Options* menu. You will see the *Project Options* dialog shown in Figure 2.13.

This is an innovative kind of multilevel, hierarchical dialog box. On the left side there is a *Topics* pane. This pane presents a *File Manager*–like tree of topics. For instance, if you click on the + sign to the left of the *Compiler* topic, that topic will be expanded to show all related subtopics (and the + sign will change into a - sign). If a topic or subtopic is displayed with a small bullet symbol to its left, then that means that by selecting it you will be allowed to set the pertaining options that will appear in the right pane of the dialog. For instance, if you click on the *Source* subtopic of the *Compiler* topic, the right pane will display to groups of options, as you can see in Figure 2.14.

In this peculiar case, these options are divided into two groups: the *Source* group and the *Language compliance* group. It is through this last group of options that you would select one language instead of another.

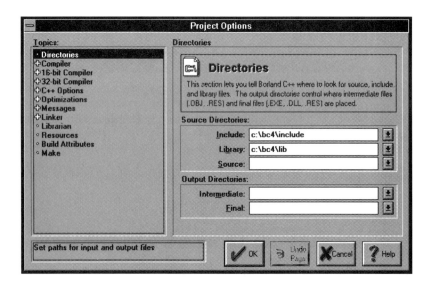

Figure 2.13 **The** *project options* **multilevel dialog box**

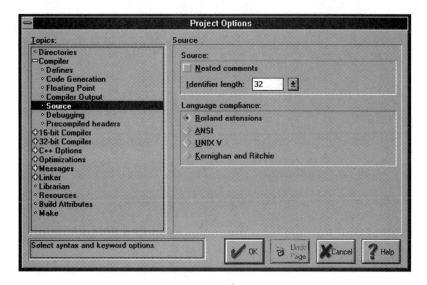

Figure 2.14 The *compiler, source* **portion of the options dialog box**

> ➤ *Note*: There might be different reasons to limit the compiler to a specific language rather than another. Usually, this kind of limitation takes place when the code has to be ported to another machine, environment, or compiler that supports only a specific language standard. Other people might use a subset of the language just because they are used to a particular C dialect, rather than learning the new constructs, which could probably not be used on different development platforms.

Since this book is about C++, and *Borland C++* in particular, we will not change the default selection of *Borland extensions*. The steps you have just completed, though, are very significant. Besides learning that you have not one language compiler, but several, you have also learned that you really have something different from an ordinary C Language compiler. That's the power of the increment (++) operator! That's how C became C++. If you want to know more, go on reading; but first close the *Project Options* dialog by pressing the *Esc* key.

A Taste of C++

The program that you copied from the help system and saved in the *time.cpp* file was actually a C Language source code program. The changes you introduced (deleting the *struct* keyword) began to transform it into a C++ code program. You will now complete this transformation.

First, make the *time.cpp* editor window active, and then save the existing source file as *time2.cpp*. To do this, you can use the *Save As* command from the file menu. Then, change the code in the *time2.cpp* window so that it becomes like the following:

```
// file TIME2.CPP                                              02\TIME2

#include <iostream.h>
#include <iomanip.h>
#include <dos.h>

int main (void)
{
    // defines a "time" structure
    time t;

    // fills the time structure with the system time
    gettime(&t);

    // outputs the fields of the time structure
    cout  << "The current time is: "
          << setw(2) << (int) t.ti_hour << ":"
          << setw(2) << setfill('0') << (int) t.ti_min << ":"
          << setw(2) << setfill('0') << (int) t.ti_sec << "."
          << setw(2) << setfill('0') << (int) t.ti_hund
          << endl;

    return 0;
}
```

After you made the changes, save the file (with the *File, Save* command).

Before you can compile (and run) the changed program, you need to update the project, since it still references the previous *time.cpp* file and not the newer *time2.cpp* file. To do this, activate the *Project* window. As we noticed before, the *time.cpp* node in the project tree now shows a + sign. This plus sign means that the node is "collapsed," and that it contains more nodes underneath it.

You can click once on the + sign, and you will see that the *time.cpp* file depends on other files, like those two that were included explicitly in it (*stdio.h* and *dos.h*) and some others (*_defs.h, _nfile.h,* and *_null.h*) that are included indirectly through those two. The expanded project tree is shown in Figure 2.15. In particular, the *[Autodepend]* that appears after all these new files indicates that these dependencies are managed *automatically* by the system. If you click again on the - sign on the *time.cpp* node, all its depending branches will collapse, and the + sign will appear again.

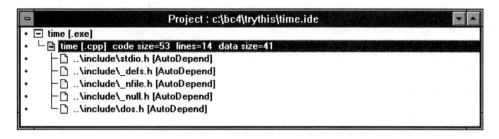

Figure 2.15 The expanded view on a project, with the include files

Local Menus

Like many other applications recently released by Borland, even the IDE allows you to *inspect* various parts of the environment. Inspecting means pressing the *Alt+F10* key combination when some item is selected on the screen, or simply pointing to the item and clicking the *right* mouse button. In either case, a *local menu* will appear, showing you the most common actions you can do with the selected item. If you now point to the *time.cpp* node in the *Project* window and inspect it, you will be presented with a menu that, in particular, will allow you to change the association between the node and the actual source file we are interested in. This command is *Edit node attributes....* By selecting it you will be presented with the *Node Attributes for time* dialog, where you can correct the *Name* from *time* into *time2*. Then, finally after clicking on *OK* to close the dialog, you will be able to compile and run the changed program.

You see that its output is identical to the previous one; the same result has been obtained by writing the program in a different way.

Surprises for C Programmers

You have already seen that it's possible to declare *t* as an instance of the type *time*. But, *cout* is an unknown entity for C programmers: It represents almost the same "thing" as C's standard output (usually the computer screen—or the *EasyWin* window in this case). In C++, the standard output *stream* serves as the destination for all output operations, which are indicated by means of the << operator.

The syntax:

```
cout  << "The current time is: "
```

might be misleading for a C programmer, since the << operator usually indicates the *left shift* operation. The expression:

```
E1 << E2
```

normally means: Take the integer *E1* and shift the bits of its binary representation *E2* places to the left. For example, the expression:

```
3 << 2
```

should result in 12. (The binary notation for 3 is 11; shifting it twice to the left results in 1100, which corresponds to the decimal number 12.)

If C++ is a super-set of C, then the result of this expression should be the same in both languages. To test it, instead of setting up a new project and writing a new program, you can use a tool of the IDE. If you select the *Evaluate/Modify...* command from the *Debug* menu, you will be presented with a dialog box of the *integrated debugger*, another significant facility of the IDE. This dialog box can be used to evaluate any expression that is valid in C++.

For instance, entering "3 << 2" in the *Expression* text box, and then clicking on the *Eval* button, the result of 12 will appear in the *Result* text box (as shown in Figure 2.16). This is precisely the correct result you would expect by knowing C!

Work Overload—No, Operator Overload

If the << operator in C++ has the same meaning of "left shift" as in C, why—in the preceding listing—could you use it to output words and numbers? The answer to this is a particular capability of C++: operator overloading. Operator overloading indicates that an operator can be used with different meanings when its operands are of different data types. In the program, the operator has been interpreted as an insertion into the standard

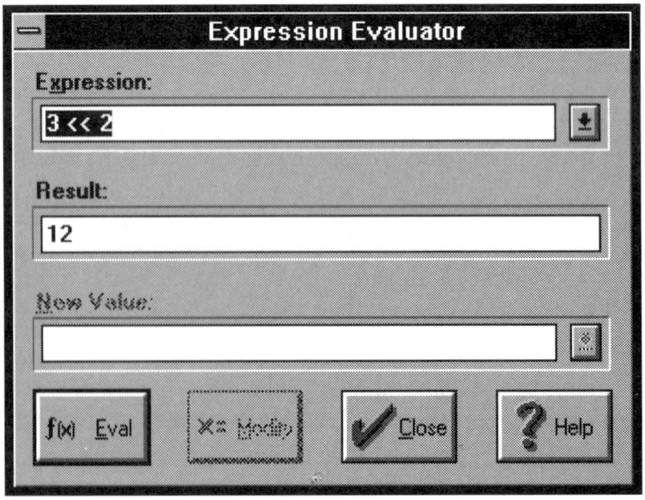

Figure 2.16 The evaluation of an expression.

output stream, since its first operand was an output stream called *cout*. In the expression 3 << 2 the operator is interpreted as left shift, since its first operand is an integer.

The most interesting aspect of the operator overloading is that its different meanings are not defined by the language, but by the programmer, as you will see shortly.

However, before we go on, we still have to explain the meaning of the last part of the program. The output instruction is made up by some data to be written, mixed with some "manipulators." One of them, for example, is *setw(2)* which sets the width of the following output field to 2. Another manipulator is *setfill('0')* which indicates to fill the possible blank spaces of the field with zero (so that a simple 9 becomes 09).

The *int* keyword within parentheses, as in C, stands for a type cast. In this case the elements of the structure are characters, and the type cast converts them into integers. However, while in C the type conversion happens implicitly, due to the *%d* format specifier in the *printf* statement, here it is explicit. The *endl* (end line) manipulator corresponds to the new line ('\n') character in the *printf* statement.

While all these manipulators are quite difficult to read, there are advantages over the corresponding *printf* statement. Many implicit operations become explicit, and therefore more clear. The position of the expression elements clearly determines the output string, without having to associate the positional format specifiers (such as *%d*) with their corresponding expression. A drawback is that the code is longer, because of the repeated manipulators.

So what is all this fuss about the advantages of C++ and its promises of shorter programs? We have actually written *more* code than in the equivalent C program: The *cout* statement is a little longer but much more *powerful*. It can even be used to output user-defined data types, as we will see in the following new version of the program. Make a copy of the actual program, saving it with the new name *time3.cpp* (using the *File, Save as* command). Remember also to edit the node attributes in the project dependency tree, in order to reference this new file. After this operation, you can change the source code into the following:

```
// file TIME3.CPP                                           02\TIME3

#include <iostream.h>
#include <iomanip.h>
#include <dos.h>

// defines a new "overloaded" << operator for the output stream
ostream& operator<< (ostream& s, time& t)
{
    return s  << setw(2) << (int) t.ti_hour << ":"
              << setw(2) << setfill('0') << (int) t.ti_min << ":"
              << setw(2) << setfill('0') << (int) t.ti_sec << "."
              << setw(2) << setfill('0') << (int) t.ti_hund;
}
```

```
int main(void)
{
    // defines a "time" structure
    time t;

    // fills the time structure with the system time
    gettime(&t);

    // outputs the structure (using the overloaded operator)
    cout  << "The current time is: "
          << t
          << endl;

    return 0;
}
```

This program begins with a function having a very strange name, really unintelligible for C programmers:

```
ostream& operator<< ( ostream& s, time& t )
```

The body of this function is almost the transcription of the *cout* statement in the previous version of the program. In the declaration of the function's parameters, *time* is used as a data type. This and the other parameter is followed by an '&' operator. The '&' (another new feature of C++) is used to indicate that the parameters are passed by reference, and not by value.

The full meaning of the function will be explained much later in the book. For now, you only need to know that it indicates the overloading of the operator <<.

Now you can write the output statement contained in the main function like this:

```
cout << "The current time is: " << t << endl ;
```

The << operator can take a time structure (such as *t*) directly as an operand.

This corresponds to an unlikely C program such as:

```
struct time t ;
...
printf ( "The current time is %t\n", t ) ;
```

which is impossible in C.

Although we had to write a new function, the body of the program becomes very short and clear, and much easier to write and read that the corresponding C program (or even the previous version of the C++ program).

In the Beginning . . . Initialization of Variables

To initialize the *t* variable, you need to call the *gettime* function, which doesn't help much to explain the *meaning* of the program. If you could avoid it, the program would become even more readable.

Usually the initialization of the variables is extremely important: Several logical errors in programs are caused by the wrong or missing initialization of a variable. If the issue were faced with an automatic method, the programmer could avoid errors and focus on the main aspects of application development. In C++ this is possible.

Of course, you must define how the data of a certain type should be initialized, through a particular function that is strictly related to the data type. Once this operation is made, then *every time* you declare a variable of that kind, the program initializes it *automatically.*

This is only one of the aspects of a typical object-oriented construct of C++: the *class.* For the moment, you can think of a class as of a data structure that contains both data and related functions.

At the End . . . It's All a Matter of Class

Although the whole issue will be described in detail in several chapters of this book, you can modify the program you have written using a class to perform an automatic initialization:

// file TIME4.CPP   **02\TIME4**

```
#include <iostream.h>
#include <iomanip.h>
#include <dos.h>

// defines a class based on the class structure
class realtime : public time
{
public:
    // the following constructor provides initialization of the class
    realtime( )
    {
        gettime ( this ) ;
    }
} ;

// Overloaded << operator for the output stream
ostream& operator << (ostream& s, time& t)
{
    return s  << setw(2) << (int) t.ti_hour << ":"
```

```
                  << setw(2) << setfill('0') << (int) t.ti_min << ":"
                  << setw(2) << setfill('0') << (int) t.ti_sec << "."
                  << setw(2) << setfill('0') << (int) t.ti_hund ;
    }

    int main(void)
    {
        // defines a realtime object (which is automatically initialized)
        realtime t;

        // outputs the realtime object (using the overloaded operator)
        cout  << "The current time is: "
              << t
              << endl;

        return 0;
    }
```

In the previous listing, the lines of code:

```
    class realtime : public time
    {
    public:
        realtime ( )
        {
            gettime ( this ) ;
        }
    } ;
```

define a new data type, called *realtime*. The *realtime* data type (a class) derives its property from the *time* structure, from which it "inherits" all the data members. This is due to the derivation or inheritance among classes, one of the most important aspects of object-oriented programming.

Also, *realtime* has a function that has same name (*realtime*). This is the function that takes care of the automatic initialization of the data. This kind of "initialization" function is called a *constructor*.

The program has some other minor differences: The overloaded operator has now a parameter of type *realtime*; the variable *t* is declared of type *realtime*; in the *main* function the call to the *gettime* function has been avoided altogether.

Now the body of the *main* function is extremely simple and easy to read: It defines a variable of type realtime, and sends it to the output after a message:

```
    int main(void)
    {
        realtime t ;
```

```
cout  << "The current time is: "
      << t
      << endl ;

   return 0;
}
```

Although the initialization function is no longer explicit, compiling and running this new program (that you can save as *time4.cpp*, always remembering to change the project's node attribute correspondingly) produces the same output of the original C code copied from the help system. In this case the call of the *gettime* function is performed during the automatic initialization of the variable *t*.

Usually, the kind of code that appears at the beginning of this last program, i.e., the code defining new classes of *objects* will be put into development libraries. Therefore, when writing the code that actually does the work, your task is much simpler, because you can now deal with much more *high-level* objects and so-called *abstract data types*. Compare this *main* function with the *main* of the original C code. You can see that it is *shorter* and *easier to understand*.

As you can see, C++ does have many new features. If you want to know more about them, keep reading.

POINTS TO CONSIDER

1. The Borland C++ package contains a number of useful tools. Their purpose is to help the development of programs, but some of them (for example, *GREP*) can also be used independently. Therefore, it might be useful to read their description in the manuals or in the documentation files and experiment with them. How about using *GREP* to find how many C++ example programs of the Borland environment contain the *printf* function or the default *cout* object?

2. You can explore some of the features of the compiler and of the language accessing the help system with the *Help Contents* commands of the IDE.

3. Use the IDE to copy (from help) the examples of the following functions: *getdate* (which retrieves the current date), *getdfree* (which returns the free disk space), *random* (which generates random numbers), *sqrt* (the square root), and *strftime* (a function used to easily output the current time and date).

4. If you want to experiment with C++, you can use the help system examples. However, most of the examples are C examples, which still work under the C++ compiler, but may not help you to understand the new language. Every time a new concept or keyword is presented in this book, the help system can serve to augment the information on the subject, and offer new examples that you can execute and modify.

3

Object-Oriented Programming and Design

Of all the monsters that fill the nightmares of our folklore, none terrify more than werewolves, because they transform unexpectedly from the familiar into horrors. For these, one seeks bullets of silver that can magically lay them to rest.

The familiar software project, at least as seen by the non-technical manager, has something of this character; it is usually innocent and straightforward, but is capable of becoming a monster of missed schedules, blown budgets, and flawed products. So we hear desperate cries for a silver bullet. [Brooks 86]

This chapter is a general introduction to the fundamental object-oriented development methods and programming techniques. To start, there is a brief overview of the main problems encountered in software development that could be solved by using a new programming model, namely programming through objects. To better understand how this can be achieved, you will see how programming languages have evolved, with particular attention to the theme of abstraction.

In the middle of the chapter, the key concepts of object-oriented programming will be described. If you have never been exposed to object-oriented programming, then this section is probably the most important of this chapter, because it summarizes at the highest conceptual level all the elements that will be examined in the rest of this book, both in terms of theoretical implications as well as in actual language constructs of the C++ language.

On the whole, this is a stand-alone chapter, but it is essential to the entire book. In fact, you can just as well read this chapter before or after the following chapters, which delve into the details of the many features of the C++ language. However, this introduction to object-oriented programming is the key to understanding all the choices made in the rest of the text. Every time we offer suggestions or practical rules for using a particular subject, we are referring to the object-oriented "philosophy" described in the following sections. This chapter provides the foundation for most of the concepts described in the book, and its comprehension will help you to more easily understand the features of C++.

Observations on the Software Crisis

The term *software crisis* was coined over 20 years ago to indicate the difficulty in developing programs while controlling costs, time schedules, and quality. Ever since, hardware has been developed at a much greater speed.

This "crisis" continues even today because, despite the many tools and methods used, the bottom-line problems remain the same, possibly because the complexity of problems that need to be solved has soared.

In particular, among the many problems that face a piece of software (that is, the various "phases" that software goes through from its formulation to its effective usage), maintenance problems appear to have become more and more severe. Among the five phases that are traditionally distinguised (analysis, design, implementation, debugging, and maintenance, shown in Figure 3.1), maintenance was once considered of secondary importance. Today, many researchers are convinced that maintenance absorbs more than half of the global costs and resources in software development.

Despite the many studies made during the past several years, not all programmers are aware of the weight, in terms of time, of this last part of a program's life cycle. Once a first-functioning version has been achieved, you still need a lot of time before it can be considered reliable. And even more time will elapse before the program is completed with other functionalities that, at first glance, were not even thought of. Often, making changes and corrections to a program will be much more burdensome

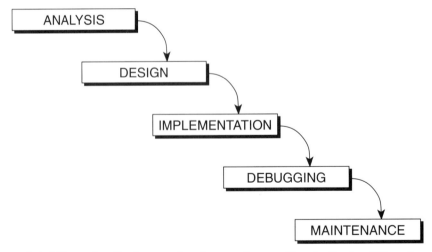

Figure 3.1 Life cycle of software development according to the traditional "waterfall" method

than you planned. Even the most well-known and successful software houses have enormous difficulties in meeting the announcement dates for the new versions of their products. Figure 3.2 shows the breakdown of costs for the different phases in a software product's life cycle.

The changes made in the evolution of programs are a weak point for traditional software development methods (thus for many of the most wide spread programming languages used today), and, conversely, is one of the strong points of object-oriented software development methods.

In 1986, with the now famous article *"No Silver Bullet"* (an excerpt of which appears in the chapter introduction), Fredrick P. Brooks claimed that there would not be any significant progress in the development of software for at least ten years, and he critically analyzed all of the most promising technologies. Even though he advocated having more faith in object-oriented programming than in any other new technology, he maintained doubts about its effective advantages.

Recently, more optimistic views have started to spread, and a solution is starting to be glimpsed for these problems. This solution is being sought in the *reusability* of *software components*, which are considered as starting blocks for the construction of programs, in a way similar to the construction of any complex object (such as an automobile) that is built through the assembly of parts.

In an answer to Brook's article, Brad Cox recently said,

> There is a silver bullet. It *is* a tremendously powerful weapon, propelled by vast economic forces that mere technical obstacles can resist only briefly. But as Brooks would agree, it is not a technology, a whiz-bang invention that will slay the soft-

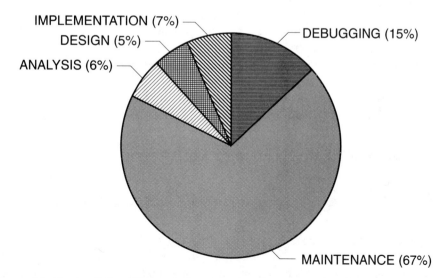

Figure 3.2 Costs of the different phases in a software product's life cycle

ware werewolf without effort on our part or vast side effects on our value systems and the balance of power between software producers and consumers.

The silver bullet is a *cultural* change rather than a technological change. It is a paradigm shift—a software industrial revolution based on reusable and interchangeable parts that will alter the software universe as surely as the industrial revolution changed manufacturing. [Cox 90]

Thus, it is not a new object-oriented programming language, but a new way of *thinking* and *designing* applications that can help solve the problems that afflict software development. The language, however, must be able to support the paradigm shift and is therefore an essential part of this "revolution." Borland C++, among the many languages available today, is one of the best vehicles for object-oriented programming.

Programming and Abstraction

To better understand the meaning of this "revolution," you will examine one of its fundamental elements: programming by abstractions.

In general, a program is no more than an abstract description of a procedure or a phenomenon that exists or happens in the real world. Often, a program mimics a human behavior or action; other times it simulates (that is, reproduces) a physical phenomenon.

However, the relationship between abstraction and programming language is two-fold: on one hand, you use the programming language to write a program that is an abstraction of the real world. On the other hand, you use the programming language to describe in an abstract way the physical behavior of the computer being used (for instance, by using decimal numbers instead of binary numbers, variables instead of explicitly addressed memory cells, and so on).

Both forms of abstraction (represented symbolically in Figure 3.3) are very important; however, most programmers have only recently become aware of this, since the very first programming languages were not able to adequately support either of these two types of abstractions. Recall that in the 1950s the only mechanism for abstraction in assembly language vs. machine language was the possibility of using symbolic names to represent memory cells.

Description of Reality Through Abstractions

The *art of programming* consists of describing to a computer in an intelligible manner (by means of a programming language) a phenomenon, an action, a behavior, or an idea.

In other words, you must explain to the computer how to perform very complex calculations, or very simple calculations that need to be executed over and over again, to reproduce on the computer a physical phenomenon of which you know the governing mathematical laws, simulating the behavior of a system.

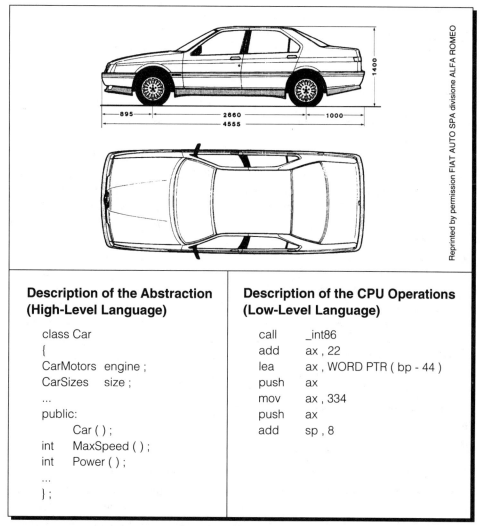

Description of the Abstraction (High-Level Language)	Description of the CPU Operations (Low-Level Language)
class Car	call _int86
{	add ax , 22
CarMotors engine ;	lea ax , WORD PTR (bp - 44)
CarSizes size ;	push ax
...	mov ax , 334
public:	push ax
Car ( ) ;	add sp , 8
int MaxSpeed ( ) ;	
int Power ( ) ;	
...	
} ;	

Figure 3.3 The twofold relationship between a programming language and abstraction

At other times, you can use the computer to emulate other machinery. For instance, it can be used as a typewriter, a drawing tool, a calculator, a personal address book, or even a national phone directory.

This list could go on almost indefinitely. It is important, though, that you get the sense of these observations. The computer needs to *behave* in a certain manner, the manner that best mimics the tasks of a certain person, machine, or tool. Therefore, the programmer needs to give the computer an *abstract* description of this behavior. A high-level programming language must enable the computer to understand a description that is close to what a programmer might give to another programmer.

The description of reality by means of abstractions is a complex subject. In later chapters, you will see concrete examples of abstractions and how to implement small programs, starting from an abstract description of a phenomenon.

Abstractions in Programming Languages

The abstractions offered by programming languages can be divided into two categories: those pertaining to data and those pertaining to control structures.

Ever since the beginning of the 1960s when the first high-level programming languages were developed, it has been possible to use the most primitive abstractions of both categories (variables, data types, procedures, loop controls, and so on).

Both categories of abstractions have spawned an enormous variety of programming languages, all of which implemented certain choices and widened some aspects of the various programming techniques.

Within this evolution—which has brought with it an increasing attention to abstractions—a particular role has been played by object-oriented programming languages, a category of programming languages that is not always well defined.

For example, there are the so-called *"pure"* object-oriented programming languages. These abandon some of the best-known constructs of classical programming languages (for instance, functions) because they are no longer necessary (and even counterproductive) for an advantageous exercise of the principles of this programming style. On the other side are object-oriented programming languages (such as C++) that offer a series of new structures and mechanisms plus a traditional procedural programming language, in which no feature is lost.

Abstraction and Data

The first steps toward data abstraction were made by languages like FORTRAN, COBOL, and ALGOL60, with the introduction of different variable types to manipulate integers, real numbers, characters, Boolean values, and so on. However, these data types were firmly set by the language, could not be modified, and did not always fit the type of usage that was needed. For instance, string handling is a well-known limitation of FORTRAN; on the other hand, the precision and reliability of FORTRAN for mathematical computation is almost legendary.

The next generation of programming languages, including Pascal, SIMULA 67, and ALGOL68, tried to offer a wider selection of data types and permitted the programmer to modify and extend the existing data types by means of specific constructs (for instance, to create records and arrays). Furthermore, SIMULA 67 was the first language to merge data and their access procedures by means of the class construct, which eventually became the basis for the development of object-oriented programming.

The concept of type, as defined in Pascal and ALGOL 68, has been a major step toward achieving a language capable of supporting structured programming. However, these languages do not fully support a methodology—in which programs are developed by problem decomposition based on the recognition of abstractions. The data abstraction useful for this purpose should not merely classify objects according to their representation structure; rather, they should be classified according to their expected behavior. Such behavior is expressible in terms of the operations that are meaningful on those data, and the operations are the only means for creating, modifying, and accessing the objects. [Ghezzi 87]

In more precise terms, Ghezzi indicates that a user-definable data type is called *abstract data type* if:

- there exists a construct of the language that allows you to associate the representation of data with the operations that manipulate it

- the representation of the new data type is hidden from the program units that use it

While the classes of SIMULA 67 satisfied only the first of these two properties, other languages were later developed that satisfied both of them; most notably, Ada and C++.

Abstraction and Control Structures

Microprocessors directly offer only two mechanisms to control the flow and execution of instructions: sequence and jump. The first high-level programming languages introduced branching statements (if) and loops (for, while, and so on). More importantly, they augmented the conceptual scope of subprograms and macro expansions, already available in some assembly languages.

Subprograms (sometimes referred to as procedures or functions, depending on the language) led to more systematic programming practices which were to become the foundation of the classical "top-down" decomposition. In all cases, subprograms make up a powerful tool for abstraction because, during their implementation, the programmer describes in detail how the subprograms operate. When the subprogram has to be called, it is enough for you to know what it does, without being concerned about how it does it. In this way, subprograms become black boxes that extend the programming language being used, making it more powerful and more specialized for the problem being faced.

Furthermore, subprograms were the first and still are the most widespread mechanism for code reuse, through collections of subprograms in libraries. We will examine this later in the chapter on code reusability.

In the subsequent future evolution of programming languages, other mechanisms for the abstraction of control are being conceived. Most notable of these are exception handling, co-routines, and concurrent units. These last two constructs will not be described because, at least for the moment, they are not part of the C++ standard.

Key Concepts of Object-Oriented Programming

Nowadays, the phrase "object-oriented" is being used (and misused) very often. What does it really mean? In this section we will try to define the fundamental concepts that relate to "object-orientedness," an issue that, as you will see, is complicated and convoluted.

The definition of "object-oriented" will be limited here to the field of programming, as it is also possible to speak about object-oriented database management systems, object-oriented operating systems, object-oriented user interfaces, and so on. Even with this limitation, it will take some effort to fully analyze and understand the basic features that distinguish an object-oriented approach to programming with respect to other, traditional approaches. It will be necessary to examine the typical methods used to design and structure programs according to object-oriented principles, and then learn how to use new tools (such as C++ and, in this case, the utilities and the development environment of Borland C++). All this will come in the remaining part of this book, but first things first.

As you will see later in this chapter, it is possible to give very precise definitions of object-oriented languages. According to these definitions, it is even possible to measure the "degree" of object-orientedness for a language. Nonetheless, without being too picky, it is possible to recognize at least three fundamental elements that must be present in any truly object-oriented language: classes, inheritance, and polymorphism.

Classes

The first key element of object-oriented programming is *classes*. Generally, a class can be defined as an *abstract description* of a *group of objects*, each of which is differentiated by a specific *state* and is able to perform a series of *operations*.

For instance, a fountain pen is an object that has a state (filled with ink or empty) with which you can perform some operations (for instance, write, put the cap on, and even refill if it is empty).

In programming, a class is a structure that contains data and procedures (or functions) that are capable of operating on that data. So the class of fountain pens could have, for instance, a variable that indicates whether it is filled or empty; another variable might contain the quantity of ink actually loaded. The class will also contain some related functions that operate or use those variables. A write function will be able to work as long as there is ink, consuming ink and eventually getting to the point where no ink is left.

Within a program, classes have two principal purposes: they can define abstractions and they favor modularity.

➤ *Note:* In the above description, we have used the terms *class* and *object* several times: what is the difference? As you will see in Chapter 5, an object describes a single element, no matter how complex it might be. A class, instead, describes a family of similar elements. In practice, a class is like a scheme that is used to define corresponding objects. It's the same kind of difference that there is between a blueprint describing how to build a car, and the number of cars built according to that blueprint that come out of a factory plant. The blueprint (a class) describes a general car. Starting with this general idea, you can actually define one or more particular cars (an object).

From a class, you can define a number of objects. Each of these objects will generally have a peculiar state of its own (a fountain pen can be filled, another can be half-empty, another completely empty), and other characteristics (like their color), although they will all share some common operations (like "write," "refill," or "put the cap on").

Classes and Abstraction

To define an abstraction means to describe a real-world entity, no matter how complex it might be, and then use this description in a program. You can think of a *class* as the extension of a record. Beyond aggregating a number of data items of different data types (as an ordinary record), a class also defines a *behavior*, which is expressed by the set of all valid values that its data items can take together with the operations (for instance, functions) that can be performed on these data items.

The idea of writing programs by defining a series of abstractions is not a novelty of object-oriented programming languages, as you saw in the previous section. However, the possibility of using classes is a great step toward managing abstractions in a programming language, because it helps to define new *user-defined data types* that can actually be thought of as an *extension* of the programming language.

Classes and Modularity

Modularity is the possibility of subdividing an application into many smaller pieces (called *modules*), each of which should be as independent as possible from the application as a whole, as well as from the other pieces of which it is a part.

The idea of modularity also derives from past experience, and it has been known and used for some time, although not always correctly. One of the most important concepts of good subdivision into modules is *encapsulation* (also known as the *principle of information hiding*). According to this idea, a key trait of every class is precisely that of "hiding" both data as well as algorithms. For this reason, classes are often thought of as *black boxes*, of which you are only allowed to know *what* they do, but not *how* they do it. You do not need to know the actual inner workings (the "implementation details" of a class) to be able to use the class; they can even be changed without affecting the program or the other modules that actually use the class. You will explore modularity further in a future section of this chapter.

The concepts of classes and objects, although fundamental to object-oriented programming, are not exclusive to it. In fact, programming with classes is simply an extension of programming with modules and programming through data abstractions. These kinds of techniques are well consolidated and used even by programmers who use methods and programming languages that are not object oriented.

To be fully object oriented, a programming language must also support inheritance and polymorphism.

Inheritance

The first really new and different element of object-oriented programming is *inheritance*. Inheritance is a feature by which it is possible to define a class, not from scratch, but in terms of another class. A class *inherits* its characteristics (both data as well as functions) from another class.

In the fountain pen example, you could define a class of cartridge-refilled fountain pens that derives from the generic class of fountain pens. All traits of a fountain pen are present even in cartridge-refilled fountain pens (you can write, refill, put the cap on, and so on), albeit with some differences (the refill operation will be simpler and faster).

Inheritance is a construct that is very powerful, but also very difficult to use—at least for beginners. One difficulty is in understanding the real *meaning* (semantics) of inheritance. In fact, several different interpretations and practical uses are possible.

- The first, and probably the simplest, interpretation is to consider inheritance as an operation by which you obtain *specialization*. In this case, a class that inherits from another class represents a subset that has some specific behavior of its own. For instance, a class that describes all managers or all secretaries of a company is a specialization of a class that describes all employees of that company.

- Another common interpretation and usage of inheritance is that of representing a *generalization*. In this case, inheritance is useful to "factor out" common elements and to simplify the description of a certain real world fact. For instance, starting with the classes of managers and secretaries, you could define a generic class of "white collars" that describes the common trait of "clerical staff." The definition of the class of white collars constitutes a generalization of the attributes (and behaviors) that are shared by many employees, each of which has its own peculiarities. Here inheritance is valuable, because once a white-collar class has been defined, it is possible to inherit from it all the characteristics that are shared by clerical employees; for instance, it would be possible to define a class of salespeople.

To sum up, inheritance is an effective tool that can be used to manage similarities and differences between classes of similar objects.

➤ *Note:* Be careful not to confuse the distinction between classes with the distinction between objects of the same class: a red car and a blue car are not objects of different classes, but objects of the same class with a different attribute.

Polymorphism

The third significant feature of object-oriented programming languages is *polymorphism*, which indicates, literally, the possibility that an entity takes *many forms*. In more practical terms—although simplified somewhat—polymorphism allows you to refer to objects of different classes by means of the same program item, and to perform the same operation in different ways, according to which object is being referenced at the moment.

For example, when describing the class of mammals, you might note that eating is a fundamental "operation" for mammals to live. So every kind of mammal must be able to perform the function *Eat*. On the other hand, a cow ruminating in a field of grass, a child enjoying chocolate fudge ice cream, and a lion devouring an antelope illustrate the *different responses* that the different mammals give to the *same function* (*Eat*).

Polymorphism is the possibility of taking an object of type (Mammal) and telling it to *Eat*; it will do that action that is most appropriate for itself. It is not a kind of "programming magic," but simply a programming technique to execute a function of an appropriate class (which must in any case have been defined and written beforehand). Polymorphism will be further explored in Chapter 8.

Classes, inheritance, and polymorphism are the three fundamental aspects of object-oriented programming that are universally recognized as essential elements of "object orientedness." However, there is no universal consensus on how these constructs should actually be realized in a programming language. For instance, inheritance can be simple or multiple; polymorphism can have very different formulations in different object-oriented languages. Beyond the technical differences, these three fundamental elements that distinguish object-oriented programming from traditional programming open the way for a new style of designing and implementing computer applications. In the rest of this chapter, these aspects will be explored in general—particularly regarding design issues—and the different flavors they take in the various object-oriented languages. In the remainder of the book, you will see how these ideas are brought into the C++ language and how they can be put to good use.

Traits of Quality Software

Before we describe some fundamental elements of software engineering, we should define this term. However, it is not that easy; software engineering indicates many different things to different people. We could say that the purpose of software engineering is to give clear guidelines and reliable tools to help programmers write high-quality software with industrial-strength features; that is, well-defined standard methods that are easily reproducible. Now the problem becomes: how do you decide if a program is of high quality? We could come up with many contradicting criteria, depending on the point of view from which we start. However, it is also possible to define some criteria that are general enough so they can be accepted by everybody.

As most programmers know, a good program must be easy to *read*. In other words, it must be possible for you to understand (from the code and the comments) how it works; it must be organized into modules, or parts that are more or less independent from one another. But to really pass muster, a good program has to be well accepted by users (and not just any user, but power users who know what they want!).

"External" Features of Software

From an "external" point of view (that of a user) the factors that determine the quality of a program could be summarized by the following, suggested by Meyer:

1. **Correctness**: a program must do exactly what it has been built to do. This might seem obvious ("a program must work, otherwise what good is it?"), but it is not. Indeed, a program might work well most of the time, but in certain unusual cases it might give rise to errors: so, strictly speaking, such a program is not correct.

2. **Robustness**: a program must be able to cope with abnormal situations. Even if a situation has not been foreseen (because data draws on "strange" values, or the user has forgotten to do a certain operation), the program must be able get out of trouble and should not just "hang."

(Together, correctness and robustness are often summarized as *reliability*.)

3. **Extendibility**: it must be easy to modify a program whenever necessary. It must be possible to make changes to the program easily, allowing for the addition of new functionality or alteration of the present features, without having to rewrite the whole program from scratch.

4. **Reusability**: a program, or a part of a program, must be readily reusable in the construction of new applications. This is very important, and therefore it will have a whole chapter dedicated to it exclusively.

5. **Compatibility**: the ease with which a program can be used with other existing products.

6. **Efficiency**: a program must make the best possible use of the computer on which it is executed; this applies to the CPU, memory, disks, and other devices, without consuming too much space or taking too much time to perform.

7. **Portability**: it must be possible to transfer and recompile a program on a different computer or under a different operating system.

8. **Testability**: it must be possible to check if a program is performing correctly and that it executes the right operations.

9. **Data integrity**: a program must ensure that data on which it operates will not be damaged, even if the user is clumsy or the computer is malfunctioning.

10. **Ease of use**: it must be an easy-to-use program, even to novice users.

11. **Interoperability**: a program should be able to cooperate seamlessly with other pieces of software, maybe even remotely through a network. [Meyer 88]

All these factors are basic criteria that indicate how a program should be written. Some might even seem obvious. Nonetheless, it's easy to forget these principles when you actually start writing code. Also, not all programming languages and methods offer the same degree of support in helping to produce programs that have all of these features.

The next step is to try to understand how to organize and structure a program to achieve these features.

Modularity

The basic principle is this: *build modular programs*. This means, approximately, that you have to subdivide a program into smaller pieces, or modules, which are generally independent from each other and can easily be "assembled" to build the whole application.

The remainder of this section provides you with a more technical and precise definition of program modularity. But first we need to focus on our choice of one of the many criteria of decomposition into modules: in fact, just by imagination, you could subdivide a program in countless ways; but only a few of these decompositions will have a real value.

Information Hiding

The criteria of modularization to which we refer is the one introduced by Parnas, in the early 1970s, also known as "Parnas's information hiding criteria."

Globally, the term *information hiding* indicates that a system should be decomposed according to "the general criteria that each module hides some design decision from the rest of the system." [Parnas 72] In other words, every module must hide a "secret"; it must effectively conceal from the other modules that make up the system at least one implementation choice (for instance, the way in which a data structure is implemented).

If a program is decomposed (or subdivided into modules) in a manner consistent with Parnas's criteria—that is, by applying the principle of information hiding—you reduce the complexity of every module that composes the solution. These are made partly independent from each other, and thus you reduce the necessity of making global choices, operations, and data.

By making choices local and hiding the design choices that might be subject to change, you reduce the problems that might occur during modifications. This way, it is possible to proceed by successive refinements, extending and varying the application or modifying parts of it independently from other parts.

However, when expressed in this way, this criterion is really too general to be useful. You need to focus on what is actually meant with a *module* and how it should be designed and used (keeping in mind that, in reality, the introduction of this criterion has been the starting point of many studies and research projects, the purpose of which has been to elaborate the principle, as well as to define programming languages based on this principle).

Rules for Modularization

In the first place, a sound design method should help the programmer subdivide the problem he or she is trying to solve into smaller subproblems, which can be solved separately from each other (these subproblems will certainly be simpler than the original problem!). It must be easy to connect the various modules to each other, inside the program you are writing. Every module has a precise meaning of its own, even if it is looked at separately from the other modules. Every module must ensure that changes to its implementation do not affect its outside (at least not much). In the same way, possible errors, boundary conditions, or erratic behaviors should not propagate beyond the module (or, at most, to the modules that are directly in contact with the one compromised).

To obtain modules with all the features that have just been exposed, you must adhere to the following rules:

1. **Linguistic Modular Units**

   The language must make available modular structures with which you can describe the various units. This way, the language (and the compiler) can recognize a module and is able to handle and govern its usage, in addition to the obvious advantages concerning the readability of the resulting code. Furthermore, these modular constructs can, as in the case of object-oriented languages, potentially exhibit features that make it easier both to structure the program as well as to write the code. In other words, we are referring to the linguistic modular units that in C++ (as well as in most other object-oriented languages) are known as *classes*.

2. **Few Interfaces**

   If the structuring of a program into units is to be beneficial, there have to be only a few interfaces; that, is only a few links between the various modules into which a program is decomposed. The interface of a module is that part of the module (data, procedure, and so on) that is visible from outside of the module (see Figure 3.4).

3. **Small Interfaces**

   The interfaces must also be small (that is, their size should be small with respect to the size of the modules involved). This way, the modules are loosely coupled; they will be linked by a small number of calls from each other (see Figure 3.5).

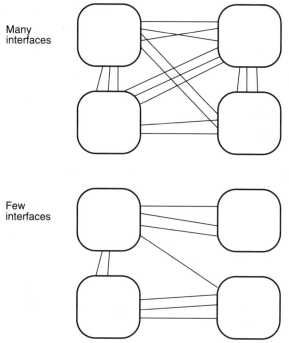

Many interfaces

Few interfaces

Figure 3.4 Few vs. many interfaces

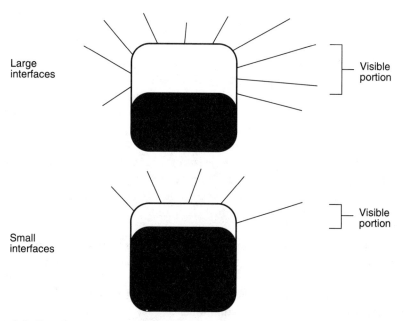

Large interfaces

Visible portion

Small interfaces

Visible portion

Figure 3.5 Small vs. large interfaces

4. **Explicit Interfaces**

The interface (the part visible externally) of a module must be declared and described explicitly: the program must specify which data and procedures a module intends to export. The others, obviously, will remain hidden from the outside. The interface must be easily readable both to the programmer (to understand how the program works) and the compiler (to check if the programmer has correctly written any code that accesses the module).

5. **Information Hiding**

Finally, all modules must adhere to the principle of information hiding: every module must conceal at least one design element (for instance, the structure of a record, an algorithm, an abstraction, and so on).

Another criterion to keep in mind in the subdivision of a system into modules, is the so-called *open-closed* principle, which was first formulated by Meyer. According to this principle, every module should be considered closed (that is, finished and thus usable from within other modules), and at the same time, it must still be open (that is, subject to changes and modifications). The open-closed principle must occur without having to rewrite all modules that already use the module being modified. Even if this criterion may seem theoretical, you will see later that the correct application of object-oriented programming will make it more practical.

Object-Oriented Design

In the subdivision of a system into modules, you must consistently apply some decomposition criteria, which are preferably encompassed by a design methodology. These methods refer to the construction phase of a program that, in the classical model, follows the definition of the requirements (analysis phase) illustrated in Figure 3.1.

The "classical" model of the life cycle of software is not the only possible model, since it is certainly possible to develop code in an evolutionary manner, by successive refinements and prototypes. We will get back to this aspect later; for the moment, suffice it to say that in these cases the design phase is compulsory, even though it may happen simultaneously with the implementation phase, instead of beforehand.

Just as there are a multitude of programming languages, many methodologies have been developed. However, they can be broken down into a few families.

A newly developed family is the object-oriented design methodologies, which contains a few dozen proposals, of which four or five methodologies are emerging as predominant.

Since this book is not deeply concerned with design issues, we won't dedicate too much space to this subject, though it is very important for sound program development and in particular for sound object-oriented program development. Therefore, we will describe only one of these methodologies, after briefly examining the traditional design methods and their intrinsic limitations.

Critique of Traditional Methodologies

Here we want to summarize briefly the limitations of some of the most widespread design methodologies for the development of large programs, and in particular the possibilities that these methodologies offer for the creation of evolutive, reusable, and extensible applications.

The following description is necessarily concise, and the limitations are stressed much more than the strong points.

According to Booch, it is possible to identify three classes of methodologies:

1. Structured top-down programming, as defined by Ed Yourdon, which focuses on the abstraction of the problem from an algorithmic point of view; this results in the definition of highly functional modules, which are particularly well-suited for sequential problems and for the topology of a language like FORTRAN.

2. Data-structure design, as developed initially by Jackson and Warnier, has had outstanding success in the description of applications like those developed in COBOL. With this technique, data structures are described first; then they are used as the foundation for a whole system.

3. Object-oriented methodologies. These have started to be developed recently, and they have been strongly influenced by the decomposition criteria of Parnas. With this technique, the algorithms get integrated with data structures. [Booch 86]

Every methodology of the first two categories, while adequate in certain cases, has weak points that are stressed with the growth in size and complexity of software projects.

The top-down design (or functional decomposition) methodologies focus on operations, and tend to neglect the importance of data structures. These are particularly suited in the case where the nature of the problem is well understood and the requirements are stable. A result of this approach is the typical topologies of first and second generation programming languages, with the usage of subprograms that produce a very limited level of abstraction and a great deal of global data that is difficult to manage even in medium-sized projects.

The data-structure design is at the opposite extreme, since it concentrates on data structures and treats operations in a global, non-structured manner. This methodology can be very complex, especially if the problem to be solved is complex. The data-structure design is suited, instead, for applications with well-defined data structures that mirror the problem at hand.

In general, when the problem to be solved is considerably large, the methodologies of the first two categories do not help the programmer manage its complexity, which will be reflected in the solution. On the contrary, these methodologies tend to add to the complexity, and tend to face the modeling and the implementation with a strict adherence to design choices that have already been made.

However, following Parnas's criteria and applying the information hiding principle, you can reduce the complexity of every single module, making every module less dependent on the others, and greatly reducing the need to make choices, operations, and data global. Furthermore, by hiding and making local the design choices, the problems are reduced. This method allows you to work by successive refinements, extending and modifying the application, or changing some of its parts independently from others.

As you can see, a methodology is needed that balances the abstraction of data as well as the abstraction of operations, or rather describes abstract objects characterized by a data structure and the operations that can be performed on that data structure. The object-oriented design methodologies intend to deliver just that.

To better understand the relationship between functions and data, consider a comparison with natural language (for instance English or Italian), which is composed of many elements, but can also convey a minimum of expressiveness when using only nouns and verbs. A methodology that is based only on data or only on procedures is similar to a language in which you use almost only nouns or almost only verbs. Only by connecting nouns to the right verbs (adhering to semantic rules, like rules of meaning) expression actually takes an intelligible form and its processing (understanding) becomes simpler.

An Object-Oriented Design Methodology

Object-oriented design methodology does not actually refer to a well-defined method, but rather to a group or a family of methodologies that can be quite different one from another. However, they all share this balance between data and functions.

The differences arise for many reasons, but the fundamental motive is that they have been conceived for different object-oriented languages—for instance, Ada (which is actually better defined not as *object oriented* but as *object based*). In this book we will present the methodology of Bertrand Meyer (described in [Meyer 88]) because it is both relevant and practical. However, the most complete and formal object-oriented design methodology is probably the one proposed by Grady Booch (described in [Booch 91]).

Meyer's methodology, while defined in less precise and less strict terms than Booch's, adheres more accurately to all the typical features of object-oriented programming languages, including inheritance and the structuring of class hierarchies. Meyer's methodology is also less restrictive regarding the implementation choices of the design as a whole. It is also much more careful regarding the issue of reusability; rather, code reusability is the central point of all choices made by this methodology.

General Properties of the Methodology

According to Meyer, "object-oriented design is the method that leads to software architectures based on the objects every system or subsystem manipulates."

But what are these "objects?" An object is an entity whose behavior is characterized by the actions it performs. More precisely, an object is defined as an entity characterized by a state; its behavior is defined by the operations it can perform; it is an *instance* of a *class*; it is identified by a name; it has a limited visibility of the other objects; it can be seen on the basis of either its specification or its implementation.

A second, more elaborate definition of object-oriented design is the following: "Object-oriented design is the construction of software systems as structured collections of abstract data type implementations." [Meyer 88]

A class of objects is the implementation of an abstract data type fulfilled by coding. The system is defined as a collection in that the classes must be designed like self-contained units, which are independent from the system to which they belong. Meyer further states that "since reusability is one of our main concerns, the abstract data type specifications, and the classes that implement them, should be as general and robust as possible." [Meyer 88]

The construction of a system thus becomes the bottom-up assembly of pre-existing classes. The structuring of the system is given by the fact that between classes there can exist a usage (client) relationship or a derivation (inheritance) relationship. With a client relationship, a class can use the objects of another class; with an inheritance relationship, a class can inherit, or derive, its defining properties from another class.

The Philosophy

As you have seen, the basis of Meyer's methodology is abstraction and information hiding. The features and the ideas that constitute its foundation are the same principles of software engineering that have been exposed in the first part of this chapter.

Following Meyer's suggestion, it is possible to expose the philosophy of object-oriented design with the following statements.

1. In a pure object-oriented sense, classes are the sole means that can be used to structure a system; they are to be considered as self-contained entities, even though they can be related by client or inheritance relationships.

2. A class is a repository of services, distinguished by the so-called *shopping list approach* in which all services are available to clients with no distinction in terms of importance, restrictions, or ordering of requests.

3. A consequence of this approach is that the only reason for limiting the number of services offered by a class is the excessive complexity that can be reached. Generally, however, if an operation has precisely defined semantics, there is no reason for excluding it, even if it were useful only for a limited number of client classes.

4. The usage of classes leads naturally to reusability, extendibility, and bottom-up assembly. The more software you develop in this way, the easier it becomes to develop new software, since you can build upon what has already been built. This is where the fundamental role of inheritance really emerges.

5. Object-oriented design leads to a distribution of the design decision throughout the whole development cycle of software, and avoids concentrating them in the first few phases. This way, it is easier to modify the outcoming program, correcting its errors and reusing parts of it in other projects.

In fact, Meyer states that "using object-oriented design, the designers will stay away, as long as possible, from the (ultimately inescapable) need to describe and implement the topmost function of the system. Instead, they will analyze the classes of objects in the system. System design will be based on successive improvements of their understanding of these object classes." [Meyer 88]

The Steps

1. **Definition of the problem domain** and understanding of its structure. You have to analyze in great detail the problem that is to be solved, describing the smallest trait, possibly in written form, and using natural language. It is necessary to draw out both the main as well as the secondary objectives, giving them priorities. In other words, it is necessary to describe a model of the reality that is being considered, from the particular point of view that has been chosen.

2. **Identification of the classes of objects**, or of the categories of objects, both real as well as abstract, of the problem domain. This means recognizing "actors, agents, and servers" of our model of reality. This identification can be made by qualifying the nouns of the problem's informal description, which was done in the previous step (although this method is sometimes questionable).

    There are essentially two kinds of classes in a system:

    • the classes that directly reflect the concepts in the application domain; that is, concepts that are used by end-users to describe their problems and solutions; and

    • the classes that are artifacts of the implementation; that is, concepts that are used by designers and programmers to describe their implementation techniques.

    Some of the classes that are artifacts of the implementation may also represent real world entities. This representation reflects the fact that a system can be viewed from several viewpoints, so that one person's implementation detail is another person's application. A well-designed system will contain classes supporting logically separate views of the system. [Stroustrup 91A]

In addition to looking for the external existing objects, real or abstract, which are significant for the application (by building a model), you can also search among the existing classes to see if the abstractions needed have already been implemented. This search can take place among both the classes of the system libraries, as well as the classes you have already developed. However, if you want to reuse the classes produced earlier, it is essential that you have built them carefully, so that they are adequately general, complete, robust, and documented. In general, you should be able to modify these existing classes, adapting them to the specific needs through the mechanism of inheritance.

3. **Analysis of objects** and definition of their functionality. At this point, you need an accurate description of the objects, looking for hierarchical structures that might be present or that might be formulated by means of abstractions and generalizations. This is necessary to characterize the behavior of an object or of a class of objects. This way, the semantics of the objects and of the operations that you can perform is established. At the end of this step, you will have a list of operations that each object should carry out.

4. **Formal description** of the main objects identified, which details all services offered by these objects and gives the most accurate semantic description possible by means of an appropriate notation. To find the interface of every object, you need to create a specification for each module by means of some kind of formal notation. This specification is necessary to capture the *static semantic* of each object (that is, its actual meaning). The formal specifications will serve as a *contract* between the clients of each object and the object itself. This description must be made in a formal manner, which can be independent and different from the physical representation actually used (that is, the actual data types used in the implementation). Therefore, it is appropriate to describe the services offered by a class by specifying an abstract data type, which will also encompass its formal properties.

   In addition, it is helpful if the specification of the abstract data type can easily be transformed into the description of the interface for the corresponding class of objects; but this requires an adequate programming language.

5. **Writing the interfaces and implementing the classes**. The development of these two steps will partly be in sequence, because once the interfaces of the classes have been specified—in relation to the class being considered—their implementation can be readily accomplished, completely or as a prototype.

   The classes of objects have to be implemented on the basis of the interfaces, which constitute a contract between the objects that are in the client relationship. To make the implementation effortless, it is important that the programming language offers constructs that are near to those used during the design phase. In other words, the programming language used should be *really* an *object-oriented programming language* (see the following section).

This scheme for a methodology should not be taken as an absolute truth; what is important is that you understand its fundamentals and then adapt it to your own needs, to the language, and to the project being developed. If you develop a large scale project, and if many programmers need to work together, it's necessary to be much more precise and careful about defining and adhering to a methodology; and it's certainly more rewarding to refer to more precise methods and techniques, for instance, like those proposed by Booch.

➤ ***Note:*** It is also worthwhile to consider what Stroustrup suggests:

Here is a series of steps that has worked for some people:

1. Find the concepts/classes and their most fundamental relationships.
2. Refine the classes by specifying the sets of operations in them: (a) classify these operations (in particular, consider the needs for construction, copying, and destruction); (b) consider minimalism, completeness, and convenience.
3. Refine the classes by specifying their dependencies on other classes: (a) inheritance; (b) use dependencies.
4. Specify the interfaces for the classes: (a) separate functions into public and protected operations; (b) specify the exact type of operations on the classes.

Note that these are steps in a repetitive process. Typically, several loops through this sequence are needed to produce a design you can comfortably use. [Stroustrup 91A]

As a matter of fact, throughout this book, these methods have been adapted to the usage of Borland C++. The ideas and techniques illustrated here will not be used in a formal and regular manner in the rest of the book, but they will serve as an underlying guide. They are present throughout this book. Even in those parts where the fundamental programming constructs offered by the language are simply explained, we have tried to direct the exposition toward object-oriented programming, with an eye on the ideas of this section.

Therefore, throughout this book, you will find "real" indications and practical rules of thumb that can serve as a guide: these are actually an attempt to extract from the general methodology described here some more specific indications for the various programming constructs and their usage. While having evident limitations, these practical indications can serve to complete the presentation given by this chapter, which, in all cases, remains an essential point of reference.

Object-Oriented Languages

Contrary to what you might think, object-oriented languages were not developed recently. The basic constructs and underlying ideas go back many years, and even the term that defines them is more than a dozen years old. In fact, the first programming language to introduce the construct of class, which has since inspired several object-oriented languages, was SIMULA 67.

The first object-oriented language to become "famous," and still probably the most well-known, was Smalltalk, whose first version was developed in 1976, followed by a second version in 1980. This language is characterized by a very high degree of dynamism and an integrated, interactive, and graphical development environment, which has been the forerunner of all modern graphical user interfaces.

Among the object-oriented languages that have been developed recently, many are extensions (by means of new object-oriented constructs) of traditional languages, like Pascal, C, and Modula2. In particular, C has had two "official" extensions: C++ and Objective-C.

C++ is characterized by the addition to C of object-oriented constructs that maintain compatibility with the original language, augmenting its static controls. This is the language on which Borland C++ is based. Objective-C, instead, introduces to C the concepts of Smalltalk and the implementation choices of this language, such as the absence of data types and a high degree of dynamism.

More recently, there has been the conviction that to correctly use the ideas of software engineering, a powerful and reliable object-oriented language was needed. There have been many attempts to define such a theoretical language. Until now, the language actually implemented that gets nearest to this ideal is probably Eiffel, conceived by Meyer. Eiffel certainly has a few limitations, but remains a language designed and implemented very well, especially considering its robustness.

Another attempt in this direction has been made with the Sather language, designed by the International Computer Science Institute of Berkeley. Sather is similar to Eiffel and is an attempt to overcome Eiffel's weaknesses.

Classification of Object-Oriented Languages

These days the phrase "object-oriented" is extremely fashionable and is used by many programmers to describe whatever language they prefer; but the term is also used for user interfaces, graphics and illustration packages, databases, and so on. So how can you actually distinguish a true object-oriented language from those that pretend to be one?

Object-oriented languages are often very different from one another, even though they might have certain common traits, like the concepts of class and inheritance. For instance, there are two very distinct categories: static languages and dynamic languages. Often static lanuages are compiled, while dynamic languages are interpreted.

Everybody, of course, would like to define his or her own ideal object-oriented language, probably based on the features of the language he or she prefers.

For these reasons, several classifications of the "presumed" object-oriented languages have been made, based on the features and the constructs offered by each language. One very widespread and largely accepted classification is the one given by [Wegner 87] illustrated in Figure 3.6. This classification identifies three categories:

1. **Object-based** languages, which support objects. That is, components characterized by a set of operations and a state.

2. **Class-based** languages, which involve objects and classes. That is, schemes for the creation of objects with common operations and behavior. A class of an object is made up of an "interface," which specifies the operations that are possible, and a "body" that implements them.

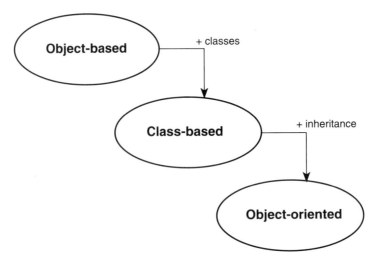

Figure 3.6 Scheme for the classification of languages proposed by Wegner

3. **Object-oriented** languages, which, in addition to objects and classes, offer an explicit mechanism for inheritance relationships between classes. That is, the possibility of deriving the operations of a class from a superclass.

This definition is quite adequate and general. Others have defined more stringent criteria for the characterization of object-oriented languages, requiring, for instance, the presence of polymorphism.

In this sense, one of the most precise and severe formulations can be found in [Meyer 88], which is also a collection of detailed indicators. These indicators can be read as a list of features that comprise a "good" object-oriented language, which all object-oriented languages should try to emulate.

According to Meyer, an object-oriented language should have the following seven features:

1. The modularization of the system takes place according to proper data structures.

2. Objects are described as the implementation of abstract data types.

3. Memory is managed automatically.

4. There is a correspondence between non-elementary data types and classes.

5. Classes can be defined as extensions or restrictions of other existing classes, through inheritance.

6. Polymorphism and dynamic binding are possible.

7. Repeated and multiple inheritance exists.

Table 3.1 "Object-oriented" features of some widespread programming languages

Programming Constructs	*Languages*			
A. Fundamental OOP Constructs	*Ada*	*C++*	*Eiffel*	*Smalltalk*
1. Modularization based on data structures	Yes	Often	Yes	Yes
2. Abstract data types	Yes	Yes	Yes	Yes
3. Automatic memory management	Yes	In part	Yes	Yes
4. "Only classes"	Yes	In part	Yes	Yes
5. Inheritance	No	Yes	Yes	Yes
6. Polymorphism (and dynamic binding)	No	Yes	Yes	Yes
7. Multiple and repeated inheritance	No	Yes	Yes	No
B. Other Constructs				
8. Genericity	Yes	Yes	Yes	Yes
9. Overloading	Yes	Yes	No	Yes
10. Abstract classes	No	Yes	Yes	In part
11. Exception handling	Yes	Yes	Yes	No

Although, according to Wegner's definition, there were no doubts, you might now wonder whether C++ is a true object-oriented language, according to this last definition.

In general, the answer is yes, even though definitions 3 and 4 are not always honored (this last one can be respected by the programmer, but it is not mandatory).

To compare some of the most well-known and widespread programming languages, refer to Table 3.1, where the seven points proposed by Meyer are listed together with some other significant features that can be present in these languages.

The C++ Language

The C++ language, by itself, is a good object-oriented programming language. It offers all the basic constructs necessary for this approach, with particular attention to efficiency and portability, features that are typical of C.

In fact, C++ preserves those features that contributed to the success of C: flexibility (the possibility of being applied in almost every application area and use almost every programming technique); efficiency (thanks to "low-level" semantics); availability on different hardware platforms; and portability of code from one machine or operating system to another.

C++ is a hybrid language that fuses object-oriented functionality with the features of a traditional and efficiently structured language, C. C++ offers the programmer and problem solver object-oriented capability without loss of run-time or memory efficiency. Production quality code can be produced on ordinary hardware. [Wiener 88]

Stroustrup, in presenting his language, outlines the advantages that are the key issues of object-oriented programming: "A programmer can partition an application into manageable pieces by defining new types that closely match the concepts of the application. This technique for program construction is often called *data abstraction*. Programs using objects of such types are often called *object based*. When used well, these techniques result in shorter, easier-to-understand, and easier-to-maintain programs." [Stroustrup 86]

C++ is a true object-oriented language, with the distinctive feature that it can be used as a "normal" language. However, in some cases it would be better if you were coerced to use the language in an object-oriented manner, without having shortcuts or other tricks handy.

Let's now examine in detail the distinctive features of this programming language, and also its limits. If, in the following description, some parts are not immediately clear, don't worry: everything will be described thoroughly in the remainder of the book.

Some History

The C++ language was conceived of by Bjarne Stroustrup at AT&T Bell Laboratories and eventually marketed by AT&T. In 1980, C was augmented with classes, strict type checking and type conversion in the parameters of function, and some other minor features. The resulting language was called "*C with Classes*."

During 1983 and 1984, "C with Classes" was further perfected and restructured, with the addition of virtual functions and operator overloading, giving birth to C++. Shortly after, the language's reference manual was published and presented in Stroustrup's first book, which extensively illustrated this new language. [Stroustrup 86]

Since then, the language has continued to evolve. The second release covered multiple inheritance, abstract classes, and many other features, which are all present in Borland C++. The reference manual has also been rewritten—always by the language's author together with Margaret A. Ellis—in which other modifications and updates are proposed and where release 2.0 is fully described.

Further development of the language was introduced in release 2.1 of C++, illustrated in [Stroustrup 91A]. This text includes the description of two proposed extensions of C++: the template construct (that defines generic classes), and exception handling capabilities. Borland C++ fully adheres to this definition of the language, also adding support for the proposed template construct.

Since 1989, a standard for the language has been under definition by the X3J16 ANSI committee, where many well-known industry and academic experts contribute their ideas. Nonetheless, the "charismatic leader" remains Bjarne Stroustrup, the inventor of the language. The ANSI committee base document is [Ellis 90].

➤ *Note:* As this book was being printed (December 1993), the ANSI X3J16 commitee, together with their international counterpart (ISO SC22/WG21), are working on an informal draft document. Most likely, during 1994, a *formal* draft will be released for public review, and eventually there will be a Standard C++ (just like there was a Standard C in 1989).

The name of the language was invented by a fellow worker of Stroustrup, Rick Mascitti, and describes in a concise manner the evolution of the language. In fact, in C, the operator ++ indicates increment, and this suggests the idea that C++ is "something more" than the C language.

General Features

"The C++ programming language is C extended with classes, in-line functions, operator overloading, function name overloading, constant types, references, free store management operators, function argument checking, and a new function definition syntax." [Stroustrup 86]

The extension that the language offers with respect to C does not always concern object-oriented programming. For instance, introducing static type checking on function arguments, "C++ provides greater type safety"; and globally the language "compensates for C's weaknesses without compromising C's strengths." [Stroustrup 88]

Some of the new features added offer the possibility of reconciling object-oriented programming with a high degree of efficiency. For instance, the possibility of *in-line* function expansion permits an intense usage of functions, even if they are very small, without incurring the overhead usually involved in function calling: the compiler will substitute the function call with the function body itself.

Another significant modification concerns the possibility of overloading operators, which "makes it possible to use the same name for different operations, in the Ada style," increasing code readability. "For example, addition functions on different data types (vectors, matrices, and so on) may all be called using the + symbols." [Meyer 88]

In general, the language "C++ was designed under severe constraints of compatibility, internal consistency, and efficiency" [Stroustrup 88] for memory usage, compile time, run time and space overheads, or development environment constraints. Furthermore, "C++ and its libraries are designed for portability." [Stroustrup 86]

Constructs for Object-Oriented Programming

C++ offers several constructs for object-oriented programming that will be described briefly here and that will be examined in great detail in the following chapters. This is only a concise "technical" description; if you do not fully understand the following notes, you can skip this section and maybe get back to it later, when all these constructs will have been introduced.

The first is the type construct class, of which single items can be "instanced" and are known as objects. A class offers services and functionality to its outside, from which it hides the internal implementation and supporting data structures.

The second is inheritance relationship between classes, that is, the possibility of defining a class using other classes as a foundation. The new class will inherit all the definitions of the existing class, in addition to all the definitions this last class might inherit from other classes. It is possible to have simple inheritance from one class, but also multiple inheritance from two or more classes at the same time.

Another construct is dynamic binding, which allows the compiler to decide at run time which among a group of procedures should answer to a certain function call, according to the class that the objects actually being involved belong to. In C++, dynamic binding is possible only for those routines that are identified as *virtual* in their original class, because static binding is used by default.

Dynamic binding is strongly related to polymorphism, that is, the possibility that one entity refers to (at run time) objects of different classes. In C++, like in all languages that perform static type checking, the mechanism is limited within the inheritance hierarchy of a class. In other words, this mechanism does not nullify data type checking, but rather, in a certain sense, it enforces it.

Like in other languages, the structure of a class consists of two parts: the interface and the collection of functions. The interface contains the information that is exported to the outside of the module; the implementation details are hidden within the functions, including the initialization details.

The subdivision in interface and implementation permits you to use the technique of separate compilation, since the compiler only needs to know the interfaces in use or inheritance relationship with the module being compiled.

The interface of a class is in turn made up of three parts. The first part specifies the *private* data structures, which represent the objects of this class and the possible private operations. The second part comprises *protected* data and functions, which are visible to the class's subclasses. The third part is where *public* functions are declared for "external" usage, to gain access to the objects of the class and thus, indirectly, to the private data structures. These last functions correspond to the operations provided by the abstraction being modeled by the class.

In addition to "normal" variables within classes, it is possible to declare (static) class variables, that is, variables of which there exists only one instance for the whole class and is, therefore, shared between all objects of that particular class. This possibility, which is not present in Eiffel, derives from Smalltalk, where the classes themselves are actually objects (defined by *metaclasses*), and can therefore have variables and methods (functions).

To complement these constructs for data-hiding in object-oriented programming, some other features have been added to C in order to circumvent them. For instance, the *friend* construct allows you to freely access the private data of a class, bypassing the rules of information hiding. The decision to introduce constructs of this kind is very questionable, but it has certainly been done primarily for the purpose of efficiency.

In the last years two new constructs have been added: genericity and exception handling. Although they do not refer directly to object-oriented programming, these new language features favor robust programming. The possibility of defining generic classes (as in Ada) is particularly useful in a language with strict type checking, and is implemented in C++ with the so-called *template* classes and functions, which are available in Borland C++ starting with version 3 (templates are part of the AT&T C++ Release 3 specifications). As we will see in Chapter 10, generic classes positively affect code reusability.

Exception handling, on the other hand, is an invaluable tool for writing robust applications. The C++ implementation of this concept, which has been approved by the ANSI committee only recently and is new in version 4 of the Borland compiler, is one of the most powerful, because it is based on objects and class hierarchies.

Not every C++ compiler includes these two important features, or for that matter other minor elements which have been added to the C++ language in the last years, such as the flexibility in the return value of virtual functions, three different character data types, and Run-Time Type Information (RTTI).

New additions to the language and some new standard libraries (such as the string library, which is already available in the Borland compilers) are expected in the next few years, as the work of the ANSI committee continues.

➤   *Note:* Most of the essential features of other object-oriented languages are present in C++, but there are some limitations.

These limitations, as a whole, do not in any way spoil the excellent performance of the language. In fact, it is difficult to find another object-oriented language that is more extensive and complete than C++, because even other languages, in comparison, suffer from other important limitations.

One inconvenience of C++ is the need to write simple functions to access the local data of a class from the outside. It's impossible to read that data directly, without allowing the data to be modified with equal directness. (This is possible, for instance, in Eiffel, where there is a uniform reference both to functions as well as data.) In practice, local data needs to be exported to the outside by means of simple functions that merely return the value of the data involved. The coding of these functions, though very simple, is certainly a nuisance. On the other hand, this is certainly no excuse for making the data public, because that would allow their direct manipulation from the outside, which is contrary to the principles of information hiding.

Much more severe, from a theoretical point of view, is the limitation imposed by C++ on dynamic binding, which has to be declared explicitly within the first class of the hierarchy where the function involved appears. This "makes it easier to implement calls efficiently, as static binding may be used for calls to nonvirtual routines," but it contrasts with the principle that "a class should always remain open for extension, which implies that it is not its business to decide which of its classes are redefinable by descendants" [Meyer 88], and thus it does not favor reusability.

Another limitation is the absence of a mechanism of *garbage collection*: the building and deallocation of objects is managed by means of pointers that have to be controlled by specific functions for their creation and destruction in order to overflow memory with inaccessible data.

Moreover, yet having the possibility of separate compilations, which favor the development of reusable software, the solution offered by C++ (similar to Ada's) is inadequate in that the interface of the class has to contain the declaration of private data elements and their internal representation. This representation is not accessible from the outside of a class, and belongs, as such, to its implementation. Apart from aesthetical and readability issues:

- The representation of data has to be determined at the same time of the specification of the interface, and this is in contrast with a correct methodological approach.

- If, among the private data members of a class there are other objects, then to compile the class it is necessary to include the interface of these other classes. And if these, in turn, contain other objects, the process has to be repeated.

- In the case of modification of a class, it is necessary to modify its interface as well, and recompile all those modules that use it.

On the other hand, this solution is very widespread, because it depends on the the compiler, and no valid alternatives have yet been found that are an acceptable solution to this problem.

POINTS TO CONSIDER

1. Think about the subject of abstraction and its relationship with the actual programming effort you have developed.

2. Consider critically the "external" features of software, adding to the list given in this chapter. Think about the consequences these could have on the development of programs, with reference to your own experience.

3. Analyze the degree of modularity in your own programs.

4. Compare the design methodology espoused in this chapter with your own preferred design practice, or with your own way of working when you approach the development of a program.

5. If you have already used an object-oriented programming language, establish which category it belongs to and which features it has (Figure 3.6 and Table 3.1).

6. Consider the merits and the limitations of C++, and compare them with the programming languages you use or know.

4

Elements of the C++ Language

*Language is the vehicle by which we express our thoughts, and the relation between those thoughts and our language is a subtle and involuted one. The nature of language actually shapes and models the way we think. Providing appropriate language constructs, we can improve the programs written using these structures. But language is **not** a panacea. A language cannot, for example, prevent the creation of obscure programs: the ingenious programmer can always find an infinite number of paths to obfuscation.* [Wulf 77]

In the previous chapter, the general ideas of object-oriented design and programming were presented, together with some considerations on object-oriented languages and C++. This chapter focuses exclusively on C++.

Although Borland C++ is actually more than a language—it's a complete development environment based on the "standard" specification of the C++ language—this chapter provides an overview of the basic constructs offered by C++. These are actually "nonobject-oriented" constructs, and most of them derive from the corresponding constructs of C.

The elements of the C++ language are introduced by describing the fundamental data types (built-in and aggregate), together with constant declarations, expressions, and operators. Then, the fundamental statements of the language will be illustrated. First there is a description of the assignment operators; then come the control statements, divided in the three generic categories of sequence, selection, and iteration. These control statements are really the "syntactic bricks" with which the programs are built. The last part of this chapter covers functions (calls, inline functions, implicit and default parameters, and parameter passing), the C++ preprocessor, and standard input/output.

There is no attempt to explain what the purpose of the various constructs is or when they are to be employed; rather, this is a presentation describing the main properties and the prominent aspects of these constructs through simple examples, so that any knowledgeable programmer will quickly get "up to speed" and recognize the fundamental constructs of C++.

Syntax Elements of C++

In this section, we will examine the basic elements of C++ and their syntax. The description here is intentionally cursory, with the sole purpose of illustrating the fundamental ideas rather than describing the language in every detail. To get more complete and comprehensive information, refer to your Borland C++ manuals.

Declarations and Definitions

In addition to the keywords defined by C++, every name in C++ can indicate an object, a function, a type, or a value. In each of these cases, the name has to be introduced in the program by means of its *declaration*, sometimes called its *prototype*. A declaration indicates what the name represents or describes the name completely (in which case it is better referred to as a *definition*).

Every name can first be declared and then defined; and while a name can be declared several times, within the program there can exist only one definition for every name being used.

Some examples (shown below) of declarations are: Functions where there is no body specified (a), the declaration of types without specifying their characteristics (b), the declarations of external objects (that is, present in some other file of which the program is made up) (c), and declarations appearing alone for the member functions within the interface of a class (d).

```
int function ( float ) ;    // declaration of a function ( a )

class MyClass ;             // declaration of a class ( b )

extern char c ;             // "external" declaration ( c )

class AnotherClass          // definition of a class
{
    ...
    int F ( ) ;             // declaration of a member function ( d )
    ...
} ;
```

In each of these cases, it is necessary that the definition of the name follow the declaration. More commonly, the two happen together, like the preceding definition of the class *AnotherClass* and the following examples:

```
int    number ;

int    Sum ( a , b )
    {
```

```
        return a + b ;
   }

struct Couple
   {
       int first ;
       int second ;
   } ;
```

Scope

Another important element is the *scope* of a name, or the set of statements of a program for which that name is known and thus usable. A name is visible only within its "scope," and remains invisible outside. In other words, the scope of a name defines its *visibility*. In C++ the visibility of a name is defined statically, and it depends on the source code text of the program and not on its execution. In particular, the following three cases are distinguished:

- **Local scope**: a name declared inside a block is visible only in that block starting from the point where it is declared.
- **File scope**: a name declared outside of any block or class can be referenced in the whole file, starting from the point where it is declared.
- **Class scope**: a class member is local to its class and can be used in the class's member functions. If the name is public or protected, then it can also be used outside the class or in the class's subclasses.

There are also some peculiar cases that will be described later. The essential element is understanding that, in general, a name is visible only inside the block that contains it (and to the other blocks that might be related to it) and only starting from the point where it is declared.

The position of the declaration, in C++, will not affect its effectiveness: in contrast to C, for instance, the names of variables do not have to be placed at the beginning of the block in which they are used; actually they can be placed anywhere. However, due to habit and for clarity, declarations are usually collected at the beginning of blocks. This also helps state clearly the initialization of variables. Figure 4.1 is an example of a variable declared inside a block, where the parts in which it is visible are clearly marked.

The Main Function

As in C, the execution of a program begins with the function *main*. Every DOS program must contain a function with this name, which marks the starting point of execution. Windows programs contain instead a *WinMain* function that is the Windows entry point.

```
    ...                    // c has not yet been declared
    {                      // beginning of a block
        int a, b ;         // other declarations
        ...
        b = a * 5 ;        // c cannot yet be used here
        ...
        int c ;            // starting point of c's visibility
        ...
        c = a + b ;
        ...
    }                      // end of the block and of c's visibility
    ...                    // outside the block c is not visible
    c = 4 ;                // ERROR!
```

Figure 4.1 Visibility of a local variable

Syntactically, a program can consist of only an "empty" *main* function, and yet still be a formally correct C++ program. Apart from this extreme case, many functionalities of the program are quite often included in the main function, and usually even its main control loop. This is legitimate, but it is not consistent with object-oriented programming.

A C++ program that is object-oriented even in appearance should have only one object declaration and its activation in the main function. This way, all functionality is transferred to the principal class of the system.

Obviously, it would be silly to take this general advice to its extreme. For this reason, even many of the most simple sample programs in this book are based on a "traditional" *main* function, although, in other examples, this rule will be applied literally.

➤ *Note:* As with all other functions, the *main* function has a return value, which is taken by default as *int*, unless the source code specifies differently. In most cases, the return value of the *main* function is indicated as *void*, which means that the function does not return any value. (The proposed C++ Standard [Ellis 90] actually states that the type returned by the main function is *implementation dependent*.)

The Elements of the Language

A C++ program consists of a series of statements, each of which is terminated by a semicolon (;). In fact, a statement can be defined as an expression followed by a semicolon. Unlike most other programming languages, the semicolon is a *terminator* symbol and not a *separator*.

It is useful for you to remember that the absence of a semicolon at the end of a statement is a very common error, especially when the statement is the last one in a block. Often, the Borland C++ compiler will indicate this kind of error in an inexact way; usually it will flag some kind of error on the line following, which is considered as the continuation of the line with the missing semicolon.

Also, the format of the source text will not affect the execution of statements. A single statement can even extend over several lines in the source text, with no problem whatsoever. The compiler will simply ignore all "white space" and "carriage returns," which actually helps make the text more readable for the programmer. We advise you to take advantage of this: a well-spaced program will be much more intelligible than the same program written in a cramped style, and you will not be slower at run time. The same is true for a program with many comments. The program comments are useful for the programmer, but they are ignored by the compiler and hardly influence compilation times. The resulting program is exactly the same as if it had no comments at all. (The actual syntax and format for inserting comments will be described in the following section.)

Many programmers find themselves discussing what kind of "layout" should be given to the source code. These discussions are trivial most of the time. "Judicious use of comments and consistent use of indentation can make the task of reading and understanding a program much more pleasant. Several different consistent styles of indentation are used. I see no fundamental reason to prefer one over another (though, like most others, I have my preferences)." [Stroustrup 91A] The important point is that "indentation is simply an additional tool to help convey the structure of the program" and that "indentation [should] be consistent across the entire file. Maintaining a program becomes extremely difficult when coding styles are mixed from one line, page, block, or function to the next." [Hansen 90]

A program consists of a sequence of statements. Some of these will be simple statements; others will be compound (that is, statements that include other statements).

It is always possible for you to create a compound statement by enclosing a series of statements within a block. A block is delimited by a pair of curly braces:

```
...
{   // beginning of the block

    ...
    // body of the block

    ...
}   // end of the block

...
```

Blocks can appear in any place inside a program wherever a single statement is legitimate and are useful to collect several statements, although the possibility of declaring variables in any place reduces their need.

The purpose of a block is to enclose a precise portion of the program. For instance, the variables declared inside a block are visible only within that block; they are "destroyed" as soon as the block is executed (although the subject of memory de-allocation is a lot more complicated than is apparent from this simple sentence).

The components of the C++ language can generally be divided into the following categories. (Each one of these will be described further in the remainder of this chapter and the following chapters. Here we will just clarify the terminology being used to better understand what follows.)

- **Data**. Data includes the declaration of the data types defined by the programmer (arrays, structures, classes, enumerations, and so on) and the declaration of variables, objects, and their initialization.

- **Classes**. A very important subcase of the statements regarding data are those statements that concern classes. Their declaration is preceded by the keyword *class* and can often be very complex. The creation of an object starting from a class can take place in several ways, but will always need the presence of a definition similar to those for other ordinary variables. Classes, in an object-oriented language, establish the foundation of every program.

- **Expressions**. Within a statement, there will very often appear an expression, which can be somewhat convoluted. Expressions can be classified according to the data type resulting from their evaluation (integer, floating point number, character, and so on) as well as to their complexity. The simplest expression consists of just a constant (for instance, an explicit integer number) or a variable (in which case the value of the expression corresponds to the value of the variable). On the other hand, a complex expression can contain many operators and sub-expressions.

- **Operators**. Operators, the ever-present elements of the language, are the set of all characters that have a meaning particular to the language, excluding only the characters that serve as punctuation (; " : ,). Among the characters used as operators, some of the most common are

    + * / - = < > . & |

    but there are many more. Furthermore, some operators are represented by a combination of two or more of these special characters, like

    && == != *= <= ++

- **Control structures**. Another basic element is the control structures of the language. These elements are special statements concerning loops (*for*, *while*, and so on) that allow you to execute one or more statements a certain number of times or until a certain condition is true. Elements containing simple branching (*if*) and multiple branching (*if-else*, *switch*) allow you to execute one statement rather than another, based on some condition.

- **Functions**. Functions are another element of C++ whose definition can sometimes be very lengthy. Functions are generally used for repeated execution of the block of statements that constitutes them. In C++, functions belong to two categories. Besides the "normal" functions known in C, there is another kind of function closely connected to classes. These functions, known as *member functions,* are an essential element of object-oriented programming.

Comments

In C++, comments are introduced by the symbol //. A comment introduced by // lasts until the end of the line. However, you can also use the commenting conventions of C, where comments are enclosed by the pair of symbols /* and */.

Usually the // is used for short notices, which generally appear at the end of a line of source code. The /* and */ are better suited for comments spanning multiple lines. For example:

```
// comment to the end of a line

/* comment to the corresponding delimiter */

// This comment is erroneous because it carries over
the end of the line where it is written.

/* This is the right
kind of comment spanning
multiple lines */

// Also this comment on
// multiple lines
// is correct.
```

The editor of Borland C++ has a feature, called *color syntax highlighting*, which allows the programmer to use a different color for the text of the comments, and thus the comments become easier to locate. This is particularly important if comments span several lines, maybe disabling a portion of the source code.

Keywords

C++, like every programming language, has a few keywords that cannot be used or redefined by the programmer. The complete list of keywords can be found in the Borland C++ manuals, or can be looked up in the online help system. This way, you will get a help window like the one shown in Figure 4.2, listing all keywords and where you can select the single items to get additional information on the usage of the different keywords.

The operators of the language (+, *, <, &, ...) can instead be redefined through overloading—allowing the operator to have different implementations depending on the type of operand(s).

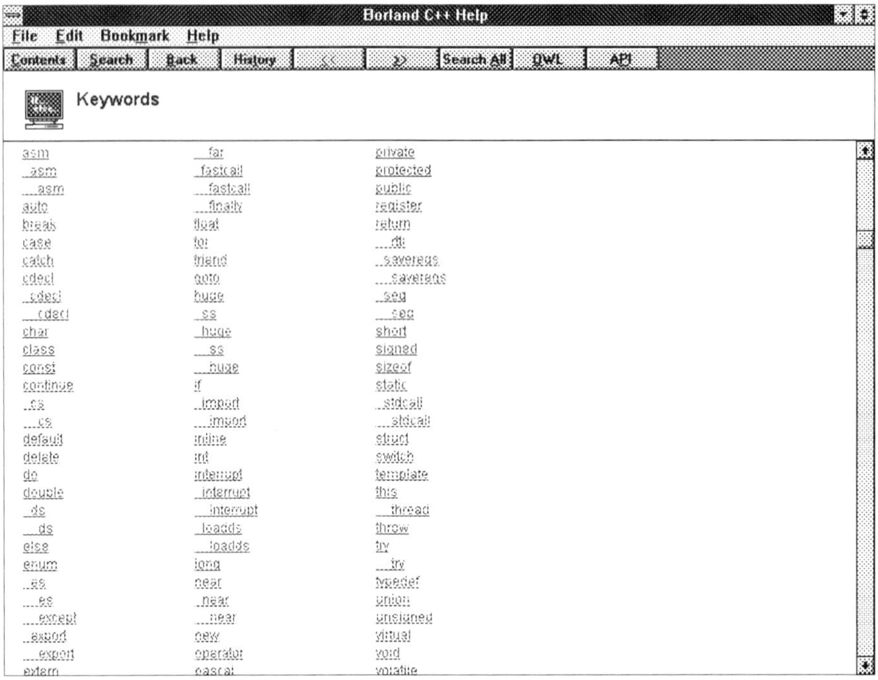

Figure 4.2 The Help window of the integrated environment of Borland C++ listing all keywords

See what happens when you use a reserved keyword. To do so, compile the following program:

```
// file KEYWORD.CPP                                    04\KEYWORD
// example of one of the error messages you get when trying to use
// a keyword inside a program ( since there isn't a proper error message )

void main ( )
{
   // simulation of a check panel
   // ...

   // there is an on/off button
   int     button ;

   // and a four-position switch
   int     switch ;

   // rest of the program...
}
```

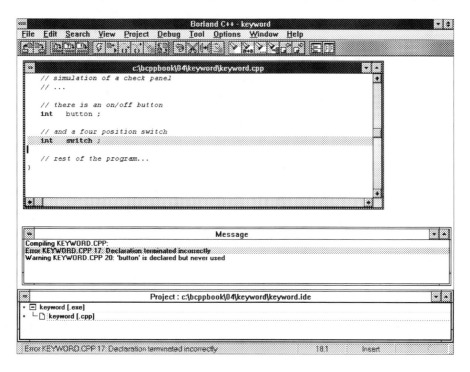

Figure 4.3 The error message that points out the problem present in the program KEYWORD.CPP

During the compilation of this program, Borland C++ issues the error message "Declaration terminated incorrectly," as shown in Figure 4.3. Although this error message does not help much in understanding what kind of error actually occurred, the *switch* keyword is clearly marked out thanks to color syntax highlighting.

C++ Data Types

Keeping in mind that classes are also data types, we'll try to outline an overview of all the data types offered by the language.

Omitting a more detailed description, we remind you that the type is one of the fundamental properties of a variable. It might be considered as the definition of the set of values that the variable can take, together with the operations that can be legitimately used to create, access, or modify these values.

You can divide C++ data types into two groups:

- built-in or defined by the language
- user-defined, by means of some construct offered by the language, which enables you to build even very complex aggregate data types

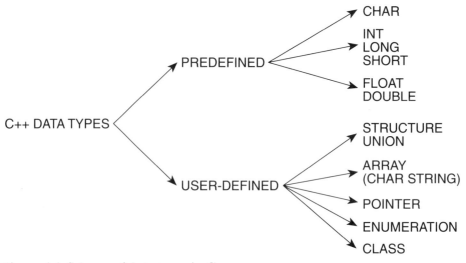

Figure 4.4 Scheme of data types in C++

A sketch of C++ data types is shown in Figure 4.4 and is described in detail in the following sections. The information, however, is not exhaustive, but gives an overall view of the data types available in C++. To have a detailed technical description of data types and their physical representation, refer to the Borland C++ manuals or to one of the technical books on C++, such as those by Stroustrup listed in the bibliography.

Built-in Data Types

The built-in data types of the C++ language, which correspond exactly to those of the C language, are called *arithmetic types*; they represent characters (*char*), integers (*int, long,* and *short*), and floating-point numbers (*float* and *double*).

Besides this list, you can annotate two particular aspects (compared with other programming languages):

1. Some data types have more than one definition, according to the precision of the computations and the range of the numbers you want to use. Having several data types, you can achieve a higher precision while in the other cases you can gain a greater efficiency (both in terms of computation speed and memory usage) by using data types with a lower number of significant digits.

2. In C++, some data types common in other languages are missing, for example, character strings and Boolean values. The absence of character strings is inherited from the C language (although a standard C++ *string* class is emerging). The same holds for Boolean values, which are handled by using integers and consider the values true and false as, respectively, nonzero and zero. The use of these data types will be shown later in several examples.

You will now look inside a program at the declarations of variables for these data types. The general structure of a simple declaration in C++ is

```
data_type   variable_name [= initial_value] ;
```

where the square brackets indicate that the assignment of an initial value is optional— it is possible but not required.

In this way, you can declare the following variables:

```
int      number = 7 ;
char     character = 'W' ;
float    other_number= 1452.13295873 ;
```

Why do you need these declarations? To be assured that, through type checking, the operations you make with these variables are legitimate. It is noteworthy, though, that in the following examples, using the preceding declarations, an incorrect operation might be accepted by the compiler, which can automatically convert an arithmetic data type into another:

```
number = 33 ;              // correct
number = 'z' ;             // incorrect
character = 3.14 ;         // incorrect
other_number = 's' ;       // incorrect
other_number = 1990 ;      // correct
number = 3.4536 ;          // incorrect
```

➤ *Note:* In this case, the incorrect operations are actually accepted by the compiler because it is capable of performing automatic conversions between arithmetic data types. In some cases, the compiler will alert you with a warning that the automatic data conversion may cause a loss of significant digits. You will see that automatic type conversion takes place only for predefined data types, and not for user-defined data types, for which the programmer must state explicit conversion operations.

Just as it is important for a variable to be associated with a data type, any variable should always have a proper value. This rule serves to avoid the error of using a variable that is defined but not initialized; that is, one to which a value has not yet been given and is therefore holding a random value. (This kind of error is much more common than you might think.) Data initialization is a way to reduce errors in a program. For this reason we will use it, in the form of variable declaration shown in the preceding examples, whenever possible.

To have a better idea of the importance of initialization, let's examine a simple program in which there is an error due to missing initialization. Obviously, this kind of error is more common if you're writing a complex piece of code.

```
// file INITIAL.CPP                                        04\INITIAL
// examples of a missing-initialization error

#include "iostream.h"

void main ( )
{
    int    a , b , c = 0 ,   // a and b not initialized
           d = 0 ;

    b = 27 ;
    d = a + b + c ;

    // shows the undefined value of variable d

    cout << "d = " << d << /endl ;
}
```

Why are such obvious ideas stressed so much? Besides the fact that they might not be so obvious for everybody (for instance, for programmers who use languages with almost no type checking at all, such as BASIC), there are also many programmers who consider the use of a data type as a kind of overhead, something the compiler needs to be efficient, but that they—clever programmers—can better do without. This way of thinking is in clear contrast with the principles of object-oriented programming explained in this book. In fact, the use of data types and of rigorous type checking is a fundamental tool for the correctness of a program, particularly if it has a certain size. At the same time, this way of thinking is the first basic step toward data abstraction and information hiding. The C language, however, doesn't support a strong type checking. Neither does C++, although it is somewhat better; with these languages, in fact, it is possible to get around type checking for example using the union (or variant record) construct.

It is the programmer who has to decide whether to be disciplined, or to do without the correctness checks offered by data types. In this book, there is a clear preference for the discipline, but it is not possible to force you to do the same!

In the C++ language, variable definitions might be coupled with some other information beyond the data type they are associated with. Here is a list of some categories of type modifiers:

- the keywords **signed** and **unsigned** might be prefixed to almost any predefined data type, to indicate if the number should or should not have a sign. If this information is missing, it is usually assumed that the value is signed.

- the storage class specifiers, including: **extern**, which indicates variables visible outside the file in which they are declared; **register**, which requests that the compiler allocate the variable in one of the CPU registers; **typedef**, which indicates the definition of a data type name instead of a variable.

- **const** and **volatile** are used respectively to define a variable that cannot change its value (a constant) or a variable whose value can be modified from the outside at run time, and therefore the compiler shouldn't make any kind of optimization or particular allocation.

- modifiers added by Borland C++: **cdecl**, **pascal**, **interrupt**, **near**, **far**, **huge**, and several others. All these keywords might be prefixed to a data type, changing the memory model to be used, the scope of a pointer, the kind of parameter passing, and so on.

A detailed description of the access modifiers can be found in the compiler's manuals, but it's probably better to try to learn them only when you have a good knowledge of the language.

Aggregate Data Types

In any programming language (that stands up to this definition) there are some constructs that allow you to define complex data structures through operations such as Cartesian product, finite mapping, sequencing, recursion, powerset, and discriminated union. Behind these names are some well-known constructs familiar to any programmer: record or structures, arrays, character strings, pointers, and sets.

Structures

Structures (in other languages called *records*) let you include different data items in a single type. For example, to define the information contained in a variable of type *Date*, you need to indicate that it is made up of a month, a day, and a year:

```
struct Date
{
    int     month ;
    int     day ;
    int     year ;
} ;
```

You can access the data inside a structure similarly to the way you access different variables: using *dot-notation* to access the single fields (or internal data) of a structure.

```
Date  d ;     // defines a variable of type Date
d.year = 1992 ;
d.day = 27 ;
int m = d.month ;
```

The above code fragment contains a subtle error. Can you spot it?

For the C programmers, we must also note that the first line of this example is equivalent to the following C code:

```
struct Date d ;
```

and is a shorthand notation peculiar to C++.

In C++, however, structures are much more powerful than in the C language, since it is possible for you to declare both data and the functions to access that data. In this way, structures become similar to classes.

The difference—and an important one—between a structure and a class is that the data of a structure, as we already noted, can (usually) be freely accessed and modified from the outside. In fact, structures usually offer no information hiding. As you will see, a structure corresponds to a class with all its data declared in the *public* section. Conversely, by declaring private all of its members, you can define a structure corresponding exactly to a class, although this last construct is more natural and clear. If the meaning of these last sentences seems obscure, don't worry; it will become clear as you progress.

Arrays

Finite mapping is usually made possible via the *array* construct, which allows you to associate the values of a domain (generally integers) to corresponding values of a fixed type.

The use of arrays is very common; their main purpose is to store sequences or groups of data, tables (with arrays having more than one dimension), and so on.

For example, to store the data related to temperature change during a day, you can declare an array of 24 integers, any one of which represents the mean temperature measured in a certain hour of the day:

```
int    temperature [ 24 ] ;
```

To access the data of the array you must indicate the element you are referring to inside a pair of square brackets.

```
temperature [ 8 ] = 62;
int maximum = temperature [ 13 ] ;
```

➤   *Note:* The indexing value of an array starts counting from 0. This means, for instance, that in the above example, you are actually accessing the ninth and fourteenth elements. The highest index value that is allowed equals the number of elements declared minus one.

This is important because a common programming mistake is to write something to the last element, using as an index the number of array elements (such as *temperature [24]*). This approach will overwrite a different variable and can cause an error that is hard to track down.

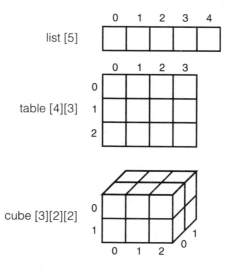

Figure 4.5 The intuitive meaning of arrays

Arrays can have more than one dimension, as shown in Figure 4.5. If they have one dimension, they look like lists; if they have two, like tables; if they have three, like parallelepipeds; if they have four or more dimensions, they look like hyper cubes (try to imagine that!) or as a list of parallelepipeds or tables of tables (if the dimensions are 4), tables of parallelepipeds (5 dimensions), parallelepipeds of parallelepipeds (6 dimensions), and so on.

This play upon words stresses that an array with more than one dimension might be seen in different ways: a bi-dimensional array might be considered as a list of objects, any one of which happens to be an array. On the other hand, it might be considered as a table of simple values.

Also, the use of tables is very common. For example, if you want to store the data regarding the traffic along a road during a week, you can count and store the number of cars passing during each hour:

```
int    cars [ 7 ] [ 24 ] ;
```

To access arrays with more than one dimension, use the following statements:

```
cars [ 3 ] [ 8 ] = 142 ;
cars [ 5 ] [ 23 ] = 57 ;
```

Character Strings

Contrary to other programming languages, C++ doesn't offer an elementary data type to hold sequences of characters, or *strings*. Nonetheless, there are several methods for handling character strings quite easily, even with C++. In the past, this was usually achieved through some functions of the C language standard libraries, but Borland C++ now supports a specific ANSI C++ *string* class, which is much simpler to use. Let us first describe how you can handle "C strings," and later look at the *string* class.

In the C language, strings are seen by the compiler as arrays of characters. The statement

```
char     s [ 20 ] ;
```

declares *s* as a string of 19 characters (you will see shortly why not 20). This string might be handled exactly as an array, modifying single characters, reading them, and so on. This method, however, is not straightforward and easy. Because of the importance of strings in programming, any C++ language compiler offers a way to handle character arrays directly, with methods typical for this data type.

A string corresponds to an array of characters, the last element of which is a null character ('\0'): that is why an array of 20 characters can contain a string having at most 19!

The declaration of a character string and its initialization might be written in the following way, using a pointer to an array (see the next section for a description of pointers):

```
char *    string = "Good afternoon to everybody" ;
```

On the variable string so defined, we can operate on it in two ways: either as a single element:

```
cout << string << endl ;
```

or as an array of elements:

```
cout << string [ 6 ] << endl ;
```

The first statement prints out the characters

```
Good afternoon to everybody
```

while the second outputs only the character

```
f
```

(that is, the seventh character, since the count begins from 0).

At the same time, it's also possible to operate in these two ways on strings declared as arrays of a fixed number of characters (such as the previous *char s [20]*). This kind of declaration is particularly useful to handle variable-length strings. In fact, declaring

```
char *    string = "Good morning";
char *    name = "Bob";
```

and changing the first string with a command like

```
strcpy (string, "Good afternoon");
```

will corrupt the second string (*name*), because the first string is too short to contain the new value provided by the *strcpy* function. Had the string been defined as

```
char  string [30];
```

no problem would have occurred.

On the whole, there are times when one or the other technique is better to declare character strings, and even times when it makes sense to combine the two types of string handling.

Several library functions are available to handle strings. In the standard input-output libraries (such as the iostream.h library) there is the object *cout*, used for output, and the object *cin*, that handles string input.

The most common string operations (concatenation, substring extraction, and length calculation) have corresponding functions predefined in the string.h library.

The ANSI String Class

Because of the lack of a built-in data type for strings, the ANSI C++ committee has defined a standard class to handle this data type. As we will see later in detail, classes are a way to define abstract data types, or to add new data types to the language. Therefore, using an object of the *string* class is not much different from using a variable of the *char* or *int* type:

```
string text = "Good morning" ;
cout << text << endl ;
```

To use the *string* class this way you need to include the header file *cstring.h*, which contains the full definition of the class. Notice that with this header file inclusion some of the code of the previous section won't compile; since *string* is now a class, you cannot use the same name for identifying an array of characters. Using the class, you can assign strings one to another (and make other operations much more simple) as in:

```
string second, third ;
second = text ;
third = "Bye" ;
```

In the rest of the book we will use both the old method derived from the C language and the new *string* class, and we will further examine this class in Chapter 14.

Pointers

Another type definition construct—the one that offers the most freedom and expressiveness—is given by pointers. This construct is also used in other situations, including function parameter passing, and—in general—the substitution of variables' names for reasons of efficiency (because of the different methods of memory addressing).

Pointers (combined with the *struct* construct) are used to allow the building of complex data structures, usually recursive.

➤ *Note:* The term "recursive" here is used to denote a data structure that is defined in terms of itself. For example, an item in a list might be defined as some data plus a pointer to an item in a list. In the same way, a node in a binary tree might be described as some data and two pointers to other binary tree nodes.

However, the most common use of the term "recursion" is to describe the definition of a function that calls itself inside its own code—to perform a series of commands over and over until a condition is met.

Quite often, to access a recursive data structure, one has to define and use recursive functions.

The declaration of pointers in C++ is made as follows:

```
int *                p1 ;    // pointer to an integer ;
float *              p2 ;    // pointer to a float ;
struct { int a ; int b ; } *  p3 ;    // pointer to a structure
```

You can operate on a pointer variable in two ways: you can operate on the pointer itself or on the value the pointer refers to.

In the first case, you use the plain variable name; in the second, the variable name must be preceded by the operator '*'.

The following code shows a sample of operations on pointers and their values. The corresponding graphical representations that appear in Figure 4.6 and the output of the program in Figure 4.7 might help you to understand them:

```
// file POINTER.CPP                          04\POINTER
// examples of usage of pointers

#include <iostream.h>

void main ( )
{

    // declarations of pointers
```

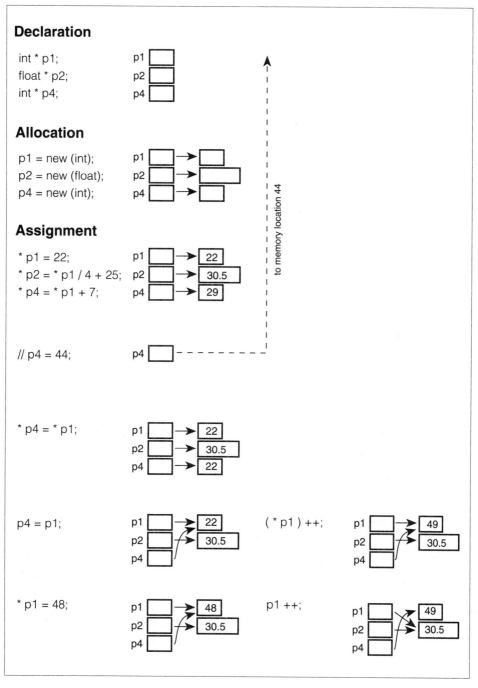

Figure 4.6 Graphic representation of some operations performed by the program POINTER.CPP

```
int *      p1 ;    // allocates memory for pointers
float *    p2 ;    // (but not the data they point to)
int *      p4 ;

// memory allocation

p1 = new ( int ) ;     // allocates memory for the data and
p2 = new ( float ) ;   // stores the address of the allocated memory
p4 = new ( int ) ;     // in the pointer memory area

// examples of pointer assignment ( '*' )

*p1 = 22 ;                     // stores numeric values in the memory
*p2 = float (*p1) / 4 + 25 ;   // locations pointed to by the pointer
*p4 = *p1 + 7 ;

// instead the following is wrong

// p4 = 44 ;     // points the pointer at memory location 44

// assignment between pointers ( see also figure )

*p4 = *p1 ;    // assigns the value pointed to by p1 to the memory location
               // pointed to by p4
p4 = p1 ;      // assignment of the pointer--p4 points to the same location as p1
```

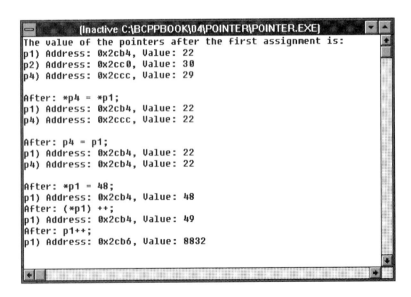

```
[Inactive C:\BCPPBOOK\04\POINTER\POINTER.EXE]
The value of the pointers after the first assignment is:
p1) Address: 0x2cb4, Value: 22
p2) Address: 0x2cc0, Value: 30
p4) Address: 0x2ccc, Value: 29

After: *p4 = *p1;
p1) Address: 0x2cb4, Value: 22
p4) Address: 0x2ccc, Value: 22

After: p4 = p1;
p1) Address: 0x2cb4, Value: 22
p4) Address: 0x2cb4, Value: 22

After: *p1 = 48;
p1) Address: 0x2cb4, Value: 48
After: (*p1) ++;
p1) Address: 0x2cb4, Value: 49
After: p1++;
p1) Address: 0x2cb6, Value: 8832
```

Figure 4.7 The output of the POINTER.CPP program

```
// increment of pointers and their values
*p1 = 48 ;      // changes the value pointed to by p1 and p4 to 48

( *p1 ) ++ ;    // increments the value pointed to by p1 and p4 to 49
cout << *p1 << " " << p1 << endl ;

p1 ++ ;         // increments the pointer from its current location to the next
                // memory location
cout << *p1 << " " << p1 << endl ;
}
```

By combining the use of pointers and records (or structures), it is possible for you to build complex and dynamic data structures (*dynamic* means that their dimensions can change according to their needs at run-time). A classic example of these structures is a simple list, which can be defined in the following way:

```
// examples of dynamic data structure created with pointers

// structure declaration
struct Element ;

// definition of a "pointer to structure" data type
typedef Element * pElem ;

// structure definition
struct Element
{
    int        data ;
    pElem      next ;
} ;
```

enum

The last construct you will examine is the *enumeration* or *set*. It is possible to both define a data type and directly indicate its domain, by writing the list of values this data type can take.

For example, if you need a variable that can have the values corresponding to the names of the weekdays, you could define its type with this construct:

```
enum    week { mon , tue , wed , thu , fri , sat , sun } ;

// declares a variable of the data type week
week    day = mon ;
```

```
// assigns the value "sat" to the variable
day = sat ;

// the following statement generates the compiler warning:
// "Assigning int to week"
day = 4 ;

// increases the value (using an explicit type casting)
day = (week) (day + 1);
```

The last two operations are possible because C++, as with the C language, treats *enums* as *ints*.

➤   *Note:* With other programming languages (notably Pascal), this construct treats enumerations as a "powerset"—that is, variables that can hold one or more elements of the set defined by listing all of its items.

Combined Constructs

All the constructs described so far can be freely combined. You can have records whose fields are arrays, pointers, or sets; you can have arrays of structures and arrays of pointers; or you can have pointers to structures or arrays. For example:

```
// array of pointers to a structure:
struct { int a ; int b ; } * pointers [ 10 ] ;

// structure containing an array
struct WithArray
{
    float   number ;
    int     array [ 28 ] ;
} ;

// structure containing pointers
struct WithPointers
{
    char       character ;
    char *     pointer ;
    float *    otherPointer ;
} ;
```

Even if they are correct, you should try to avoid the following kind of declarations:

```
/* definition of a list of eight pointers to structures made of
a tridimensional array of real numbers ( threeD ), another
```

```
much simpler structure ( couple ) and a pointer with double
indirection ( doubleP ) */

struct
{
    float *                   threeD  [ 20 ] [ 15 ] [ 15 ] ;
    struct { int a ; int b ; }   couple ;
    char * *                  doubleP ;
}
* list [ 8 ] ;
```

When you need to define such complex data structures, it's much better to define intermediate data types, using the *typedef* construct, then combine the different parts in the main structure. With the monolithic declaration, it is not possible for you to declare temporary variables to store only parts of the structure, or to pass these parts as parameters to functions; this can only be done with data types having a defined name.

You can rewrite the preceding data structure in the following way:

```
typedef float * [ 20 ] [ 15 ] [ 15 ]    Table ;

typedef struct { int a ; int b ; }       TwoInt ;

typedef char * *                          Double ;

typedef struct
{
    Table    threeD ;
    TwoInt   couple ;
    Double   doubleP ;
}
ComplexData ;

ComplexData *   list [ 8 ] ;
```

Constant Declarations

Besides declaring variables, in C++ you can also declare constants (data that hold a value that is set when initialized and that cannot be changed later on). To declare a constant, you follow basically the same rules for variables declaration, the only difference being that you add the keyword *const* before the data type. Constants can be used exactly as variables of the corresponding data type, with the only obvious difference being that their values cannot be changed.

```
// constant definitions
const float      pi = 3.14 ;
```

```
const char      five = '5' ;

// constant use
float           i = 27 * pi ;

// trying to assign a value to a constant
five = '7' ;   // will generate the error: "Lvalue required in function ..."
```

➤ *Note:* For most purposes, you can treat variables and constants almost alike. However, the compiler will perform consistency checks on the usage of constants, ensuring that they are not modified directly or by side effects. You can think of the compiler as actually replacing any constant with its literal value, while a variable will always refer to a real memory location.

Expressions and Operators

An *expression* is a sequence of operators and operands. The evaluation of an expression determines its value and its type. In fact, even though the operands present in an expression can be of different types, every expression results in its own specific type.

The following are a few examples of numeric expressions (with an indication of the type of the expression—that is, the type of the result):

```
( 4 - 2 ) * 3                   // -> int
16.4 / 23.7                     // -> float
3 + 5 + 6 + 7 + ( 12 * 34 )     // -> int
13.8 * 12 + 31                  // -> float
```

The values that appear within an expression can be "literal" values (like in the preceding examples) or variable and constant values; or they can also be the result of a function. By means of operator overloading (which will be described in Chapter 6), expressions can also operate on objects or on compound data types.

To familiarize yourself with the order in which the evaluation of expressions takes place, you need to consider several factors: First, the precedence rules between operators, in which a multiplication is calculated before an addition; then, the presence of parentheses, which can alter the precedence rules; and finally, the associative property of operators, since some of them are evaluated from left to right, while others are evaluated from right to left.

Order of Precedence Between Operators

Likewise in a mathematical expression, the operators of C++ have different "precedence"; that is, some of them are evaluated before others. As you have already seen, for instance, multiplication takes precedence over addition: 3+2*5 equals 13. While for the arithmetical and logical operators, the precedence corresponds to the customary rules in math and algebra, the remaining operators of the language might give rise to some doubts concerning their evaluation order.

For this reason, it is worthwhile to take a look at the online help system of Borland C++, where a very detailed table on the priority of operators can be found, as seen in Figure 4.8.

To change the evaluation order of operators according to the meaning you want to give to an expression, you can use parentheses, which can be nested any number of times.

Parentheses mean that the subexpression (the expressions embraced by parentheses) is calculated before the whole expression is calculated. For instance:

```
3 + 4 * 5      equals 23
( 3 + 4 ) * 5  equals 35
```

In the second example, the subexpression (3 + 4) is calculated first, then the whole expression is completed as if it were 7 * 5.

Expressions can be made up of very complex formulas, and generally they contain several references to variables or to other values. Sometimes it is preferable not to make an expression too complex. Instead, divide it into smaller expressions and calculate partial results. While there may be a slight performance loss, using smaller expressions will lower the risk of making subtle errors.

The same is true for readability: you should always write an expression in a way that makes it easy to comprehend. For this reason, it is worthwhile to subdivide a complex expression into simpler subexpressions, and, above all, format the source code (with spaces, carriage returns, and even redundant parentheses) to help clarify the meaning. This will help readability without introducing any inefficiency. For instance, compare the following formulations of the same expression:

```
total  =  (a*x*x*x+b*x
           *x+c*x+d)/(e*
           x*x+f*x+g)

total  =  ( a*x*x*x + b*x*x + c*x + d ) /
            ( e*x*x + f*x + g )
```

Semantic Meaning of Operators

To fully utilize a programming language, you need to have a detailed knowledge of the meaning of every operator, the type of data with which it can be used, and the properties that characterize it.

A summary of these features is given in Figure 4.8. While the meaning of some operators is immediately obvious (for instance, the arithmetic operators), others are not. A

1. Highest

()	Function call
[]	Array subscript
->	C++ indirect component selector
::	C++ scope access/resolution
.	C++ direct component selector

2. Unary

!	Logical negation (NOT)
~	Bitwise (1's) complement
+	Unary plus
-	Unary minus
++	Preincrement or postincrement
--	Predecrement or postdecrement
&	Address
*	Indirection
sizeof	Returns size of operand, in bytes
new	Dynamically allocates C++ storage
delete	Dynamically de-allocates C++ storage

3. Member access

.*	C++ dereference (direct)
->*	C++ dereference (indirect)

4. Multiplicative

*	Multiply
/	Divide
%	Remainder (modulus)

5. Additive

+	Binary plus
-	Binary minus

6. Shift

<<	Shift left
>>	Shift right

7. Relational

<	Less than
<=	Less than or equal to
>	Greater than
>=	Greater than or equal to

8. Equality

==	Equal to
!=	Not equal to

9. Bitwise AND

&	Bitwise AND

10. Bitwise exclusive OR

^	Bitwise XOR

11. Bitwise OR

		Bitwise OR

12. Boolean product

&&	Logical AND

13. Boolean sum

||	Logical OR

14. Conditional

?:	a ? x : y means "if a then x, else y"

15. Assignment

=	Simple assignment
*=	Assign product
/=	Assign quotient
%=	Assign remainder (modulus)
+=	Assign sum
-=	Assign difference
&=	Assign bitwise AND
^=	Assign bitwise XOR
|=	Assign bitwise OR
<<=	Assign left shift
>>=	Assign right shift

16. Comma

,	Evaluate

Figure 4.8 Table of precedence and meaning of operators in C++

complete description, with complete examples of their usage, can be found in the Borland C++ manuals; the online help system of the integrated environment is another excellent reference. In this section, you will just be given some general guidelines.

To analyze the various operators in a concise manner, it is useful to classify them into the following categories.

a. Operators that belong directly to the syntax of the language or that access data. A pair of parentheses can denote a function call; a pair of square brackets encloses the indexes of arrays.

The selection of components inside a structure (or a class) is accomplished by means of two different operators: **.** (dot) and **->**, according to whether the component is accessed directly (via a variable) or indirectly (via a pointer). These can both be combined with the indirection operator *****, which accesses a data item referenced by a pointer. On the other hand, the **&** operator returns the address of a variable, and is used to pass parameters by reference to functions.

b. The mathematical operators, which have an obvious meaning, like the arithmetic operators (addition, subtraction, division, multiplication, remainder); the logical operators (and, or, not); the binary operators (complement, shift, and, or, xor) and relational operators (less than, greater than, equal, not equal).

c. Some "unusual" operators, like **sizeof**, **new**, **delete**, the conditional operator *(?:),* and the comma operator *(,).* The first, **sizeof**, returns the quantity of memory (expressed in number of bytes) consumed by a variable (simple or compound). The operators **new** and **delete** allocate and de-allocate memory for pointer variables.

The conditional operator (**?:**) is similiar to the immediate if (iff) function available in most well-known spreadsheet and database programs; if is used to select between two mutually exclusive values based on the result of a logical expression, and is usually a shorthand notation for a conditional statement (*if-else*), as shown in the following example:

```
// file CONDOPER.CPP                              04\CONDOPER
// example of conditional operator

// includes input/output library
#include <iostream.h>

void main ( )
{
    // declaration of variables

    char *    phrase ;
    int       value = 0 ;

    // requests the input of a number
```

```
cout  << "Input a number: " ;
cin   >> value ;

// if the value is higher than 50, the variable phrase receives
// the first character string, otherwise the second one

phrase = ( value > 50 ) ? "higher than 50" : "lower than 50" ;

// outputs the full sentence

cout << "The number you have typed is " << phrase << endl << endl ;

// ... but if value equals 50 the sentence is wrong!
}
```

The use of this operator is subject to certain limitations, which are clearly specified in the help system of the IDE and in the Programmer's Guide of Borland C++.

Even the comma operator (,) is peculiar to the C language: it lets you write a sequence of expressions, have them evaluated one at a time from left to right, then gives as a result the value of the last expression. For instance, in the expression

```
expr1 , expr2 , expr3
```

the first expression to be calculated is *expr1*, then *expr2*, and finally *expr3*, whose value is given to the whole expression. The intermediate results of the first two sub-expressions are simply ignored. This operator is useful for only producing controlled side effects. In the example

```
b = 5 , a = ( ++b ) + 4 , a + b
```

the value of this expression is 16 (because when the last subexpression is calculated, *b* has the value of 6 and *a* has the value of 10).

One reason for using this operator in place of a sequence of statements is to write the code in a shorter and more readable fashion. Sometimes this helps you to avoid having to use additional variables to hold intermediate results. Furthermore, an expression containing the comma operator can appear in place of any other "ordinary" expression; in particular, it can appear in place of expressions that control loops or conditions. In these cases, using additional statements would actually be more difficult, as illustrated in the section on the *for* loop.

It is important to stress that you can use the comma both as an operator as well as a separator. The comma acts as a separator, for instance, when it appears between the parameters of a function. These two cases are very distinct: the comma operator can be used even inside a list of parameters, but it has to be marked out by an additional pair of parentheses.

➤ *Note:* Be aware that the comma operator is valid even inside the indexing expression of an array. This might give rise to subtle misinterpretations if you are used to other high-level programming languages like Pascal and Ada. For example, the expression

```
array [ 8 , 9 ]
```

is perfectly valid in C++, but has a different meaning in Pascal (where, in this instance, the comma is a separator and thus the expression addresses the ninth element in the eighth row of a bi-dimensional array).

Can you figure out what the expression means in C++? What kind of indexing expression should you use in C++ to address an element in a bi-dimensional array?

Type Conversions

Parentheses, in addition to denoting function calls by enclosing a parameter list, can also be used to perform explicit type conversions. (In fact, the compiler itself often performs implicit type conversions, which do not need to be indicated in the source code.) In this case, more commonly known as *type casting*, the data type desired must appear within parentheses. An alternative notation introduced by C++ allows you to write the type conversion as a function call.

The simplest kind of type casting is the one concerning numeric data. For instance, you can convert an *int* to a *float*, and vice versa, with the following expressions:

```
int     integer = 5 ;
float   decimal = 3.45 ;

int     integer2 = ( int ) decimal ;
float   decimal2 = ( float ) integer ;
```

The same two type conversions can also be written with the following functional notation:

```
int     integer2 = int ( decimal ) ;
float   decimal2 = float ( integer ) ;
```

These conversions, if not indicated explicitly, would be performed by the compiler. If the expressions instead involve data types defined by *typedef*, *enum*, or other constructs, the conversions would have to be explicit (otherwise the compiler will issue a *warning* or an *error* message, according to the particular case).

Likewise, it is possible to perform conversions between all data types of the language, predefined or defined by the programmer. Keep in mind, though, that the values resulting from the conversion are not always easy to identify.

In particular, a case of complex and subtle conversions can take place between pointers. In fact, it is possible to convert pointers to elementary types, like

```
pDecimal = ( float * ) pInteger ;
```

but it is also possible to convert pointers to compound data types, like entire objects! This case is particularly subtle because by typecasting you can get around some of the rules of C++, specifically those regarding type checking. Therefore, it is necessary to use this kind of typecasting only in "extreme" cases. Usually, it would be wise to employ safer methods, like those made possible by polymorphism, which will be described in Chapter 8.

Assignment Operators

Of all operators, the assignment operators play a special role, one that characterizes the statements (or expressions) in which they appear to such an extent that these statements are called *assignment statements* (or *assignment expressions*).

➤ *Note:* An assignment statement is an assignment expression followed by ';'. Assignment expressions. however, are not limited to these statements, but can appear whenever an expression is legal.

These operators allow you to assign to a variable (which can be indicated directly, as part of an array or a record, and so on) a value given by an expression. Unlike other languages, which have only one assignment operator, C++ has several.

The basic operator is =.

```
int    total ;
int    first , second ;
...
total = 25 ;
...
total = first + second ;
...
total = ( first + 4 ) * 31 - ( second * 4 + 7 ) * 2 + 23 ;
```

To the left of the equal sign, you must have the variable to which the value is to be assigned. More generally, you must have an *lvalue* (*left-value*) that is the reference to a memory location that will receive the expression's value. To the right of the equal sign you must have an expression, the result of which will be assigned to the variable. Obviously, the variable and expression must be compatible.

The possible *lvalues* can be quite different one from another and can even be very complicated if the structure of the data type to which they belong is complicated, as shown below:

```
number = 3 ;          // a variable
number [ 8 ] = 3 ;    // an element of an array
data.number = 4 ;     // a field of a structure
*pNumber = 7 ;        // memory location referenced by a pointer
```

The result of an assignment expression is the value being assigned; this can be used directly by other statements or expressions. An example of this possibility is given by multiple assignments. The statement

```
first = second = 5 ;
```

is equivalent to

```
second = 5 ;
first = second ;
```

because the result of the expression *second = 5* gets assigned in turn to *first*. More precisely, the compiler will understand the expression as though it were written like

```
first = ( second = 5 ) ;
```

and it will generate optimized code that will run much faster than what would be possible with two separate assignments.

A bizarre programmer could delight in writing much more convoluted assignment statements, like

```
first = 34 + 5 * ( second = 23 * 7 ) - 15 ;
```

But the readability of this certainly suffers (it is not easy to understand exactly what gets assigned to *second*), and the advantages of efficient code generation, like in the previous example, get lost (because the operations are much more elaborate to perform).

In general, it is best for you to avoid using the result of an assignment inside complex statements or expressions, particularly if parameter passing to functions is involved, or inside a control expression (*if, while,* and so on).

You should also be aware that an assignment between objects calls (implicitly) the object constructor (described in the following chapters), which can bring with it some undesired side effects.

The Family of Assignment Operators

The = assignment operator is usually available in every programming language, although it might be represented by a different symbol. (Note that the = symbol of C and C++ corresponds to the := symbols in Pascal, while the = symbol of Pascal is represented in C and C++ by the double symbol ==.) In addition to this operator, however, C++ and C have several other assignment operators that allow you to speed up the assignment operations that modify the value of a variable by means of recalculating the new value on the basis of the same variable. For instance, to add a certain value to a variable, the operator += can take the place of a more convoluted expression, as shown below:

```
// classical method, though still usable:

total = total + 5 ;

// shorthand notation:

total += 5 ;
```

The same is true for subtraction (-=), multiplication (*=), division (/=), remainder (%=), right shift (>>=), left shift (<<=), AND (&=), XOR (^=), and OR (l=).

The use of these operators is more efficient (the compiler can generate better code, without further need for optimization) as well as more readable. It also avoids the risk of making errors when copying parts of expressions, for instance, variables with complicated names:

```
// classical:

total_expenditure [ *date.day ] = total_expenditure [ *date.day ] + 23 ;

// with the '+=' operator:

total_expenditure [ *date.day ] += 23 ;
```

Increment and Decrement

Finally, even the unit increment (++) and decrement (--) operators belong to the family of assignment operators. The unit increment of a variable, such as *total*, can be expressed by the following statements, which are all equivalent to each other:

```
total ++ ;
total += 1 ;
total = total + 1 ;
```

The operators ++ and -- appear as a prefix or as a postfix; the value of the variable will be incremented or decremented by one unit, no matter where you place the operator. The difference, though, is the value of the resulting assignment expression, as illustrated by the following program:

```
// file INCREMEN.CPP                               04\INCREMEN
// example of prefix and postfix increment operator

// includes input-ouput library
#include <iostream.h>

void main ( )
{
    // variables definition

    int    before, after ;
    int    sum = 1 ;

    // postincrement:
    after = ( sum++ ) ;

    // restores the value
    sum = 1 ;

    // preincrement:
    before = ( ++sum ) ;

    // outputs the two values
    cout  << "Postincrement value is " << after << endl
          << "while preincrement value is " << before << endl ;
}
```

The above example shows that in the case of a postfix operator, the value of the variable *sum* is incremented after the assignment (the variable *after* will thus have the value of 1); on the other hand, in the case of a prefix operator, *sum* is incremented before the assignment to the variable *before* (which will thus hold the value of 2). In practice, the result of the assignment statement is different in the two cases, but the effect of incrementing the variable is the same in both cases.

Control Statements

Among the most important statements of any programming language are those that allow you to control the "flow" of execution in a program; that is, the constructs that establish the order and criteria of execution of the statements in a program.

The control statements can be divided into two broad categories: "in the small" and "in the large." Control statements in the small control the flow of operations within a limited area of a program; control statements in the large globally organize the various parts of a program and their order of execution.

The control statements in the small can be further subdivided into three fundamental categories: sequence, selection, and iteration. Every programming language must have at least one statement of each category, otherwise it would be impossible to write any algorithm. This has been proved by the result of a theorem by Bohm and Jacopini.

A visual scheme of the various statements that control flow of execution is shown in Figure 4.9.

As you will see shortly, C++ offers more than one statement for selection and iteration; this makes programming easier and programs much more readable, intelligible, and efficient.

The programming construct in the large can be subdivided into several categories, the three most important of which are: subprograms and function calls; the definitions of classes; and the creation of concurrent program units (which are not available in C or in C++).

In addition to these programming constructs, which allow the logical subdivision of a program, is the possibility of a "physical" subdivision into distinct source files, which should reflect the logical subdivision. In object-oriented programming, this subdivision is usually achieved by making each file correspond to a distinct class.

Sequence

In C and C++, you can indicate a sequence, where two or more statements have to be executed one after the other, by enclosing the statements within curly braces. This actually defines a compound statement, or a *block*. Inside a block, the statements are simply listed one after the other, in the order they should be executed. For instance, the following compound statement:

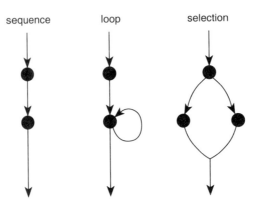

Figure 4.9 Scheme of control flow statements

```
{
    firstStatement
    secondStatement
}
```

actually means "carry out the first statement, and then the second one." It is always possible to replace one statement with a compound statement. It is also possible to write more statements on one line, although to improve the program's readability, it is customary to start each statement on a new line.

Every statement—even those inside a block and even the last statement of a block—must be terminated by a semicolon.

➤   *Note:* In the preceding and the following statement diagrams, we are using a simplified notation. To get to know the exact syntax of the various control structures and other constructs of the language, refer to [Ellis 90], *Chapter 17 Grammar Summary*, where the precise definition of every language element is given. For instance, where we use the generic indication of "*statement*," it should be understood that a statement can actually be a labeled statement, an expression statement, a compound statement, a selection statement, an iteration statement, a jump statement, or a declaration statement. In turn, all these items are made up of more specific elements. For instance, an expression statement is actually an optional statement (so it can also be missing!) followed by a semicolon. (This means that the semicolon alone is actually a statement, the null expression statement!) Some of these items are even described in recursive terms. For instance, a compound statement (that is, the block described above) is made up of an opening brace followed by an optional (even missing!) statement list and then a closing brace; and a statement list is described as a statement, followed by a statement list that is followed by yet another statement!

All this might sound complicated, but for all practical purposes, every time you see the term *statement* in the following syntax diagrams, you can think of it either as an expression followed by a semicolon, or as a block of statements (as defined above).

Selection

Often, instead of executing statements in sequence, you must select among two or more statements to perform. The choice will usually depend on the value of a variable, or—more generally—on the value of an expression. In C++, there are three kinds of selection statements (sometimes referred to as conditional statements), which are indicated by the keywords: *if, if-else,* and *switch*. Figure 4.10 gives a general idea of the way these statements work.

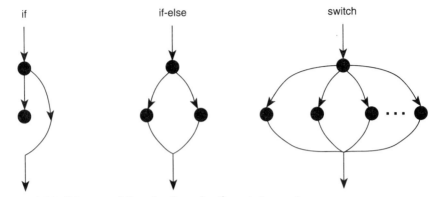

Figure 4.10 Scheme of flow in the selection statements

Simple Selection (if)

The most simple selection statement is *if*:

```
if ( expression )
    statement
```

If the indicated *expression* is true (that is, nonzero), then the indicated *statement* is executed. Otherwise, execution jumps directly to the following part of the program, skipping and ignoring the indicated *statement*. For instance:

```
if ( grade == 'A' )
    cout << "excellent" ;
```

If the variable *grade* is equal to *A*, then the program will output the string "excellent"; otherwise, it won't do anything. To test this, assign some values to the variable *grade* and look at the result. Of course, the statement to be performed when the test is true can also be a compound statement, that is, a block of statements enclosed within curly braces.

➤ *Note:* In a testing expression, the == operator has to be used instead of the more intuitive = operator. It is a common error to use the assignment operator (single =) by mistake and thus change a variable instead of testing its value. The compiler in such a case will issue only a warning (and not an error) since the testing expression can legally be any expression, even an assignment expression. In some cases, this is what the programmer actually wants.

Two-way Selection (if-else)

Somewhat more elaborate is the *if-else* statement:

```
if ( expression )
    statement1
else
    statement2
```

This selection statement differs from the preceding one in that if the *expression* is false (that is, equals zero) then *statement1* is ignored—just as before—but *statement2* gets executed instead (which is commonly referred to as the *else* branch). The two statements (which can be simple or compound) are simply two mutually exclusive alternatives, because only one of the two gets executed according to the value of the expression.

To continue with the preceding example:

```
if ( grade == 'A' )
    cout << "excellent" ;
else
    count << "pass mark" ;
```

This solution, though, is still unsatisfactory. It would be better to have a greater number of choices than just two. You get more choices by concatenating more *if-else* statements, like this:

```
if ( grade == 'A' || grade == 'B' )    // 'll' is the logical operator
    cout << "excellent" ;
else if ( grade == 'C' )
    count << "pass mark" ;
else
    cout << "below standard"
```

Even this solution might not always be adequate. If you wanted to select from many different cases, it would be a nuisance to have to write several *if-else* statements, and you would be much more likely to make an error.

Multiple Selection (switch)

The alternative is to use the *switch* statement, which has the syntax

```
switch ( expression ) {

case value1 :
    statement1
```

```
case value2 :
   statement2

...

default :
   defaultStatement
}
```

The switch statement works like this: first, the value of the *expression* is evaluated (which must result in an integral type), then the list of values written after the *case* keywords (which must be constant values and not expressions) is searched for a value matching that of *expression*. If a matching value is found, then the corresponding statement is executed; otherwise, a predefined default statement, written after the *default* keyword, will be executed.

To break out of the switch statement after a matching value has been found and the corresponding statement has been executed, you have to write a *break* keyword before the subsequent *case* keyword (unless, of course, you wish to continue executing the statements immediately following). This means that you can list several statements to be executed for each *case* branch without having to resort to the definition of a block within curly braces.

The preceding example could have been written and completed like this using a *switch* statement:

```
switch ( grade ) {

case 'A' :
   cout << "excellent" ;
   break ;

case 'B' :
   cout << "good" ;
   break ;

case 'C' :
   cout << "pass mark" ;
   break ;

case 'D' :
   cout << "below standard" ;
   break ;

default : // in all other cases ( 'E', but also 'F' and 'Z'! )
   cout << "unclassifiable" ;
   break ;
}
```

Loops

The last group of control statements "in the small" are for making loops; that is, statements that repeat the execution of a block of statements several times. The number of times a loop is executed can be predefined (in a *for* loop) or it can depend on the value of an expression or a variable (*while* and *do-while* loops).

while

The *while* loops have the following syntax:

```
while ( expression )
    statement
```

This example means that the *statement* (which can be simple or compound) will be executed repeatedly so long as the *expression* is true (that is, nonzero). In other words, the *expression* is evaluated; if it is true, the *statement* is executed, then the whole thing starts over again; if, on the other hand, the *expression* is false, execution continues with the statements following the loop.

For instance, in the loop

```
int i = 1 ;

while ( i <= 10 ) {

    // statements to be repeated go here
    i++ ;

}
```

the statement in the block is executed 10 times, because the expression (*i<=10*) will remain true until *i* reaches the value of 11, which happens after 10 iterations through the loop (unless, of course, some other statement inside the loop does not change the value of the control variable *i*). As you will see shortly, to write a definite loop like the one above, it is much better to use a *for* loop. The *while* loop, though, is more convenient in many cases, especially when the controlling expression is complicated or when it is a Boolean expression that signals some condition.

The following example demonstrates the full meaning of this kind of loop (keeping in mind the actual, linguistic meaning of the word "while"). This example was inspired by a similar example in [Eckel 89].

```
// file WHILE1.CPP                                        04\WHILE
// example of while loop: GUESS THE NUMBER
```

```
#include <iostream.h>      // includes the input-output library
#include <stdlib.h>        // includes random and randomize function prototypes
#include <conio.h>         // includes kbhit ( ) declaration

void main ( )
{
    int    secretNumber = 0 ;
    int    guess = 0 ;

    // function activating the random number generator

    randomize ( ) ;

    // assign a number from 1 to 20
    secretNumber = 1 + random ( 20 ) ;

    // while guess is different from the secret number
    while ( guess != secretNumber ) {

        // ask the user to input a number

        cout << endl << "Try to guess the secret number (range 1-20): " ;
        cin >> guess ;
    }

    // when the two numbers are equal exit from the loop
    // and print an appropriate phrase

    cout << endl << "OK! You win! It was truly " << secretNumber << endl ;
}
```

The *while* loop is an open loop. This means that it is not possible to decide before-hand how many times it will be executed. It is therefore possible to create infinite loops, which get executed an unlimited number of times.

➤ *Note:* If you ever get caught in an infinite loop in DOS you will always be able to break out by pressing the *Control-Break* keys. If you are running a EasyWin application those same keys will not work.

   If you are running the program in Borland C++ 4.0 integrated dubugger or under Turbo Debugger for Windows, you can break out of an endless loop by hitting *Ctrl-Alt-SysReq* keys. Otherwise, if you are running it under Windows 3.1, it's always possible to interrupt the current task by pressing *Ctrl-Alt-Del*, while under Windows 3.0 in a similar circumstance you had to reboot the computer!

A demonstration of this is given by the last loop in the preceding example. In just a matter of seconds, the loop is executed many times. This is better illustrated by the following program:

```
// file WHILE2.CPP                                              04\WHILE
// example of the speed of the while loop

// Inclusion of library
#include <iostream.h>
#include <conio.h>

void main ( )
{
    // counter for the number of loop executions ( the type is long
    // instead of int since the counter can reach large values )

    long  loops = 0 ;

    // Print the usage instructions

    cout << "The loop is running... press any key to stop it!" << endl ;

    // loop until a key is pressed

    while ( ! kbhit ( ) ) {

        loops ++ ;  // increment the counter variable

        // uncomment following line ( deleting the // ) to put a dot on the screen
        // cout << "." ;
    }

    // Report the final data

    cout << endl ;
    cout << "The loop has been executed " << loops << " times!" << endl ;
}
```

A more complex example of an infinite loop, which illustrates how much care is needed not to write one accidentally, is the following:

```
int    total = 0 ;
int    sum = 10 ;

while ( total < 100 ) {
```

```
        total = sum ;

        // more assignments might go here ...
        sum = 23 + total % 8 ;

        // more statements might go here ...
        total += sum ;
    }
```

It seems that *total* is increased every time through the loop, but this is not true. If you don't believe us, run the program providing some output (as in the statement *cout << total;*) to understand what is going on, but take care. If you don't run the program in the debugger, to quit an infinite loop you might need to halt the application using the *Ctrl-Alt-Del* keys (which might be good in Windows 3.1, but terrible in Windows 3.0). Running the application in the debugger, instead, you can see how the variables change their values during the loop execution using a *watch*.

do-while

The *do-while* loop is similar to the *while* loop in that it is an open loop, and it has the following syntax:

```
do
    statement
while ( expression ) ;
```

The different order in which the *statement* and the *expression* are written indicate the difference between the two types of loops: the test on the value of the *expression* will be performed after the execution of the *statement* (in other words, at the end of the loop instead of at the beginning). In practice, the difference is that the code represented by the simple or compound statement of the *do-while* loop will be executed at least once (while the statement of the *while* loop can even be skipped altogether, if the value of the controlling expression is false to begin with).

The *while* loop is actually a *do-while* loop preceded by an *if* statement. For example,

```
while ( expression )
    statement
```

is equivalent to

```
if ( expression )
    do
        statement
    while ( expression ) ;
```

for

The *for* loop has the syntax

```
for ( expression1 ; expression2 ; expression3 )
    statement
```

and is equivalent to the following code:

```
expression1
while ( expression 2 ) {
    statement
    expression3
}
```

The first of the three expressions initializes the loop; the second expression is the condition being tested for at the beginning of each iteration; the third generates some kind of change that must be executed at the end of the loop (usually, an increment or a decrement). This might seem confusing, but the following will help to clarify the meaning of this loop:

```
for ( int cout = 0 ; count < 10 ; count++ )
    statement
```

This example means that the *statement* (which, again, can be simple or compound) will be executed because at the beginning *count* is less than 10; the variable *count*, which initially was set to 0, will be incremented by 1 (by evaluating the expression *count++*) until it becomes 10. At this point the control expression *count < 10* will evaluate to false and the loop ends. In other words, as indicated above, this loop is equivalent to the following code:

```
int count = 0 ;

while ( count < 10 ) {
    statement
    count ++ ;
}
```

In general, you can determine beforehand how many times the *for* loop will be repeated (in this example, 10 times). An exception is when some statements directly change the counting variable or another variable that appears in the controlling expression (which should generally be avoided or done with extreme caution).

Even with the *for* loop, though, it is possible to generate an infinite loop. In its simplest form, it is enough to write:

```
for ( ; ; )
    ;   // Note the null statement!
```

The expressions of the *for* loop are an excellent example of where it is useful to resort to the comma operator. For instance, you can define loops with two counters:

```
for ( int i = 0 , int j = 0 ; i + j < 100 ; i++ , j++ )
    ...
```

This feature can be used in several particular situations and provides an immediate usefulness and terseness of coding of the *for* loop, especially if the counter is not an integer but a more elaborate variable (even an object).

Jumping with break, continue, and goto

Before closing this section on loops, it is important to note that there are a couple of statements that force loops to behave in different ways:

- The *break* statement immediately stops the execution of a loop and forces execution to proceed with the statements following the loop. This statement is also commonly used with the *switch* statement to indicate the end of a *case* branch.
- The *continue* statement forces the execution to continue immediately with the controlling statement in a *while* or *do* loop, or with the increment statement in a *for* loop, even if the block of statements of the loop has not been completely executed.

Using these statements, which sometimes are invaluable, must be limited to those cases where they are logical and natural. It is always a good idea to search for alternate and more appropriate solutions so that you do not use these statements in a "dirty" way (that is, trying to simplify the program by avoiding some parts of code).

Likewise, it is a good idea not to abuse the unconditional jump statement, *goto*, which usually is a sign that the program is badly structured.

All of these unconditional jump statements can, in fact, undermine the readability of a program, and, even worse, induce the programmer to commit severe errors, especially when there are many complicated and nested loops.

Function Calls

Among the programming constructs "in the large," in this section, we will examine functions. In the next chapter we will introduce the class construct, one of the pillars of object-oriented programming.

Possible Meanings

The original meaning of a function call corresponds to the invocation of a *subprogram* (usually denoted by the CALL instruction in assembly language). A subprogram is nothing more than a block of statements identified by a name, that can be executed several times on demand. Furthermore, a subprogram can take some parameters, which are established before its call, and determine its actual execution.

From a completely different point of view, the function call can be seen as the extension of the programming language with new constructs and new operators, so that the language becomes more powerful and more specialized for the application or the family of applications to which the function belongs. As you will see, a function can be shared among several programs and constitutes one of the simplest but most often used examples of code reuse. Actually, this is the basis for the creation of function *libraries*.

Another definition of function is closely related to the algebraic-mathematical meaning of function: a function is a rule that relates the members of two sets. It creates a relationship between the elements of a source set (domain) and the elements of a target set (co-domain). Even the functions of a programming language can be interpreted in this manner, though only in a limited number of cases. (In particular, some programming languages are actually founded on this concept, like LISP.)

Yet another interpretation of a function is that of the abstraction of a behavior, an algorithm, or a procedure, that can be generalized and applied on different occasions. The structuring of a program into functions, which often happens in a top-down sequence (that is, by first defining the highest-level function of the system, then subdividing it into ever more elementary functions until you eventually reach the final implementation), has for a long time been one of the most widespread and well-known methods for developing programs. Even today, it is one of the most used methods; and there is an intense debate regarding if and when this method should be used, if it should be completely or partly abandoned, if and when it deserves some validity, and so on.

Attributes of Functions

Generally, every function has the following three distinctive attributes:

1. a name that identifies it
2. the type of its result; that is, the type of the value returned by the function
3. the function's parameters and their types

All of these attributes must be indicated precisely when you define a function, and are strictly checked by the compiler. Note, though, that the return value can be omitted, in which case the compiler will assume that the return value is of type *int*.

Precise attribute specification is especially important for the parameters that are passed to functions, which in C++ are even rigorously type checked (as opposed to the looser requirements in ordinary ANSI C and the almost total lack thereof classical K&R C). The declaration (and the definition) of a function must therefore specify the number of its parameters and the type of each. A difference between a function declaration and its definition is that a function declaration can be written without naming its formal arguments (only indicating their type), while its definition needs them.

In C++, if a function is lacking parameters, they can simply be omitted from the function's definition; alternatively, you can clearly state their absence by using the keyword *void*, as is customary in Standard C. Instead, in C++ a function that does not return a value has to be defined of type *void*.

```
// declaration of a function without parameters

int     current_day ( ) ;

// or equivalently

int     current_day ( void ) ;

// declaration of a function without a return value

void   print ( int number ) ;

// declaration of a function without parameters
// and without a return value

void  play ( ) ;
void  play ( void );
```

Inline Functions

One of the attributes that functions can have is that of being declared as *inline*. This means that the compiler, instead of generating the code that calls the function to be executed, will, whenever possible, substitute every occurrence of a call to that function with the actual code of the function itself. The declaration of *inline* is not a dictum for the compiler, it is only a suggestion; the compiler will decide what is the best solution, whether to use a call to the function or whether to use the actual code of the function itself. (In Borland C++, the use of inline functions can also be enabled or disabled by a compiler option.)

Usually, when the compiler encounters the definition of a function, it will generate the corresponding code and will store the starting point (address) of this code. When the compiler later encounters a call to this function, it issues a jump instruction so that the computer can execute the instructions found at the function's address.

With an *inline* function, the compiler will store the definition of a function, instead of generating its code; every time it encounters a call to that function, it will copy all instructions in place of writing a jump instruction. This way, the compiler can avoid all the instructions that actually carry out the function call (which perform state suspension, memory allocation, and set up some internal pointers), which are generally referred to as *function call overhead*. These two distinct ways of handling function invocation will generate code in very different ways, as illustrated in Figure 4.11.

We must stress that inline functions are similar to a literal text substitution, like those that can be achieved by a preprocessor macro expansion. However, they are also very different, because the compiler will perform on them the same kind of type checking reserved for ordinary functions, while no type checking is performed in the case of literal text substitution.

The decision to introduce *inline* functions in C++ was due to efficiency; in fact, in the case of very simple functions (those containing only a few statements), the resulting code performs much better, since it is no longer necessary to execute the function call overhead instructions. Therefore, you might wonder if it wouldn't be worthwhile to make all functions *inline*.

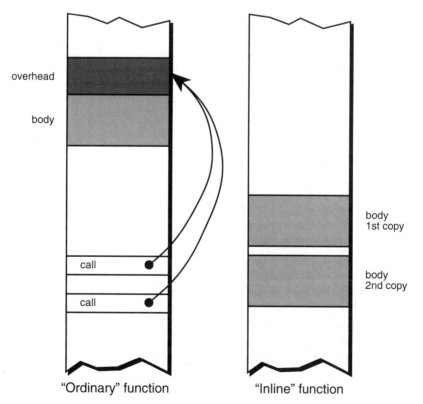

Figure 4.11 Graphic representation of the code generated by the compiler at function invocation for a "normal" function call and for an inline function

The answer is no. In fact, the size of the resulting code would be much larger if the same functions were called several times, and if they were of considerable size to start with, its code would be replicated at every function call.

To decide whether it is better to declare a function *inline* or not, you should consider the following guidelines:

- An inline substitution does not always increase the size of a program: a function call consumes both execution time as well as memory space, because it requires that some instructions get inserted into the code to perform the function call.
- On the other hand, "the saving from inlining any but the simplest functions is minimal." [Ellis 90]
- Obviously, the best *inline* functions are those that simply return a value (which are very common in classes with private data members, as you will see in the following chapters), functions that perform one or two simple operations (like an addition, a multiplication, or a data access), or functions that simply call another function.
- Additionally, there is at least one negative aspect: modifying the implementation of a function requires you to recompile those parts of the code that call it if the function is inline; if the function is an ordinary function, this recompilation will not be necessary.

Although inline functions can effectively be used like ordinary functions, their real value emerges when they are used as class member functions; and in this sense, they are best considered as an enhancement of the object-oriented constructs of the language. For this reason, the language specification states that the member functions defined inside a class definition should automatically be considered as inline functions by the compiler.

Implicit and Default Parameters

In this section, function parameters will be examined again. As noted earlier, a function can be defined with any number of parameters of a predefined type; the function calls have to honor these parameters by indicating a corresponding number of variables or expressions of the appropriate type.

However, it is not strictly mandatory that the number of parameters match exactly. In fact, some parameters can have a default value assigned to them whenever an explicit value is absent.

For instance, you can have a function that sums up three numbers, where, if you supply only two of them, the third number will automatically be taken as zero (and ignored). The declaration and the definition of this function need to contain, after the type and the name of the parameter, an assignment expression that states its default value, as shown below:

```
int sum ( int a , int b , int c=0 )
{
```

```
    return ( a+b+c );
}
```

The call

```
sum ( 2 , 3 , 4 );
```

will give the expected result of 9. However, if you code the call

```
sum ( 8 , 12 );
```

contrary to what might be expected, there will be no compilation error reported, and the value of the function will actually be 20 (8+12+0).

A function can also have more than one default parameter. For instance, it is possible to define the function

```
int sum ( int a = 0 , int b = 0 , int c = 0 , int d = 0 )
{
    return ( a+b+c+d );
}
```

which can be called with no, one, two, three, or four parameters:

```
sum ( 3 , 5 );
sum ( 6 , 7 , 8 , 1 );
```

Also the following is acceptable, which will return a value of zero:

```
sum ( );
```

In the above example, all parameters are of the same type (but this has been done here only for simplicity). It is important to note that the parameters are assigned in the order they are written: the first with the first, the second with the second, and so on. At the end, for all those parameters that might be missing, if they all have a stated default value, they will take that value; otherwise the compiler will report an error.

The following rules govern the definition of default parameters:

- Only the last parameters of a function can have a default value (that is, after one default parameter has been stated, there cannot be any other parameters unless they are also default parameters).
- When a function is called, any number of default parameters can be missing, but only starting from the last one. This rule means that if a function has three default parameters, then it can be called with all three parameters, with the first two only, with the first one only, or with none; but it cannot be called, for instance, with the third parameter alone.

Parameter Passing by Reference and by Value

Another very important issue, both from a theoretical point of view and for its practical implications, is that of parameter passing to functions. In most programming languages, there are several ways with which a parameter can be passed from a program to one of its subprograms. The two most common techniques (which are also available in C++) are

- parameter passing by value, where a parameter is actually a copy of the variable indicated
- parameter passing by reference, where the memory address of the variable, instead of its value, is copied

The C language allows only parameter passing by value; however, it allows a programmer to pass as a parameter the pointer to a variable (which in practice is equivalent to passing by reference). However, C++ introduces an explicit notation for the indication of parameter passing by reference. In this way, both methods of parameter passing are available, directly and transparently as shown below:

```
// parameter passing by value:

    // function definition

    int product ( int a , int b )
        {
            return a*b ;
        }

    // function call

    int x ;
    x = product ( 5 , 10 ) ;   // meaning: x is equal to the product between 5 and 10

// parameter passing by reference:

    // function definition

    void  multiply ( int &a , int b )
        {
            a *= b ;
        }

    // function call

    int x = 5 ;
```

```
multiply ( x , 10 ) ;    // meaning: x is 5, multiplied by 10
```

```
// parameter passing by pointer:
```

```
// function definition
```

```
void   multi ( int *a , int b )
   {
       ( *a ) *= b ;
   }
```

```
//  function call
```

```
int *px ;
*px = 5 ;
multi ( px , 10 ) ;  // meaning: px points to the value of 5, multiplied by 10
```

```
// second (commonly used) form of function call
// using the "address of" operator &
```

```
int x = 25;
multi (&x, 8);
```

The function definition and the function call are almost the same in the first two cases (function *product* and function *multiply*), while the third function (*multi*) must make explicit use of pointers. To denote parameter passing by reference (instead of by value) it is only necessary to place the & symbol in front of the name of the variable, as in:

```
void multiply (int &a, int b)
```

Naturally, when the function is called, the parameters passed by reference must be matched by variables, even though it is not possible to indicate their value explicitly (which, however, is possible in the case of parameter passing by value).

Parameter passing by pointer is very similar in meaning and functionality to parameter passing by reference; however, it imposes the direct manipulation of the pointer, both inside the function, as well as for the value passed and returned. The introduction of an explicit notation for parameter passing by reference transfers the burden from the programmer to the compiler, and therefore is generally preferred.

The differences between the two ways of passing parameters (by value and by reference) and their respective advantages are summarized below:

- With large parameters, passing by value (which implies the creation of a copy) becomes slower and takes up (temporarily) a larger amount of memory space (with the risk of severe consequences, such as program crashes due to memory shortage, especially on 8086 processors with segmented memory models).

- Small parameters, such as an integer variable, might even be smaller than their pointers, and passing them by value could be faster.

- Passing by reference allows you to modify the variable being passed. This technique might be useful, but is often bad programming, and you should not abuse it. The direct manipulation of a parameter by a function is referred to as a side effect.

- Passing by value, on the other hand, lets you modify and use a parameter as you please, without any risk of altering the original value.

- Since an array name is actually a pointer to an array, when an array is passed as a parameter to a function it is always passed by reference, as is done with pointers, and the items of the array are not copied. So, if the value of the elements of an array is changed inside a function, this new value affects the value of the array even outside of the function (as is the case with pass by reference). This behavior is shown in the following program:

```
// file ARRAY-P.CPP                                    04\ARRAY-P
// example of passing an array as parameter to a function

#include <iostream.h>

// defines a new data type: an array of ten integers
typedef int numList[10] ;

// defines a functions to sum an integer to each
// of the items of a numList array
void add (numList nl, int n)
{
    for (int i = 0; i < 10; ++i)
        nl [i] += n ;
}

void main ( )
{
    // defines an array (notice the form of the initialization)
    numList  numbers = {12, 3, 4, 5, 6, 7, 8, 22, 9, 10} ;

    // output the value of the array elements

    cout << "Values of the array elements:" << endl ;
    for (int i = 0; i < 10; ++i)
        cout << i << ". " << numbers [i] << endl ;
    // add 5 to each item of the array
    add (numbers, 5) ;

    // output the array elements (to see their final value)
```

```
        cout << endl << "Final values of the array elements:" << endl ;
        for (i = 0; i < 10; ++i)
            cout << i << ". " << numbers [i] << endl ;
    }
```

If you run this program it will produce the output shown in Figure 4.12.

Preprocessor Directives

A C++ source file, in addition to the statements proper to the language, can also contain instructions (or directives) for the preprocessor. Originally, the preprocessor was a kind of filter on the source file that preceded the action of the compiler, processing the source text and giving certain useful functionalities.

In Borland C++, the preprocessor is integrated with the compiler, and the two operations—preprocessing and compiling—happen at the same time, and not in sequence, as is customary.

These directives can perform the following three types of operations:

1. **File inclusion**: at the point at which the command *#include* is found, the preprocessor automatically includes the text of the specified file, which can be a stan-

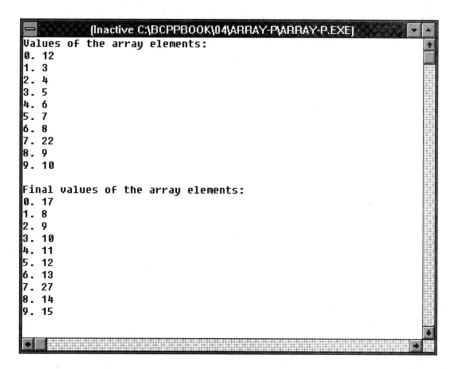

Figure 4.12 The output of the program *ARRAY-P.CPP*

dard header file of the system or a file peculiar to the program being developed. The name of the file is enclosed by < > or by " ", according to whether it should be sought for only in the standard *include* paths, or in the current source directory and then in the standard *include* paths. (The *include paths* can be set with the *Options Directories* command of the IDE.)

2. **Macro expansion**: a text string can be substituted every time it appears in the text with another string, defined beforehand. This mechanism is very useful, because it is much more powerful than is apparent at first sight. In the past, before the *const* variable type and *inline* functions were available, macro expansion played this fundamental role; today, however, it is less important, although it has not completely lost its usefulness.

3. **Conditional compilation**: a part of source code can be compiled only in certain cases, according to whether a certain parameter has been defined (*#ifdef*) or not defined (*#ifndef*) with the specific directive (*#define*). One case in which conditional compilation is particularly useful is to avoid the inclusion of the interface of a class or a library more than once in the same file. This can happen easily if the *#include* directive is used repeatedly, and can cause compilation errors. By reading the text in the standard header files (files with a *.h* extension under the *include* directory of Borland C++), you can see that this method is used very often.

Macro Substitutions in Borland C++

After this introduction on preprocessor directives you can experiment with one of the traditional constructs to achieve the reusability available with Borland C++: macro substitutions.

Macros let you replace the text of a properly defined word with a character string. It's also possible to handle some parameters in a way similar to functions, although conceptually very different. In both cases, to indicate a macro you use the *#define* compiler directive, as in the following example:

```
// file MACRO.CPP                                    04\MACRO
// examples of macro definitions

// example 1: constant macro
#define ONE_MILLION 1000000

// example 2: macro function ( attention: blanks are relevant! )
#define max(a,b) ((a>b) ? a : b)

void main ( )
{
    float  num1 = 9000 ;
    float  num2 = ONE_MILLION ;
    float  greater ;
```

```
    greater = max(num1, num2) ;
}
```

To verify the transformation that takes place to the source file before the code compilation, with the proper processing of *#define* and the other compiler directives, Borland C++ includes a utility equivalent to the integrated preprocessor, called CPP. You can run this tool from the DOS command line or use the local menu (right mouse button) on a file containing source code inside the project window and select *Special, Preprocess* (as in Figure 4.13).

CPP MACRO.CPP

the following *macro.i* file is generated:

```
macro.cpp 1:
macro.cpp 2:
macro.cpp 3:
macro.cpp 4:
macro.cpp 5:
macro.cpp 6:
macro.cpp 7:
macro.cpp 8:
macro.cpp 9:
macro.cpp 10: void main ( )
macro.cpp 11: {
macro.cpp 12: float  num1 = 9000 ;
macro.cpp 13: float  num2 = 1000000 ;
macro.cpp 14: float  greater ;
macro.cpp 15:
macro.cpp 16: greater = ((num1 > num2) ? num1 : num2);
macro.cpp 17: }
macro.cpp 18:
macro.cpp 19:
```

Note that this file can be used only to explore the effect of the directives, since it cannot be compiled due to the presence of the line numbers. (You could, if you wish, disable the generation of line numbers by giving an appropriate command line option to the CPP utility. You can discover what command line options are available to CPP by executing it with no additional arguments on the command line.)

This use of macros might seem quite obvious and useless, since it's always possible to use search and replace tools to substitute words in the text. Certainly, it's better not to abuse macros, particularly with C++, but there are times when they can be very useful.

A common use for macros is to define mnemonic constants (as in the first example above). It's easier to remember a name than a value, and much easier to globally change it (where there can be several occurrences). This use of macros is particularly

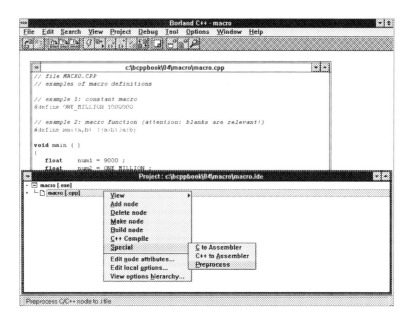

Figure 4.13 To see the result of the preprocessing on a source code file, you can select the proper operation using a local menu.

important for the applications developed for the Windows environment, which uses numbers to indicate almost all of its elements (as you will see in Chapter 15). The possibility of associating names to those numbers makes the programs much more readable and easier to modify. To make them even more clear, write the names of the macro definitions completely in uppercase.

However, for the definition of fixed numeric values it's better not use macros. Instead, you can define constants with the proper language construct, avoiding the use of the preprocessor. The use of a C++ keyword instead of the preprocessor substitution offers higher control of the code (for example, for checking that the type corresponds exactly) without any overhead in compilation or run time.

Similarly, it's better to use functions (perhaps inline functions) than parametric macros, since the first method ensures that the parameters and the return value have the proper type, thus reducing the possibility of making errors.

For more information on macro substitutions, refer to the Borland C++ manuals. The *#include* directive, which is the most commonly used directive, will be used often in the examples that follow, but its usage is quite elementary.

Standard Input and Output

In C++, input and output generally take place through the standard classes defined in the library *iostream.h*. Alternatively, a C programmer can continue to use the standard *printf* and *scanf* functions, although we strongly recommend the use of the new C++

streams because they provide a better and stronger type checking. In this section we introduce only some of the features of this library, because we are going to use it often in the following chapters. Thanks to the Borland *EasyWin* library, we can use plain input and output streams under Windows, all the input and the output takes place in a *teletype-like* window. A more detailed description of the *iostream* library can be found in Chapter 15.

The *iostream* is a class library, since it defines a number of classes to support input and output operations. The library instantiates also some default objects: the *cin* object for input and the *cout* object for output. Using these streams is very simple because, thanks to operator overloading, they are independent of the data type being used. To be more precise, there is a definition of the input and output operators for each standard data type of the language, and a programmer can also write new operators for the user-defined data types and classes (as we already saw in Chapter 2).

The standard *printf* requires the text with some positional formatting codes and the corresponding values, as in:

```
printf ("He is %d years old", age) ;
```

The use of the output stream, instead, requires a list of variables and constants, divided by the << operator:

```
cout << "He is " << age << " years old" ;
```

As you can see, there is no need to indicate that *age* is a decimal, as with the *%d* of the *printf* call. The compiler determines which output function is needed by looking at the data type of the parameter. The same holds for the input, as in:

```
int age ;
cout << "Input the age: " ;
cin >> age ;
```

Among the various elements of a *cout* statement, you can add some *output manipulators*, which affect the output of the text. The most common manipulators is *endl* (end line) which adds a newline character ('\n') to the output stream and forces the display of any text stored in a buffer. Other manipulators allow to set the width of an output field and the filling character, change the base of an integer (decimal, octal, or hexa-decimal) or the number of decimal digits of a floating point value. You can find some details on manipulators in Chapter 15, and even more in the compiler documentation and on-line help.

The use of the input output streams is illustrated by the following example, where the input and output of two different types of values is performed, without worrying whether they are integers or floating point values. The example also shows how to use the *#include* directive, mentioned in the previous section.

```
// file CINCOUT.CPP
// short example of cin and cout streams for input and output

#include <iostream.h>

void main ( )
{
    int     number ;
    float   decimal ;

    cout  << endl ;                              // moves to a new line
                                                 // corresponds to: cout << "\n" ;
    cout  << "Type in an integer number: " ;     // asks for input
    cin   >> number ;                            // gets input
    cout  << endl ;                              // moves to a new line
    cout  << "Type in a decimal number: " ;      // asks for another input
    cin   >> decimal ;                           // gets the input

    cout  << endl << "You have typed: "          // final output
          << number << " and " << decimal ;      // of the two numbers
}
```

Running this program results in a window with an output similar to the one in Figure 4.14.

POINTS TO CONSIDER

1. Compare the set of operators offered by C++ with the set of operators from other programming languages that you know (excluding C). Consider the advantages and disadvantages that come with such a large number of operators.

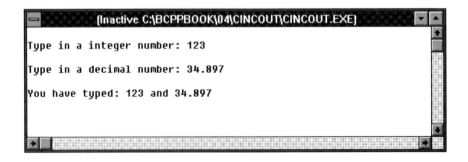

Figure 4.14 The output of the program *CINCOUT.CPP*

2. Compile an empty main function, like the one illustrated in the following example, to verify that it is the shortest "legal" program you can write:

```
// file EMPTY.CPP
// a program with an empty main function

void main ( )
{
    /* there is nothing but a comment */
}
```

3. At the opposite extreme, try to write and compile a program without *main* (just compile any "empty" text).

4. Correct the program CONDOPER.CPP by also considering the case of equality (in other words, if the value entered is equal to 50). You might want to use two nested conditional operators, or you might use a conditional *if-else* statement.

5. Corroborate with some example when a conditional statement (*if*) can be replaced with the conditional operator (*?:*) and in which cases it is not possible for you to use it.

6. Compare the data types of C++ with those of other programming languages that you might know. You might want to compare single data types: both the predefined data types and the aggregate data types. For instance, what differences can you spot between integers or real numbers in C++ and those in your favorite programming language?

7. Examine which data structures you're accustomed to using, and compare them with the corresponding structures in C++.

8. Compile and run one of the infinite loops indicated in the text, maybe even entering one or more statements in the loop. Recall that it is always possible to interrupt execution by pressing *Ctrl-Alt-SysReq* under the debugger or *Ctrl-Alt-Del* under Windows 3.1 (but not Windows 3.0).

9. Compare the control statements of C++ (loops, selection) with those of other programming languages you might know.

10. Rewrite the three examples regarding the *while* loop by using a *do* and/or a *for* loop instead.

11. Explore the ANSI standard C libraries that contain the definitions of the procedures that operate on character strings (first of all "strings.h") and that are collected under the "include" directory of Borland C++.

PART TWO

Object-Oriented Language Constructs

5

Abstract Data Types, Classes, and Objects

*The most fundamental notion of object-oriented design and program-
ming is that the program is a model of some aspects of reality. The
classes in the program represent the fundamental concepts of the
application and, in particular, the fundamental concepts of the "reality"
being modeled. Real-world objects and artifacts of the implementation are represented by objects of these classes.* [Stroustrup 91A]

In this chapter, we reconsider abstraction as a means of building programs, showing
how this approach to problem solving is different from traditional ones. In object-
oriented design, the focus is neither on functions (as in functional design) nor on data
(as in data-structure design): the focus is on objects, considered as logical aggregates
of related data and functions, structured to form a single entity.

At the beginning of this chapter, you'll find a detailed description of data abstraction, based on some examples. Then, there is a section about classes, objects, and the
differences between the two.

The second part of this chapter discusses data types in C++, particularly the class
construct. This second part of the chapter contains some annotated examples that show
how to implement classes with Borland C++.

Abstract Models of Reality

In Chapter 3, you saw the role of abstraction and its double meaning (the programming
language as an abstraction of the physical machine, and the program as an abstraction
of the real world) with particular attention to the first of the two meanings.

Now you will see what it means to write computer programs through data abstraction. In short, this means building an abstract model of reality with a trustworthy
description of real objects and events. (Here the term "real" denotes both tangible
entities, such as a computer, as well as abstract entities, such as a program, an idea, or
an algorithm.) But there's more to it than this short statement.

127

We might try to express a clear description of an object, first with words, and later with a high-level programming language. The verbal description is certainly far from ideal, because it may give rise to misinterpretations caused by incompleteness or ambiguity or even inconsistency, but for our needs it might be considered good enough.

For each entity we examine, we need to know its behavior, in order to be able to implement it on a computer, and simulate the consequences of different conditions.

A First Example: The Queue

The first example of an abstract data type is a classic one that any programmer will already be familiar with: the queue. Imagine that you have to describe, inside a program, the behavior of a line of people waiting at a counter. The basic working model is very simple: if there is a queue and people comply with it, they form a line and wait. The first person to arrive is the first in line and is then the first to be served. When the first person finishes, the next in line is served, and so on.

The working model of a queue might be much more complex, but we will only consider a simplified situation, which adequately describes the process from an external point of view. As each person arrives, he or she joins the queue; when the clerk is free, the clerk serves the first person, who thus will exit from the queue. For the moment, we are not concerned about processes internal to the queue (such as people cutting in line or grouping themselves into parties larger than one person, etc.).

We thus need to describe just these two operations—addition or deletion of an element—or at most add a third one, to answer the question: How many people are in the queue at this moment?

Since queues are useful in several fields of programming, you might already know how they work and how they can be implemented. If not, it's not very complicated. The two operations of adding elements to and extracting elements from a queue are known, respectively, as *push* and *pop*. A queue and its working model are illustrated in Figure 5.1.

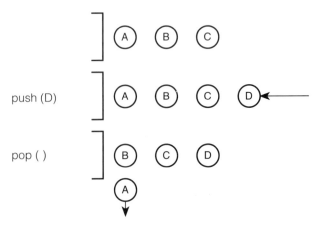

Figure 5.1 Operating scheme of a queue

Also, the following outline illustrates the action taken by the queue.

```
Class          queue
Operations     push    → adds an element
               pop     → returns the first element
               number  → the number of elements
```

Naturally, it will be necessary to translate these operations into function definitions; to be able to implement the class, we also need a way to describe the internal data types (that is, the people waiting in the queue). This procedure will be explained in detail in the last part of this chapter, in which you will build a C++ class describing queues of people, based on the following class definition:

```
class Queue
{
    // private data definition (invisible from the outside)
    ...

    // member functions definition (visible from the outside)
public:
            Queue ( ) ;
    void    Push ( ... ) ;
    ...     Pop ( ) ;
    int     Number ( ) ;
};
```

A Second Example: The Car

Now let's try to describe the abstraction that corresponds to the concept of an automobile. This problem is much more difficult than the previous one (the queue), but we will see that it's possible to manage it through a simplified approach.

In point of fact, we don't need a detailed description of what a car is or how it works: we just need to describe the car from a particular functional point of view. Of course, depending on the point of view, you will have a different description of the abstraction. For example, the driver of a car equipped with an automatic transmission might speed up, brake, turn right, or turn left (plus some other minor operations, such as use the turn signals, honk the horn, or get out of the car). This is a minimal description of the car from the driver's point of view.

To a race car driver, what matters most are the engine's revolutions per minute, the amount of fuel consumed, the power delivered, and so on.

From the point of view of a pedestrian, a car might be best described by its position, speed, and direction. These are the main characteristics. The pedestrian is not concerned who the driver is, how the engine is built, or if it is an automatic or stick. The pedestrian might be interested in the color of the body, the model, or the license number.

Is this information really important? It really depends on the pedestrian. If he is a policeman, he might be interested in the license plate; if, by looking at the car, the pedestrian decides to buy a similar one, he might be interested instead in the model and the color. Most pedestrians, though, are interested in establishing a single fact—is the car likely to hit me? To determine this, let's assume that the pedestrian is more interested in knowing the automobile's speed and whether it is increasing or decreasing, rather than knowing whether the driver is pushing the accelerator or the brake pedal (although the pedestrian would likely assume that this was the reason for the change of speed).

From this point of view, the car might therefore be described by the following list of operations/data:

- present speed
- speed increase
- speed decrease
- present direction
- change of direction
- position along the road

The position (which may be expressed by the distance from a particular starting point—maybe that of the pedestrian) changes continuously according to speed and direction, which in turn might be changed with the corresponding operations. These operations might also have some limits. For example, if the car is at full speed it won't be able to make a U-turn without going off the road. All these aspects can be represented in the fundamental information on which the abstraction is based.

Thus, a single entity has several descriptions, which depend mainly on the point of view you choose and on the degree of detail and precision desired in the description and in the subsequent computer model.

For clarity, the descriptions contained in this chapter (and also in the rest of the book), are all very simple and short, but in case you have to face the description of a real, complex system, it is possible to identify hundreds of abstractions, any one described by several parameters and characteristics.

The Concepts of Class and Object

Before we go on describing the object-oriented data types of the language, it is necessary to define with the highest possible precision the difference between two terms that have already been used several times: class and object.

Although these two terms are often (mis)used interchangeably, there is a great difference between them: the class is the data type, while the object is the instance of the data type—the actual variable—the type of which is determined by the corresponding class. It's the same as the difference in other programming languages between a data type and a variable.

In C++, there are additional ways to look at this difference: the concept of class is static, because its definition is written in the code of the program. The concept of object, instead, is dynamic—because it exists only at run time and denotes a location in the computer's memory.

While this is true for C++, in other object-oriented programming languages, particularly Smalltalk, the difference is more subtle and complex because classes can also exist dynamically. (In Smalltalk, classes are themselves objects, their class being some metaclasses. This difference is because in Smalltalk everything is dynamic, and everything is considered to be an object, even the compiler and the system itself.)

You can describe the difference between classes and objects (or instances) with the comparison proposed by Cox, the author of Objective-C: "The concept of class and instance will already be familiar. 'Betsy is a cow' is just a short way of saying 'Betsy is an instance of class cow.' In programming, the same concept is often called type … Betsy is a cow, but Betsy is also Betsy, the individual. She is like cows in most ways; yet different in ways that set her apart from the herd. The instance, Betsy, is a tangible, flesh and blood creature, but cow, the class is an abstraction. Betsy, the instance, can moo, but cow, the class, cannot." [Cox 86]

The Class

The simple and compound data types described in the previous chapter are the data types common to both C and C++. C++ adds the construct of class, similar to C's structure, but also radically different in that it offers the power of information hiding (and several other aspects, including inheritance, that will be described later).

The class makes it possible to define abstract data types through the declaration of the data needed to represent them and the operations available on them.

The following is an example:

```
// first full definition of class Date

class Date
{

    // declaration of private data

    int    month ;
    int    day ;
    int    year ;

public:   // declaration of public functions

    // constructor: ( the strange syntax will be explained later )
```

```
Date ( int m , int d , int y ) :
        month ( m ) ,
        day ( d ) ,
        year ( y )
        { }

// functions that return the values of day, month, year

int Month ( )
    {
        return month ;
    }

int Day ( )
    {
        return day ;
    }

int Year ( )
    {
        return year ;
    }
} ;
```

In the above listing, you can see that a class—almost like an ordinary C structure—can contain data items (*data members*). But a class can also contain—very differently from an ordinary C structure—functions (*member functions*). It is by means of this construct that C++ realizes the strong coupling between data and functions, which was indicated as one of the fundamental traits of object-oriented languages. The actual meaning of member functions will be explored in greater detail in the next chapter; however, for the moment we want to concentrate on the more general consequences of this coupling.

What are the advantages you can obtain by using a class instead of a structure to handle a date? Data encapsulation offers a higher degree of security, forbidding direct access to the private data of a class. This isn't an arbitrary restriction: it's fully intentional and "legal." Suppose, for instance, that a program using dates decides erroneously that today is February 30, 1999. If the data is public (that is, if you use a structure), you can make the assignments

```
d.month = 2 ;
d.day = 30 ;
d.year = 1999 ;
```

and the program might continue to run. Though it might be odd for a programmer to make the preceding assignments purposefully, the assignment might just be:

```
        d.day = 30 ;
```

and nothing more. If the month previously stored is February, the error would be invisible.

Another way to obtain a potentially nonexistent date is by trying to calculate tomorrow's date in the statement

```
        d.day = d.day + 1 ;
```

(or more typically in C *d.day++;*).

To avoid this risk, you must take some precautions. For example, any time you increment a date, you might precede this operation with a test, to see if the current date is the last day of the month. Therefore, you need to know if the current month has 30 or 31 days, or if it's February 28 or 29. In this occurrence, you must also test if the year is a leap year, which isn't a trivial operation.

To write this multitude of tests, you need several lines of code. Then, you will need several more lines of code to increment the date in the different occurrences.

It is a good idea to write all this just once, and enclose it in a function, which you might call *IncreaseDate*. With C++, you can place this function inside the class that describes dates; if the data members of this class are private, the only way to increase the date is by using this function. While it might seem more difficult, it is much more secure.

Adding the function *LeapYear ( )*, *DaysInMonth ( )*, *IncreaseDate ( )* and a couple of functions for printing, the class might become the following:

```
// file DATE1.H                                           05\DATE
// second definition of class Date
// with some new functions

#include <iostream.h>

class Date
{

    // private data

    int    month ;
    int    day ;
    int    year ;

public:

    Date ( int m , int d , int y ) :
        month ( m ) ,
        day ( d ) ,
        year ( y )
```

```
       { }

   int Month ( )
      {
         return month ;
      }

   int Day ( )
      {
         return day ;
      }

   int Year ( )
      {
         return year ;
      }

      // returns 1 ( TRUE ) in case of a leap year,
      // 0 ( FALSE ) in the opposite one ( int stands for Bool ) :

   int LeapYear ( )
      {
         if ( year % 4 != 0 ) return 0 ;
         else {
            if ( year % 100 != 0 ) return 1 ;
            else if ( year % 400 != 0 ) return 0 ;
            else return 1 ;
         }
      }

      // return the number of days of the actual month

   int DaysInMonth ( )
      {
         switch ( month ) {
         case 2:
            if ( LeapYear ( ) ) return 29 ;
            else return 28 ;
         case 4:
         case 6:
         case 9:
         case 11:
            return 30 ;
         default:
```

```
            return 31 ;
        }

        //  Note that there are no break statements
        //  because return stops function execution,
        //  returning the exit value that is present
    }

    // turns the date into that of the following day

    void  IncreaseDate ( )
      {
        if ( day < DaysInMonth ( ) ) day ++ ;
        else {
           day = 1 ;
           if ( month != 12 ) month ++ ;
           else {
              month = 1 ;
              year ++ ;
           }
        }
      }

    // sends the date to the output device

    void  PrintDate ( )
      {
        cout  << endl
           << "Date : "
           << month << "/"
           << day << "/"
           << year ;
      }

    // prints a phrase indicating whether the year is a leap year

    void  PrintLeap ( )
      {
        cout << endl << "The year " << year ;
        if ( LeapYear ( ) ) cout << " is a leap year" ;
        else cout << " is not a leap year" ;
      }


};
```

To see if this class works correctly, you can compile and run the following code:

```
// file DATE1.CPP                                              05\DATE
// test program for the class Date with the new functions

#include "DATE1.H"

void main ( )
{
    // defines the object newYearsDay, then makes some operations...

    Date  newYearsDay ( 1 , 1 , 2000 ) ;

    newYearsDay.PrintDate ( ) ;
    newYearsDay.IncreaseDate ( ) ; // the variable loses its meaning
    newYearsDay.PrintDate ( ) ;
    newYearsDay.PrintLeap ( ) ;

    // creates the object d of class Date, then makes some operations...

    Date  d ( 4 , 30 , 1991 ) ;

    d.IncreaseDate ( ) ;
    d.PrintDate ( ) ;
    d.PrintLeap ( ) ;

    // defines and prints a list of dates

    for ( Date dd ( 2 , 25 , 1992 ) ; dd.Day ( ) < 3 || dd.Day ( ) > 10 ; dd.IncreaseDate ( ) )
        dd.PrintDate ( ) ;
}
```

The above program will produce the following output:

```
Date : 1/1/2000
Date : 1/2/2000
The year 2000 is a leap year
Date : 5/1/1991
The year 1991 is not a leap year
Date : 2/25/1992
Date : 2/26/1992
Date : 2/27/1992
Date : 2/28/1992
Date : 2/29/1992
Date : 3/1/1992
Date : 3/2/1992
```

➤ ***Note:*** Compiling the above example, you will receive the warning "Functions containing switch are not expanded inline." As noted in Chapter 4, this is a practical demonstration of the fact that the compiler will try to treat the member functions defined inside a class definition as *inline* functions, but this will not be possible if the functions are overly complicated (for instance, if they contain *for* loops or *switch* statements). This kind of warning message will be seen even during the compilation of many other examples in this book. You might just as well ignore this message, since it will not affect the functionality delivered by the programs.

Constructors and Destructors

Among the member functions of a class, two have a particular role: the constructor(s) and the destructor of the class. (There can be more than one constructor, and there are also several other particular class member functions, such as those corresponding to assignment and equality operators.)

The constructors, which can be recognized because they have the same name as their class, are the functions that are called (automatically) whenever the objects need to be initialized. It is a good rule to avoid creating objects (or variables) and assigning a value only later; it's much better to create the objects (the variables), assigning them a value at the very same time.

For example, the class date should have a constructor such as:

```
Date ( int m , int d , int y ) ;
```

Therefore, to declare an object of type *Date* and initialize it, you must use the following statement:

```
Date  Christmas ( 12 , 25 , 1990 ) ;
```

Alternatively, it is possible to use a pointer. In this case an object can be declared and initialized with the two following statements:

```
Date *   pDate ;
pDate = new Date ( 10 , 12 , 1992 ) ;
```

The constructor, in the class definition, could have been defined in the following way:

```
Date ( int m , int d , int y ) :
   month ( m ) ,
   day ( d ) ,
   year ( y )
   { }
```

After the name and the parameters list, enclosed in parentheses, comes a colon character. After that is a comma-separated list of private data members with the values they must receive upon initialization, enclosed in parentheses. As you will see later, there can also be a list of constructors of the classes from which the actual class is derived. At the end, enclosed in curly braces, there is the usual function code for the initialization. This initialization code might be absent if all the necessary initialization operations have been made in the previous lines of code.

Again, we stress the importance of a proper initialization, which can be achieved with the previous definition in which all the private data members are defined at the same time and, if possible, at the declaration. On the other hand, when using a structure it is possible to have the following (invalid!) initializations:

```
Date Christmas ;

...

Christmas.month = 12 ;
Christmas.day = 25 ;

...

// here the variable Christmas is meaningless
// because the value of the year is undefined

...

Christmas.year = 1990 ;
```

Between the declaration of the variable Christmas and the last definition of its member (that of the year), the structure contains a meaningless value, though it can still be used by the rest of the program as any other variable. The initialization problem, once again, shows its importance.

A class may have more than one constructor, thanks to the C++ property of overloading of function names (described in Chapter 6).

For example, you can add the following constructors to the class *Date*:

```
// partial definition of class Date with several constructors

class Date
{
    int    month ;
    int    day ;
    int    year ;

public:

    // "standard" constructor

    Date ( int m , int d , int y ) :
```

```
            month ( m ) ,
            day ( d ) ,
            year ( y )
            { }

        // default constructor ( i.e. without parameters ) :

        Date ( )
        {
            // the compiler will assign zero to the internal data
            // that is left undefined ; so:
            month = 1 ;
            day = 1 ;
            year = 1900 ;
        }

        // functions added because their structure must
        // be known by the following constructor, which uses them

        int     Month ( ) ;
        int     Day ( ) ;
        int     Year ( ) ;
        void   IncreaseDate ( ) ;

        // "oddball" constructor... creates a date nn days after d

        Date ( Date d , int nn )
        {
            month = d.Month ( ) ;
            day = d.Day ( ) ;
            year = d.Year ( ) ;
            for ( int i = 1 ; i > nn ; i++ )
                IncreaseDate ( ) ;
        }

        // other functions...
    } ;
```

As we have seen, a class can have several constructors, or have none of them. In this case, the compiler adds to the class a default constructor having no parameters, which simply initializes all the members to default values (usually zero). This constructor is called automatically each time you declare an object of that class, as in:

```
    class Foo
    {
```

```
        // data and functions but no constructor
    }

    Foo   f ;
```

However, if you add a constructor of any kind to a class, then the compiler doesn't add the default constructor anymore, and you always have to provide the proper parameters. The following code won't be compiled, because there isn't a default constructor for the class *Foo*.

```
    class Foo
    {
        // data and functions

    public:
        // constructor with one parameter
        Foo (int i)
        {
            // some code...
        }
    }

    Foo   f ;        // ERROR
```

The opposite of a constructor, a destructor, is a function that is automatically called at the end of the "life" of the object (that is, when it goes out of scope).

This function provides the cleanup of the memory used by the object: it is automatic for the parts of the object that were automatically allocated. If, on the other hand, some parts of the object were created with the keyword *new* (generally inside a constructor), the destructor must provide the proper *delete* statements to free up the allocated memory, or the objects will continue to occupy (and waste) that portion of memory.

Therefore, each class having pointers as data members should have constructors to allocate memory to the pointers and a destructor to free it:

```
    class FooWithPointer
    {
        // data and functions...
        int *   pNumber ;

    public:
        // default constructor
        FooWithPointer ( )
        {
            pNumber = new int ;
            *pNumber = 0 ;
```

```
    }

    // constructor with one parameter
    FooWithPointer (int i)
    {
        pNumber = new int ;
        *pNumber = i ;
    }

    // destructor
    ~FooWithPointer ( )
    {
        delete pNumber ;
    }
} ;
```

However, in these classes some problems occur when you copy an object to a similar one. We will face this and some related problems in the next chapter.

Private, Protected, and Public

We have repeatedly stressed the importance of information hiding and that classes are a means that allow you to implement it.

We will now examine in detail how this can be done. The class members, either data or functions, belong to one of three categories, according to how much external visibility they have. The visibility from within another class will also be determined by the relations between the classes, according to the scheme shown in Figure 5.2. (The full sense of which will be clear only after you will have seen the construct of inheritance. However, this figure delivers an overall picture of the visibility of the private, protected, and public data members of a class.)

If the data members cannot be modified and function members cannot be called externally, then these members are said to be *private*, and their declaration will be preceded by the keyword *private*.

If data members (if any!) can be freely accessed and the function members can be called from outside the class, then these members are said to be *public*, and their declaration will be preceded by the keyword *public*.

You will see later that there is a third category of function and data members that are only partially visible (in particular, only from within those classes that derive from the class where they have been declared) and that are known as *protected*. Their declaration will be preceded by the keyword *protected*. This will be covered later on. For now, we will focus on the first two categories of members.

The class construct has, by default, *private* members. Therefore, if you omit a specific keyword, the declared members will be private. Once you indicate one of the three possible keywords, all members, data, or functions declared thereafter will be

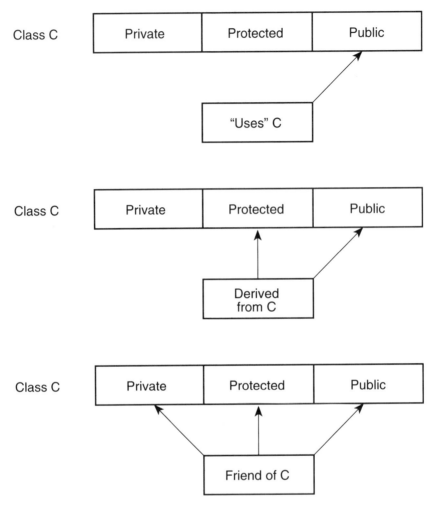

Figure 5.2 Visibility from other classes of the declarations in the various sections of the interface of a class

characterized by the corresponding category until you specify a different keyword (from the three possibilities).

At this point, you might ask what should be public and what should be private? The simplest answer is: leave everything private, unless it has to be public! In other words, once you have listed the services (the functionality) that a class should deliver to the outside world, everything else that needs to be added for "internal" purposes needs to be hidden.

To this general rule, we can add the following rules:

- Data members should never be changed directly from the outside (that is, they should generally be private, sometimes protected).

- In general, constructors and destructors should be public.

- The functions used for internal data manipulation, and called from other functions of the same class, should be private or protected.

- All other functions, such as those defined for correct (and safe) data manipulation (input, processing, and so on), will be public.

Later on, we'll complete this list with other cases that will be encountered in the next few chapters.

Interface and Body of a Class

The definition of a class is made up of two parts: the interface and the body. This subdivision is not mandatory, but for complex classes it is best to always apply it. The interface of a class corresponds to its declaration, which comprises its name, the definition of the internal data members of the class, and the declaration of the function members. The body of a class consists of the collection of member functions.

Every time you write a moderately complicated program, you should place the interface and the body of a class in two distinct files. Usually, in this text we'll indicate the files containing the interface of a class with the extension ".*h*", and the files containing the body of a class with the extension ".*cpp*" (the latter being the same extension used for sample programs and, generally, for files containing the main function).

➤   *Note:*   Usually the selection of a *.c* or *.cpp* extension for the filename determines which kind of compiler should be used to process the file. However, in any project you can change the *Node Attributes* to specify which operation should be performed on the file.

To use the objects of one class in another, or to derive a new class from another, you only need to know the interface of the original class and include its text. The subdivision between an interface file and a definition file for all functions will allow you to compile the different classes separately and create the corresponding object files that can later be linked together in an executable file. Even better, you can take full advantage of the project tool.

Generally, the compilation can be done directly; however, subdividing the class into different files gives you the advantage of better organization, the trade-off being a greater number of files to manage. This, however, should not be a problem if you're using Borland C++: the IDE can open several source files at once, and the project tool can organize them in a consistent way.

This fine-grained subdivision can even help you to quickly find the various parts of a program, making them more independent, and—above all—allow you to easily change a part of the implementation without having to change the class interface or the classes that use it. In fact, while it is enough to know the interface of a procedure during the first compilation phase, at link time it is necessary that the body of every function used in other parts of the program be compiled.

Keeping this in mind, you could rewrite the interface of the class Date, described earlier. This time, however, you'll declare all the functions that have been added in the meantime. You can then collect all functions separately (that is, build the body of the class). Below are the two files that result:

```
// file DATE2.H                                              05\DATE
// full interface definition of class Date

class Date
{

    // private data

    int     month ;
    int     day ;
    int     year ;

public:

        // creates a date from day, month and year

    Date ( int m , int d , int y ) ;

        // creates a default date

    Date ( ) ;

        // creates a date nn days after date d

    Date ( Date d , int nn ) ;

        // returns the day of the month

    int     Day ( ) ;

        // returns the month of the year

    int     Month ( ) ;

        // returns the year

    int     Year ( ) ;
```

```
                // return 1 if it's a leap year, 0 if not

    int     LeapYear ( ) ;

                // returns the number of days in the actual month

    int     DaysInMonth ( ) ;

                // increase the date of one day

    void   IncreaseDate ( ) ;

                // sends the date to the current output

    void   PrintDate ( ) ;

                // sends to the current output a phrase stating
                // if the current year is a leap year or not

    void   PrintLeap ( ) ;

} ;



// file DATE2.CPP                                                05\DATE
// "out-of-class" definition of the member functions of class Date
// which interface is inside the file DATE2.H

#include <iostream.h>
#include "date2.h"

Date :: Date ( int m , int d , int y ) :
    month ( m ) ,
    day ( d ) ,
    year ( y )
    { }

Date :: Date ( )
{
    month = 1 ;
    day = 1 ;
    year = 1900 ;
}

Date :: Date ( Date d , int nn )
{
```

```
     month = d.Month ( ) ;
     day = d.Day ( ) ;
     year = d.Year ( ) ;
     for ( int i = 1 ; i > nn ; i++ )
        IncreaseDate ( ) ;
}

int Date :: Month ( )
{
   return month ;
}

int Date :: Day ( )
{
   return day ;
}

int Date :: Year ( )
{
   return year ;
}

int Date :: LeapYear ( )
{
   if ( year % 4 != 0 ) return 0 ;
   else {
      if ( year % 100 != 0 ) return 1 ;
      else if ( year % 400 != 0 ) return 0 ;
      else return 1 ;
   }
}

int Date :: DaysInMonth ( )
{
   switch ( month )
   {
   case 2:
      if ( LeapYear ( ) ) return 29 ;
      else return 28 ;
   case 4:
   case 6:
   case 9:
   case 11:
      return 30 ;
   default:
```

```
        return 31 ;
     }
   }

void Date :: IncreaseDate ( )
{
   if ( day < DaysInMonth ( ) )
      day ++ ;
   else {
      day = 1 ;
      if ( month != 12 ) month ++ ;
      else {
         month = 1 ;
         year ++ ;
      }
   }
}

void Date :: PrintDate ( )
{
   cout  << endl
         << "Date : "
         << month << "/"
         << day << "/"
         << year ;
}

void Date :: PrintLeap ( )
{
   cout << endl << "Year " << year ;
   if ( LeapYear ( ) ) cout << " is a leap year" ;
   else cout << " is not a leap year" ;
}
```

As you can see from the second file in the preceding program, if you wish to define a member function from the outside of a class, you just need to indicate the class to which it belongs and, after the scope resolution operator **::**, the function you wish to define. Naturally, the parameters and the return value must match those given in the class interface.

The only difference between an internal and an external definition of a member function is that in the first case the compiler will generate, if possible, an *inline* function. So if you intend to make the two kinds of definitions exactly the same, you'll need to precede the second one (the one defined externally) by the keyword *inline*, as in the following example:

```
inline void Date :: PrintDate ( )
{
    cout  << endl
          << "Date: "
          << month << "/"
          << day << "/"
          << year ;
}
```

The this Pointer

You have seen in the preceding examples that from within a class (that is, in its member functions) you can reference data and other functions belonging to the object on which you're operating, simply by naming the interested members. For instance, the statement

```
if ( LeapYear ( ) ) ...
```

means that the member function has to be applied to the current object.

In fact, for each class the compiler generates a "pointer to the current object" that can be referenced explicitly by means of the keyword *this*. In practice, the compiler will consider the above statement as if it were written:

```
if ( this -> LeapYear ( ) ) ...
```

These two statements are exactly equivalent. The first merely is easier to write. The effective use of the *this* pointer is usually limited to the case in which you need to process data structures with pointers that define links between objects. For instance, if another object needs to point to the current object, you can reference the current object by using the *this* pointer.

How to Create and Use Objects

You can create an object (an instance) of a class in one of two ways by using one of its constructors. In fact, the object you create can be processed directly by means of a variable, or indirectly by means of a pointer.

In the first case, you can declare a variable and, at the same time, initialize it like this:

```
ClassName    VariableName ( ConstructorParameterList ) ;
```

That is, in our example:

```
Date    midAugust ( 8 , 15 , 1994 ) ;
```

Alternatively, the two operations—declaration and initialization—can be separate, such as

```
ClassName *  PointerName
PointerName = new ClassName ( ConstructorParameterList ) ;
```

which in the previous example correspond to

```
Date *   pMidAugust ;
pMidAugust = new Date ( 8 , 15 , 1994 ) ;
```

In both cases, the corresponding access to member functions is made as shown by the next two calls:

```
midAugust.IncreaseDate ( ) ;
pMidAugust->IncreaseDate ( ) ;
```

Obviously, using this technique you will only be allowed to access this way those function members or data members that have been declared as public.

Another possibility is to create "constant" objects, which are characterized by the fact that their values cannot be changed. A constant object is declared simply by prefixing the *const* keyword to its declaration. For example:

```
const Date  NewYear ( 1 , 1 , 1994 ) ;
```

You cannot use a member function to access a constant object, unless it has explicitly been declared as a read-only function (by using the same *const* keyword, as will be explained in Chapter 6).

Class Data and Class Functions

Generally, as you have seen, you can access functions and data in a class only by creating objects (instances) of that class and by operating on that object. Sometimes, though, it may be useful to have functions that refer to the class as a whole that can be called even when there is no instance of that class.

These functions (and data) are designated in C++ by the keyword *static*. This construct is not present in all object-oriented languages but is heavily used in others like Smalltalk, in which you have class methods (functions) and class variables (data). In fact, the whole issue is debated among computer scientists: as to whether the capabilities given by class functions and class data are really needed, or if the same operations can be implemented without class functions and class data.

For instance, the class *Date* could be assigned a function that checks if a given year is a leap year by reusing the function already written to check if a specific *Date* object is a leap year.

```
// example of class function
// the following code should be added to the interface of the class Date

// check whether a certain year is a leap year

static int IsYearLeap ( int year )
{
    // defines a date in the year

    Date      d ( 1 , 1 , year ) ;

    // returns whether it's a leap year or not

    return d.LeapYear ( ) ;
}
```

This could have also been done in other ways, such as:

- by means of a C++ function that isn't tied to any class at all. However, this function makes sense only as long as it remains related to the class and to the way the class defines dates, rather than to a general definition of dates that does not exist. Furthermore, even if this reason is trivial, it is certainly simpler and easier to maintain the definition of this function within the unit that defines the class Date. The whole point of tying functions and classes is that they implement and rely upon the same data hiding.

- by means of an object initialization function that might either succeed or fail, based on the correctness of the parameter. This method, however, besides not being very natural, is unnecessarily more complex and contrived than the preceding. However, some object-oriented languages rely on such a method.

Another example of the use of a static class function is the following program, which is also illustrated in Figure 5.3. All objects of the class share a common value (the integer variable *num*), while the remaining variables (in the example, the only variable *ch*) have one copy for every object. The value common to all objects of the class can be initialized and checked through class functions. It is necessary, however, to define the static data member outside of the class, so that the compiler can allocate the correct amount of memory to it. At the same time, this definition can be used to initialize the value of the static data member.

➤   *Note:* Actually, the static data member can only be declared inside a class, and not defined. Furthermore, despite the fact that in the class, we have only a *declaration*, this declaration is mandatory. "Static members obey the usual class member access rules except that they can be initialized (in file scope)." [Ellis 90]

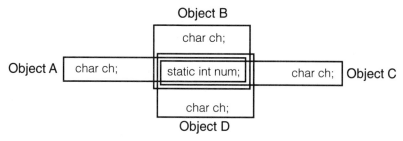

Figure 5.3 The sharing of static data between objects of the same class

```cpp
// file LETTERS.CPP                                    05\LETTERS
// example of class having class data members and destructors

#include <iostream.h>

// definition of class Letters
class Letters
{
    // private data:
    char     ch ;
    static int num ;

public:
    Letters (char c) :
        ch (c)
        {
            num ++ ;
            cout << "New letter " << c
                << ", the total number is " << num
                << endl ;
        }

    ~Letters ( )
        {
            num — ;
            cout << "Letter " << ch << " destroyed, " ;
            if (num == 1)
                cout << "1 letter remains" << endl ;
            else
                cout << num << " letters remain" << endl ;
        }

    char  Value ( )
        {
```

```
            return ch ;
        }

    static int Number ( )
        {
            return num ;
        }
} ;

// out-of-class definition of the class variable

int Letters :: num = 0 ;

// example of class usage

void main ( )
{
    // the following call of static function refers
    // to the class as a whole, and not to a specific object
    cout << "Program begins..." << endl ;
    cout << "Number of letters at the beginning: "
        << Letters::Number() << endl ;

    // creates four objects of class Letters
    Letters   A ('a') ;
    Letters   B ('b') ;
    Letters   C ('c') ;
    Letters   D ('d') ;

    cout << "Number of letters after declarations: "
        << A.Number() << endl ;
    // (this situation is shown in a Figure 5.3)

    cout << endl ;
    cout << "Entering a new block..." << endl ;
    {
        Letters   E ('e') ;
        Letters * pF ;
        pF = new Letters ('f') ;

        cout << "Total number of letters inside the block: "
            << A.Number() << endl ;

        cout << endl ;
        cout << "Leaving the block..." << endl ;
```

```
      }
      // end of block (K is destroyed; L is not, but it's unaccessible!)

      cout << endl ;
      cout << "Total number of letters after the block: "
            << Letters::Number ( ) << endl ;
}
```

The above program produces the output shown in Figure 5.4. As you can see, the static data member can be accessed directly from within the class (for example in the constructor). Outside of the class a proper static member function is used. This function can be called either by using an object as in

```
      A.Number ( )
```

or by referring to the class as a whole, as in

```
      Letters::Number ( )
```

at the beginning of the program, when there are still no objects.

In this example, the problem of initializing class variables is solved directly: a starting value is specified with the out-of-class definition. Alternatively, you could have defined a class function that would take care of this initialization (this function, though, would be no substitute for the out-of-class definition).

```
[Inactive C:\BCPPBOOK\05\LETTERS\LETTERS.EXE]
Program begins...
Number of letters at the beginning: 0
New letter a, the total number is 1
New letter b, the total number is 2
New letter c, the total number is 3
New letter d, the total number is 4
Number of letters after declarations: 4

Entering a new block...
New letter e, the total number is 5
New letter f, the total number is 6
Total number of letters inside the block: 6

Leaving the block...
Letter e destroyed, 5 letters remain

Total number of letters after the block: 5
Letter d destroyed, 4 letters remain
Letter c destroyed, 3 letters remain
Letter b destroyed, 2 letters remain
Letter a destroyed, 1 letter remains
```

Figure 5.4 The output of the program LETTERS.CPP.

You should use a class function for initializations, especially when there are many different variables or when there are many classes to initialize, because the various initialization functions can call one another (this happens very often in Smalltalk programs).

Generally, this construct is useful because the "out-of-class definition" of the static variable must be in the same file as the class, preferably right after the class definition. On the contrary, initialization functions (where the supplied parameters are often of vital importance) should be concentrated in a unique place of the source code, preferably at the beginning of the *main* function, or in a separate function (preferably the initialization function of the main classes) called at that point.

With the method just described, the static class variables should be used to reduce the number of global data in the program:

A static data member acts as a global variable for its class. Two advantages of a static data member over the use of a global variable are the following:

1. Information hiding can be enforced. A static member can be made nonpublic; a global variable cannot.

2. A static member is not entered into the program's global "name space"; thus removing the possibility of an accidental conflict of names. [Lippman 89]

Furthermore, "the association between the static members and their class is explicit and obvious, whereas the use of global variables and functions for similar purposes is neither." [Ellis 90]

The Class Queue

We will now get back to the description of the queue that was given at the beginning of this chapter, and describe it through a class. The initial information we have available is that shown in Figure 5.2, where a scheme of the class interface was outlined.

The first problem is how to define the type of object that makes up this queue. Since this was a queue of people, we'll define a very simple class, *Person*, using the ANSI C++ string class for the name. Here is the code:

```
// file PERSON.H                                    05\QUEUE
// definition of the class Person

// include standard C++ string class
#include <cstring.h>

class Person
{
    string name ;

public:
```

```
    Person (string n) :
        name (n)
        { }

    Person ( ) :
        name ( string( ) )
        { }

    string Name ( )
        {
            return name ;
        }
} ;
```

Now that we have defined the objects, we need to specify in which way these data are stored: we'll go along the simplest possible line, and that is by using an array of elements, defined in this way:

```
Person   line [ 20 ] ;
```

This code indicates that you have an array named *line* consisting of 20 objects of class *Person*.

At this point, you can fully describe the interface of the class *Queue* as the following:

```
// file QUEUE.H                                           05\QUEUE
// definition of the interface of class Queue

#include "person.h"

class Queue
{

    // private data definition (invisible from the outside)
    Person   line [ 20 ] ;
    int      number ;

    // member functions' definition (visible from the outside)
public:

    Queue ( ) ;

    void     Push (Person p) ;
    Person   Pop ( ) ;
    int      Number ( ) ;
};
```

To complete the class, we still need to define the four member functions. But first, we will make a few implementation choices on how to achieve a FIFO ("First In, First Out") mechanism that characterizes the queue. Again, we will choose the simplest route. Although it is certainly not the most efficient, it is the easiest to understand, since it mimics a "real" queue. Since we are interested only in implementing the abstraction, rather than making the most efficient implementation, we will content ourselves with this simplistic approach. When we execute a *Push*, a person is added to the end of the queue in a new position that is computable on the basis of the number of people already in the queue. When we execute a *Pop*, we will take the first person in the queue (that is, in the 0 position of the array), and then all remaining people will advance one position. The following are the function definitions:

```
// file QUEUE.CPP                                        05\QUEUE
// definition of the member functions of class Queue

#include <iostream.h>
#include "queue.h"

Queue :: Queue ( )
{
    // assigns the number of people present at the beginning

    number = 0 ;
}

void Queue :: Push (Person p)
{
    // adds the person at the end of the queue
    // incrementing the total number of people
    line [ number ] = p ;
    number ++ ;

    // describes the event
    cout << p.Name ( ) << " has joined the queue" << endl ;
}

Person   Queue :: Pop ( )
{
    // selects the person to be extracted (the first one in the "line")

    Person   p = line [ 0 ] ;

    // rearranges the line, advancing every person

    for (int i = 1; i < number; i++)
        line [ i-1 ] = line [ i ] ;
```

```
    // decreases the total number of people in the queue

    number -- ;

    // describes the event

    cout << p.Name ( ) << " has left the queue" << endl ;
    // return the first person in the line,
    // already stored in temporary variable p

    return p ;
}

int Queue :: Number ( )
{
    // returns the number of people present in the queue

    return number ;
}
```

To test that this queue class is really working, you can try out the following short example.

```
// QUE-USE.CPP                                        05\QUEUE
// example of use of class Queue

#include <iostream.h>
#include "queue.h"

void main ( )
{
    Queue       q ;

    // prints the number of people in the queue
    cout << "In the queue there are "
        << q.Number () << " people" << endl << endl ;

    // adds some people to the queue
    q.Push ( Person ("John") ) ;
    q.Push ( Person ( "Francis") ) ;
    q.Push ( Person ( "Paul") ) ;
    q.Push ( Person ( "Richard") ) ;
    cout << "In the queue there are "
        << q.Number ( ) << " people" << endl << endl ;
```

```
// extracts the first person in the queue
q.Pop ( ) ;
cout << "In the queue there are "
    << q.Number ( ) << " people" << endl << endl ;

// adds to the queue Billy
q.Push ( Person ("Billy") ) ;
cout << "In the queue there are "
    << q.Number ( ) << " people" << endl << endl ;

// empties the queue
cout << "Everyone leaves the queue..." << endl ;
while (q.Number ( ) > 0)
    q.Pop ( );
cout << "In the queue there are "
    << q.Number ( ) << " people" << endl << endl ;
}
```

To compile this program you need a project with two files, *QUEUE.CPP* and *QUE-USE.CPP*, as shown in the bottom of Figure 5.5, below the output of the program.

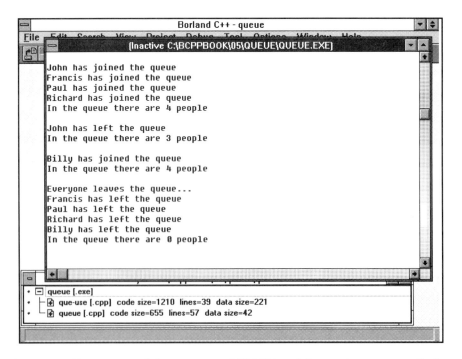

Figure 5.5 The output of the program *QUEUE* and the project to compile it

How to Choose Your Classes

Now that you have seen the class construct and an example of its usage, let's try to define a few "rules of thumb" that might guide us in designing new classes. These rules are inspired by similar ones provided by Jossman. [Jossman 90]

As said in Chapter 3, these rules are no substitute for a design methodology, but are useful as general reference criteria.

The first rule to remember is a very common (and "obvious") one: *keep your classes as simple as possible*. It's the good old programmer's KISS ("*Keep It Simple, Stupid*"), which is even more valuable in object-oriented programming, because every class should describe one—and only one—abstraction. The abstraction must be defined in the most complete and exhaustive way (so it can easily be reused). But you also need to limit its complexity by defining the abstractions of the objects that constitute the class, then use a client relationship or an inheritance relationship to assemble the various concepts that you want to represent with the class.

For example, you could easily define a class of cars if you already had available a class of engines and a class of drivers.

A second rule is: *better small than scattered*. In other words, it is better to create small classes that contain only a couple of function or data members, rather than leave them global (or "scattered"). You don't have to describe a complex abstraction to allow yourself to call it a class! What really matters is that every class describes a well-defined concept, even a simple one. An extreme is this: it is certainly better to have a class with only one function than a global function.

For instance, in the previous program on queues, we described a very simple class, *Person*. Nonetheless it was a very significant class: it would have been possible to define this element in even simpler terms (just like a simple string, for instance), but we prefer to enclose this abstraction in a class. This class can be extended later, without having to make other changes to the classes that use it (like the queue of people).

We also suggest this rule: *don't make personal questions*. In other words, don't have data in classes that identify their type, or parameters that might determine which functions should be called under different circumstances. In these cases, you have to rely blindly on the mechanism of polymorphism, which you can achieve through inheritance and dynamic binding (virtual functions) that will be described later.

The last rule: *don't make too many friends*. You must reduce to a minimum the usage of the *friend* construct, because it lets you violate the rules of information hiding. Use of this construct must be limited only to certain cases, as will be shown in the next chapter.

Stroustrup suggests:

When you program, you create a concrete representation of the ideas in your solution to some problem. Let the structure of the program reflect those ideas as directly as possible: (a) if you can think of 'it' as a separate idea, make it a class; (b) If you can think of 'it' as a separate entity, make it an object of some class; (c) if two classes have something significant in common, make that commonality a base class; (d) if a class is a container of objects, make it a template. [Stroustrup 91A]

POINTS TO CONSIDER

1. Describe and implement in a simple way other abstractions similar to the queue; for instance a LIFO ("Last In, First Out") stack. Use this last abstraction to describe cars entering a narrow blind alley.

2. Develop further the abstraction of a car and implement a simple class to describe it.

3. What is the difference between a class and an object? What do they have in common, and what distinguishes the two concepts? (This is a very important point, and it must be thoroughly understood!)

4. Invent, analyze, describe, and implement the interface and the body of a class. Start with the bare minimum functionality and then expand on that. Take examples from the real objects or phenomena that you can observe: chairs, tables, people, boxes, discs, books, binders, and so on.

5. Write a sample program that uses the *Date* class defined in the previous examples and compile everything (as in the compilation of QUE-USE.CPP).

6. Think about the meaning and the usage of class functions. Add a class function to some classes you have already implemented.

7. Expand (using your imagination) the class *Queue* with new functionality: the possibility that someone gets tired of waiting and goes away, that someone else rudely tries to get into the middle of the queue, and so on. Write some other program that uses the class.

8. Rewrite the class *Queue* with other elements: instead of people, describe a queue of numbers, books (with their title and author), or cars (with all their features). How many changes do you have to make in order to modify one type of object (in this case, Person) with another within a class?

6

Functions and Object-Oriented Programming

In object-based and object-oriented programming languages, opera-
tions that clients may perform upon an object are typically declared
as methods, which are part of the declaration of the class of the
*object. C++ uses the term **member function** to denote the same*
concept. . . .

    *The terms **operation**, **method**, and **member function** evolved from*
three different programming cultures (Ada, Smalltalk, and C++, re-
spectively). They all mean virtually the same thing. [Booch 91]

In this chapter, we will concentrate on functions and on how they relate to the object-oriented constructs of C++. Functions have already been covered in Chapter 4, but there they were considered exclusively from a "traditional" point of view. You will now see how the function construct has been adapted to the object-oriented features of the language.

Member functions—the object-oriented siblings of ordinary functions—are described in detail, together with the meaning of functions with respect to object-oriented programming principles. This chapter also describes function and operator overloading, the use of the *friend* construct, and some typical programming errors related to functions (side effects, aliasing, and dangling references).

Functions and Member Functions

In C++, functions can be divided into two distinct categories: "ordinary" functions and member functions.

    Ordinary functions correspond to the functions of C, those of a procedural programming language. Essentially, they allow you to describe subprograms, as outlined in Chapter 4.

    Member functions are defined as "members" of classes. These are functions that can be applied only to the objects defined by the corresponding classes. You have already seen some examples of member functions in the previous chapter, in the various sample classes.

Member functions can be further divided into two categories: those that actually can be applied to objects and the so-called *static* class functions (of which some examples were given in Chapter 5), which are associated not with a particular instance (object) of a class, but with the class itself (whether the class actually has real instances, in this case, does not matter).

The following code illustrates how each type of function can be implemented. In all three cases, the same operation is performed. This way, the syntactic differences between the different cases stand out better, since the difference in meaning of the various categories of functions is deliberately ignored (in particular, the meaning of class functions).

```
// file FUNCS.CPP                                    06\FUNCTION
// example of functions of different kind
// that accomplish the same operation ( triple a number )

#include <iostream.h>

// non-member ( "ordinary" ) function definition

int Triple1 ( int number )
    {
        return number*3 ;
    }

class Number
{
    int    n ;
public:

    // constructor

    Number ( int num ) :
        n ( num )
        { }

    // member function definition

    void   Triple2 ( )
        {
            n *= 3 ;
        }

    int    Value ( )
        {
            return n ;
```

```
        }

    // class member function definition

    static int Triple3 ( int num )
        {
            return num*3 ;
        }
} ;


void main ( )
{
    int          intNum = 5 ;
    Number       objNum ( 5 ) ;
    int          triple ;

    // the following function calls have the same result
    cout <<"shows the result of three corresponding functions" << endl;

    // non-member function call

    triple = Triple1 ( intNum ) ;
    cout <<triple << endl;

    // class ( static ) member function call

    triple = Number :: Triple3 ( intNum ) ;
    cout <<triple << endl;

    // member function call and value retrieval

    objNum.Triple2 ( ) ;
    triple = objNum.Value ( ) ;
    cout <<triple << endl;
}
```

Nonstatic member functions do not always return a value. As in the above example, these functions merely change the value of the objects to which they are applied. This behavior is quite common, since (nonstatic) member functions usually represent operations to be performed on objects. In any case, you can get the resulting object's value by using the ordinary data access functions.

➤ *Note:* If the definition of a member function happens within the declaration of a class—as in the preceding example—then the language will consider it equivalent to the definition of an *inline* function (outside the class), even though in the first case the *inline* keyword is not present. The reason is that often many short functions are declared inside a class—for example, for accessing data—which are always good candidates for *inline* functions. (*Inline* functions were described in Chapters 4 and 5.)

In examining the different categories of functions in C++, it is important to notice the profound difference between "ordinary" functions typical of traditional programming languages and member functions and class functions that are distinctive features of object-oriented languages. In certain cases (for the so-called pure object-oriented languages, like Smalltalk, Eiffel, or Actor), the first type of function call is not available at all—only the last two categories exist (and, in some cases, only the second one, like in Eiffel).

By merging the traits typical of an object-oriented programming language with a procedural language like C, the C++ language lets you simultaneously use all three kinds of function calls. The language, therefore, does not force you to use a pre-arranged choice, but allows you to program in an object-oriented manner, a classical manner, or even a hybrid manner. The different kinds of functions available in C++ allow you to choose the one that best describes the behavior of the system and its parts.

Whether this freedom of choice is positive or not is a highly controversial issue. On one side are programmers who feel that this freedom is good because it allows a "seamless" transition from traditional programming to object-oriented programming. Others consider it to be a severe drawback because, if not forced to do otherwise, the programmer will tend to continue to program in a traditional way and will only use the new constructs marginally (and probably incorrectly).

In fact, "many programmers who make the transition to hybrid OOP languages, such as C++, continue to write hard-to-reuse procedural code rather than take advantage of the reusability OOP offers." [Duff 90]

Functions and Programming Styles

The choice of the C++ language for a project thus does not imply the adoption of a particular style of programming. It is important, though, that during the design and implementation (that is, during the actual writing of the code) it must be clear which model is to be used. You must decide whether to use functions (and traditional methodologies), classes and member functions (and an object-oriented methodology), or a mix of the two.

In point of fact, this latter route is often preferred by several programmers having the common doubt whether to use member functions exclusively when classes are involved. The following two observations can be drawn:

- The advantages of object-oriented programming (code reusability, information hiding, abstraction, and so on) can be achieved only by applying these techniques correctly and rigorously.

- The problem is not so much in the selection of programming constructs, but in the combination of these with an appropriate programming style.

Naturally, with a hybrid object-oriented language like C++, you can write programs based on procedures (which, for instance, is impossible in Smalltalk!). In this case, though, it might be more convenient to continue using a traditional programming language than to climb up a steep learning curve to master new constructs and then lose all of their advantages.

While you can write object-oriented programs with traditional procedural programming languages, you will have to do somersaults to achieve what object-oriented languages deliver directly, and you will have to renounce the automatic checks that a compiler of such a language can perform on the code. This is not to say that this should never be done; it is simply not worthwhile to use this approach as an ordinary programming practice.

Even by using a language like C++ that allows many "dirty tricks," you can still assert a few guidelines that should be helpful to those people learning this programming methodology:

1. "Ordinary" functions should be used very infrequently: often, what can be performed with a function can also be achieved with a member function (and sometimes with a class function).

2. If it is really necessary to write a function, or if you have to create a new class to accommodate a new function, probably the design decisions can be improved. It is almost always possible to modify the design in such a way that the functions that you do not know where to place become integrated.

3. All functions (and in particular, member and class functions) should be devoid of "side effects" to allow a looser coupling between classes and make them more modifiable and reusable. (The term "side effects" usually refers to the modification of some nonlocal data by a function.)

Const Member Functions

A member function can be declared as *const*, which means that the function will be able to access the data members of the objects for which it is called, but it will not be able to modify them. Think of this as a "read-only" function for the private data members. This property is checked by the compiler, which will detect any errors. Constant functions are allowed to call other member functions only if they are also constant.

Differently from ordinary member functions, a *const* member function can be applied even to constant objects, which is why you should always explicitly indicate the constant functions if you intend to use constant objects.

To declare a constant function, you just have to place the keyword *const* between the function's argument list and its body, as in the following example:

```
// file CONSTFN.CPP
// example of constant function

class A
{
    int    n ;

public:

    A ( int m ) :
        n ( m )
        { }

    int Read ( ) const      // Constant function
        {
            return n ;
        }

    // if you were to declare const the following
    // function, you would get a compilation error

    void   Change ( int m )
        {
            n = m ;
        }
} ;

void main ( )
{
    A   a1 ( 5 ) ; // Ordinary object

    a1.Change ( 4 ) ;
    a1.Read ( ) ;

    const A a2 ( 8 ) ;  // Constant object

    a2.Change ( 6 ) ; // generates a warning !
    a2.Read ( ) ;
}
```

Constant Functions and Constant Arguments

Constant functions should not be confused with constant arguments. Constant arguments are used when a pointer or a reference is passed as a function argument, and their purpose is to deliberately signal to the compiler (and the reader) that the function does not have any kind of side effect on the addressed argument. In other words, the function implementation decides that the addressed argument will not be changed by the function, and the compiler checks for this condition.

A constant argument is declared simply by writing the *const* keyword before the formal argument in the function declaration, such as

```
void read ( const pObject * ) ;    // constant pointer

void read ( const rObject & ) ;    // constant reference
```

or even within member functions like this:

```
class One
{
    ...
} ;

class Two
{
    ...
    int  Compare ( const One * pOne ) ;

    int  Compare ( const One & rOne ) ;
    ...
} ;
```

Both constant functions and constant arguments are tools that you can use to write better interfaces between functions and their invocations, and therefore improved class interfaces.

Side Effects, Aliasing, and Dangling References

As you have seen, functions can have "side effects," which are often exploited by experienced programmers, but which can also open the way to significant errors that are difficult to identify, unless extreme care is taken. We will now examine these aspects of function calls in more detail, and also some other causes of common errors: aliasing and dangling references.

These problems are discussed in the belief that a "clean" programming style is the basis for writing programs that are easy to modify and extend; a basis onto which object-oriented programming can easily be built.

Each subject will be illustrated by short examples to show both intent and risks. In reality, when these problems arise in large programs, they are often the cause of elusive errors, because the various parts of the program can be correct, but still do not work well together.

The best way to avoid these types of errors is "prevention." Use a great deal of care when using these "tricks of the trade."

Side Effects

The term "side effect" usually indicates the modification of some nonlocal data by a function. This can happen, in particular, when the program uses pointers, or if parameters are being passed by reference.

An example of a side effect of this kind is present in the listing below, which is further illustrated in Table 6.1. Inside the following code, the function *multiply* inadvertently modifies a variable passed by reference; in other words, it modifies the value of the parameter that it has passed, in this case the variable *a*.

```
// file SIDE.CPP                                        06\SIDE-EFF
// example of side effect in a function

#include <iostream.h>

// the multiplying function is correct, but can modify some nonlocal data
// changing the value of the reference parameters
int multiply ( int &x , int &y )
    {
        x *= y ;
        return x ;
    }

void main ( )
{
    // initialization and value assignment
    int    a = 5 ,
           b = 3 ,
           c = 0 ;

    // expression yielding a wrong result because of the side effect
    c = a + multiply ( a , b ) ;

    // the output highlights the error
    cout << "5 + 3 * 5 = "<< c ;
}
```

The above program produces the following output:

```
5 + 3 * 5 = 30
```

In some cases, side effects can be useful, but you should not abuse them. Above all, they should be used to modify only well-defined local data—for instance, other data

Table 6.1 Scheme of side effects present in the program SIDE.CPP

		a	*b*	*c*
1.	Initialization and value assignment	5	3	0
2.	" multiply (a, b) "	**15**	3	0
3.	" c = a + ... "	15	3	**30**

items of the same class (though this is an operation that should be avoided). The most dangerous case is that of the alteration of data passed as parameters, because it is not possible to anticipate all possible ways the function will be called and if and how that data will be referred to again after the function call.

Aliasing

The problem of aliasing arises when, in a certain area of a program, two names refer to the same entity, making it possible to access the same data item by using two different notations. This case is illustrated in the following example, where the variables *b* and *c* refer to the same piece of data, thereby creating a program that is not very readable, and in which operations will be performed differently from what you might expect at first sight.

```
// file ALIAS.CPP                                    06\SIDE-EFF
// tiny example of aliasing

#include <iostream.h>

void main ( )
{
    int a = 2 ;
    int b = 10 ;

    int &c = b ; // c is an alias for b

    cout << endl << "b equals to " << b << endl ;

    // the following instruction changes the value of b
    c = a * b ;

    // b should not have changed ( it has never been an lvalue... )
    cout << endl << "now b equals to " << b << endl ;
}
```

The above program produces the following output:

```
b equals to 10

now b equals to 20
```

Apart from its simplicity, this example shows that you should avoid creating variables that share the same memory with other variables. If this is unavoidable, you should at least try not to use both references in the same program segment.

Another very common case of aliasing, although less evident than this one (and therefore more dangerous), can happen with parameters passed by reference, when the same variable is passed more than once. For instance, in the function call

```
int Funct ( int &x , int &y ) ;
```

you could pass the same parameter twice, like this:

```
Funct ( a , a ) ;
```

In the body of this function there would be two distinct variable names, both referring to the same memory location (that is, the memory location occupied by the variable *a* at the moment the function is being called). Even this potential source of errors, which might seem trivial, can actually occur in very complicated situations, in which it is virtually concealed.

Generally, writing programs that rely on aliasing is bad programming practice, and should be avoided at all costs. In fact, this type of error is quite easy to prevent, but is far more difficult to catch and correct once its symptoms are detected.

Dangling Reference

Another very common error, which can also be a consequence of aliasing, is the *dangling reference*, which denotes the existence of a pointer that references a memory location not currently allocated to any data. This error can occur because of a missing initialization of a pointer (but in this case it is more accurate to call it a missing initialization error). It can also occur, in particular, when a memory location can be accessed by means of two or more pointers, and one of these gets de-allocated, thus freeing the memory to which other (still usable) pointers are allowed access. This type of dangling reference is shown in Figure 6.1.

The following example illustrates how this can happen:

```
// file DANGLE.CPP                                    06\SIDE-EFF
// example of dangling reference

#include <iostream.h>

void main ( )
{
```

```
// declaration of pointers to integers
int    * a ;
int    * b ;

// the new operation reserves space in memory for the integer variables
a = new ( int ) ;
b = new ( int ) ;

// some miscellaneous operations...
*a = 10 ;

// b is assigned to the same location of a ( aliasing )
b = a ;
cout << endl << "The original value of b is " << *b << endl ;

// the following instruction ( the deletion of a ) , causes the value of
// b to become random, since its memory location is de-allocated
delete ( a ) ;
cout << "After the de-allocation of a the value of b becomes " << *b << "\n" ;

// following operations on b, although correct, are meaningless
*b *= 2 ;
cout << "Multiplying b by 2 yields the value of " << *b << "\n" ;
}
```

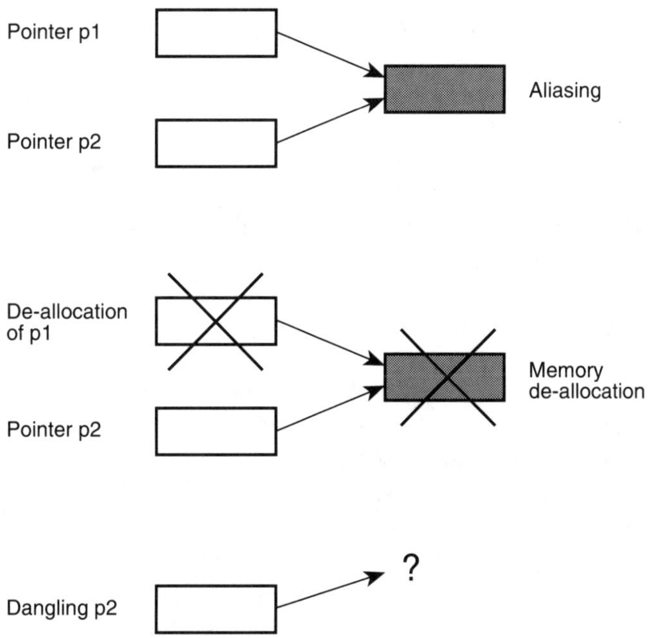

Figure 6.1 Scheme of dangling reference

The above program might produce the following output:

```
The original value of b is 10
After the de-allocation of a the value of b becomes 14146
Multiplying b for 2 yields a value of 28292
```

➤   *Note:*   The values in this example obviously depend on the state of the computer at run time. Therefore, you will probably get different values from those shown.

It is certainly necessary to exercise great care when writing programs that are not linear! But what does this really mean? On one hand, we state that exercising care does not necessarily mean that you should not use these techniques (or tricks), as long as you know what potential errors you might face. On the other hand, we state that dangerous constructs or techniques should never be used to avoid abandoning good programming practice.

The bottom line is simple: every programmer has to decide which approach he or she prefers.

Function Overloading

It is said (without proof) that every person has at least two or three doppelgängers in the world; and it is certainly an uneasy thought that you might walk down a street and see your mirror image approaching from the other direction. Some people look alike as twins and differ only in minor respects. In C++ that is true for functions as well.

In C++, functions can be *overloaded*. Function overloading is when several distinct functions are all identified by the same name. These functions—whether ordinary, member, or class functions—differ only in their *argument signature*—the number and the types of their parameters. C++ allows function overloading as long as the functions have different parameters, so that you can identify which function is being called by examining the number and the types of parameters present (considering also the various combinations that might arise if there are default parameters).

Although these functions all have the same name, you can determine which is being called and distinguish between the overloaded functions simply by examining their unique argument signatures. C++ accomplishes function overloading through name mangling, which changes the internal function name to include the representation of the types of its parameters. Therefore, even the linker can distinguish among the different versions of the same function. An effect of this approach is that the same checks are performed by the linker onto ordinary (that is, not overloaded) functions; this useful behavior is known as *type safe linkage*.

In the following example, there are several functions that share the same name but have different parameters: some of them are member functions (like *Complex::Add*), others are ordinary functions (like *Multiply* and *Print*). In particular, note how the functions that calculate the product or the sum of complex numbers have one parameter inside and the other outside the structure. This is possible because the structure has all public data members. The function *Print* instead is simply a rewrite of *cout*. Although there are certainly better ways to solve the same problem—for instance, by overloading the << operator (operator overloading will be described later in this chapter)—this represents an interesting case in which the same function is being used in very different ways (to print strings, numbers, complex numbers, or just to print a new line if it is called with no parameters).

```
// file OVERLOAD.CPP                              06\OVERLOAD
// examples of function overloading

#include <iostream.h>

struct Complex        // i.e. a class with public members
{
    int    r ;        // real portion of the number
    int    i ;        // imaginary portion of the number

    // overloaded member functions

    void  Add ( Complex c )
       {
           r += c.r ;
           i += c.i ;
       }

    void  Add ( Complex * pc )
       {
           r += ( *pc ) .r ;
           i += ( *pc ) .i ;
       }

    void  Add ( int a , int b = 0 )
       {
           r += a ;
           i += b ;
       }
} ;

// overloaded nonmember functions

Complex Multiply ( Complex c1 , Complex c2 )
    {
        Complex    c3 ;
```

```
        c3.r = c1.r * c2.r - c1.i * c2.i ;
        c3.i = c1.r * c2.i + c1.i * c2.r ;

        return c3 ;
    }

Complex Multiply ( Complex c , int n )
    {
        c.r *= n ;
        c.i *= n ;
        return c ;
    }

// other example of overloaded nonmember functions

void   Print ( Complex c )
    {
        cout << c.r << "+" << c.i << "i" << endl ;
    }

void   Print ( int n )
    {
        cout << n << endl ;
    }

void   Print ( char * string )
    {
        cout << string << endl ;
    }

void   Print ( )
    {
        cout << endl ;
    }

// the main function uses the overloaded functions just defined:
// Add, Multiply and Print ( in the various versions )

void main ( )
{
    Complex    x = { 3 , 1 } ;
    Complex    y = { 1 , 2 } ;
    int        v = 7 ;
    int        z = 4 ;
    Complex    product1 , product2 ;
```

```
Print ( "Sum of the complex numbers:" ) ;
Print ( x ) ;
Print ( y ) ;

// sum of two complex numbers: first version of Add ( )

x.Add ( y ) ;

Print ( "----" ) ;
Print ( x ) ;

// sum of a complex and a real number: third version of Add ( )

y.Add ( z ) ;

// calculates two products, using two different functions

product1 = Multiply ( x , y ) ;
product2 = Multiply ( x , v ) ;

// prints the starting and resulting values

Print ( ) ;

Print ( ) ;
Print ( "x equals to:" ) ;
Print ( x ) ;

Print ( ) ;
Print ( "y equals to:" ) ;
Print ( y ) ;

Print ( ) ;
Print ( "v equals to: " ) ;
Print ( v ) ;                    // call a different function than Print ( x )

// prints the multiplication results
Print ( ) ;
Print ( "x * y = " ) ;
Print ( product1 ) ;

Print ( ) ;
Print ( "x * v = " ) ;
Print ( product2 ) ;
}
```

The above program will produce the following output:

```
Sum of the complex numbers:
3+1i
1+2i
----
4+3i


x equals to:
4+3i

y equals to:
5+2i

v equals to:
7

x * y =
14+23i

x * v =
28+21i
```

This program defines several global functions with the same name. If you look at them using the *View Globals* menu command of the Borland IDE, a list of functions with the same name appears. Selecting each one of these functions, you'll see the detailed description, with the proper parameters.

It can be interesting to see name mangling in action in the previous program. This is possible by issuing:

```
TDUMP -m -oiPUBDEF OVERLOAD.OBJ
```

on the DOS command line, where the -m parameter serves to retrieve the names in *mangled* format, and the -oi is used to select a portion of the information about the object file. This command produces a list of the global functions (with C++ generated names) of the compiled file, with some information on their position in the code segment:

```
0013F4 PUBDEF '@Multiply$q7Complext1'    Segment: _TEXT:0000
001486 PUBDEF '@Multiply$q7Complexi'     Segment: _TEXT:0036
0014C3 PUBDEF '@Print$q7Complex'         Segment: _TEXT:0056
001502 PUBDEF '@Print$qi'                Segment: _TEXT:00AB
001536 PUBDEF '@Print$qpc'               Segment: _TEXT:00D2
```

```
00156F PUBDEF  '@Print$qv'                    Segment: _TEXT:00F5
0015A6 PUBDEF  '_main'                        Segment: _TEXT:0101
```

Avoiding the -m parameter, the output changes considerably, becoming much more readable but less precise, since you do not see the information actually present in the *obj* file, which should be used when linking with code written in another language (including plain C):

```
0013F4 PUBDEF  'Multiply(Complex,Complex)'    Segment: _TEXT:0000
001486 PUBDEF  'Multiply(Complex,int)'        Segment: _TEXT:0036
0014C3 PUBDEF  'Print(Complex)'               Segment: _TEXT:0056
001502 PUBDEF  'Print(int)'                   Segment: _TEXT:00AB
001536 PUBDEF  'Print(char near*)'            Segment: _TEXT:00D2
00156F PUBDEF  'Print()'                      Segment: _TEXT:00F5
0015A6 PUBDEF  '_main'                        Segment: _TEXT:0101
```

As you can see there is a direct correspondence between the two descriptions: the i above stands for int, pc for pointer to char, v for void, and Complex for itself. Notice, however, that this internal representation is compiler dependent.

In C++, the functions that get overloaded most often are probably the class constructor functions; this allows you to build new objects starting with different parameters. For instance, you can define the objects of a class that describes a line by indicating two points belonging to the line, by listing the coordinates of both of these points with a pair of integers, or with an appropriate data structure (*Point*). You can also identify a line by a point and its slope. The declaration of these two constructors is shown in the following example:

```
// example of overloaded constructors

struct Point { int x ; int y ; } ;

class Line
{
   // private data...
public:

   Line ( Point p1 , Point p2 ) ;
   Line ( int x1 , int y1 , int x2 , int y2 ) ;
   Line ( Point p1 , int angle ) ;
   Line ( int x1 , int y1 , int angle ) ;

   // function definitions...
} ;
```

Overloaded Function Calls Resolution

The only limit of function overloading is the availability of a function to be called. Each call of an overloaded function requires that there is one and only one actual function with matching parameters to be called. This definition seems simple but can get quite confusing in case of default values and automatic type conversions.

The call of an overloaded function can result in three different situations:

1. The match of one function: this can be an exact match, a match through a parameter promotion, a standard conversion, a user-defined conversion.

2. No match at all.

3. An ambiguous match, in case more than one function definition corresponds to the call, perhaps because of a parameter promotion or conversion.

If you find it difficult to understand how an ambiguous match can occur, consider the following code:

```
void   f (int x, char c) ;
void   f (char c, int x) ;
...
f (12, 15) ;
```

The call is ambiguous because both *f* functions can be called after a standard conversion. Since both matches require a conversion of the same kind, the compiler cannot decide which of the two functions to call. On the other hand, in the following case:

```
void   f (int x, char b, char c) ;
void   f (char c, int y, int x) ;
...
f (12, 13, 15) ;
```

the call is correct, because the second function requires one conversion while the first function requires two casts from *char* to *int*. The compiler can easily determine the *nearest* function (the second in this case) and call it.

➤ *Note:* The Borland C++ compiler checks for ambiguously overloaded functions only when a call—and not the definition—is actually encountered. This ambiguity results in a error message reporting a misleading error line (which refers to the call and not to the definition of the function). A class containing such an error will be compiled flawlessly: the error will be reported only when some other piece of code uses the overloaded function of that class.

Operator Overloading

In addition to the overloading of functions, C++ allows you to redefine the meaning of the operators of the language. This technique is also known as *operator overloading*.

Usually in a programming language, an operator has a very precise predefined meaning. In some programming languages, though, it is possible for you to give several meanings to the same operator, based on the context in which it appears. For instance, the operator + between two integers could mean "add these two numbers," while between two strings it could mean "concatenate these two strings." In this case, the *semantics* (or meaning) of the operator has been overloaded, because there exists more than one meaning, according to the context.

With binary operators (i.e. operators that act upon a pair of operands), operators are represented with infix notation; but operators can also appear with a prefix or postfix notation, especially if they are unary operators.

The fundamental difference between ordinary functions and operators is the appearance of the function call

```
// function

a = sum ( b , c ) ;

// operator

a = b + c ;
```

which in the second case is much more readable and immediately understandable, especially if the operation is part of a complex expression. For instance, the sum of three numbers would be expressed in the following way:

```
// function

a = sum ( b , sum ( c , d ) ) ;

// operator

a = b + c + d ;
```

Operators can be defined either like member functions or like ordinary functions (as in the C language) outside of the class. However, with ordinary functions, one of the parameters of the operator must be a class. Therefore, you cannot redefine, for instance, the sum of two integers. The C++ language allows overloading of most operators, including the array subscript, [ ], the function call, ( ), the indirect class member access, ->, and the *new* and *delete* operators. The only operators you cannot overload are:

.   .*   ::   ?:

Operator > Between Dates

To see how a "member" operator can be implemented in a class, let's refer to the base class *Date* as defined in Chapter 5, of which the interface code is reproduced in the listing below, with the addition of the declaration of the *operator >*.

In this example, you will add the *operator >* to the class *Date*. This operator will determine whether one date is greater than another date, chronologically. The operator must return a Boolean value of true or false, that is, one of the two corresponding values of 1 or 0.

To add this operator to the class, you must first insert the following line of code to its interface:

```
int    operator> ( Date d ) ;
```

as shown in the shaded portion of the following listing:

```
// file DATE3.H                                              06\DATE
// full interface definition of class Date ( as in file DATE2.H, Chapter 5 )
// with the addition of the operator >

class Date
{
    // private data

    int    month ;
    int    day ;
    int    year ;

public:

    // creates a date from day, month and year

    Date ( int m , int d , int y ) ;

    // creates a default date

    Date ( ) ;

    // creates a date nn days after date d

    Date ( class Date d , int nn ) ;

    // returns the day of the month

    int    Day ( ) ;
```

```
// returns the month of the year

int     Month ( ) ;

// returns the year

int     Year ( ) ;

// return 1 if it's a leap year, 0 if not

int     LeapYear ( ) ;

// returns the number of days in the actual month

int     DaysInMonth ( ) ;

// increase the date of one day

void   IncreaseDate ( ) ;

// sends the date to the current output

void   PrintDate ( ) ;

// sends to the current output a phrase stating
// if the current year is a leap year or not

void   PrintLeap ( ) ;

// returns true ( 1 ) if the actual date is after
// d, otherwise returns false ( 0 ) if it is before

int     operator > ( Date d ) ;
} ;
```

In the above listing, the interface of the class Date, described in the previous chapter, is complemented with the addition of an overloaded operator. Next, the operator must be implemented, such as in the following way:

```
// portion of the file DATE3.CPP                              06\DATE

// The operator > between two dates corresponds to the
// same operator between year, month, or days.

int Date :: operator > ( Date d )
{
```

```
        return Year ( ) == d.Year ( ) ?    //  if the years are equal,
(
        Month ( ) == d.Month ( ) ? //  if the months are equal
        Day ( ) > d.Day ( ) :       //  check the days
        Month ( ) > d.Month ( ) ) :  //  else check the months
    Year ( ) > d.Year ( ) ;         //  else check the years
}
```

At this point, once objects of the class *Date* have been created, these can be compared with an expression like

```
( d1 > d2 )
```

which is similar to what you would write in order to compare two variables of predefined types, like *int* or *float*.

Remarks on Operator Overloading

To sum up, one can see that it is useful to overload operators only if the new meaning is
similar to the old meaning (although this is not mandatory). In fact, the greater than
operator could just as well have been identified with the symbol "<" (which would
undoubtedly give rise to confusion), "+", "%", or with the name of any other operator
available in the language. This identification is legitimate and permitted by the compiler, though it would not be a particularly good idea.

The fundamental purpose of operator overloading is to improve the readability and
understandability of a program. Operator overloading will also ease the actual writing
of the code of a program, because you can avoid having to constantly remember the
names of obscure functions, and can replace them with appropriate operators. Thus,
the code can be written in a more natural and concise way.

Furthermore, using operators gives the "feel" of actually having extended the language with a new data type, on which it is possible to "operate" just like on the
predefined data types of the language.

However, if the names of the operators were not intuitive, or even worse, not the
same as their semantic meanings, then operator overloading could actually be counterproductive and harmful by undermining readability and understandability.

Overloading the ++ Operator

Overloading the increment and decrement operators involves some peculiar aspects.
The ++ (and --) operator can be used in two different situations: It can be either prefix
or postfix. As we saw in the *INCREMEN.CPP* example in Chapter 4, the two versions
of the operator have a slightly different meaning. Overloading the ++ operator with the
statements

```
class Date
{
    ...
public:
    ...

    operator ++ ( ) ;
} ;
```

will actually overload only the prefix version of the increment operator and not the postfix version. If you then use the operator in postfix notation, the compiler will accept it and generate the correct code, but it will also issue the warning message *"Overloaded prefix 'operator ++' used as a postfix operator"*.

However, it is possible to define both prefix and postfix increment operators in the following way:

```
class Date
{
// private data as in previous example...

public:
// constructors and member functions as in previous example...

// prefix increment operator
Date &      operator ++ ()
    {
    // calls the IncreaseDate member function
    IncreaseDate ();
    return * this;
    }

// postfix increment operator
Date &      operator ++ (int)
    {
    IncreaseDate ();
    return * this;
    }
};
```

The only difference between the two definitions is the *int* type parameter of the postfix version, which is almost useless. This parameter is just a place holder: No deeper meaning is implied and it cannot be used to pass a value in any way. The two operators can be called with the usual notation or with the functional notation, in which case the parameter has to be supplied to distinguish between the operators:

```
Date  d;
++d;                    // prefix operator
d++;                    // postfix operator
d.operator++ ( );       // functional notation for the prefix version
d.operator++ (0);       // functional notation for the postfix operator
```

By using this "strange" notation it is possible to define two different increment operators. This is, in fact, the usual behavior, since the return values of the two operators in the "predefined" arithmetic version are different. One is the value before the increment, while the second is the value after the value resulting from the increment. You can take advantage of this by implementing a different "postfix" version, compliant with the behavior of ordinary arithmetic postfix operators. For instance, in the previous example:

```
Date    operator ++ (int)
   {
   Date theOldOne = *this;
   IncreaseDate();
   return theOldOne;
   }
```

Overloading the Assignment Operator

The assignment operator is the only operator which is not inherited by a derived class and that has a default definition for each class. In fact, you can write:

```
Date d1, d2 ;
d2 = d1 ;
```

even if you haven't defined the = operator for the *Date* class. The default behavior of the assignment operator added to each class by the compiler is the member wise assignment: Each member of the destination object (*d2* in the example) receives the value of the corresponding member of the source object (*d1* in the example). If the members are object themselves, their assignment operator is called and the process is repeated over and over.

It's really useful for us that the compiler adds a default assignment operator to every class we write, but sometimes we need a different behavior to avoid aliasing and dangling references. These problems may arise if we have a class with a pointer as a member. In this case the default behavior of the assignment operator is to copy the members, that is, the pointers and not the values they point to. After a copy we end up with two objects having a member referring to the same memory location. If one of the objects changes this value, it affects both of them. If one of the objects goes out of scope and its destructor is called, the destructor might delete the pointer (and free the corresponding memory location). In this case the reference in the second object is dangling.

The declaration of the assignment operator for a class is quite simple:

```
class Data
{
    ...
    Data&      operator = (const Data& source) ;
    ...
};
```

Each class having pointers should redefine the assignment operator (and the copy constructor, too, as we will see in the next section). For the moment being, the class *FooWithPointer* of the last chapter can be rewritten as follows:

```
class FooWithPointer
{
    // data and functions...
    int *  pNumber ;

public:
    // default constructor
    FooWithPointer ( )
    {
        pNumber = new int ;
        *pNumber = 0 ;
    }

    // constructor with one parameter
    FooWithPointer (int i)
    {
        pNumber = new int ;
        *pNumber = i ;
    }

    // destructor
    ~FooWithPointer ( )
    {
        delete pNumber ;
    }

    // overloaded assignment operator
    FooWithPointer& operator = (const FooWithPointer& source)
    {
        // copy the pointed value, not the pointer
        *pNumber = *(source.pNumber) ;
```

```
            // the other members should be copied, too
    }
} ;
```

Conversion Operators

Among the operators that can be defined for a class there are some which are not based on operators of the language! The conversion operators, in fact, are based on keywords specifying the arithmetic data types of C++.

Suppose you have a class of *Numbers*, such as:

```
class Numbers
{
    int n ;

public:
    ...
} ;
```

How can you convert an object of class *Number* in an integer value and vice versa? The conversion of an integer into a number is straightforward, because you can use a constructor:

```
class Numbers
{
    int n ;

public:
    Numbers (int value)          // converts from int to Numbers
    {
        n = value ;
    }


    ...
} ;
```

You can use a constructor each time you need to convert a data type into a user-defined data type (because the user-defined data type, a class, can have any number of constructors). However, you cannot use a constructor to convert a data type into an arithmetic data type, since you cannot have a constructor for integers! In the latter case you need to add to the class *Number* a conversion operator, which is an operator having no parameters and no return value at all (as a constructor), although it needs a return statement. The general form of a conversion operator is:

```
operator <data-type> ()
```

If we add such an operator to the class *Numbers*, we obtain:

```
// portion of file CONV-OP.CPP                          06\OVERLOAD
class Numbers
{
    int n ;

public:
    Numbers (int value)          // converts from int to Numbers
    {
        n = value ;
    }

    operator int ( )             // converts from Numbers to int
    {
        return n ;
    }

    ...
} ;
```

Both the conversion defined through the constructor and the one that is based on the operator can be called automatically (and implicitly) by the compiler each time a conversion is required, as in:

```
int i = 7 ;
Numbers    n (12), n1 = 15 ;

i = abs (n) ;
n1 = 3.14 + i ;
```

The last two statements generate implicit calls to the conversion operator and to the *conversion constructor,* respectively. It's important to notice that implicit constructors can cause an unexpected behavior, as a missing type error or as an ambiguous over-loaded function call. Therefore, conversion should be limited to the cases in which you really need it.

Copy Constructor

Parameter passing of objects can take both forms that were explained in Chapter 4 for ordinary functions (that is, by reference and by value) and even in this case, the same rules as for ordinary scalar parameters still apply. However, there are a few significant differences:

- If the objects have only *private* or *protected* data members, their modification can happen—in any case—only through member functions.
- If an object is being passed by reference to a function, the function can be compiled even without the compiler knowing the class of the object. However, a similiar function cannot operate on the parameter, which becomes almost useless.

An interesting aspect that arises when dealing with functions and objects is that when an object is being passed as an argument to a function or when a function returns an object, that object is assigned to another object of its same class (either the actual argument of the function in the first case, or a variable of the same class as the returned object in the second case). During this assignment, although a "new" object is being instanced, its ordinary constructor function (provided by the class designer) is not called. Instead, the initialization happens through the call of a special constructor function—the so-called *copy constructor*.

If you don't add this special constructor to a class, with the syntax

```
class Test
{
public:
    Test (Test& t1) ;
} ;
```

the compiler provides it automatically, using the same kind of *memberwise copy* of the assignment operator.

Memberwise initialization is really something more than a straightforward copy of each member. Sometimes an object can contain other objects as members. When there are member objects, they are subject to another memberwise initialization. In other words, the memberwise initialization is applied recursively to all member objects, then to the member objects of the member objects, and so on until all "sub-objects" have been initialized.

An object can be built from another of the same class, using the copy constructor, in three different cases:

- The explicit initialization of an object, with another one of the same class:
  ```
  Test    t2 = t1 ;
  ```

- The passing of an object by value as function parameter:
  ```
  void    Print (Test t) ;
  ```

- The passing of an object as return value of a function (always by copy):

```
Test       NextTest ( ) ;
```

If you pass an object to a function or return a value by reference instead of by copy, then the copy constructor is not called, because no *new* temporary object is build.

When Is the Copy Constructor Called?

To gain a better understanding of the implicit calls of a copy constructor, you can look at the following self-descriptive example. The class *Test* has both a default constructor and an assignment operator, which output their name and the state of the object. Each new object, including temporary objects used for the parameters and return values, has a different number. This numbering scheme determines the need to write a specific copy constructor and assignment operator, because the memberwise copy made by the system would affect both the value and the number of the object, leading to a wrong result.

```
// file SHOWCOPY.CPP                               06\SHOWCOPY
// Self describing examples, showing the calls of a copy constructor

#include <iostream.h>

class Test
{
int    value ;    // value of the object
int    obj_number ;   // number of the object
static int last_obj ;        // number of the last object

public:
    // standard constructor, with one parameter
    Test (int n)
    {
        value = n ;
        obj_number = ++last_obj ;
        cout  << "Standard constructor (object no."
                << obj_number
                << ") : value = " << value
                << endl ;
    }

    // copy constructor
    Test (const Test& t)
    {
        // we need to copy the value because if we provide
        // a copy constructor the default copy is not done
        value = t.value ;
```

```
    // although it has the same value it is another object
    obj_number = ++last_obj ;
    cout  << "Copy constructor (object no."
          << obj_number
          << ") : value = " << value
          << endl ;
}

// destructor
~Test ( )
{
    cout  << "Destructor (object no."
          << obj_number << ")"
          << endl ;
}

// assignment operator
Test& operator= (const Test& t)
{
    // we need to copy the value because if we provide
    // an assignment operator the default copy is not done
    value = t.value ;
    cout  << "Assignment operator (from object no."
          << t.obj_number << " to object no." << obj_number
          << ") : value = " << value
          << endl ;
    return (*this) ;
}

// increment operator
int operator ++ ( )
{
    return ++value ;
}
} ;

// external definition of the static member
int Test::last_obj = 0 ;

// global function printing the increased value
// parameter and return value are passed by copy
Test PrintNext (Test t)
{
    cout << "New increased value = " << ++t << endl ;
    return t ;
}
```

```
// main function: creates some objects
void main ( )
{
    cout << "1. New object" << endl ;
    Test  t1 (25) ;

    cout << endl ;
    cout << "2. New object... copied" << endl ;
    Test  t2 = t1 ;

    cout << endl ;
    cout << "3. New object... increased" << endl ;
    Test t3 = PrintNext (t1) ;

    cout << endl ;
    cout << "4. Assignment of increased object" << endl ;
    t2 = PrintNext (t3) ;

    cout << endl ;
}
```

To show the calls of the copy constructor there is a global function having as parameter and return value an object of the *Test* class. As you can see, the main function defines some objects, in different ways. Notice that the statements:

```
Test  t2 = t1 ;
Test  t3 = PrintNext (t1) ;
```

call the copy constructor, not the assignment operator, because they are used to build a new object. Looking at the output of the program (Figure 6.2) you should be able to understand what happens in it.

Several temporary objects are created and, after a while, destroyed: the *PrintNext* function parameters are passed by copy, and the same holds for its return value. Passing these parameters by reference instead of by copy affects the output of the program, since no temporary objects will be created. Using the function:

```
// portion of file SHOWCPY2.CPP                    06\SHOWCOPY
Test& PrintNext (Test& t)
{
    cout << "New increased value = " << ++t << endl ;
    return t ;
}
```

the output of the program becomes the one of Figure 6.3.

```
[Inactive C:\BCPPBOOK\06\SHOWCOPY\SHOWCOPY.EXE]
1. New object
Standard constructor (object no.1) : value = 25

2. New object... copied
Copy constructor (object no.2) : value = 25

3. New object... increased
Copy constructor (object no.3) : value = 25
New increased value = 26
Copy constructor (object no.4) : value = 26
Destructor (object no.3)

4. Assignment of increased object
Copy constructor (object no.5) : value = 26
New increased value = 27
Copy constructor (object no.6) : value = 27
Destructor (object no.5)
Assignment operator (from object no.6 to object no.2) : value = 27
Destructor (object no.6)

Destructor (object no.4)
Destructor (object no.2)
Destructor (object no.1)
```

Figure 6.2   Output of the program SHOWCOPY.CPP

```
[Inactive C:\BCPPBOOK\06\SHOWCOPY\SHOWCPY2.EXE]
1. New object
Standard constructor (object no.1) : value = 25

2. New object... copied
Copy constructor (object no.2) : value = 25

3. New object... increased
New increased value = 26
Copy constructor (object no.3) : value = 26

4. Assignment of increased object
New increased value = 27
Assignment operator (from object no.3 to object no.2) : value = 27

Destructor (object no.3)
Destructor (object no.2)
Destructor (object no.1)
```

Figure 6.3   Output of the program SHOWCPY.CPP, using reference parameters

Copy Constructor in a Class with Pointers

Usually you need to override the default copy constructor only for a class having member pointers. As a matter of fact, the default behavior of the copy constructor is known as *shallow copy*, because the objects are copied as they are, regardless of their meaning. The definition of a copy constructor for a class with pointer turns it into a *deep copy*, because the code makes a copy of the pointed object, too.

In the following example (a portion of the file POINTCLS.CPP) the constructor of the class with a pointer allocates new memory for it, and its destructor deletes it, as it frequently happens.

```
// file POINTCLS.CPP (first part)                    06\POINTCLS
class PointerClass
{
    int number ;
    int *  pointer ;

public:
    // constructor
    PointerClass (int a, int b)
    {
        number = a ;
        pointer = new int ;
        *pointer = b ;
        cout  << "New pointer - address:" << pointer
              << ", value:" << *pointer << endl ;
    }

    // destructor
    ~PointerClass ( )
    {
        cout  << "Deleting pointer - address:" << pointer
              << ", value:" << *pointer << endl ;
        delete pointer ;
    }

    void Print ( )
    {
        cout  << "The pointer value is " << *pointer
              << " and its address is " << pointer << endl ;
    }
} ;
```

This code works correctly only if the copy constructor (or the assignment operator) is never called. On the other hand, if you call it, the class becomes unstable and you risk having dangling references. It is quite easy to develop a main function that causes problems using this class as in the POINTCLS.CPP example:

```
// file POINTCLS.CPP (second part)                   06\POINTCLS
void main ( )
{
    cout << "Creating Object A" << endl ;
    PointerClass   objA (5, 8) ;

    {
        cout << endl ;
```

```
        cout << "Creating object B" << endl ;
        PointerClass   objB = objA ;
        objB.Print ( ) ;

        cout << endl ;
        cout << "Object B is going out of scope" << endl ;
    }

    cout << endl ;
    cout << "Object A has a dangling pointer" << endl ;
    objA.Print ( ) ;

    cout << endl ;
    cout << "Object A is going out of scope" << endl ;
}
```

If you look at this main function, when *objB* goes out of scope (at the end of the enclosed block) the pointer inside *objA* becomes dangling, because the memory address it points to is deleted by the *objB* destructor. The behavior of this program is demonstrated by its output (Figure 6.4) and the graphical description of Figure 6.5.

To avoid this kind of problem, you need to define a copy constructor for every class having a pointer as member data. The copy constructor should allocate a new pointer and then copy the value instead of its address (as the default member wise copy does). A possible copy constructor of the previous *PointerClass* is the following (which is part of POINTCL2.CPP):

```
// excerpt from file POINTCL2.CPP                          06\POINTCLS
// (the rest is the same of POINTCLS.CPP file)


PointerClass (const PointerClass& pc)
```

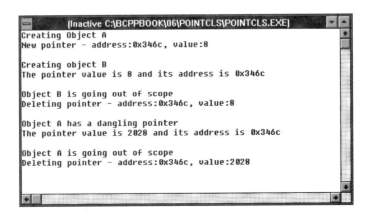

Figure 6.4 Output of the POINTCLS.CPP program

```
{
    // copy the members
    number = pc.number ;

    // allocates a new pointer and copies the pointer value
    pointer = new int ;
    *pointer = *(pc.pointer) ;
    cout  << "New pointer - address:" << pointer
        << ", value:" << *pointer << endl ;
}
```

With this new version of the class, the output changes considerably, as shown in Figure 6.6.

> *Note:* The solution presented in this section for avoiding dangling references is only one of many. It is quite simple, but has two drawbacks. A first one is practical: it wastes a lot of memory, because each referenced object must be replicated. A second one is semantical: sometimes you really do need to reference the *same* object from within two or several other different objects.
>
> In order to avoid the first problem an elegant solution is using a *copy-on-demand* strategy. This means making a copy of the referenced object only when it is changed on behalf of one of the objects that references it. You can find an example of this approach in the ANSI *string* class, as implemented in the Borland compiler.
>
> A solution for the second problem is implementing a *reference counting* mechanism: the object keeps track of how many other objects point to it, and its destructor is smart enough to allow actual deallocation only when there are no more references to it.

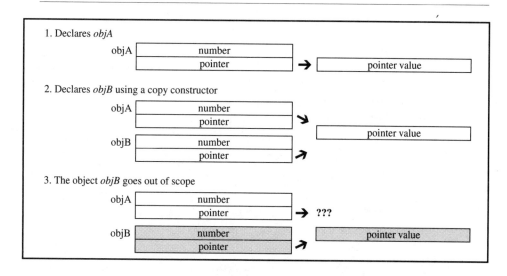

Figure 6.5 Copying an object with a pointer can result in a dangling reference

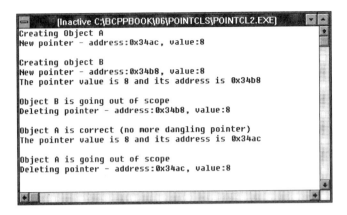

Figure 6.6 Output of the POINTCL2.CPP example.

The Copy Constructor in Action

A real world example of the definition of a copy constructor is shown in the following listing, which fully describes a class of *Boxer*, using pointer to array of characters as member data. A better solution would have been to use the proper ANSI C++ string class, but the example requires the pointers to work properly (using a string the copy constructor is not required).

```
// file BOXER.CPP                                        06\POINTCLS

#include <iostream.h>
#include <string.h>

class Boxer
{
char  * name;

public:
    // ordinary constructor taking one argument
    Boxer (char * n)
    {
    name = new char [20];
    strcpy (name, n);
    cout << "*** Ordinary constructor called ***" << endl;
    }

    // copy constructor
    Boxer (const Boxer& b)
    {
```

```
        name = new char [20];
        strcpy (name, b.name);
        cout << "*** Copy constructor called ***" << endl;
        }

        // destructor
        ~Boxer ()
        {
        delete name;
        }

char *    GetName ()
        {
        return name;
        }

void   SetName (char * n)
        {
        strcpy (name, n);
        }
};

void main ()
{
// defines two objects of class Boxer
Boxer ChampionOfTheSixties ("Cassius Clay");
Boxer TheBestEver = ChampionOfTheSixties;

// changes the name of the first boxer
ChampionOfTheSixties.SetName ("Mohamed Ali");

// outputs the name of the first one
cout  << "The champion of the sixties "
      << ChampionOfTheSixties.GetName ()
      << endl;

// outputs the name of the second one
cout  << "The best boxer is "
      << TheBestEver.GetName ()
      << endl;
}
```

If you run the program, you will see that both constructors are called (producing the output in the first part of Figure 6.7) and that the last output statement is correct. If you modify the source code by eliminating the copy constructor or by enclosing it in a comment, and then run the program again, you will notice that the "ordinary" constructor is called only once, since the default constructor is invoked for the second initialization. But the final output (see the second part of Figure 6.7) will be wrong, since changing the name of one of the boxers affects both of them: the two objects contain a pointer to the same memory location.

Friends

As we have seen, there are several precise rules that govern access to the internal data members of a class, according to their access qualifiers: private, protected, or public. However, there is one exception to these rules: in C++, and only in this language, it is possible to access freely all data members and function members of a class by means of the friend construct.

A class can have, among other functions and other classes, some "friends" who are allowed to know its "secrets," such as the implementation of data, and who are allowed to access even private data and functions in that class. This runs contrary to the rules of information hiding (where every class should have at least one "secret" of its own).

Why has this friend construct been added to C++? There are many reasons: mainly because C++ has been designed with a strong emphasis on efficiency. Direct access to private data members can make a program faster and/or reduce its size. This access, however, makes sense only when efficiency is the "critical" element in an application. In all other cases, the advantages are small. And, as we will see in Chapter 14, the fact

Figure 6.7 The correct output of the program BOXER.CPP (above) and the wrong output, after the changes suggested in the text.

that Borland C++ is an optimizing compiler can actually boost the performance of object-oriented constructs (mainly *inline* data access member functions) to levels that are comparable to those of a traditional direct access construct. In this case, efficiency has very little to gain with the friend construct.

Are there other reasons for using the friend construct? Many books on programming in C++ describe this construct as necessary to perform certain operations on complex data structures, such as when you have to operate on a pair of similar objects and one of them has to be external, and you can access its data only through its functions. However, there is almost always an alternative, more "object-oriented" way to solve this problem; even though it might not be easy to find and might be somewhat less efficient.

In some cases, the friends construct is quite useful and even correct from a theoretical point of view. An important example is that of the subdivision of an abstraction in two classes: one class serves as the interface to the abstraction, while the other serves as the implementation. Think about why it might be useful to make such a subdivision. As said before, among the elements of criticism of C++ is that private data members of a class are declared in its interface, and when you need to modify its implementation you have to recompile all classes that use that class. Thus, it is better to divide a class in two: one outer interface class (that is not subject to changes) and one inner implementation class (where changes do not affect other parts of the program).

Below is an example to illustrate this concept. First, you need to define the interface of the class, where you list its functions and insert, as sole private data member, a pointer to the implementation class:

```
// file NOTE.H                                              06\NOTE
// interface of class Note, that uses for its
// implementation the friend class NoteImpl

class Note
{
    class NoteImpl * ni ;

public:
    Note ( int pitch , int duration ) ;
    ~Note ( ) ;
    void   Sound ( ) ;
    void   Increase ( int delta ) ;
    void   Modulate ( int cycles ) ;
} ;
```

➤ *Note:* By putting the declaration of the *NoteImpl* class inside the *Note* class, you ensure that other pieces of code that include the interface of the *Note* class (that is, the NOTE.H file), will not be allowed to use the implementation class.

Also note that the usage of the keyword *class* in this declaration is mandatory, because otherwise the compiler will not understand that *NoteImpl* is a user-defined data type.

Next, you have to actually implement the abstraction, by describing fully the implementation class and defining the procedures of the *Note* class. The sound functions we are going to use are the old Windows functions to drive the speaker. Although they are considered obsolete, using the new multimedia functions is too complex for this example. Since we use some functions of the Windows API, the application needs to include the *windows.h* file in the source code.

```
// file NOTE.CPP
// implementation of class Note through
// the definition of class NoteImpl

#include <windows.h>
#include "note.h"

class NoteImpl
{

    friend    Note ;

private:

    int pitch ;      // Hertz
    int duration ;   // milliseconds

    NoteImpl (int p, int d) :
        pitch (p),
        duration (d)
        { }

    void Sound ( )
        {
            // sounds the note

            OpenSound ( ) ;
            SetVoiceNote (1, pitch, 32, duration) ;
            StartSound ( ) ;
            WaitSoundState (S_QUEUEEMPTY) ;
            StopSound ( ) ;
            CloseSound ();
        }
} ;
```

```
// Member functions of class Note:

Note :: Note (int pitch, int duration)
{
    ni = new NoteImpl (pitch, duration) ;
}

Note :: ~Note ( )
{
    delete ni ;
}

void Note :: Sound ( )
    {
        ni -> Sound ( ) ;
    }

void Note :: Increase (int delta)
    {
        // direct access to private data of a different class

        ni -> pitch += delta ;
    }

void Note :: Modulate (int cycles)
    {
        for (int i = 1; i <= cycles; i++) {
            ni -> pitch ++ ;
            ni -> duration = 1 + i%2 ;
            ni-> Sound ( ) ;
        }
    }

/*
// the preceeding member function could be rewritten using
// Windows' sound function more correctly either in the following
// way or adding a Modulate member function to the NoteImpl class:

void Note :: Modulate (int cycles)
    {
        OpenSound ( ) ;
        for (int i = 1; i <= cycles; i++) {
            ni -> pitch ++ ;
            ni -> duration = 1 + i%2 ;
            SetVoiceNote (1, ni->pitch, 32, ni->duration) ;
```

```
        }
    StartSound ( ) ;
    WaitSoundState (S_QUEUEEMPTY) ;
    StopSound ( ) ;
    CloseSound ( ) ;
}
*/
```

Since this is a true Windows application, it requires a *WinMain* function instead of a *main* function as entry point. We will return to *WinMain* and the details of its parameters in the chapters on Windows programming at the end of the book. Notice, however, that this is quite a strange Windows application, since it creates no main window.

There are just a couple of message windows made using the *MessageBox* function, which requires as second parameter the text displayed, as third parameter the title of the message window, as fourth parameter some flags describing the buttons (MB_OK stands for a message box with only the OK button). The first parameter of the function refers to the main window of the application, which does not exist. Therefore, we can use NULL (i.e., zero) as value.With this information, you can understand the following:

```
// file NOTE-USE.CPP                                          06\NOTE
// example of use of the double-class Note

#include "note.h"
#include <windows.h>

// this window application uses no "window interface"

int PASCAL WinMain (HINSTANCE, HINSTANCE, LPSTR, int)
{
    Note  n (5, 32) ;

    // ouputs a window with a message
    MessageBox (NULL, "Press the button to play the sound", "NOTE", MB_OK) ;

    // play the sound
    n.Sound ( ) ;
    n.Increase (5) ;
    n.Sound ( ) ;
    n.Modulate (50) ;

    // output a final message
    MessageBox (NULL, "Press the button to end the program", "NOTE", MB_OK) ;

    return TRUE ;
}
```

In this example, note the distinction between the class and the program that uses this class (and knows only its interface). To compile this program, you'll have to open a project using the Project menu in the Borland IDE, insert the two files (NOTE.CPP and NOTE-USE.CPP) into the project, compile them, and link them. The project target, however, must be "Application" and not "Easy Win," since this is a full-blown Windows application, although somewhat strange.

You can now modify the implementation of the class, changing the procedures, and even the private data members, without having to recompile the NOTE-USE.CPP program that uses the class; you only need to relink. You can try, for example, to change the type of data being referenced (for instance, changing an *int* into *long*), recompile the class, relink, and then run the program. The object code file NOTE-USE.OBJ (that is, the compiled code) will not be modified! This approach is convenient when dealing with very large projects and many programmers, where each one of them can independently produce different object modules and still modify the private members of their classes.

We can make some further theoretical considerations on the usage of the "friends" construct in this example. First of all, the two classes are tightly coupled; in fact, the class NoteImpl authorizes the class Note to access its hidden parts. Although *this certainly is a violation* of the principles of information hiding, it is a disciplined violation because the access of the internal parts of the class *NoteImpl* is permitted, but only for a class identified explicitly through the friend statement.

From another point of view, you could observe that the principles of object-oriented programming are still enforced, because the example implements an abstraction that is completely contained in a module divided in two files, of which it is not allowed to know the internal information and implementation. Indeed, the classes that use this double-class are even more unaware of its implementation than what happens normally (in the previous example you could extensively modify the implementation, changing even the class's private data).

The constructs of a language like C++ are not all specifically designed for object-oriented programming. However, they can be easily exploited for this type of programming. When a programmer has acquired a certain way and habit of thinking, and has adopted a discipline and rules, he or she will be able to correctly use all constructs offered by the language at hand, consistently with the chosen methodology.

Overloading the Input-Output Operators

We have already used several times an expression such as:

```
cout << n ;
```

Now we can try do explain its meaning in detail. We know that << is an operator of the C++ language meaning *left shift* (that is, all the bits of the representation of the value are shifted to the left *n* times). However we know that the << operator can be overloaded by a class, and it is actually overloaded by the classes of the stream library. This operator (and the corresponding >>) was probably chosen both for its visual appeal (a kind of arrow toward the *cout* object) and for its infrequent use. In C++, << and >> are almost considered as input and output operators, regardless of their C language origin.

It's quite easy to imagine how these operators have been defined in the *ostream* and *istream* classes: there is probably a pair of these operators for each predefined data type of the language. But how can we add standard input and output support for our own classes? We cannot change the original stream classes, and it won't be easy to derive new classes from them, adding new operators. The best way to add support for user-defined data types is to define some new *global, non-member,* operators.

These operators should have two parameters, the stream and the data, and return the stream to allow chaining the operators. In case of the *Date* class, we can write:

```
ostream& operator << (ostream& s, Date d) ;
```

The stream object is passed and returned by reference, avoiding local copies, but not as a constant, since the operation modifies the value of the stream object. The code of this operator might be very simple:

```
ostream& operator << (ostream& s, Date d)
{
    s << d.Month ( ) << '/' << d.Day ( ) << '/' << d.Year ( ) ;
    return s ;
}
```

This definition allows us to use the operator by itself, or chained with other operators:

```
Date  d1 (10,12,1492) ;
cout << d1 ;
cout << "What happened on " << d1 << " in America?" << endl ;
```

The definition of an input operator is somewhat more difficult, because you need to collect the values for the month, the day, and the year, check if they are correct, then call a member function of the class (such as *SetDate*) to change its value. Of course, you need to pass the *Date* object by reference for the changes to have effect.

```
istream& operator >> (istream& s, Date& d)
{
    int m, d, y ;
    s >> m >> d >> y ;
    // make some cheks...
    d.SetDate (m, d, y) ;
}
```

Another approach is to declare the overloaded << and >> operators as friend functions of the class they refer to. In this case, the usage of the *friend* construct is valuable and theoretically sound, since the input and output operations for the object of a class are logically part of the class itself.

In the following example the two operators are initially defined as members of a class describing complex numbers. Later, a second structure is defined, containing three complex numbers and named *Triple*. Both classes declare the operators as friend functions.

```cpp
// file INOUT.CPP                                    06\OVERLOAD
// Example of overloading of the input-output operators >> and <<

#include <iostream.h>

class Complex
{
    float   real ;
    float   imag ;

public:

    Complex ( )
    { }

    Complex (float re, float im)
    {
        real = re ;
        imag = im ;
    }

    float   Re ( )
    {
        return real ;
    }

    float   Im ( )
    {
        return imag ;
    }

    friend istream& operator >> (istream& s, Complex& c) ;
    friend ostream& operator << (ostream& s, Complex c) ;
} ;

istream& operator >> (istream& s, Complex& c)
```

```
   {
      s >> c.real >> c.imag ;
      return s ;
   }

   ostream& operator << (ostream& s, Complex c)
   {
      s << "(" << c.real << ", " << c.imag << ")" ;
      return s ;
   }


   class Triplet
   {
      Complex   one ;
      Complex   two ;
      Complex   three ;

   public:
      Triplet ( )
      { }

      friend istream& operator >> (istream& s, Triplet& t) ;
      friend ostream& operator << (ostream& s, Triplet t) ;
   } ;

   istream& operator >> (istream& s, Triplet& t)
   {
      cout << "First element:" << endl ;
      s >> t.one ;
      cout << "Second element:" << endl ;
      s >> t.two ;
      cout << "Third element:" << endl ;
      s >> t.three ;
      return s ;
   }

   ostream& operator << (ostream& s, Triplet t)
   {
      s << t.one << ", " << t.two << ", " << t.three ;
      return s ;
   }

   void main ( )
   {
```

```
Triplet   t ;

cout << "Input a ""triplet"" of complex numbers..." << endl ;
cin >> t ;
cout << endl << endl ;
cout << "You have input the ""triplet"": " << t ;
}
```

POINTS TO CONSIDER

1. Rewrite—in an "object-oriented" manner—a small program that you have implemented in a traditional fashion with top-down decomposition. Analyze the differences between the two projects (which depend on the type of problem being solved and on your own ability to "forget" the top-down version when you implement the object-oriented version).

2. Judge the different parameter passing mechanisms available in C++; build a few examples and assess the relative speed and memory requirements. Compare the C language's pointer passing mechanism with C++'s reference passing mechanism.

3. Analyze operator overloading as it has been implemented in the standard libraries available in Borland C++. In particular, look at the header file *complex.h* and *iostream.h*, which are usually located under the *include* directory. These files define, respectively, the class of complex numbers and the classes of input/output (*cin* and *cout*), which rely heavily on operator overloading.

4. Complete the class *Line*, mentioned in the section *Function Overloading*, by defining a private data structure and the code of the constructor, and adding some additional functions. Devise an example of usage of the class.

5. Look for errors caused by side effects, aliasing, or dangling references. Experimenting with similar problems might help you avoid them in your programs.

6. As shown in the text, the TDUMP utility can be used to see the mangled names produced by the C++ compiler in an object file. Try to use the same technique to examine some other program beside OVERLOAD.CPP.

7

Inheritance

*Just as a child inherits traits from its parents, a derived class (also called a **subclass**) inherits traits from a base class (also called a **superclass**). With derivation, you are saying "this new class is that old one with some changes." For instance a **skyscraper** is a **building** with many floors.* [Eckel 89]

This chapter introduces one of the most powerful tools available in object-oriented languages: inheritance. This construct allows you to model more precisely the reality that you wish to emulate in your program, abstracting common behavior between similar objects through a mechanism of generalization. This, in turn, provides a greater detail of description, starting from more global classes and progressing through increasingly specialized and specific subclasses.

In other words, inheritance allows you to create many classes that are similar to each other, without having to rewrite the similar parts every time; it lets you combine several classes into one or to modify an existing class without actually altering the original code. Inheritance is the heart of object-oriented programming and constitutes the first basic building block for code reuse. The second basic building block is polymorphism, which will be described in the following chapter as a pleasant consequence of inheritance.

A First Example of Inheritance

Suppose you need to write a class into which you want to store a person's date of birth, so that you can generate a reminder in time to send a card or present. In Chapter 5, you wrote a class named *Date*, which might be useful now since the case is somewhat similar. You can try to derive the class *BirthDate* starting from the class *Date*. Recall that this class has been built in a series of steps and consecutive examples, and that its complete interface was listed in the preceding chapter.

The class you construct is a specialization of the class *Date*; it will extend its functionality in ways that would only make sense for the specialized category of birth dates.

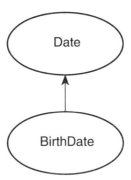

Figure 7.1 Graphic notation used to represent inheritance relation between classes

The syntax used to state the derivation is simple: the heading of the class (the keyword *class* and the class name) is followed by a column (:) and the name of the class from which it is derived (or a list of names of classes). These class names may be preceded by the keywords *public*, *private*, or *protected*.

Several different notations can be used to visually represent the inheritance relation that ties the two classes. Here we will use the notation depicted in Figure 7.1, where an arrow points from the derived class to the base class.

To calculate a person's age and birthday, you need to add the functions listed below:

- *Age (Date)* function, which, taking a date as parameter, returns the age that a person born on the current birth date will be on the indicated date.
- *Birthday (Date)* function, which indicates whether the day passed through the parameter is the birthday of the person.
- *DaysToBirthday ( )* function, which returns the number of days left until the next birthday.

The interface of the class could be the following:

```
// file BIRTHDAT.H                                    07\BIRTHDAY
// derivation of class BirthDate from class Date

#include "date3.h"

class BirthDate : public Date
{

// new private data members might be declared here

public:
```

```
BirthDate ( int m , int d , int y ) :
    Date ( m , d , y )
    { }

    // returns the age of a person born on the current birth date
    // at date d ( i.e. the years from current date to d )

int    Age ( Date d ) ;

        // return 1 ( TRUE ) if d is the birthday of the person
        // born on the current date

Int    Birthday ( Date d ) ;

        // returns the days from date d to the next birthday of
        // the person born on the current date

int    DaysToBirthday ( Date d ) ;
} ;
```

The following file, instead, holds the definition of the function members of the class *BirthDate* described above:

```
// file BIRTHDAT.CPP
// definition of member functions of class BirthDate

#include <iostream.h>
#include "birthdat.h"

int    BirthDate :: Age ( Date d )
        {
            // this year's birthday

            Date    birthday ( Month ( ) , Day ( ) , d.Year ( ) ) ;

            // years from current birth date to d

            int     years = ( d.Year ( ) - Year ( ) ) ;

            // if birthday is after date d, the age is lower than the
            // difference in years between the two dates

            if ( birthday > d )
                years -- ;
```

```
            return years ;
        }

int     BirthDate :: Birthday ( Date d )
        {
            // it's the birthday if both days and months are equal

            return ( ( d.Day ( ) == Day ( ) ) &&
                ( d.Month ( ) == Month ( ) ) ) ;
        }

int     BirthDate :: DaysToBirthday ( Date d )
        {
            int days = 0 ;

            // adds a day until the birthday is reached

            while ( ! Birthday ( d ) ) {
                days ++ ;
                d.IncreaseDate ( ) ;
            }
            return days ;
        }
```

You can try to use this new class by compiling and running the following program. In its main function, you can apply to objects of class *BirthDate* both the functions of their classes and the functions of the base class *Date*.

```
// file BD-USE.CPP                                    07\BIRTHDAY
// Example of use of class BirthDate

// includes definitions of class BirthDate and Date

#include "birthdat.h"

// includes a system library and the input-output library
#include <dos.h>
#include <iostream.h>

void main ( )
{

    // temporary variables

    int    m , d , y ;
```

```
// calculates the correct value of today using the getdate function,
// defined in dos.h

struct date      da ;

getdate ( &da ) ;

Date      today ( da.da_mon , da.da_day , da.da_year ) ;

// input and definition of the date the user was born on ( birth )

cout  << endl ;
cout  << "Input your birthdate:" << endl ;
cout  << "Month ( number ) : " ;
cin   >> m ;

cout  << "Day: " ;
cin   >> d ;

cout  << "Year: " ;
cin   >> y ;

BirthDate   birth ( m , d , y ) ;

// prints some information: the age and the days to the birthday

cout  << endl ;
cout  << "You are " << ( birth.Age ( today ) ) << " years old"  << endl ;

if ( birth.Birthday ( today ) )
    cout  << "Today is your birthday. Congratulations!" << endl ;
else
    cout  << "There are still "
          << ( birth.DaysToBirthday ( today ) )
          << " days to your next birthday"
          << endl ;

}
```

You can compile the program DB-USE.CPP using a project that contains the files BD-USE.CPP, BIRTHDAT.CPP, and DATE3.CPP.

When you run the program, you produce an output similar to the following (depending on the input you give it; here you see two consecutive executions with different data):

```
Input your birthdate:
Month (number): 10
Day: 7
Year: 1963

You are 30 years old
There are still 205 days to your next birthday


Input your birthdate:
Month (number): 3
Day: 16
Year: 1965

You are 29 years old
Today is your birthday. Congratulations!
```

Two "Classical" Examples of Inheritance

Before examining the subject of inheritance in depth, and analyzing its advantages and risks, let's look at two "classical" examples of this construct. These examples do not reveal the full potential of inheritance, but they help you get a better understanding of its meaning, especially if you are a newcomer to object-oriented programming.

Squares and Rectangles

First, we will describe—by means of a class—rectangular shapes, so that you can define their position and size (assuming their sides are parallel to the reference axis).

A rectangle can be described by a pair of coordinate values that indicate the position of its lower-left corner and its base and height. It might also be useful for you to know its perimeter and areas. We might then need to move the rectangle or to change its size.

It would be easy to identify even more characteristics, in addition to these, to make the description of the class more complete; but for our purpose (illustrating inheritance) these are enough, so we can avoid having to handle and understand an overly complicated class.

The code of the class rectangle could be the following:

```
// file RECTANG.H                                          07\SQUARE
// definition of class Rectangle

#include <iostream.h>

class Rectangle
```

```
{
private:

    // base, height and position of the bottom left corner
    int base, height ;
    int x_pos, y_pos ;

public:

    // constructor
    Rectangle (int b, int h, int x = 0, int y = 0)
    {
        base = b ;
        height = h ;
        x_pos = x ;
        y_pos = y ;
    }

    int Base ( )
    {
        return base ;
    }

    int Height ( )
    {
        return height ;
    }

    int Perimeter ( )
    {
        return ((base + height) * 2) ;
    }

    int Area ( )
    {
        return (base * height) ;
    }

    // moves the rectangle
    void Moves (int delta_x, int delta_y)
    {
        x_pos += delta_x ;
        y_pos += delta_y ;
    }
```

```
    // changes the scale
    void Scale (float scale)
    {
        base *= scale ;
        height *= scale ;
    }
} ;

ostream& operator << (ostream& s, Rectangle r)
{
    s << "Rectangle: Base = " << r.Base ( ) << ", Height = " << r.Height ( ) << endl ;
    s << "\tArea = " << r.Area ( ) << ", Perimeter = " << r.Perimeter ( ) << endl ;
    return s ;
}
```

This class can be used directly in a program like this:

```
// file RECT-USE.CPP                                        07\SQUARE
// example of use of the class Rectangle

#include "rectang.h"

void main ( )
{
    // define a rectangle
    Rectangle   rect (10, 18) ;

    cout << "This is the rectangle" << endl ;
    cout << rect << endl ;

    // double the rectangle
    rect.Scale (2) ;

    cout << "The rectangle has doubled" << endl ;
    cout << rect << endl ;

    // example of a definition of a square
    Rectangle   square (22, 22, 12, 35) ;

    cout << "Here is a square" << endl ;
    cout << square << endl ;


}
```

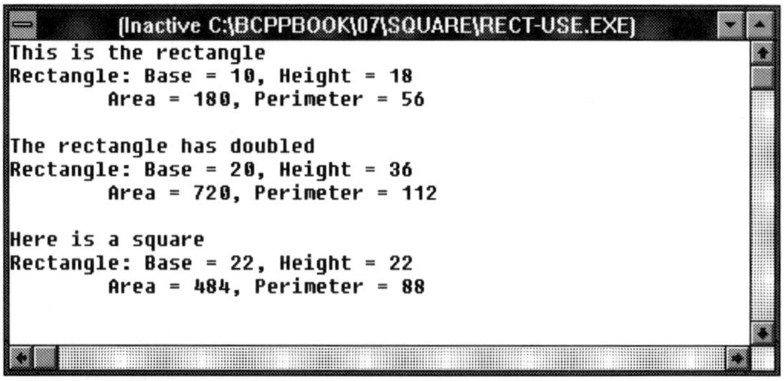

```
[Inactive C:\BCPPBOOK\07\SQUARE\RECT-USE.EXE]
This is the rectangle
Rectangle: Base = 10, Height = 18
         Area = 180, Perimeter = 56

The rectangle has doubled
Rectangle: Base = 20, Height = 36
         Area = 720, Perimeter = 112

Here is a square
Rectangle: Base = 22, Height = 22
         Area = 484, Perimeter = 88
```

Figure 7.2 The output of the program RECT-USE.CPP

The program produces the output shown in Figure 7.2. In the last portion of the program we have used the class *Rectangle* to create a *square* object, since squares are rectangles with all sides equal. While this approach is possible, it would also be extremely inefficient and inconvenient. Furthermore, there is no kind of provision for automatic controls. For instance, if the two values differed (they must both be the same for a square), then your *square* would actually be a rectangle.

To make the code more readable, efficient, and reliable, there are two possible alternatives:

- Classical: rewrite a completely new class that describes squares.

- Object oriented: derive a class *Square* from the class *Rectangle*.

In the second case, without worrying too much about efficiency (you will shortly), you could quickly come up with:

```
// file SQUARE1.CPP                                    07\SQUARE
// derivation of class Square from class Rectangle
// ( first version )

#include "rectang.h"

class Square : public Rectangle
{
public:
    Square ( int side , int x_pos = 0 , int y_pos = 0 ) :
        Rectangle ( side , side , x_pos , y_pos )
        { }
} ;

void main ( )
{
    Square  squ ( 15 , 12 , 18 ) ;
```

```
    cout << "Square perimeter is " << squ.Perimeter ( ) << endl ;
}
```

The above program produces the following output:

```
Square perimeter is 60
```

To make this new derived class more efficient, you could rewrite its key procedures: those that have the most differences in the two cases or that are used more often. It might seem necessary to rewrite almost all of them, and this is actually true for this example. However, for the purpose of illustration and clearness, the functionality of this class is reduced to what is minimally acceptable. In a more complete class that could easily have thirty or more member functions, only a few key procedures would need rewriting and most of the functions could actually be common to the two classes.

```
// file SQUARE2.CPP                                            07\SQUARE
// derivation of class Square from class Rectangle
// (second version)

#include "rectang.h"

class Square : public Rectangle
{
public:
    Square (int side, int x_pos = 0, int y_pos = 0) :
        Rectangle (side, side, x_pos, y_pos)
    { }

    // function redefined for efficiency (is it really faster?)

    int Perimeter ( )
    {
        return (Base ( ) * 4) ;
    }

    // function added (it's a calculation typical of squares)

    float Diagonal ( )
    {
        return (Base ( ) * 1.4142) ;
    }
} ;
```

```
ostream& operator << (ostream& s, Square sq)
{
    // statement using a function of class Rectangle
    s << "Square: Side = " << sq.Base ( ) << endl ;

    // statement using a new function of class Square
    s << "\tDiagonal = " << sq.Diagonal ( ) << endl ;

    // statement using a function of class Rectangle
    s << "\tArea = " << sq.Area ( ) << endl ;

    // statement using a function of class Rectangle
    // redefined in class Square
    s << "\tPerimeter = " << sq.Perimeter ( ) << endl ;

    return s ;
}


// main function
void main ( )
{
    int side ;

    cout << "Input the value of the side (or 0 to end): " ;
    cin >> side ;
    cout << endl ;

    while (side != 0)
    {
        Square   sq (side) ;

        cout << sq << endl ;

        // request a new value
        cout << "Input the value of the side (or 0 to end): " ;
        cin >> side ;
        cout << endl ;
    }
}
```

The output of the program, which clearly depends on your input, should be similar to that of Figure 7.3.

```
┌─────────────────────────────────────────────────────────┐
│ ▬  ▓▓▓  [Inactive C:\BCPPBOOK\07\SQUARE\SQUARE2.EXE] ▓▓▓ ▼ ▲ │
│ Input the value of the side (or 0 to end): 5            ▲ │
│                                                           │
│ Square: Side = 5                                          │
│         Diagonal = 7.071                                  │
│         Area = 25                                         │
│         Perimeter = 20                                    │
│                                                           │
│ Input the value of the side (or 0 to end): 12            │
│                                                           │
│ Square: Side = 12                                         │
│         Diagonal = 16.9704                                │
│         Area = 144                                        │
│         Perimeter = 48                                    │
│                                                           │
│ Input the value of the side (or 0 to end): 100           │
│                                                           │
│ Square: Side = 100                                        │
│         Diagonal = 141.42                                 │
│         Area = 10000                                      │
│         Perimeter = 400                                   │
│                                                           │
│ Input the value of the side (or 0 to end): 0             │
│                                                         ▼ │
│ ◄ ▬▬▬▬▬▬▬▬▬▬▬▬▬▬▬▬▬▬▬▬▬▬▬▬▬▬▬▬▬▬▬▬▬▬▬▬▬▬▬▬▬▬▬▬▬▬▬▬▬ ► │
└─────────────────────────────────────────────────────────┘
```

Figure 7.3 The output of the program SQUARE2.CPP

Colored Rectangles

Let's now examine a second example, which is quite different from the first one, though it reuses the code of the class *rectangle* defined before.

Suppose that you had to deal with rectangular geometric shapes characterized by a color. This could be useful, for instance, to display the shapes on the computer's screen. To handle colors, we use simply an integer code, as shown in the following listing:

```
// file RECTCOL.H                                          07\SQUARE
// derivation of a class of colored rectangles from class Rectangle

#include "rectang.h"

class ColorRect : public Rectangle
{

    int color ;      // the int stands for a color number

public:
    ColorRect (int b, int a, int c = 4, int x = 0, int y = 0) :
        Rectangle (b, a, x, y),
        color (c)
    { }
```

```
    void Color (int c)
    {
       color = c ;
    }

    int Color ( )
    {
       return color ;
    }
} ;

ostream& operator << (ostream& s, ColorRect cr)
{
    // output the ColorRect as if it was a Rectangle
    s << (Rectangle) cr ;

    // output the specific data (the color)
    s << "\tColor = " << cr.Color ( ) << endl ;

    return s ;
}
```

There are two aspects of this code that are worth describing. The first is the form of the two new member functions of the class *ColorRect*, which both have the same name, although one of them is used to change a data member, the other to access it. We could have called them *SetColor* and *GetColor*, but it's much better to overload the same name for both operations. This is easier to remember and to use, and is becoming a standard way to name member functions.

The second aspect is the form of the output operator, which is based on the one defined for the class *Rectangle*. You cannot make a direct call to this operator, but it will be executed automatically for each object of the corresponding class. Therefore, to call it we can convert our *ColorRect* object into a *Rectangle* object or, more precisely, extract from the *ColorRect* object its *Rectangle* "base sub-object."

Here is some code to use for this class:

```
// file RECTCOL.CPP                                07\SQUARE
// example of the use of class ColorRect

#include "rectcol.h"

void main ( )
{
    // defines a colored rectangle
    ColorRect cr (10, 15, 5) ;
```

```
cout << "This rectangle has color" << endl ;
cout << cr << endl ;

// change the color
cr.Color (8) ;

cout << "The color has changed" << endl ;
cout << cr << endl ;
}
```

There is a substantial difference between this and the previous example of inheritance: In the first case you derived a specific class (squares) from a general class (rectangles); in this second case, instead, you added new functionality to an existing class (avoiding to modify the original code of that class directly).

Advantages of Inheritance

Now that you have seen these two examples of inheritance, it might be useful to see a summary of the main advantages of this construct before going into greater detail:

1. The first advantage is the economy in the actual writing of the code. This might seem a trivial point: any good text editor can copy and paste a section of code, and it's easy to make changes on the copy. But that is not the point—with inheritance, code can be reused without directly modifying the existing code or copies of it.

2. The code that is being reused is more likely to be correct because it has been used and tested several times before, and the possible errors that might arise are probably due to the new parts of the code, which are—in any case—independent of the part being reused.

3. You can reuse parts of the code of a class without having to actually understand how it works by referring to the declarations in its interface or to any detailed documentation of the various functions.

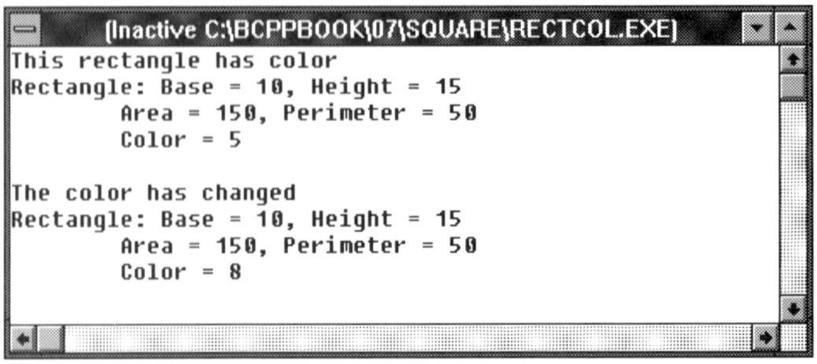

```
[Inactive C:\BCPPBOOK\07\SQUARE\RECTCOL.EXE]
This rectangle has color
Rectangle: Base = 10, Height = 15
         Area = 150, Perimeter = 50
         Color = 5

The color has changed
Rectangle: Base = 10, Height = 15
         Area = 150, Perimeter = 50
         Color = 8
```

Figure 7.4 The output of the RECTCOL.CPP program

4. Generally, you can reuse entire modules of code (that might contain very complex classes) without having the original source code at hand, by using class libraries—and still be able to freely modify the classes of the libraries that are being reused. This feature provides for much more flexible usage of class libraries vs. traditional function libraries (as will be seen in Chapters 15 to 17).

5. You can easily create programs that are extendible by adding new functionalities to modules that have already been implemented. This gives rise to a rather unique programming style, which allows you to develop applications incrementally. Starting from a simplified prototype that you can produce quickly, you can then extend the prototype by modifying the classes, which will only have to be optimized for final efficiency—and not at all for functionality. (Prototyping and evolutionary development are described in Chapter 13; efficiency and optimization are discussed in Chapter 14.)

6. Inheritance, together with dynamic binding, lets you exploit polymorphism (which will be described in the next chapter); allowing a very "dynamic" style of programming without having to renounce strict type checking by the compiler.

7. Inheritance allows you to define hierarchies of classes. This definition of hierarchies is so important that these structures are often the fundamental *framework* of a typical object-oriented program. The development of applications through the definition of classes and hierarchies of classes radically changes the traditional design criteria, as described in Chapter 3.

8. From a theoretical point of view, inheritance lets you apply the *open-closed* principle. In fact, a class is already a closed structure, that is, well defined and fully usable by other modules (as long as its interface and its compiled code are available). At the same time, though, the class continues to be an open structure, that is, you are free to modify and extend the class as you wish, since this can be achieved through the derivation of a new class without affecting the modules that use the original class.

Access to Inherited Data Members

It is important that you understand how you can access data and functions in the original class, both from within derived classes, as well as from functions that use the class (from the outside).

The general member access rules are listed below:

- The *private* members of the original class cannot be accessed by any other class.
- The *protected* members can be accessed only by derived classes.
- The *public* members can be accessed by any other class.

When a class is derived from a base class using public derivation, the functions and data members inherited by the class maintain the same access specifier, that is, they remain in the same category as the base, either *private, protected,* or *public.* Obviously, the private data members of the original class will not be accessible to its derived offspring, because the offspring constitute new and distinct classes. A scheme of these rules, which apply to the most frequent case of *public* inheritance, is shown in Figure 7.5.

To better understand how the access rules actually work, particularly the *protected* access specifier, let's examine the example of colored rectangles once again.

The following code adds a function to the class *ColorRect*, which inherits from *Rectangle*. However, the possibility of accessing the data members of the base class depends solely on the fact that these have been declared in the *private* or in the *protected* sections. If you attempt to compile it, Borland C++ will report the error, indicating that the *base* and *height* data members of class *Rectangle* are not accessible, as shown in Figure 7.6.

```
// portion of file RECTCOL2.H                          07\SQUARE
class ColorRect : public Rectangle
{
    // ... before

    void IncreaseAll ( )
    {
        ++ color ;
        ++ base ;
        ++ height ;
    }
} ;
```

To compile the function *IncreaseAll,* you have to replace the access to the private data members of the *Rectangle* class with the use of some public member functions having the corresponding effect, such as:

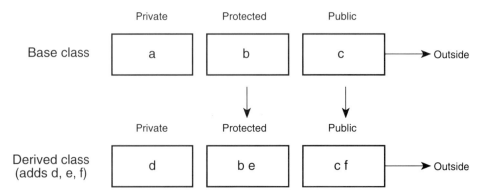

Figure 7.5 Modification of the access specifiers in the most common type of inheritance (*public*)

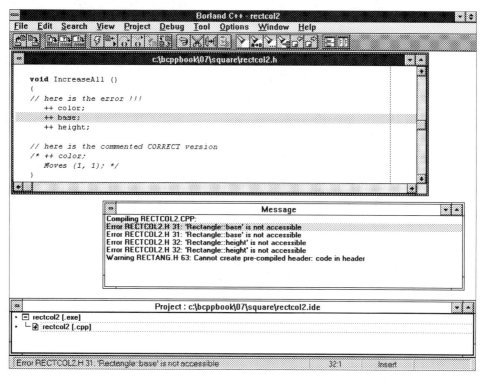

Figure 7.6 The compilation error in the modified code of class *ColorRect*

```
void IncreaseAll ( )
{
    ++ color ;
    Moves (1, 1) ;
}
```

However, in such a case the real solution is the definition of the *height* and *base* data members of class *Rectangle* in the protected section, so that they are directly accessible to the derived classes.

Public, Private, and Protected Inheritance

In addition to public inheritance, there are two other types of inheritance: *private* and *protected*. The different kinds of inheritance determine the accessibility of the member functions and data. The default inheritance is *private* (with one exception: it is *public* if the base "class" is a *struct* declaration and not a real *class* declaration).

By now, you probably have noted that the name of the base class from which one inherits will usually have the keyword *public* in front of it. This is not mandatory, though, because this keyword can also be *private* or *protected*. In this usage, the three keywords are also referred to as *access modifiers* because, according to which one is actually present, the kind of access to data members and member functions in the base class changes.

The "public derivation" leaves the specifiers of the members unchanged; "protected derivation" reduces the access possibilities because *public* members are reduced to *protected*; and in "private derivation" both *protected* and *public* members are reduced to *private*, according to the following scheme:

"Public Derivation"
private	$\rightarrow$	(not accessible)
protected	$\rightarrow$	protected
public	$\rightarrow$	public

"Protected Derivation"
private	$\rightarrow$	(not accessible)
protected	$\rightarrow$	protected
public	$\rightarrow$	protected

"Private Derivation"
private	$\rightarrow$	(not accessible)
protected	$\rightarrow$	private
public	$\rightarrow$	private

Protected and private derivation can also be represented by the schemes in Figures 7.7 and 7.8, which are similar to the one in Figure 7.5 regarding public inheritance.

While the first form of inheritance might seem completely useless, in practice there are many cases in which it can be significant. One example is when you want to change the names of the inherited functions or need to make heavy changes to the services

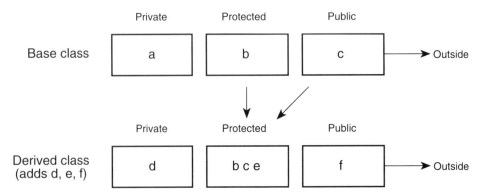

Figure 7.7 Changes made by the access modifiers in the case of protected inheritance

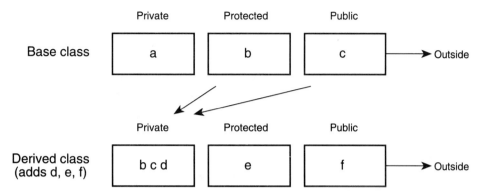

Figure 7.8 Changes made by the access modifiers in the case of private inheritance

offered by the class (in other words, to the set of functions delivered by the class). While there are times when this sort of change is useful, it can also be inconsistent within a given hierarchy (discussed in Chapter 9), where you must be able to perform the operations available in the base class in every derived class (this will be much clearer in Chapter 8, which examines polymorphism).

Using private inheritance can be a shortcut for not using a client relation, that is, for not declaring an object as a private data member in that class.

The differences between "inheritance" and "client" relationships will be examined more closely in a subsequent section of this chapter.

➤ *Note:* Private and protected inheritance in C++ offer also a way to derive only a portion of the public interface of a base class. Suppose that we already have a class like:

```
class Base
{

private:
    ...

public:
    int first ;
    int second ;
} ;
```

If we want a derived class having the *first* integer but not the *second,* we can use private or protected inheritance, making both members inaccessible; then we can use an *access declaration* to make the *first* public again:

```
class Derived : protected Base
{
```

```
public:
    Base :: first ;
}
```

Of course, you cannot use an access declaration to restrict access to a member that is accessible in the base class, nor to provide access to an inaccessible member: You can only adjust the access of a member that has become inaccessible because of protected or public derivation.

An Example of Multiple Inheritance

In addition to simple derivation from a class, C++ provides you with multiple inheritance, which means that you can declare a class in such a way that it derives its characteristics from more than one other class, adding up features from all its base classes.

Assume that you have already defined the class *Circle* and the class *Color* with very limited characteristics, like in the following two files:

07\CIRCLE

```
// file CIRCLE.H
// definition of class Circle

class Circle
{

public:
    Circle (int x, int y, int r = 20) :
      X_center (x) ,
      Y_center (y) ,
      radius (r)
      { }

    // changes position of the center

    void  Center (int x, int y)
    {
       X_center = x ;
       Y_center = y ;
    }

    // changes the radius

    void  Radius (int r)
    {
       radius = r ;
    }
```

```
    // functions returning private data

    int Radius ( )
    {
        return radius ;
    }

    int XCenter ( )
    {
        return X_center ;
    }

    int YCenter ( )
    {
        return Y_center ;
    }

    // describes the circle (should paint it using graphics)

    void   Paint ( )
    {
        cout << "Circle in (" << X_center << ", " << Y_center
            << "), radius is " << radius ;
    }

    // increases dimension and position

    void   operator ++ ( )
    {
        radius ++ ;
        X_center ++ ;
        Y_center++ ;
    }

// private data are the x and y coordinates of the center and the radius

private:

    int X_center ,
        Y_center ;
    int radius ;
} ;
```

```
// file COLOR.H
// definition of class Color
```
07\CIRCLE

```
class Color
{
    int    color;

public:
    // defines some local constant for the colors:
    enum {BLACK, RED, BLUE, GREEN, YELLOW, WHITE} ;

    Color (int c = BLACK) :
        color (c)
    { }

    // functions to modify and read the private data

    int Col ( )
    {
        return color ;
    }

    void Col (int c)
    {
        color = c ;
    }

    // increment operator (using the modulus operator)

    int operator++ ( )
    {
        color = (color + 1) % (WHITE + 1) ;
        return color ;
    }
} ;
```

These two classes are very simple, but complete: There are functions to read and change their data members, as well as functions to output some information on circles. Furthermore, both classes have been enhanced with the ++ operator, to illustrate once again the usage of overloaded operators (and to be able to build, despite the shortness of the code, a significant example).

Now, with these two classes at hand, you can easily generate colored circles, which derive from both of these classes, according to the relationship scheme shown in Figure 7.9. This is simple, as you can see from the definition of the *ColorCircle* class, which is followed by a sample program using it. The only problem we face is the redefinition of the ++ operator, to avoid an ambiguity in the *ColorCircle* class, which derives from two classes, both having the same operator.

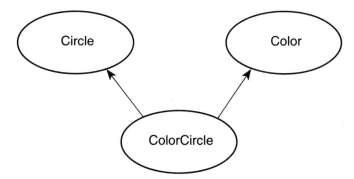

Figure 7.9 Relationship diagram of multiple inheritance

```
// file CIRCLEC.H                                          07\CIRCLE
// definition of class ColorCircle, derived from both
// class Circle and class Color (multiple inheritance)

class ColorCircle : public Circle, Color
{
public:
    ColorCircle (int x, int y, int r = 20, int c = Color::RED) :
        Circle (x, y, r) ,
        Color (c)
    { }

    void   Paint ( )
    {
        Circle :: Paint ( ) ;
        cout << ", the color number is " << Col ( ) ;
    }

    void   operator ++ ( )
    {
        Color :: operator++ ( ) ;
        Circle :: operator++ ( ) ;
    }
} ;
```

```
// file MAINCC.CPP                                         07\CIRCLE
// main function of the ColorCircle example

#include <iostream.h>
#include "circle.h"
#include "color.h"
#include "circlec.h"
```

```
void main ( )
{
    int nRad1, nRad2 ;
    cout << "Input starting and final radius: " ;
    cin >> nRad1 >> nRad2 ;

    for (ColorCircle cc(30, 30, nRad1, Color::RED) ;
         cc.Radius ( ) < nRad2 ;
         ++cc)
    {
        cc.Paint ( ) ;
        cout << endl ;
    }
}
```

➤   ***Note:*** Observe the *for* loop at the end of the listing. This code is a typical example of how a class can be used as a counter of the *for* loop. Note also the use of the overloaded increment operator in the last expression of this *for* loop. The result is terseness in code writing, without any loss in readability.

Besides the output (shown in Figure 7.10), this sample exhibits some interesting features of multiple inheritance. You've created a new class by writing only the minimum amount of new code: The constructor of the class does nothing more than call the constructors of the two base classes, while the *Paint ( )* function calls the corresponding function in the class *Circle* and outputs the current color.

Note also the **++** operator, which simply invokes the corresponding **++** operators in its two base classes.

The difference between this example and the one that implemented colored rectangles is interesting. With the rectangles, the color was added as an attribute to a

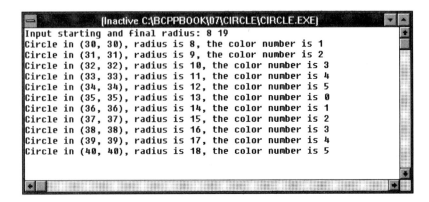

Figure 7.10 Output of the program CIRCLEC.CPP

subclass. Now we have defined a new *Color* class and derived *ColorCircle* from that. Which of these two methods is best depends on the circumstances.

The second solution offers a greater degree of flexibility (because you can reuse the class *Color* in other contexts), while the first one is simpler and somewhat more efficient.

On the other hand, if you created a "well-constructed" color class with, for example, a dozen member functions, it would certainly be much more convenient to reuse this class in the various cases. This reuse can be accomplished by inheriting from the class or using it as a member data. In the first case the derived class already has all the member functions of the base class (the *Color*), while in the second case you need to define again all the member functions you want to use as calls to the corresponding member functions of the member object.

Some Observations on Multiple Inheritance

In recent years, multiple inheritance has been the subject of many debates among object-oriented programming experts and authors of object-oriented languages. For some, this construct is considered completely superfluous, and is introduced only for convenience, but is in contrast with the rules of "good" object-oriented programming. For others, multiple inheritance, apart from some cases of abuse, is a construct that is theoretically sound and practically convenient.

Both parties' arguments are numerous and cannot all be listed here: the issue is very complex. In the first releases of C++ this construct was absent but it was added later, because its lack was perceived as a real deficiency.

However, the advantages of multiple inheritance, beyond its practical convenience of usage, are a greater degree of flexibility, simplicity, and elegance in defining new classes starting from existing classes. It is thus easier to define "small" and simple classes, (which can possibly be merged together later in more complex classes) that are not obliged to cater to all possible future aspects in their initial conception. Furthermore, you can "factor out" specific elements (like the color in the previous examples) that recur frequently, parts of some data structures, or yet other items.

Multiple inheritance clearly favors reusability, for the very reason that it allows more liberty in defining new classes from existing ones. This construct also lets you create entire class hierarchies more easily, without restricting the relationship class hierarchy to singular cases. In this sense, multiple inheritance favors a much more flexible approach to the design of applications.

Furthermore, multiple inheritance makes it easier to change the implementation of a class while leaving its interface untouched. You could in fact change the part of a class that corresponds to one of its base classes simply by inheriting from a different base class that achieves the same functionalities in different ways, thereby obtaining a different implementation of the same abstraction.

However, you should also note that these advantages are somewhat less significant in the most recent release of C++, due to the presence of another construct, templates (which are described in Chapter 10) that provide genericity—a further level of abstraction for code models.

➤ *Note:* In the absence of the template construct, inheritance could effectively be used to simulate it. Obviously, inheritance and templates simulated through inheritance could not be used simultaneously if you had only simple inheritance.

➤ *Note:* As a real-world example of the use and benefits of multiple inheritance, see the second version of the ObjectWindows Library (included with the Borland C++ 4.0 compiler) which uses *mixin* classes to add to a class a number of properties of another class (*mixing* their behavior) . See Chapter 16 and the compiler manuals for more information on multiple inheritance in OWL.

Virtual Base Classes and Repeated Inheritance

As you can see from the previous example of multiple inheritance, the syntax of this construct is very simple and results from a direct extension of the syntax used for simple inheritance. It is sufficient to list, after the class name, all base classes with the only limitation being that they cannot be repeated.

A legitimate doubt can be raised at this point about how the compiler behaves if one class is a base class more than once, indirectly, like in this case:

```
class A ;
class B1: public A ;
class B2: public A ;
class C: public B1 , public B2 ;
```

Here, class *A* is present twice in the list of base classes of *C*: first as a base class of *B1*, then as a base class of *B2*.

Generally, the compiler will generate two copies of the duplicate base class, which will be independent of each other and produces a structure that can be represented by Graph A, shown in Figure 7.11.

In this case, you must be careful because the call of a member function or the access to a public data member of *A* inside the class *C* is ambiguous: it would be unclear which of the two objects the call refers to. For this reason, you must refer to the scope of the member by writing the name of the class from which it is directly inherited (that is, in this example, *B1* or *B2*) in front of it, thus resolving any ambiguity.

If inside *A* there is the definition

```
public:
int    data ;
```

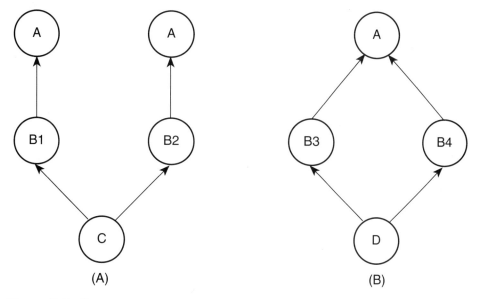

Figure 7.11 Graphs that represent repeated inheritance in the default case (A), and in the case of virtual base classes (B)

you could reference this variable inside the class *C* by writing *B1::data* or *B2::data* (not simply by indicating *data* or *A::data,* because these last two expressions are both ambiguous).

Although the compiler will usually duplicate the class that is inherited twice, you can force it to generate only one copy of any repeated base class by using the keyword *virtual,* as in the following example:

```
class A ;
class B3: virtual public A ;
class B4: virtual public A ;
class D: public B3 , public B4 ;
```

This type of derivation is illustrated by Graph B in Figure 7.11, in which there is only one copy of the data corresponding to class *A*, thus resolving any ambiguity.

These two different kinds of repeated inheritance correspond to two very different meanings of this construct, which can be illustrated by two simple examples.

The first is with a class that describes a person (through a series of personal data and other information). You can describe the class of university professors (in which there will be additional data about the university to which they belong and the courses they teach). You can also derive a class of all authors of books (in which there will be the titles of the books written, maybe with a short abstract, by that person). At this point, you can find some professors who are also authors of books: to describe this situation it is sufficient to describe a class that derives from both preceding classes, according to Figure 7.12.

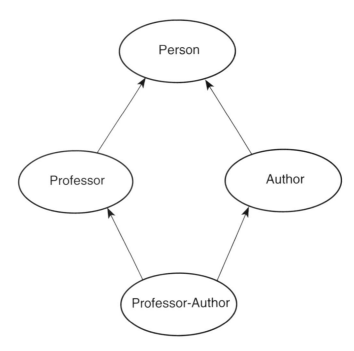

Figure 7.12 Inheritance graph of professors and authors

In this case, it is more correct to use the class that describes the person as a virtual base class for authors and professors, because an author-professor is, after all, one person (and not two!) and his or her private data does not have to be duplicated.

The following is another example: from the class that describes a person, you can derive two classes that describe men and women. From these, by means of multiple inheritance, you can derive a class that describes a married couple. In this case, the couple consists of two persons, not one. The class *person* must be present twice, so in this case this class must not be virtual (see Figure 7.13).

Inheritance Relation and Client Relation

Now that you know what inheritance is and how to use this construct, you are ready to treat a fundamental problem that is very important in object-oriented programming. If a class *A* needs to refer to another class *B*, then you can use two fundamentally different methods:

- A **client relation**, with which you declare that, among the members of the class, there is an object of type *B*.

- An **inheritance relation**, with which you declare that class *A* derives from class *B*, so every object of type *A* is also an object of type *B*.

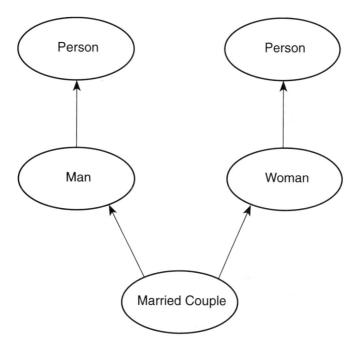

Figure 7.13 Inheritance graph of a married couple

A question naturally arises: are there any criteria for deciding whether it is better to use an inheritance relation or a client relation? The answer is, unfortunately, no! However, it is possible to give some general indications that can *help* to decide which of the two solutions is better.

Generally, the two relations correspond to two very different concepts: inheritance relation corresponds to *being*, while client relation corresponds to *having*. For instance, a square *is a* rectangle and a birth date *is a* date (inheritance); a person *has an* address and *has a* birth date (client).

This distinction is of fundamental importance, but is not always easily understood immediately. For example, a colored circle *is a* color or *has a* color? Most prefer the second hypothesis; but semantically the situation is misleading—it might just be a problem of terminology (what about if we called it "circle with color," or "circle-shaped color," or "circular color"?).

In these cases, it is important to consider other issues, such as efficiency. Efficiency is greater in the case of inheritance, especially if the hidden data items are *protected*, because then they are directly accessible even from within derived classes, just like the derived classes' own proper data member. Other issues might include the simplicity in deriving one class from another; flexibility in redefining or modifying a class, and greater protection and minor coupling between the code of classes in client relation.

So, although there is a rather simple conceptual criterion (*is a* vs. *has a*), it is not as easy to apply it. The final decision depends a lot on your own preference and ideas, since there is seldom a single solution to the problem. For example, the main concern might be efficiency, importance of modularity, definition of autonomous classes or parts that are easy to reuse, or development time.

A Complex Example of Multiple Inheritance

We will now build a more complex example in which multiple inheritance will be put to good use.

The subject we are addressing (in other terms, the problem domain) is an implementation of the legal concept of the "juridical person." This description allows us to describe entities such as corporations, individuals, and groups of either.

Although the implementation is reduced to its minimal terms, it illustrates some important ideas regarding the two cases of multiple derivation that are present. To better understand the properties of this example, you can refer to the schema of classes shown in Figure 7.14, where both the inheritance relations as well as the client relations are shown.

The first case of multiple inheritance is found in the class *JuriPerson* (juridical person), which is simply the sum of all data in the two classes from which it derives (*Person* and *JuriData*) and their corresponding access functions. This example shows how you can use multiple inheritance to "sum" classes, without having to redefine anything. This usage is perfectly legitimate, because a juridical person can be thought

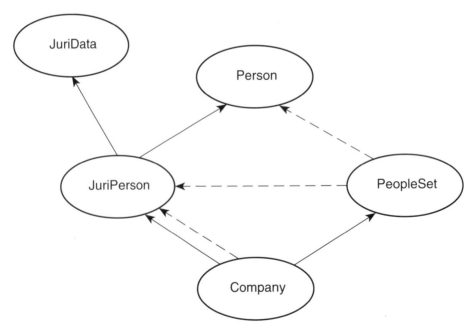

Figure 7.14 Classes of the example MULTIPLE.CPP (the inheritance relations are shown by a solid line, while the client relations are shown by dashes)

of as the composition of its personal data with its juridical data. Naturally, you could object that a person is not a Social Security number; but then you could also argue that a person is not a name nor an address, but has a name and has an address. It really all depends on the *point of view* from which you examine the problem!

The second case of multiple inheritance is more complex. It can be found in the class *Company*, which is a juridical person that consists of a set of people (or even other companies). This class, which has many inherited data and function members, is defined by means of derivation from the classes *PeopleSet* and *JuriPerson*. Note that there is an indirect self-reference (that is, recursion): a company is a set of juridical persons, and at the same time it is a juridical person in its own right. This same situation can be found in other examples like a display window, which can consist of a set of windows that are similar to itself.

Another observation about the program is that before the definition of one of its functions, *Print ( )*, there is the keyword *virtual*, which, in this case, does not define a virtual base class, but a virtual function. Apart from the usage of the same keyword, these two constructs have nothing else in common: virtual functions allow dynamic binding between the function call and its code, and this is a very complex issue that will be explained in the following chapter. For now, you only need to know that this allows you to insert inside *PeopleSets* objects both of type *Person* as well as of type *JuriPerson*, as indicated by the client relations in Figure 7.14.

```
// file MULTIPLE.CPP                              07\MULTIPLE
// program with two examples of multiple inheritance

#include <iostream.h>
#include <cstring.h>

// definition of a class describing a person

class Person
{
    string name ;
    string address ;
    int addrdef ;    // boolean: address defined

public:
    Person (string n) :
        name (n)
    {
        addrdef = 0 ;
    }

    Person (string n, string a) :
        name (n) ,
```

```
        address (a)
    {
        addrdef = 1 ;
    }

    void Address (string a)
    {
        address = a ;
        addrdef = 1 ;
    }

    string Address ( )
    {
        return address ;
    }

    void Name (string n)
    {
        name = n ;
    }

    string Name ( )
    {
        return name ;
    }

    virtual void Print ( )
    {
        cout << name << endl ;

        // the address is printed only if defined
        if (addrdef)
            cout << address << endl ;
    }
} ;

// class containing juridical data of a person

class JuriData
{
    string juriCode ;   // the juridical code (could be social security number)

public:
    JuriData (string jc) :
        juriCode (jc)
```

```
        { }

        string JuriCode ( )
        {
            return juriCode ;
        }

        void JuriCode (string jc)
        {
            juriCode = jc ;
        }

        void Print ( )
        {
            cout << "Juridical code: " << juriCode << endl ;
        }
} ;

// class JuriPerson, derived from both Person and JuriData,
// describes the person from the juridical point of view

class JuriPerson : public Person, public JuriData
{

public:
    JuriPerson (string n, string jc) :
        Person (n) ,
        JuriData (jc)
    { }

    JuriPerson (string n, string a, string jc) :
        Person (n, a) ,
        JuriData (jc)
    { }

    void Print ( )
    {
        Person :: Print ( ) ;
        JuriData :: Print ( ) ;
    }
} ;

// class defining a group of at most 20 people
class PeopleSet
{
```

```cpp
        Person * group [20] ;
        int number ;

    public:
        PeopleSet () :
            number (0)
        { }

        void AddP (Person * p)
        {
            group [number] = p ;
            number ++ ;
        }

        Person * SelectP (int n)
        {
            return group [n] ;
        }

        int MembersNumber ( )
        {
            return number ;
        }

        void   Print ( )
        {
            cout  << "The group is made of "
                  << number << " members:" << endl ;

            for (int i = 0; i < number; i++)
            {
                // print a sequence number, a delimeter
                // and member's data
                cout << (i+1) << "." << "\t" ;
                group [i] -> Print ( ) ;
            }
        }
} ;

// multiple inheritance: a company corresponds to a juridical entity
// (or person) but is also a group of people and/or other companies
// all of which have their own juridical data

class Company : public PeopleSet, public JuriPerson
{
```

```
            string     companyName ;
            Person *    leader ;

        public:
            Company (string s, string n, string jc) :
                JuriPerson (n, jc) ,
                companyName (s)
            {
                leader = new Person ("undefined") ;
            }

            void CompanyName (string cn)
            {
                companyName = cn ;
            }

            string CompanyName ( )
            {
                return companyName ;
            }

            Person * Leader ( )
            {
                return leader ;
            }

            void   Leader (Person * p)
            {
                leader = p ;
            }

            void   Print ( )
            {
                cout << "Company: " << companyName << endl << endl ;
                JuriPerson :: Print ( ) ;
                PeopleSet :: Print ( ) ;
            }
        } ;

// demo of the use of the classes just defined:
// description of a company with a certain number of members

void main ( )
{
    // defines a company and its address
```

```
Company       a ("PDC", "Penguin Dalambertian Club", "PDCPOLI86") ;
a.Address ("by Room B67, Polytechnic of Milan") ;

// adds a list of members

a.AddP (new JuriPerson ("Marco", "MRCBRT34")) ;
a.AddP (new JuriPerson ("Luca", "LCANNN74")) ;
a.AddP (new JuriPerson ("Andrea", "NDRBRR47")) ;
a.AddP (new JuriPerson ("Giulio", "GLOLPR67")) ;
a.AddP (new JuriPerson ("Diana", "DNABND84")) ;
a.AddP (new JuriPerson ("Massimo & Lella", "MSSLLLPCT27")) ;
a.AddP (new JuriPerson ("Francesco & Camilla", "FRNCMLRCC28")) ;
a.AddP (new JuriPerson ("Graziano", "GRZRVZ76")) ;
a.AddP (new JuriPerson ("Flavio & Flavio", "FLVCSTBSN54")) ;
a.AddP (new JuriPerson ("Lorella", "LRLCLM58")) ;

// prints the company data

a.Print ( ) ;
}
```

The above program produces the following output:

```
Company: PDC

Penguin Dalambertian Club
by Room B67, Polytechnic of Milan
Juridical code: PDCPOLI86
The group is made of 10 members:
1.    Marco
Juridical code: MRCBRT34
2.    Luca
Juridical code: LCANNN74
3.    Andrea
Juridical code: NDRBRR47
4.    Giulio
Juridical code: GLOLPR67
5.    Diana
Juridical code: DNABND84
6.    Massimo & Lella
Juridical code: MSSLLLPCT27
7.    Francesco & Camilla
Juridical code: FRNCMLRCC28
8.    Graziano
Juridical code: GRZRVZ76
```

9. Flavio & Flavio
Juridical code: FLVCSTBSN54
10. Lorella
Juridical code: LRLCLM58

The Order of Initialization of Base Classes

When you declare a new object of a class, something happens behind the scenes: a constructor is called. It might be an explicit constructor, with some parameters, or a default implicit constructor, but this operation is always accomplished.

If a class has a base class, the situation is more complex. The base class is initialized before the derived class, using either a default constructor or a constructor with parameters depending on the code of the constructor of the derived class. The following constructor of the *Derived* class invokes the constructor of the *Base* class, which is executed before the constructor code of the *Base* class.

```
class Derived : public Base
{
public:
    Derived (...) :
        Base (...)
        {
            // constructor code ...
        }
};
```

If the constructor of the *Derived* class doesn't call one of the constructors of its base, then the base's default constructor is used. The order of the initialization of the base classes and of the member objects is quite important, because the code of the constructor may depend on it. For example, in the constructor of the previous *Derived* class you could use any member function inherited from the *Base* class, because the so-called *base sub-object* has already been built and is in a properly initialized state.

The rule of the C++ language for initialization is:

- The base classes are initialized first, in the order they appear in the list of the base classes, and not in the order in which their constructors are called. (Virtual base classes have a special precedence as described later.)

- Then the member objects are initialized, in the order they appear in the class's declaration.

- Finally the code of the constructor is called.

Let us describe this rule with an example, where each capital letter stands for a different class:

```
class A : public B, public C, public D
{
    G  g ;
    H  h ;
    K  k ;

public:
    A (...) :
        C (...),
        B (...),
        k (...)
        g (...),
        D (...),
        h (...),
    {
        // code
    }
} ;
```

To initialize an object of class A, the sequence of calls is:

- Base classes as they appear in the list of base classes: B, C, D
- Member objects, in the order of the class declaration: g, h, k
- The object itself (using the code between braces)

If one of the base classes has base classes or member objects, the same rule is applied recursively.

```
┌─────────────────────────────────────────────────────────────────────┐
│ ═      [Inactive C:\BCPPBOOK\07\INITIAL\INITIAL.EXE]             ▼ ▲  │
├─────────────────────────────────────────────────────────────────────┤
│ Defining an object of class A                                         │
│ Constructor of class A                                                │
│                                                                       │
│ Defining an object of class B                                         │
│ Constructor of class A                                                │
│ Constructor of class B, derived from A                                │
│                                                                       │
│ Defining an object of class C                                         │
│ Constructor of class A                                                │
│ Constructor of class C, derived from A                                │
│                                                                       │
│ Defining an object of class D                                         │
│ Constructor of class A                                                │
│ Constructor of class C, derived from A                                │
│ Constructor of class A                                                │
│ Constructor of class B, derived from A                                │
│ Constructor of class A                                                │
│ Constructor of class B, derived from A                                │
│ Constructor of class D, derived from B and C, having a B object inside│
│                                                                       │
├─────────────────────────────────────────────────────────────────────┤
│ ◄ █                                                              ►    │
└─────────────────────────────────────────────────────────────────────┘
```

Figure 7.15 The output of the program INITIAL.CPP

The presence of virtual base classes changes the order slightly, since the virtual base classes are initialized before any non-virtual base class. If there is more than one virtual base class, the order of their initialization is determined by their position in the inheritance graph from top to bottom and left to right.

The call of the destructor for a derived class follows the same rules, but in the reverse order. The destructor of the class is called first, then those of its member objects, then the base classes, and eventually the virtual base classes.

If you are still puzzled, a self-referencing example might help you. In the following program each constructor and destructor outputs its name, to show that it had been called. If you can read the code and guess what the output is going to be, you can be quite certain you have the hang of it. If not, don't worry, and check the output of Figure 7.15.

```
// file INITIAL.CPP                                          07\INITIAL
// Example of the order of initialization of base classes

#include <iostream.h>

class A
{
public:
    A ( )
    {
        cout << "Constructor of class A" << endl ;
    }
} ;

class B : public A
{
public:
    B ( )
    {
        cout << "Constructor of class B, derived from A" << endl ;
    }
} ;

class C : public A
{
public:
    C ( )
    {
        cout << "Constructor of class C, derived from A" << endl ;
    }
} ;
```

```
class D: public C, public B
{
B  b ;
public:
  D ( )
  {
      cout << "Constructor of class D, derived from B and C,"
          << " having a B object inside" << endl ;
  }
} ;

void main ( )
{
    cout << "Defining an object of class A" << endl ;
    A  aa ;

    cout << endl ;
    cout << "Defining an object of class B" << endl ;
    B  bb ;

    cout << endl ;
    cout << "Defining an object of class C" << endl ;
    C  cc ;

    cout << endl ;
    cout << "Defining an object of class D" << endl ;
    D  dd ;
}
```

If you change the repeated base class A into a virtual base class in the definition of the classes B and C, as in the code below, the output becomes a little different, as shown in Figure 7.16.

```
// changes to the previous program, INITIAL.CPP

class B : virtual public A
{
public:
  B ( )
  {
      cout << "Constructor of class B, derived from A" << endl ;
  }
} ;

class C : virtual public A
{
```

```
public:
  C ( )
  {
     cout << "Constructor of class C, derived from A" << endl ;
  }
} ;
```

Exploring Classes with the Browser

During the implementation of a project, or when you need to use classes collected in some library, you might have to deal with very complicated class hierarchies. This term usually denotes a structure (graph or tree) that consists of a set of classes in inheritance relation among themselves, as you will see in Chapter 9.

To analyze these hierarchies, you can use the "*class hierarchy browser*" tool, or *browser* for short. In several object-oriented development environments (following the guidelines set by Smalltalk, which introduced this tool), the browser is actually the central piece of the whole environment, and it incorporates even the functionality of a source code editor. This happens in Borland C++ with the Class Wizard.

Generally, however, the browser allows you to explore the classes of the hierarchy, their member functions, and their data, letting you modify them or add new ones, compile the various classes, and save the code in one or more files.

Borland C++, which offers a more traditional integrated development environment (based on files) for "nonObjectWindow" development, is essentially similar to other environments of procedural language compilers (like C or Pascal). Despite this, it has a browser which allows you to analyze the hierarchies of the classes of an application once you have compiled it. On the other hand, if you build ObjectWindows applica-

```
┌────────────────────────────────────────────────────────────────────┐
│  ═          (Inactive C:\BCPPBOOK\07\INITIAL\INITIAL.EXE)        ▼ ▲ │
├──────────────────────────────────────────────────────────────────┬─┤
│Defining an object of class A                                      │▲│
│Constructor of class A                                             │ │
│                                                                   │ │
│Defining an object of class B                                      │ │
│Constructor of class A                                             │ │
│Constructor of class B, derived from A                             │ │
│                                                                   │ │
│Defining an object of class C                                      │ │
│Constructor of class A                                             │ │
│Constructor of class C, derived from A                             │ │
│                                                                   │ │
│Defining an object of class D                                      │ │
│Constructor of class A                                             │ │
│Constructor of class C, derived from A                             │ │
│Constructor of class B, derived from A                             │ │
│Constructor of class A                                             │ │
│Constructor of class B, derived from A                             │ │
│Constructor of class D, derived from B and C, having a B object inside│▼│
├──────────────────────────────────────────────────────────────────┴─┤
│  ◄ ░░░░░░░░░░░░░░░░░░░░░░░░░░░░░░░░░░░░░░░░░░░░░░░░░░░░░░░░░    ►      │
└────────────────────────────────────────────────────────────────────┘
```

Figure 7.16 The output of the modified version of the program INITIAL.CPP

tions you can use the Class Wizard, which is really a powerful browser. The class browser can be invoked by the development environment with the menu command *View, Classes* once you have generated the executable file for a project. One of its most interesting features is the graphical representation of the hierarchy of classes, something that other development environments do not offer. A similar tool exists in the DOS-based TurboDebugger, although it lacks most of the graphics.

Under Windows, for instance, browsing the executable code of the SQUARE1.CPP program seen at the beginning of this chapter would give you a screen like the one shown in Figure 7.17. You can see the hierarchy of the two classes defined in the program and the several classes imported from the *iostream.h* library.

The *ObjectBrowser* window, in addition to allowing the examination of the inheritance relations between classes, makes it easy to access to their description. By selecting a class, you can get a list of all its data and function members. As you can see in Figure 7.18, there are both the functions defined by the class itself and those inherited by the base classes. Selecting the proper filters at the bottom of the window, the program will list, for example, only the functions, or only the non-inherited members. You can further access the full definition of an item (including the parameter list for the functions), and eventually jump to the definition in the source code.

Besides these very simple examples, the usefulness of the browser can better be appreciated with complex hierarchies and programs with many classes, or for examining the classes present in a library.

For instance, compiling the following program, you can get a browser with many classes, as shown in Figure 7.19. In the program, a series of classes is defined for describing various animals; these classes are organized in a hierarchy that is quite easy to understand. For each of these classes, it is necessary to create at least one object, to which a value must be assigned, otherwise the corresponding class will not be inserted in the executable code (it would be completely useless) and will not be displayed in the browser.

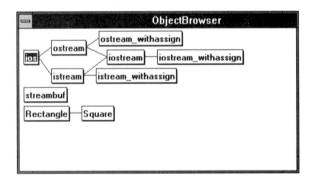

Figure 7.17 The class hierarchy of the SQUARE1.CPP example under the Windows-hosted IDE

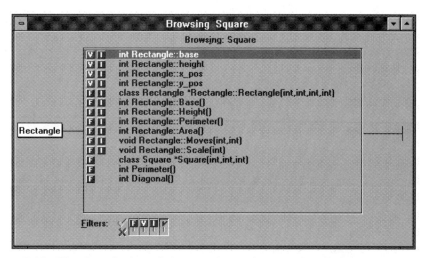

Figure 7.18   The description of the members of a class in the ObjectBrowser

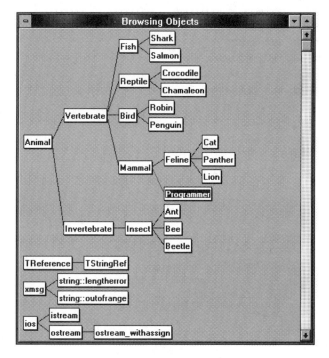

Figure 7.19 The scheme of classes in BROWSE.CPP

```
// file BROWSE.CPP                                    07\BROWSE
// definition of a hierarchy of classes to describe animals
// vaguely based on scientific classification, but much simplified

#include <cstring.h> #include <iostream.h>
class Animal
{
public:
string        name;
};

class Vertebrate : public Animal {};
class Mammal : public Vertebrate {};
class Programmer : public Mammal {};
class Feline : public Mammal {};
class Cat : public Feline {};
class Panther : public Feline {};
class Lion : public Feline {};
class Bird : public Vertebrate {};
class Robin : public Bird {};
class Penguin : public Bird {};
class Reptile : public Vertebrate {};
class Crocodile : public Reptile {};
class Chameleon : public Reptile {};
class Fish : public Vertebrate {};
class Shark : public Fish {};
class Salmon : public Fish {};
class Invertebrate : public Animal {};
class Insect : public Invertebrate {};
class Ant : public Insect {};
class Bee : public Insect {};
class Beetle: public Insect {};

// in the main program you must declare an animal for any
// of the terminal classes of the hierarchy
void main ()
{
Programmer   insane ;
insane.name = "steve" ;
cout << insane.name << endl ;

Programmer   crazy ;
crazy.name = "marco" ;
cout << crazy.name << endl ;

Cat          cat ;
cat.name = "kitty" ;
```

```
        cout << cat.name << endl ;

        Panther        panther ;
        panther.name = "pinky" ;
        cout << panther.name << endl ;

        Lion           lion ;
        lion.name = "richard" ;
        cout << lion.name << endl ;

        Robin          robin ;
        robin.name = "chirpy" ;
        cout << robin.name << endl ;

        Penguin        penguin ;
        penguin.name = "pengo" ;
        cout << penguin.name << endl ;

        Crocodile      crocodile ;
        crocodile.name = "dundee" ;
        cout << crocodile.name << endl ;

        Chameleon      chameleon ;
        chameleon.name = "007" ;
        cout << chameleon.name << endl ;

        Shark          shark ;
        shark.name = "jaws" ;
        cout << shark.name << endl ;

        Salmon         salmon ;
        salmon.name = "smokey" ;
        cout << salmon.name << endl ;

        Ant            ant ;
        ant.name = "redeye" ;
        cout << ant.name << endl ;

        Bee            bee ;
        bee.name = "bumble" ;
        cout << bee.name << endl ;

        Beetle         beetle ;
        beetle.name = "ugly beast" ;
        cout << beetle.name << endl ;
        }
```

Comparison Between C++ and Other Languages

This final section draws some general conclusions on the constructs provided by C++ for the definition of classes and inheritance relation, compared to what is offered by other object-oriented languages. Some observations have already been made during the presentation of the language, in Chapter 3; but now that some of its object-oriented constructs have been introduced, a more precise critique can be given.

1. One interesting feature of the classes of C++ is given by the access specifiers, which are not present in other object-oriented languages. Although it is possible, in other languages, to indicate which data and function members should be private and which should be public (that is, visible from the outside, from whatever other class or function) C++ also lets you hide or reveal parts of a class to its subclasses, thanks to the *protected* access specifier and to the *private* and *protected* derivations. These constructs are very useful, because they let you decide whether a part of a class (data and functions) should be visible to its subclasses; a possibility which is usually not available in other languages.

   In this way, C++ compensates for the absence of a redefinition construct, which implies both the possibility of changing the name of a member as well as modifying its visibility directly. In fact, this operation can take place directly for a group of functions and data, and is useful, thanks to the possibility of dividing the members into three distinct categories according to which of them should be used and modified by the subclasses.

2. Another important aspect is the possibility of defining static data items inside a class (that is, data items that are shared between all object instances), a tool that is very valuable for getting rid of global data from programs, simply by transferring this data to appropriate classes. Furthermore, some of this data can be hidden inside the class and manipulated by means of static member functions. In this way, you can fulfill the requirements of having the data visible in the whole program, as well as adhering to the principle of information hiding, which is being able to modify the implementation of this data without having to change the code that uses it.

3. We can consider C++ as a language that is extremely different from C (because it supports an extremely different programming style), although it does have a similar syntax. This certainly eases the transition from C to C++: there are only a few constructs and the keywords that have been added, but they offer a completely new kind of potential.

4. C++ could be defined as "a programming language with many models." In fact, instead of deciding for the programmer how to define and implement a certain construct, the inventor of C++ preferred to supply different versions of them, thus giving you the freedom to use the version that best matches your needs.

Other languages, instead, end up imposing a solution, with no possibility for other choices.

- One case where this is evident is with repeated inheritance, which can come in two flavors (according to whether there is normal or virtual derivation).

- Another case, already mentioned, is the three different ways to pass data to subclasses (according to whether there is *public*, *protected,* or *private* derivation).

- In traditional languages, binding is always static. In object-oriented languages, it is always dynamic (except, maybe, through optimizations applied by a compiler). In C++, it is defined by the programmer.

This "choice of not choosing," but rather giving you the freedom to make a decision by giving several versions of the same construct, can sometimes be counterproductive, but is one of the most unique traits of C++ compared to other object-oriented languages.

POINTS TO CONSIDER

1. Identify, in the programming languages that you know and that do not have inheritance, some kind of mechanism and construct that allow you to simulate inheritance.

2. Evaluate the impact that classes and inheritance could have had in a project that you completed with traditional methods.

3. Rewrite one of the classes defined by inheritance in the examples of this chapter as an autonomous class (that is, as a class that is not derived from any other class). Point out the differences between the resulting class and the one defined by derivation in the text.

4. Identify some other example of inheritance relation and try to recognize the corresponding classes. Try to reuse some of the classes you have come across so far in this text, and think about how they could be extended or modified.

5. The class of colored rectangles was derived from the class *Rectangle* with the addition of the color attribute. Redefine the same class by means of multiple inheritance deriving from the class *Color*, as was done in the example of colored circles.

6. Modify some of the inheritance relations you have already seen or implemented by using private derivation and/or protected derivation; examine the differences with respect to the ordinary public derivation.

7. Examine the file MULTIPLE.CPP where persons, groups, companies, and juridical persons were defined. The example is only sketched, so it can be extended in various directions, by enriching it with new data and function members (beyond those strictly necessary for accessing data).

Describe other abstract elements: a corporation with a department of employees and managers; an association of different members, maybe also with employees; a group of holdings with many subgroups of companies, geographical territories, departments, work groups, directors, mangers, workers, and so on.

8. Play with the browser and examine the hierarchy of the MULTIPLE.CPP example, where you can also find the classes of the library *iostream.h* in addition to those defined with multiple inheritance.

You should also play around with the hierarchies in the file BROWSE.CPP, determining under which circumstances a class defined in the source code is actually present in the executable file, and when, instead, the classes are discarded because—although being defined—they are never used in any part of the program.

8

Polymorphism and Dynamic Binding

Dynamic binding of functions to function names is one key to flexibility and extensibility of object-oriented languages. It allows new code to be called from unaltered old code by passing data of new types to old operations or assigning them to old variables. It is implemented by dynamic dispatch in which run-time type information is used to lookup, or bind to, the proper function. Dynamic dispatch makes functions and procedures polymorphic, that is, applicable to different kinds of data. [Schmidt 91]

This chapter introduces the second basic building block of object-oriented programming: polymorphism. This term, derived from Greek, means "many shapes," and denotes the possibility for an entity to refer to instances of different classes at run-time. We have already seen an analogy of polymorphism in Chapter 3: every animal responds to the eat function in a different way.

The language construct that makes polymorphism possible is *dynamic* (also known as delayed, deferred, or late) *binding* between function calls and effectively executed procedures.

However, all this happens without modifying type compatibility rules, which allow static type checking on the data used (that is, checking is performed at compile time, not at run time). To demonstrate this, the first section serves as an introduction, through examples, to type compatibility rules for data in Borland C++.

Type Compatibility Rules

Basically, C++ follows a name-equivalence rule: two variables are type-compatible if their types have the same name. The only exception to this rule applies to class pointers: a pointer to a base class is type-compatible with any pointer to classes derived from that base class.

The following example shows how the *typedef* construct can be used to define several variables of the same type (that is, having a type with the same name). To see if the variables are compatible it's enough to try to assign them to each other.

```
// file TYPE1.CPP                                              08/TYPE
// this file demonstrates the type compatibility rules of C++:
// typedef assigns a name to the type ; that name is later used to type-check

#include <iostream.h>

void main ( )
{
    // defines the type twoChars ( a structure , with all the data public )

    typedef
       struct
       {
           char  first ;
           char  second ;
       }
    twoChars ;

    // defines two variables of this type

    twoChars    state1 ;
    twoChars    state2 ;

    // assigns a value to state1

    state1.first = 'M' ;
    state1.second = 'N' ;

    // the two variables are of the same type

    state2 = state1 ;

    // as this is public data you can freely manipulate structures:
    // so Minnesota can turn into Missouri in a strange way...

    state2.second ++ ;

    // prints the values of the two structures

    cout  << "Original structure: "   << state1.first
          << state1.second            << endl
          << "Changed structure: "    << state2.first
          << state2.second            << endl ;
}
```

The previous program produces the following output:

```
Original structure: MN
Changed structure: MO
```

The second example, shown below, is very similar to the first: the only difference is that the two variables, although equal, have independent declarations, without a proper type definition. Therefore, the following main program won't be compiled; Borland C++ will stop with an error message, as shown in Figure 8.1.

```
// file TYPE2.CPP                                              08/TYPE
// this file demonstrates the type compatibility rules of C++:
// without a common definition, even equal structures are
// considered different. The example is similar to the previous one.

#include <iostream.h>

void main ( )
{
    struct
    {
        char  first ;
        char  second ;
    } state1 ;

    struct
    {
        char  first ;
        char  second ;
    } state2 ;

    state1.first = 'M' ;
    state1.second = 'N' ;

    // ERROR! the two variables are NOT of the same type

    state2 = state1 ;

    state2.second ++ ;

    cout  << "Original structure: "      << state1.first
          << state1.second               << endl
          << "Changed structure: "       << state2.first
          << state2.second               << endl ;
}
```

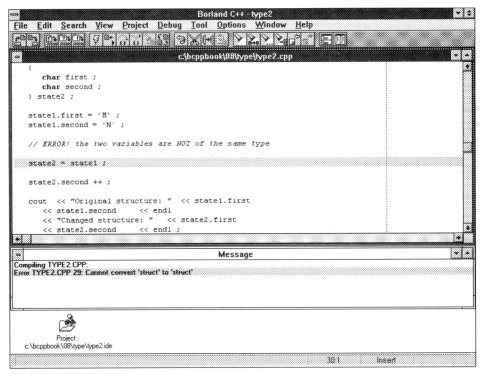

Figure 8.1 The compiler error message in program TYPE2.CPP

The third example, shown below, is similar to the preceding two: it shows how the previous error can be avoided by declaring the two variables with the same statement; this technique relies on the way the compiler builds internal type names of the object it manipulates. The declaration of a structure is converted to a random internal name, which is the same for all the variables defined in the same statement. In the previous example, the same structure was assigned two different internal type names by the compiler, because it was present twice in two different statements.

```
// file TYPE3.CPP                                         08/TYPE
// this file demonstrates the type compatibility rules of C++:
// declaring two variables with the same statement gives them
// the same type ( but don't abuse this trick )

#include <iostream.h>

void main ( )
{
    struct
    {
```

```
        char  first ;
        char  second ;
    } state1 , state2 ;

    state1.first = 'M' ;
    state1.second = 'N' ;

    // OK: the two variables are of the same type

    state2 = state1 ;

    state2.second ++ ;

    cout  << "Original structure: "   << state1.first
          << state1.second            << endl
          << "Changed structure: "    << state2.first
          << state2.second            << endl ;
}
```

The last two examples are different from the previous three in that they deal with type-compatibility rules for pointers to classes. While two objects are usually of the same type only if they are declared to be of the same class, in case of pointers to objects, there are exceptions to the base rule of name equivalence.

Usually, pointers to different classes cannot be assigned one to the other, as the following code demonstrates. The program, when compiled, generates two errors (one for each of the two assignment statements), as shown in Figure 8.2.

```
// file TYPE4.CPP                                                08/TYPE
// this file demonstrates the type compatibility rules of C++
// for pointers to classes: instances of two classes, although equal,
// have different type, because their name is different

class TwoChars
{
    char  first ;
    char  second ;

public:

    TwoChars ( char f , char s ) :
        first ( f ) ,
        second ( s )
        { }
} ;
```

```
class StateCode
{
    char  first ;
    char  second ;

public:

    StateCode ( char f , char s ) :
        first ( f ) ,
        second ( s )
        { }
} ;

void main ( )
{
    // defines two pointers

    StateCode *    pState1 ;
    TwoChars *     pState2 ;

    // pointers' allocation and initialization

    pState1 = new StateCode ( 'C' , 'A' ) ;
    pState2 = new TwoChars ( 'H' , 'I' ) ;

    // assignment between the variables is impossible

    pState2 = pState1 ;  // ERROR !
    pState1 = pState2 ;  // ERROR !
}
```

The last example shows that for derived classes you can assign a pointer-to-a-derived-class to a pointer-to-a-base-class, but not vice versa. In fact, while the derived class can handle any function of the base class (inheriting all of them), the opposite is not true: if the derived class has a new member function $A ( )$, the call $p \rightarrow A ( )$ has no meaning for a pointer to its base class (unless a member function with the same name was already defined in that class).

```
// file TYPE5.CPP                                              08/TYPE
// this file demonstrates the type compatibility rules of C++
// for pointers to classes: the pointer-to-a-derived-class may be assigned
// to a pointer-to-a-base-class, but not vice versa

class TwoChars
{
```

```
        char  first ;
        char  second ;

public:

        TwoChars ( char f , char s ) :
            first ( f ) ,
            second ( s )
            { }
} ;

class StateCode : public TwoChars
{
public:
        StateCode ( char f , char s ) :
        TwoChars ( f , s )
            { }
} ;

void main ( )
{
    // defines two pointers

    StateCode *    pState1 ;
    TwoChars *     pState2 ;

    // pointers' allocation and initialization

    pState1 = new StateCode ( 'C' , 'A' ) ;
    pState2 = new TwoChars ( 'H' , 'I' ) ;

    // assignment to a superclass pointer is possible

    pState2 = pState1 ;      // Correct

    // while the opposite is not

    pState1 = pState2 ;      // ERROR!

    // it's even possible to assign a new value of a different type

    pState2 = new StateCode ( 'A' , 'R' ) ;
}
```

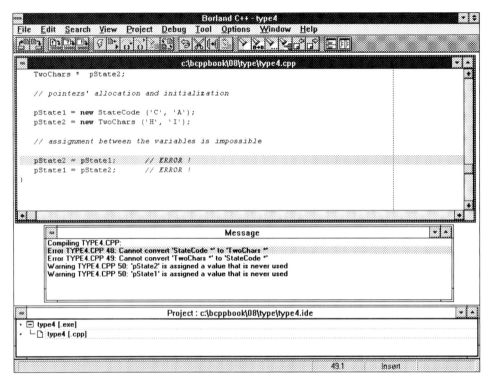

Figure 8.2 Compilation errors produced by TYPE4.CPP

Introduction to Dynamic Binding

Before proceeding with a detailed description of dynamic binding and an analysis of its main uses, we will study an introductory example; it is based on two classes with an inheritance relationship.

The first class, *Person*, has a simple data structure to hold the name of the person and a function to print that name. The second class, *Foreigner*, is derived from class *Person* and is extremely similar to it. The only difference is in the phrase preceding the name inside the modified printing function.

```
// file FOREIGN.CPP                                    08/FOREIGN
// example of polymorphism between derived classes

#include <iostream.h>

class Person
{

protected:
```

```
      char *   name ;

public:

    Person ( char* n ) :
       name ( n )
       { }
    // virtual function, using dynamic binding

    virtual void Print ( )
       {
          cout << "My name is " << name << endl ;
       }
} ;

class Foreigner : public Person
{
public:
    Foreigner ( char* n ) :
       Person ( n )
       { }
    // redefined virtual function

    void   Print ( )
       {
          // the foreigner happens to be an Italian!
          cout << "Il mio nome e'" << name << endl ;
       }
} ;


void main ( )
{
    Person *   man ;
    Person *   woman ;

    // initialization

    man = new Person ( "John" ) ;
    woman = new Foreigner ( "Paola" ) ;

    // prints the names

    cout << "Prints the name of the man:" << endl ;
    man -> Print ( ) ;
```

```
        cout << "Prints the name of the woman ( a foreigner ) :" << endl ;
        woman -> Print ( ) ;

        // it's possible to assign to the variable man a pointer to an object
        // of class foreigner, derived from Person

        man = new Foreigner ( "Mario" ) ;
        cout << endl ;
        cout << "Reprints the name of the man after the new assignment:" << endl ;
        man -> Print ( ) ;
}
```

Although this example is somewhat ridiculous (as shown by the following output), it demonstrates the basics of dynamic binding and polymorphism.

```
Prints the name of the man:
My name is John
Prints the name of the woman (a foreigner):
Il mio nome e' Paola

Reprints the name of the man after the new assignment:
Il mio nome e' Mario
```

Note that in the class *Foreigner* a function is redefined; in class *Person* the definition of that function was preceded by the keyword *virtual*, which lets the compiler use dynamic instead of static binding for the function.

In this example, two pointers to objects of type *Person* (thus able to handle both objects of class *Person* and of derived class *Foreigner*) are created and, after the initialization, printed. However, the function call

```
woman -> Print ( ) ;
```

used to invoke a member function with a pointer of type *Person*, doesn't call the function

```
Person :: Print ( )
```

but calls the function

```
Foreigner :: Print ( )
```

How is this possible? The compiler decides which of the two functions is to be called only at run time, and the choice depends on the value assigned to the pointer *woman*.

In the preceding lines, the pointer *man* was associated with an object of class *Person*, so the compiler called the function of this class; on the other hand, the pointer *woman*, still of type *Person*, was associated at runtime with an object of class *Foreigner*, so the compiler called the function of this class.

In the last part of the program, the pointer *man* was associated with an object of the derived class; so the second time the statement

    man -> Print ( ) ;

was encountered, the program called a different function than the first time.

To understand the whole process better, look at Figure 8.3, which shows the bindings of the variables with the class along the program execution.

The dynamic binding mechanism is not very easy to grasp, but if you can fully understand this example, you will be on your way to understanding the whole of this chapter and one of the most powerful elements of object-oriented programming.

Static Binding and Dynamic Binding

At this point, it's important for you to understand in detail what dynamic binding is and the differences between it and the ordinary static binding.

Remember, "binding" generally denotes the connection between an entity and its properties. Limited to functions, the main connection is between the function call and the code that is executed because of this call.

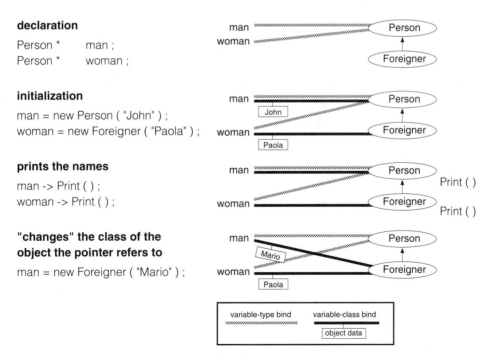

Figure 8.3 Analysis of the FOREIGN.CPP program

With static binding (also known as early binding), which is the norm in most programming languages (in particular, in procedural languages), the compiler and the linker directly define the fixed address of the code to be executed on every function call.

With dynamic binding (also called late binding), the compiler does not define the address of the Function to be called, instead it waits until run time to decide which of a list of addresses is the actual one. Only during the execution of the program some value (usually that of a pointer to a class) will be used by a run-time mechanism to determine the effective address among the several that are possible (one for every derived class). This concept is exactly what you have already seen at work in the previous example related to the classes *Person* and *Foreigner*, with the dynamic function *Print ( )*.

The main advantage of dynamic binding vs. static binding is that dynamic binding gives you a higher degree of flexibility and several practical advantages, the most relevant of which is the opportunity to define and handle class hierarchies in a very simple way.

Among the disadvantages is that dynamic binding is less efficient than static binding, although the difference is small compared to the ordinary function call overhead, and seldom noticeable unless the function is extremely short.

In fact, the implementation of dynamic binding in C++ is very efficient and requires just a couple of memory accesses (dereferencing operations) and not the traversal of a class hierarchy tree, as happens in other object-oriented programming languages (particularly in dynamic languages such as Smalltalk).

Virtual Functions

By default, C++ functions have static binding; you must explicitly request dynamic binding by preceding the function declaration with the keyword *virtual*, as you have already seen.

The following is another example of virtual functions, which presents this construct in a general way. This example can be defined as "self-referencing," since the program does nothing other than describe itself, showing the statements that are executed, the functions that are called, and the effects of these calls.

```
// file BINDING.CPP                                    08/BINDING
// self-explanatory and self-referencing example of the difference
// between static and dynamic binding

#include <iostream.h>

// defines a class A with two functions that print their names

class A
{
public:
    A ( ) { }
```

```
    virtual void Dynamic ( )
       {
           cout << "- Dynamic function of class A" << endl ;
       }

    void   Static ( )
       {
           cout << "- Static function of class A" << endl ;
       }
} ;

// defines a class B, derived from A, redefining both functions

class B : public A
{
public:
   B ( ) { }

    void   Dynamic ( )
       {
           cout << "- Dynamic function of class B" << endl ;
       }

    void   Static ( )
       {
           cout << "- Static function of class B" << endl ;
       }
} ;

void main ( )
{
    // definitions

    A      * a ;
    B      * b ;

    // initialization

    a = new A ( ) ;
    b = new B ( ) ;

    cout << "Functions of object a of class A" << endl ;
    a -> Dynamic ( ) ;
    a -> Static ( ) ;
    cout << endl ;
```

290 Borland C++ 4.0 Object-Oriented Programming

```
        cout << "Functions of object b of class B" << endl ;
        b -> Dynamic ( ) ;
        b -> Static ( ) ;
        cout << endl ;

        // thanks to polymorphism, variable a can take as a value
        // a pointer to an object of class B

        a = b ;

        cout   << "Functions of the object a of class A" << endl
               << "to which has been assigned a value of class B" << endl ;
        // calls the virtual function of class B

        a -> Dynamic ( ) ;
        // calls the nonvirtual function of class A
        a -> Static ( ) ;
}
```

The output of the BINDING.CPP program is as follows:

```
Functions of object a of class A
- Dynamic function of class A
- Static function of class A

Functions of object b of class B
- Dynamic function of class B
- Static function of class B

Functions of the object a of class A
to which has been assigned a value of class B
- Dynamic function of class B
- Static function of class A
```

In C++, virtual functions follow a precise rule: the function must be declared as *virtual* in the first class in which it is present (following the order of derivation). This rule means that usually the virtual functions are declared in the highest level class of a hierarchy.

Note: You cannot redefine a function as *virtual* in a derived class if the function was already declared without the *virtual* specification in a base class. Therefore, you cannot make a function *virtual*, if that wasn't specified when the base class interface was designed in the first place, unless you can modify the base class itself (which is not always possible, particularly when using class libraries). Declaring the functions as virtual in the base class is a drawback to the flexibility of class hierarchies. In fact, to change the behavior of a function in a derived class, you have to modify the source code of the base class (and recompile it, along with all the modules that use the class). This drawback depends on how dynamic binding is implemented by the C++ compilers. (Other object-oriented programming languages offer slightly better solutions.)

Instead of placing the address of the function code to be executed inside the call instruction, the compiler (in collaboration with the linker) will add the address to a table that has one entry for every function redefinition of the virtual function in the derived classes. When the function is called, a table look up will occur at the proper location to fetch the correct address of the code to be executed.

To redefine a virtual function in a derived class you need to provide a function matching *exactly* the previous one: It must have the same parameters (same number and data-type), otherwise the compiler thinks you want to overload the virtual function with another one, having the same name but different parameters.

In the past the virtual function had to be redefined with the same return type as the original, too. In fact it was not allowed to have a function with the same name and parameters and a different return type, since this isn't a correct overloading. Now the specification of the C++ language has slightly changed to allow a kind of "polymorphism" in the return type of virtual functions. If the original function returns a pointer to a class A, the redefined function might return a pointer to a class derived from A.

For example, if the virtual function of a class returns a pointer to its class, you can redefine the function in a derived class and have it return a pointer to the derived class, instead of a pointer to the base class. This is possible only with virtual member functions: There is nothing similar for non-virtual member functions or regualar non-member C-style functions.

Regardless of the presence of some complex details, virtual functions are the key to the powerful polymorphism mechanism of C++. In fact, you can have class hierarchies in which the same function name corresponds to different "incarnations" of the function. Also, since you're able to refer to all of the objects of a hierarchy with a base class variable, you can choose in a totally dynamic and transparent way, from among these functions, the one that actually needs to be called at run time.

Advantages of Polymorphism

Polymorphism makes your system flexible without losing any of the static type checking that takes place at compile time.

Other object-oriented programming languages choose an unlimited polymorphism, which clashes with the idea of type checking. While they may offer you more flexibility and freedom, they tend to avoid almost any check on the source code, deferring them at run time. You have more freedom to play "what-if" programming, but you will also have the potential to make more errors. As a result, the code produced with other object-oriented languages is less secure, because the function calls that are encountered may not be defined for some objects, for reasons ranging from a simple spelling error to a conceptual or logical error. (The resulting program also tends to be slower, because of the many checks that need to be made at runtime.) Using the terminology of Smalltalk (which ignores static type checking), a message might not have a corresponding method, but the environment will catch the problem only when it tries to execute the faulty instruction.

Although it gives you less freedom, the polymorphism of C++ is a very powerful tool, and one that you can use in many different situations. The following list shows the three most frequent uses of polymorphism.

a. **Specialization of derived classes.** The most common use: once a class has been defined, you can derive a specialized class, which is defined as a subset of the objects described by the base class. In the next section, for example, you will see an example of the classes describing rectangles and squares: the second is a specialization of the first, since it is defined as a subset of the objects (any square is also a rectangle). This kind of polymorphism increases subclass efficiency, while retaining a high degree of flexibility and allowing a uniform way to handle rectangles and squares.

b. **Heterogeneous data structures.** Often, it's useful for you to be able to manipulate a set of similar—but not perfectly equal—objects. There are several alternatives: handle them differently (writing several very similar functions); enclose them in a single data type, writing functions that have a different behavior based on a tag field (but this kind of complex function is hardly modifiable); or try to handle the situation directly by using dynamically allocated structures and complex pointer schemes (the increased complexity will require a very skilled programmer, who will be the only person able to modify the resulting program).

There is, however, an object-oriented alternative: with polymorphism you can easily create and handle heterogeneous data structures, which are easy to design and modify, without losing a proper type checking of the elements used. Later in this chapter, you will see a solution for this kind of problem.

c. **Class hierarchy management.** Another situation in which polymorphism helps a lot, and that can be considered as a follow-up of the preceding two, is class hierarchy management. Class hierarchies are highly structured collections of classes with inheritance relationships that can be easily extended. As you might remember from Chapter 3, class hierarchies are the basis of the object-oriented design of applications, and set this methodology apart from the others. The next chapter will be fully devoted to this subject.

Specialization of Derived Classes

To illustrate the specialization of derived classes, we will return to the example of the hierarchy of animals, used to illustrate the browser. We are going to build a smaller set of classes, adding some member functions to those bare classes.

We will describe the animals from a particular point of view. Each animal can move around, jumping near his current location, and *speak* or utter some sound. The generic class *Animal* has the member functions corresponding to these operations.

To handle the position of the animal on the screen (and output the "sound" in the corresponding location), we need a class for points, in terms of *x* and *y* coordinates. Once we have defined the class *Point*, one of its instances can be a member of class *Animal* to describe the position of the animal itself.

```
// file point.h
// interface of class Point with inline functions
class Point
{
public:

    Point (int xp = 0, int yp = 0) :
       xPos (xp) ,
       yPos (yp)
    { }

    int x ( ) { return xPos ; }

    int y ( )   { return yPos ; }

    void x (int px)  { xPos = px ; }

    void y (int py) { yPos = py ; }

    void operator += (Point p)
    {
       xPos += p.xPos ;
       yPos += p.yPos ;
    }

   private:
      int xPos, yPos ;
};
```

The class *Point* is used as one of the members of the *Animal* class:

```
// file animal.h
// interface of class Animal

#include "point.h"
```

```
class Animal
{
public:
    Animal (Point p = Point ( )) ;

    // the "speak" function is redefined by each derived class
    virtual void Speak ( ) ;

    // two different "moving" functions
    void JumpBy (int x, int y) ;
    void MoveTo (Point newPosition) ;

protected:
    // the current location of the animal
    Point position ;

    // selects the location for the following output operations
    void MoveOutput ( ) ;
} ;
```

Here is the code of the member functions of the class. They use some library functions to change the output of the text, but luckily these functions are supported by the *EasyWin* library, so we can run this program under Windows.

```
// file animal.cpp                                    08/ANIMAL
// member functions of the class Animal

#include <conio.h>
#include <iostream.h>
#include "animal.h"

Animal :: Animal (Point p) :
    position (p)
{ }

void Animal :: Speak ( )
{
    cout << "The animal is making his verse" << endl ;
}

void Animal :: JumpBy (int x, int y)
{
    position += Point (x,y) ;
}
```

```
void Animal :: MoveTo (Point newPosition)
{
    position = newPosition ;
}

// protected member function
void Animal :: MoveOutput ( )
{
    gotoxy (position.x( ), position.y( )) ;
}
```

The class of the animals needs some further refining. It describes every kind of animal in general terms, without specifying any detail. For instance, it doesn't know what to do to make an animal *speak*. A typical solution is to add a member data holding the kind of animal, then write a *switch* statement to provide the corresponding *output* for each animal. This is exactly what we would like to avoid!

The alternative is to add a number of derived classes, describing the specific animals, such as cows, dogs, cats, lions, and so on. Each of these derived classes needs a specific constructor and a proper member function to override the default behavior of *Speak*. Here, as an example, is the definition of a couple of these classes, in a single file.

```
// file cow_dog.h                                    08/ANIMAL
// classes Cow and Dog, both derived from Animal

class Cow : public Animal
{
public:

    Cow (Point p = Point (10, 10)) ;
    void Speak ( ) ;
} ;

class Dog : public Animal
{
public:

    Dog (Point p = Point (20, 20)) ;
    void Speak ( ) ;
} ;
```

```
// file cow_dog.cpp                                  08/ANIMAL
// member functions of the classes Cow and Dog

#include <iostream.h>
#include "animal.h"
```

```
#include "cow_dog.h"

// class Cow

Cow :: Cow (Point p) :
   Animal (p)
{ }

void Cow :: Speak ( )
{
   MoveOutput ( ) ;
   cout << "moo" ;
}

// class Dog

Dog :: Dog (Point p) :
   Animal (p)
{ }

void Dog :: Speak ( )
{
   MoveOutput ( ) ;
   cout << "arf" ;
}
```

Once we have defined some classes derived from *Animal*, we can write:

```
Animal * pAnimal = new Cow ( ) ;
pAnimal -> Speak ( ) ;
```

The effect of the call *pAnimal->Speak()* really depends on the type of the object currently assigned to the pointer. In this case it corresponds to a call of the function *Cow:: Speak ()*. Changing the first statement to:

```
Animal * pAnimal = new Dog (pos) ;
```

the output changes, because a different function is executed, *Dog :: Speak ()*. But what really matters is that the compiler doesn't need to know which function to call, such as in:

```
Animal * pAnimal ;

if ( value < 10)    / * some condition, perhaps based on the input */
   pAnimal = new Cow ( ) ;
```

```
else
    pAnimal = new Dog ( ) ;

pAnimal -> Speak ( ) ;
```

Here we do not know which function will be executed by the last statement: This can be determined only at run-time. We can include a similar piece of code (which might be used with different data types) in a function having a pointer to an *Animal* as one of his parameters:

```
void RunSpeaking (Animal* pAnimal, int nSteps)
{
    for (int i = 0; i < nSteps; ++i)
    {
        pAnimal -> JumpBy (1, 1) ;
        pAnimal -> Speak ( ) ;
    }
}
```

The function can use the pointer, and thus refer to an object of the class *Animal* and each of its derived classes (as *Cow* and *Dog*), and call each of the member functions of the class *Animal*. However, these calls may refer to virtual functions redefined by the derived classes. Since all the classes derived from *Animal* know how to respond to the member functions of the base class, we can use as parameter a pointer to an object of any class derived from it.

The same can be accomplished using a parameter passed by reference, instead of a pointer, because polymorphism works with references, too. In the function

```
void RunSpeaking (Animal& a, int nSteps) ;
```

the *a* parameter can refer to generic animals, cows, and dogs. The following file contains the source code of a similar function and a *main* calling it a couple of times with different parameters. The program produces an output similar to that of Figure 8.4.

```
// file running.cpp                                              08/ANIMAL
// Animals running around the screen

#include <iostream.h>
#include <stdlib.h>
#include "animal.h"
#include "cow_dog.h"

// a "polymorphic" global function, using a reference to an Animal
void RunSpeaking (Animal& a, int nSteps)
{
```

```
        randomize ( ) ;
        for (int i = 0; i < nSteps; ++i)
        {
            int x = random (5) - 2 ;
            int y = random (5) - 2 ;

            a.JumpBy (x, y) ;
            a.Speak ( ) ;
        }
    }

    // a sample of the use of the polymorphic RunSpeaking function
    void main ( )
    {
        Cow cow (Point (20, 10)) ;
        Dog dog (Point (10, 20)) ;

        RunSpeaking (cow, 5) ;
        RunSpeaking (dog, 28) ;
    }
```

To compile the program you need a project containing the files *animal.cpp, cow_dog.cpp,* and *running.cpp*, as shown in Figure 8.5.

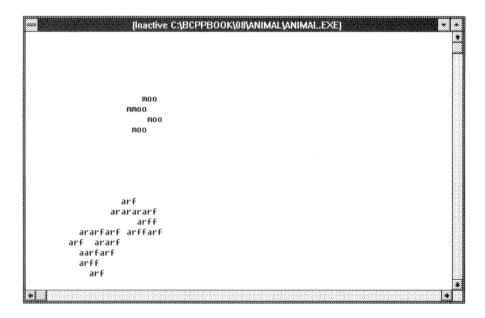

Figure 8.4 The output of the program ANIMAL

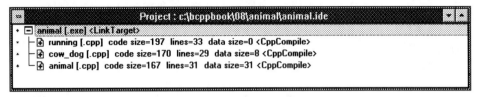

Figure 8.5 The project used to compile the *animal* example

The importance of this example lies in the fact that the function *RunSpeaking* has no knowledge of the objects it is going to work on, and of the member functions it is going to call. It knows nothing about cows and dogs. You can easily add new animals deriving new classes, and the function will go on running without a glitch. Although there is a run-time mechanism in action, if the program compiles without errors you can feel confident that no run-time error will appear! Run-time errors are known to be the most dangerous, because you risk missing them during testing. Compile-time errors, extensively supported by C++, are much safer, since the programmer has more information about what went wrong and is pretty sure to *see* them in the first place.

This example stressed two different aspects of polymorphism:

- The same message (member function call) sent to different objects (of derived classes)
- Objects of different classes used as parameters of a function (such as *RunSpeaking*) that uses only member functions common to those classes (the member functions of the base class)

Heterogeneous Data Structures

Usually, with a strongly typed programming language like C++, you can have only homogeneous data structures.

For example, you can declare arrays of integers, characters, pointers to integers, and character strings (arrays), but you cannot have an array containing entities of several different types. In C, this rule is somewhat possible through unions; while still a possibility in C++, we strongly advise you not to use that kind of construct, because then you must handle all the related problems by yourself. Often this situation leads to the decision to avoid heterogeneous structures altogether, even when you need them.

Returning to the example presented in the previous section, you can attempt to solve this problem in an object-oriented way using an array of objects of a class:

```
Cow herd [ 10 ] ;
```

With this statement, you define an array of ten cows named *herd*. Using this data structure is similar to using any other array. Having defined the elements, you can *hear* the fourth cow (remember the indexing of array elements starts from 0) with the following statement:

```
herd [ 3 ] . Speak ( ) ;
```

What if you wanted an array of dogs? The situation is similar. Then, what if you want to handle an array containing both cows and dogs? You can use polymorphism to declare and use the following data structure:

```
Animal * mixedFlock [ 10 ] ;
```

This array holds ten pointers to objects of class *Animal*, or pointers that are type-compatible with pointers to objects of class *Animal*. You can manipulate the array elements using all (and only) the member functions of class *Animal* (both virtual or not).

You can then build a small program that uses the classes defined in the previous section. In the following example, you define an array, insert some animals, hear any of them speak, then make all of them jump around while speaking.

```
// file HETERO.CPP                                          08/ANIMAL
// example of an heterogeneus data structure

#include <iostream.h>
#include <stdlib.h>
#include <conio.h>

#include "animal.h"
#include "cow_dog.h"

// the usual "polymorphic" global function, using a reference to an Animal
void RunSpeaking (Animal& a, int nSteps)
{
    randomize ( ) ;
    for (int i = 0; i < nSteps; ++i)
    {
        int x = random (5) - 2 ;
        int y = random (5) - 2 ;

        a.JumpBy (x, y) ;
        a.Speak ( ) ;
    }
}

void main ( )
{
    // array of pointers
```

```
Animal * mixedFlock [10] ;

// pointers' initialization

mixedFlock [ 0 ] = new Cow ( ) ;
mixedFlock [ 1 ] = new Dog ( ) ;
mixedFlock [ 2 ] = new Dog (Point (12, 24)) ;
mixedFlock [ 3 ] = new Dog (Point (2, 12)) ;
mixedFlock [ 4 ] = new Dog (Point (22, 4)) ;
mixedFlock [ 5 ] = new Cow (Point (7, 7)) ;
mixedFlock [ 6 ] = new Cow (Point (7, 11)) ;
mixedFlock [ 7 ] = new Cow (Point (11, 13)) ;
mixedFlock [ 8 ] = new Animal (Point (1, 1)) ;
mixedFlock [ 9 ] = new Dog (Point (7, 19)) ;

// first loop: each animal speaks, then wait for a key to be pressed

for (int i = 0; i < 10; i++)
    mixedFlock [ i ] -> Speak ( ) ;

getch ( ) ;
clrscr ( ) ;        // clears the screen

// second loop: each animal speaks jumping around

for (i = 0; i < 10; i++)
    RunSpeaking ( * mixedFlock [ i ], 8) ;
}
```

To compile this program you need a project containing the files ANIMAL.CPP, COW_DOG.CPP, and HETERO.CPP. Its output is shown in Figure 8.6.

Notice that the ninth pointer is quite strange: It refers to an object of class *Animal*, but what does it represent? Probably it's nonsense to allow the instantiation of objects of the class *Animal* itself, since the idea of animal is only a human abstraction. To avoid this problem we might think of declaring the constructors of class *Animal* protected. In this way, they cannot be called directly from other code, but the constructors of the derived classes can use them. We will describe this subject in detail in the next chapter.

POINTS TO CONSIDER

1. Investigate type compatibility rules, modifying the examples of the first section of the chapter.
2. Enlarge the example FOREIGN.CPP, adding new member functions to the classes (and possibly figuring out a "useful" main program).

```
┌─────────────────────────────────────────────────────────────────┐
│ ▬              [Inactive C:\BCPPBOOK\08\ANIMAL\HETERO.EXE]     ▼ ▲ │
├─────────────────────────────────────────────────────────────────┤
│                                                                   │
│                                                                   │
│                          arf                                      │
│                         arfarf                                    │
│                          arf                                      │
│            moo          aarff                                     │
│           moomoo         arf                                      │
│            moo                                                    │
│           mmooo                                                   │
│          moooomoo                                                 │
│ arf moomoooo                                                      │
│ ararf moomooThe animal is making his verse                        │
│ The animal is making his verse                                    │
│ The animal is making his verse                                    │
│ The animal is making his verse                                    │
│ The animal is making his verse                                    │
│ The animal is making his verse                                    │
│ The aarfal is making his verse                                    │
│ The arfarf is making his verse                                    │
│           arf           arfarf                                    │
│          aarff           arf                                      │
│          arf            aarff                                     │
│            aarfrff   arf                                          │
└─────────────────────────────────────────────────────────────────┘
```

Figure 8.6 The final output of the HETERO program

3. Discern the difference between the redefinition of "normal" function (with static binding) and virtual function (with dynamic binding)? What are the effects of the two operations?

4. Create and implement a short example in which dynamic binding is useful.

   Suggestions: You can design classes describing geometrical shapes, each with a specific paint function; classes of people greeting in several languages; classes of clocks, each with its own ticking and alarm sounds; or classes of transportation. In any example you implement, evaluate if it was equally easy to have the same effect with a different method (perhaps having a member data containing the output string) if this tends to become too complex.

5. Modify the function *RunSpeaking*, or write a similar "generic" function that works independently from the class of the object passed as a parameter.

6. Derive new classes from *Animals*, and pass the corresponding objects to the *RunSpeaking* function (without modifying it).

7. Define a new heterogeneous data structure, using one of the class hierarchies you have already created (for example, one of those requested by the fourth example).

9

Class Hierarchies and Abstract Classes

*Abstract superclasses are created when two classes share a part of their descriptions and yet neither one is properly a subclass of the other. A mutual superclass is created for the two classes, which contains their shared aspects. This type of superclass is called **abstract** because it was not created in order to have instances.* [Goldberg 83]

Now that we have gained a sufficient knowledge of C++ in order to fully understand and define class hierarchies, we will examine them in greater detail, focusing on the comprehensive description of sets of classes, whose common features are drawn from inheritance relationships.

Class hierarchies play an essential role in object-oriented programming. Thus, the examples in this book are very important in helping you to switch from traditional programming (even if based on classes) to a style of programming that is really object oriented. This will actually allow you to put into practice some of the theoretical ideas introduced in Chapter 3.

In this chapter, you will be introduced to more language constructs of C++ including pure virtual functions and abstract classes.

Designing Class Hierarchies

In Chapter 3 when abstraction was introduced, one important aspect was left out: the problem of classification. To give an exhaustive and detailed description of reality, every scientific study resorts to some kind of classification. The most well-known examples come from biology: the animal and vegetable worlds are customarily described by means of an elaborate classification schema that shows a hierarchy of elements. We have seen a similar classification in Chapter 7, where we used it to understand the properties of the browser in the program BROWSE.CPP.

We can use a similar classification system to provide clear and precise descriptions of objects in terms of similarities and differences, instead of resorting to an exhaustive method of description, which will be repetitive.

For instance, to describe an ink-jet printer, you could state that it is similar to a dot-matrix printer, except that instead of pins that strike an inked ribbon, there are several nozzles that fire small drops of ink. In this way, you define the object in terms of another object, without having to repeat the description of the common traits, and by stating only the differences. With the right choice of initial object for comparison, the list of differences will generally be shorter than the full description. This operation can be described as follows:

- examine a known object, leave out some of its features, and obtain something that is abstract.

- add some other specific features, thus attaining the new real object.

These steps are illustrated in Figure 9.1A.

Often, however, you must give a detailed description of the starting object. In this case, it might be easier for you to proceed linearly by describing an abstract object (a generic printer), which has traits common to all printers, then describe the specific differences, as shown in Figure 9.1B. You can add features later to describe more distinct printer objects.

These two approaches are used to *classify* objects that have common traits and that can be described in a hierarchical way.

When you program an application by following an object-oriented methodology, you use an approach similar to the previous examples. The identification of common elements brings forth the definition of classes that are related to one another, and often leads to the identification of "abstract" elements that describe common parts of several objects. These generic and "useless" classes (because no real object can be instanced from them) allow us to speak about hierarchies when we refer to collections of classes in inheritance relationships. However, this distinction is subtle.

In object-oriented programming, the use of hierarchies has several purposes:

1. The description of actual object classifications.
2. The abstraction of common elements between classes (generalization).
3. The creation of "variants" of a class (distinguished by different implementations, for example).

In all of these cases, there will exist some "abstract" classes. In C++, an abstract class has at least one member function that is declared but not defined, because the definition will be provided only by derived classes. Since an abstract class has at least a function that cannot be called, it cannot be instantiated. This behavior can be implemented with a specific construct that is described in the following sections.

Generalization of Classes

The term "generalization" has already been used a few times: let's try to understand what it means through some examples.

(A)

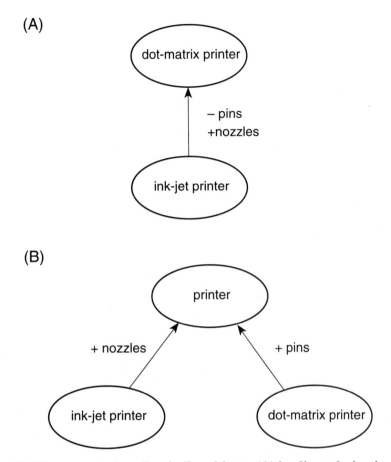

(B)

Figure 9.1 Two ways to describe similar objects: (A) by direct derivation, (B) by derivation from an abstract entity

To describe a collection of cars, trucks, and motorcycles, each with its own features, you would probably note that some of their components are common: all have wheels and an engine; all need fuel, and so on. Thus, you can think of the description of all common elements in terms of a specific class that will describe all vehicles in a generic way.

From this generic class you can form subclasses that correspond to the various vehicles; from these, in turn, you can derive specialized classes for describing vans, coupes, mopeds, and so on to obtain a hierarchy like the one shown in Figure 9.2.

In every subclass you must redefine only the features that have been added to the class from which they derive, without having to repeat the description of the common features. The elements present in all cases will be described only once in the generic class vehicle. This class will provide a common interface to all subclasses. This common interface, which usually consists of virtual functions, is a fundamental item, because it allows you to make a *uniform reference* to all classes of the hierarchy, which are always free to redefine the various functions as deemed necessary.

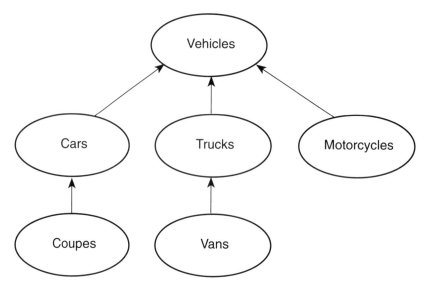

Figure 9.2 Hierarchy of motor vehicles

Similarly, you could apply this approach to extend our discussion at the end of the last chapter on squares and rectangles to cover circles, triangles, and other geometric shapes. In this case, you could create an abstract class called, for example, *Shape* that is a generalization of circles and rectangles. This abstract class describes geometric shapes in general. The definition of this new class will let you handle any type of shape.

At this point, you're probably wondering how it is possible to define an abstract class in C++; before we can address that, however, we need to know more about virtual functions.

Pure Virtual Functions

Pure virtual functions are virtual functions the declaration of which is not followed by a definition. In fact, they are functions that "do nothing." However, virtual functions are different from empty functions (that is, functions whose bodies do not contain any statements) since the compiler handles them differently, such as checking that they are never called. As far as syntax is concerned, the difference between a pure virtual function and an empty virtual function is this:

```
virtual int    empty_function ( int number ) { }

virtual int    pure_function ( int number ) = 0 ;
```

From a semantic point of view, the difference lies in the fact that a pure function cannot be called: if that happens, the compiler will issue an error message. If, due to the presence of pointers and explicit typecasting, a call to a pure function occurs, Borland C++ will issue a run time error.

So, if a pure function cannot be called, what good is it? You use pure functions to declare, within an abstract class, those functions with a definition deferred to some derived class.

At the same time, pure virtual functions define abstract classes, as you will see in the following section. They are used only for this purpose and nothing else.

Abstract Classes

From the point of view of the language, a class is an abstract class if it has at least one pure virtual function. An abstract class cannot be instanced (that is, there cannot exist any object of that class), but it has a meaning only as a base class for other classes, as shown in the following example:

```
// file ABSTR1.CPP                                        09/ABSTR
// example of the definition of an abstract class:
// a call to its constructor generates a compiler error

class Printer
{
public:
    Printer ( )
        { }

    virtual void Method ( char * buffer ) = 0 ;
    virtual int Dpi ( ) = 0 ;
} ;

void main ( )
{

    // if you uncomment the following statement the compiler shows the message:
    // "Cannot create instance of abstract class 'Printer'"

    // Printer pri ;

    // the following definition is correct

    Printer *    pPri ;

    // if you uncomment the following statement the compiler shows the
    // same message again

    // pPri = new Printer ( ) ;

}
```

The preceding example shows how an abstract class can be used only through pointers: it is not allowed to define an instance of the class (that is, define an object). Likewise, it is not possible to initialize a pointer with a value of that class, since the constructor of the class, although present, cannot be called.

We are only allowed to define pointers and references to the abstract class and pass them to functions, as in the following example:

```
class Printer
{
public:
    Printer ( )
        { }

    virtual void Method ( char * buffer ) = 0 ;
    virtual int Dpi ( ) = 0 ;
} ;

// objects of class Printer can be passed to functions only
// by reference or with a pointer, not directly

// void function1 ( Printer pr ) ;
void function2 ( Printer& pr ) ;
void function3 ( Printer * pr ) ;
```

Of course, objects corresponding to an abstract class can be passed to functions only by reference or using pointers, and not by value. In this last case, in fact, the compiler needs to make a copy of the object, but even the copy constructor of an abstract class cannot be called.

Every class—derived from an abstract class—that provides a definition for *all* of its pure virtual functions yields a "concrete" class (a class that is not abstract). The objects of this last class can be used directly or even through a pointer to the abstract base class, as the following code demonstrates:

```
// file ABSTR2.CPP                                    09/ABSTR
// example of the derivation of a "concrete" class from an abstract one

// includes sprintf function prototype
#include <stdio.h>

#include <iostream.h>

class Printer
{
public:
    Printer ( )
```

```
        { }
    virtual void Method ( char * buffer ) = 0 ;
    virtual int Dpi ( ) = 0 ;
} ;


class DotMatrixPrinter : public Printer
{
int    nDots;
public:
    DotMatrixPrinter ( int n ) :
        nDots ( n )
        { }

    void   Method ( char * buffer )
        {
            sprintf ( buffer , "Dot matrix printer with %d pins" , nDots ) ;
        }

    int    Dpi ( )
        {
            switch ( nDots ) {

            // almost random values

            case 8: return 150 ;
            case 9: return 160 ;
            case 24: return 300 ;
            default: return 100 ;
            }

        }
} ;

void main ( )
{
    char   description [40];

    // definition of dot-matrix objects

    DotMatrixPrinter   dmp ( 24 ) ;

    dmp.Method ( description ) ;
    cout  << description << endl
          << "DPI: " << dmp.Dpi ( ) << endl
          << endl ;
```

```
// definition of a pointer to generic printers

Printer *      pPri ;

pPri = new DotMatrixPrinter ( 9 ) ;
pPri -> Method ( description ) ;
cout  << description << endl
        << "DPI: " << pPri -> Dpi ( ) << endl
        << endl ;
}
```

The above program produces the following output, in which the two printers are handled in two different ways: with an object of class *DotMatrixPrinter*, and with a pointer to the abstract base class *Printer*.

```
Dot matrix printer with 24 pins
DPI: 300

Dot matrix printer with 9 pins
DPI: 160
```

If a class does not provide an actual redefinition for all of the pure virtual functions of its base classes, it is considered to be abstract itself, as demonstrated by the following example:

```
// file ABSTR3.CPP                                          09/ABSTR
// a class derived from an abstract one, and which does not redefine
// all of its virtual pure functions is considered abstract

class Printer
{
public:
    Printer ( )
        { }

    virtual void Method ( char * buffer ) = 0 ;
    virtual int Dpi ( ) = 0 ;
} ;

class LaserPrinter : public Printer
{
public:
    LaserPrinter ( )
        { }
```

```
        int  Dpi ( )
          {
              return 300 ;
          }
};

void main ( )
{
    // since the class LaserPrinter is still abstract
    // it cannot be used directly, but only through pointers

    // the first of the two declarations results in the compiler error:
    // "Cannot create instance of abstract class 'LaserPrinter'"

    LaserPrinter    lp1 ;     // wrong
    LaserPrinter    * lp2 ;   // ok, but useless
}
```

Abstract classes correspond to general concepts, which are not easily translated into specific objects, but are useful for providing a description of all common features of objects that might be very different from each other. For this reason, even if abstract classes define their functionalities, they seldom implement them.

This construct is also very important in polymorphism and dynamic binding; in fact, abstract classes are usually those at the highest level in the hierarchy, and they "abstract" the behavior (and thus the functions) common to all their subclasses.

Abstract classes are also useful for making partial implementations—classes that implement part of their functionalities—deferring the remainder to their subclasses.

Let's now see a complete interface of an abstract class that solves a problem we discussed earlier: The class *Animal* we wrote in the last chapter can be rewritten as an abstract class, since we do not know how to write the code of the member function *Speak* for a generic animal.

```
class Animal
{
public:
    Animal (Point p = Point ( ));

    // the "speak" function is redefined by each derived class
    virtual void Speak ( ) = 0;

    // two different "moving" functions
    void JumpBy (int x, int y);
    void MoveTo (Point newPosition);
```

```
protected:
    // the current location of the animal
    Point position;

    // selects the location for the following output operations
    void MoveOutput ( );
};
```

Which Classes Are Abstract?

The preceding example should give you a better understanding of the use of abstract classes in object-oriented programming.

An abstract class cannot have any instance, but serves mainly to provide a common interface to derived classes, of which—naturally—it will be possible to declare objects. In other words, abstract classes declare the member functions that have to be implemented in the derived classes. In this sense, they can be thought of as the skeleton of a program: its backbone, around which the hierarchy is built by defining and implementing the specific classes.

A class that is not abstract is sometimes referred to as "concrete." In principle, it is better to inherit from an abstract class rather than from a concrete class. In fact, a concrete class must define its own representation of its private data, while some of its derived classes will probably need a different data representation. Instead, usually abstract classes do not have a data representation of their own, or if they do, it will only be partial, and thus all its "concrete" subclasses will be allowed to define their own private data items without the risk of conflict or of inheriting useless parts of other classes.

Creating new abstract classes is very important, though not simple. It is always simpler to reuse a well-constructed abstraction rather than to create a new one. In any case, this activity is fundamental to good object-oriented programming. However, it is very important that you always try to inherit from another class that is already available before defining a new class, attempting in this way to build new hierarchies of increasing size in which there might be more than one top-level class that is "concrete."

At this point, an experienced programmer might consider reorganizing the hierarchy by putting an abstract class at the highest level, into which the whole meaning of the hierarchy might be enclosed and reused the greatest number of times.

As you might guess, it is difficult to give definite rules or suggestions regarding the choice of abstract classes or the structuring of hierarchies, because the various cases that you might encounter will probably represent very different situations. Despite this, one can at least try to set some basic criteria (shown below), which are mainly drawn from [Johnson 88], which will certainly help "newcomers" design their first hierarchies.

1. **The class hierarchies must be narrow and deep.** A well-structured class hierarchy must be several levels deep (9.3A), and cannot be resolved in a "flat" structure of only a couple of levels (Figure 9.3B).

(A)

(B)

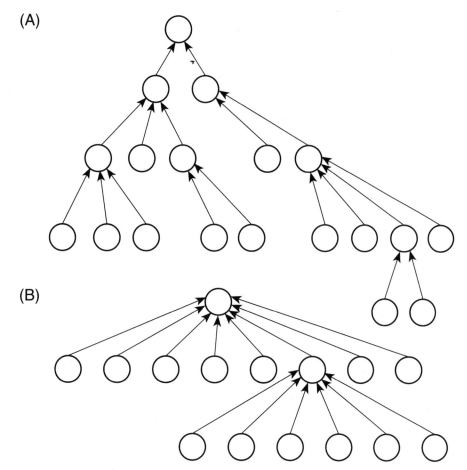

Figure 9.3 Example of (A) a "narrow-and-deep" hierarchy, and (B) a "shallow-and-wide" hierarchy

---

➤ *Note:* While *one* shallow-and-wide hierarchy usually indicates bad design, sometimes it might be worthwhile to consider not one but a "number of discrete interconnected hierarchies" that "cooperate closely. Do not make the mistake of equating the size and number of class hierarchies with their quality or with their object-orientedness. A soundly designed, object-oriented class library can consist of a number of small shallow hierarchies rather than a single deep one. The two styles of libraries are simply different approaches to design, and both have their places." [Mansell 92]

---

2. **The highest level class in the hierarchy must be abstract.** You have already seen one reason for this rule: it is always better to inherit from an abstract class. Generally, if more than one class has to redefine an inherited method, then it might be

preferable to move the common part to a new abstract class from which all classes can inherit. The abstract class is thus described, in a sense, like the intersection of the two classes, each of which will implement only its own specific elements.

3. **Minimize access to variables.** Since one of the differences between concrete and abstract classes is the presence of data, the classes can be made "more" abstract by reducing (or even eliminating) their reliance on that data, or rather on a specific representation of that data.

   In this sense, it is preferable that you access variables by means of functions, rather than directly. In this way, you will be able to change the data representation easily by changing just the access functions, and leaving untouched the code that uses them. For instance, an abstract class with public data would not make much sense.

4. **Derived classes must be specializations.** You should be able to think of every component of a derived class as a component of the base class, and all objects belonging to a hierarchy as objects of the highest level (abstract) class. The use of abstract classes in the structuring of the hierarchy will in any case favor the specialization of the concrete classes.

5. **All intermediate classes should be abstract,** while only the terminal classes should be concrete. In terms of a hierarchical tree, all nodes should be abstract classes, and all leaves should be concrete classes, as shown in Figure 9.4. This is not always possible, nor is it always the "best" solution; however it is an "ideal" point of reference that is very important and can serve as a guideline during the design of a new hierarchy.

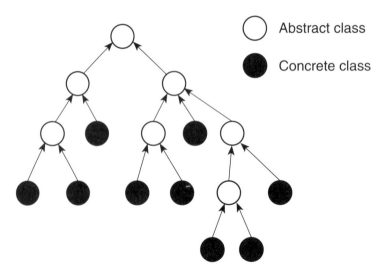

Figure 9.4 Concrete classes and abstract classes in an "ideal" hierarchy

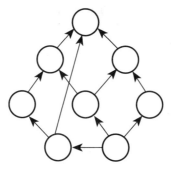

Figure 9.5 The DAG of a hierarchy with multiple inheritance

The hierarchies presented so far are all based on single inheritance, hence they are in the form of trees. However, multiple inheritance can also be used to design hierarchies, in which case they can be described by Directed Acyclic Graphs (DAGs), as shown in Figure 9.5.

Virtual Destructors

Using polymorphism to refer to objects of different classes might cause problems during their deallocation. In the following code fragment:

```
Animal * pa ;
pa = new Dog ( ) ;
...
delete pa ;
```

an object is referenced using a pointer to its base class. When the last statement is executed, what happens? The static type of the pointer *pa* refers to the base class, so the destructor of the base class is erroneously called instead of the destructor of the derived class (the dynamic type of the object). Dynamic linking, in fact, takes place only for virtual functions.

The solution is quite obvious: The destructor of the base class should be virtual, thus allowing dynamic binding of the proper destructor at run-time. This behavior, however, is quite strange, since the name of the destructors of the different classes are different! In this particular case different functions with the same meaning are regarded as a single redefined virtual function.

The following example shows the calls to the constructors and destructors of two derived classes. When the destructor is virtual, as in the code, the program is correct and generates the output shown in Figure 9.6. If you remove the virtual keyword from the destructor, you end up with the output of Figure 9.7, which highlights the error.

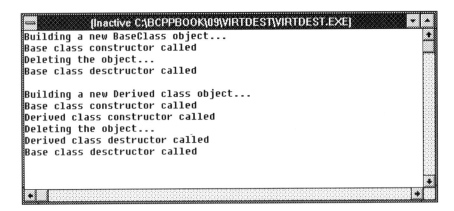

Figure 9.6 The execution of the correct version of the *virtdest.cpp* program

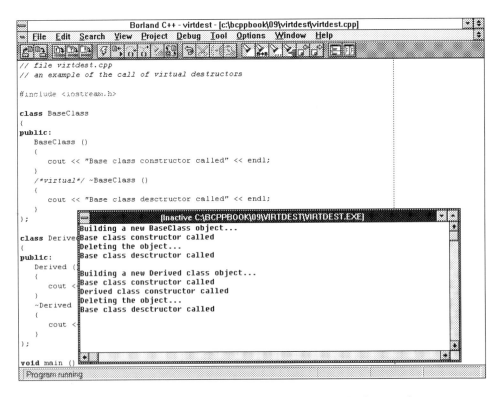

Figure 9.7 Without the virtual destructor the program *virtdest.cpp* is wrong, as shown by its output.

```
// file VIRTDEST.CPP                                    09/VIRTDEST
// an example of the call of virtual destructors

#include <iostream.h>

class BaseClass
{
public:
   BaseClass ( )
   {
      cout << "Base class constructor called" << endl ;
   }
   virtual ~BaseClass ( )
   {
      cout << "Base class desctructor called" << endl ;
   }
};

class Derived : public BaseClass
{
public:
   Derived ( )
   {
      cout << "Derived class constructor called" << endl ;
   }
   ~Derived ( )
   {
      cout << "Derived class destructor called" << endl ;
   }
} ;

void main ( )
{
   BaseClass * pbase ;

   cout << "Building a new BaseClass object..." << endl ;
   pbase = new BaseClass ;

   // ... use the pbase pointer

   cout << "Deleting the object..." << endl ;
   delete pbase ;
```

```
    cout << endl << "Building a new Derived class object..." << endl ;
    pbase = new Derived ;

    // ... use the new pbase pointer

    cout << "Deleting the object..." << endl ;
    delete pbase ;
}
```

With regard to the problem of virtual destructors, the interface of the class *Animal* becomes:

```
class Animal
{
public:
    Animal (Point p = Point ( )) ;
    virtual ~Animal ( ) ;

    // the "speak" function is redefined by each derived class
    virtual void Speak ( ) = 0 ;

    // two different "moving" functions
    void JumpBy (int x, int y) ;
    void MoveTo (Point newPosition) ;

protected:
    // the current location of the animal
    Point position ;

    // selects the location for the following output operations
    void MoveOutput ( ) ;
} ;
```

Of course you do not always need to add a virtual destructor for each class having virtual member functions: It is only required if the class really needs its destructor to be called. If the class doesn't need a destructor, the virtual destructor is not needed.

A Hierarchy of Graphical Classes

Now we would like to put the preceding ideas to work by building a significant example of a class hierarchy. A very interesting case, although quite common, is that of a hierarchy of graphical classes. We can define a generic base class (an abstract class) called *shape*, then derive from this a number of classes for the different closed geometrical forms, such as rectangles, squares, ellipses, circles, triangles, and so on.

However, the problem is that our graphic application cannot use the *EasyWin* library: We need to write a full-blown Windows application, something you will learn in the last chapters of the book, where you will find the example of a hierarchy of graphical classes.

➤   *Note:* Besides using Windows graphic, it's still possible to write a DOS-based application using the Borland Graphics Interface (BGI). An example of a hierarchy of BGI-based graphical classes is available on the companion disk together with some text explaining it (see file SHAPE.TXT).   **09/BGI-HIER**

POINTS TO CONSIDER

1. Analyze some common objects; describe a hierarchy that expresses their similarities and common traits. You could describe animals, plants, people, buildings, and so on. Try to define abstract classes that generalize the shared elements and a base class for the hierarchy that provides a common interface to all shared functions.

2. Define an abstract class that describes a common interface to the member functions of one of the hierarchies you defined in the preceding exercise, then implement it in C++.

3. Describe in C++ one of the hierarchies you have found in the first exercise, by implementing a significant part of the hierarchy and then creating an example that uses the hierarchy.

4. Check the hierarchies you described in the preceding exercises against the general rules exposed in this chapter. While you are learning how to design a hierarchy, you should always try to draw this kind of comparison. Do this to give a better structure to your classes, but also to criticize these same rules that are inevitably too general. This analysis will help you to value your own experience better.

10

Genericity and Templates

The notion of templates provides what is sometimes called param-eterized types or generics. It resemble features from Clu and Ada.
[Stroustrup 91A]

The type checking provided by C++ is useful for improving the correctness of the code, which increases with the number of checks done by the compiler. We have already stressed the positive aspects of this approach, showing how it differs from that of other object-oriented programming languages, which rely on a more dynamic concept of type.

You might think that the type checking of C++ is also a nuisance since it limits your independence. In real world programming, when you define a class or a function, you may want to be able to use it with objects of different types, without having to rewrite the code several times (or just cut and paste, replacing some items). The C++ type checking facilities strongly discourage this practice. This was a serious limit of C++, one that many programmers disliked. Therefore, the C++ language has been improved to overcome it.

Now you can declare a class without specifying the type of one or more data members: this operation can be delayed until an object of that class is actually declared or defined. Similarly, you can define a function without specifying the type of one or more parameters until the function is called.

To do this, a new keyword has been added to C++: *template*. Templates were first formally introduced in the *draft* ANSI standard [Ellis 90] and are supported by the current versions of AT&T C++, Borland C++, and Turbo C++.

You can use the template clause to declare a whole family of classes or functions, instead of just one. With templates, you only need to select the proper class of the family.

This chapter is dedicated entirely to templates. The first section introduces you to the concept of genericity and the different forms it takes in programming languages. Next, you will see how to emulate templates with macros and inheritance; then the construct is described in detail. An analysis of genericity provided by templates and polymorphism ends the chapter.

The Concept of Genericity

Before describing C++ templates in detail, it is worth analyzing the underlying concept, known as *genericity*, which is present in several other programming languages as well.

Genericity is a very important construct in object-oriented programming languages, particularly with regard to the issue of reusability. Nonetheless, the concept of generic modules was borrowed from other languages and was not present in the first object-oriented systems. We will soon see the reason for that, but it's better to start by defining what genericity is:

> "Genericity is the ability to define parameterized modules. Such a module, called a generic module, is not directly usable; rather, it is a module pattern. In the most common case, the parameters stand for types. Actual modules, called instances of the generic module, are obtained by providing actual types for each of the generic parameters." [Meyer 88]

This definition corresponds precisely to generic classes in C++ (which are a kind of module). In other programming languages, the term module takes on a different meaning.

The purpose of genericity is to define a class (or a function) without specifying the type of one or more of its members (parameters). This way, you can change the class to fit the different uses without having to rewrite it. We call a class of this type a *container class*. Suppose you had to write the code for a set of elements (such as a list, a queue, or a stack). You could define a set of integers and use it. If, later on, you also had to define a set of dates, how could you proceed? Different languages have solved this problem in different ways.

As Booch points out, "There are basically four ways to build container classes" [Booch 91] such as those just mentioned.

- With some languages you have to use macros to compile a class several times, each time providing a definition of the type actually being used.

- Other languages, such as Smalltalk, avoid type checking altogether. In Smalltalk (and other dynamic languages), polymorphism is not limited to hierarchies as in C++, and any class can be substituted for another. Therefore, any container is totally heterogeneous.

- This approach can be slightly changed adding checks to the polymorphic containers of Smalltalk with some code that performs the missing type checking (during run time), following the example of Object Pascal.

- The last approach is the use of generic modules. Some languages provide a mechanism for parameterized classes similar to that introduced by Clu and adopted by Ada, Eiffel, and recently, C++.

The first object-oriented programming languages did not provide genericity because they didn't need it, since they did not have the concept of type. With the introduction of typed object-oriented languages, generic modules have become very important; they are still not considered essential (as Meyer has demonstrated [Meyer 88]), though their value must not be underestimated.

Two things should be clear to compare the different object-oriented languages:

- Genericity is only meaningful in typed languages.
- "The possibility of parameterizing user-defined abstractions provides a still more flexible and powerful tool for expressing abstractions in a programming language." [Ghezzi 87]

Since C++ is a typed language offering good type-checking features, genericity is very useful to express commonality between classes operating on different data types. But the concept has been extended even more: in C++ there are both template classes and template functions; the parameters usually stand for types, but can also be in place of constant values.

Emulating Genericity with Macros

As we have seen, you can use macros to define generic modules. In fact, you can use them to define classes with a parametric data type. These generic classes are similar to those you can obtain with the new *template* construct, which will be described shortly. Although using the proper construct is much better (for reasons you will soon see), this example is useful both for owners of older versions of the compiler (that do not support templates) as well as to understand how templates are implemented.

As an example of a generic class defined with a macro, the following declaration of a LIFO (Last In First Out) stack is provided:

```
// file STACK1.H                                    10/STACK1
// interface of a stack of generic objects obtained through the
// macro expansion of the TYPE definition
// the stack is made of an array of 50 elements

class Stack
{
    TYPE    data [ 50 ] ;
    int     nElements ;

public:

    Stack ( ) :
        nElements ( 0 )
        { }

        // adds an element to the stack

    void  Push ( TYPE elem ) ;

        // gets an element from the stack
```

```
TYPE    Pop ( ) ;

    // number of elements actually on the stack

int      Number ( ) ;

    // is the stack empty?

int      Empty ( ) ;
} ;
```

The member functions of the class are contained in the following source file:

```
// file STACK1.CPP
// member function definition of generic class Stack

#include "Stack1.h"

void Stack :: Push ( TYPE elem )
    {
        data [ nElements ] = elem ;
        nElements ++ ;
    }

TYPE Stack :: Pop ( )
    {
        nElements -- ;
        return data [ nElements ] ;
    }

int Stack :: Number ( )
    {
        return nElements ;
    }

int Stack :: Empty ( )
    {
        return ( nElements == 0 ) ;
    }
```

This generic class can become an effective class through the definition of its parameter and can be used in different situations. Of course, the previous code cannot be compiled by itself without a proper definition of the parameter. This definition should precede the inclusion of the files, as in the following example:

```
// file STA1-USE.CPP                                    10/STACK1
// example of an instance of class Stack

#include <iostream.h>

// definition of a stack of integral numbers
#define TYPE int
#include "Stack1.cpp"

void main ( )
{
    Stack intStack ;

    // adds values to the stack

    intStack.Push ( 500 ) ;
    intStack.Push ( 1992 ) ;
    intStack.Push ( 33 ) ;
    intStack.Push ( 1024 ) ;

    // prints the elements while emptying the stack

    while ( ! intStack.Empty ( ) )
        cout << intStack.Pop ( ) << endl ;
}
```

When the preprocessor processes this file, it generates a very long text, including the full *iostream.h* header file. One of the effects of the preprocessor (and of the CPP program) is to insert in the source code the files named in the *include* directives. To use the preprocessor and see how the preceding program is translated, you need to open the project with this file, and run the preprocessor via the *Special, Preprocess* command of the source file local menu. This operation produces a very long output file (with more than 700 lines included from *iostream.h*), so the following code contains only some excerpts of the original *sta1-use.i* file.

```
sta1-use.cpp 1:
...
c:\borlandc\include\iostream.h 1:
...
c:\borlandc\include\iostream.h 721:
...
Stack1.cpp 1:
...
Stack1.h 1:
```

```
...
Stack1.h 5:
Stack1.h 6: class Stack
Stack1.h 7: {
Stack1.h 8: int data [ 50 ] ;
Stack1.h 9: int nElements ;
Stack1.h 10:
Stack1.h 11: public:
Stack1.h 12:
Stack1.h 13: Stack ( ) :
Stack1.h 14: nElements ( 0 )
Stack1.h 15: { }
...
Stack1.h 19: void Push ( int elem ) ;
...
Stack1.h 23: int    Pop ( ) ;
...
Stack1.h 27: int    Number ( ) ;
...
Stack1.h 31: int    Empty ( ) ;
Stack1.h 32: } ;
...
Stack1.cpp 5:
Stack1.cpp 6: void Stack :: Push ( int elem )
Stack1.cpp 7: {
Stack1.cpp 8: data [ nElements ] = elem ;
Stack1.cpp 9: nElements ++ ;
Stack1.cpp 10: }
Stack1.cpp 11:
Stack1.cpp 12: int    Stack :: Pop ( )
Stack1.cpp 13: {
Stack1.cpp 14: nElements -- ;
Stack1.cpp 15: return data [ nElements ] ;
Stack1.cpp 16: }
Stack1.cpp 17:
Stack1.cpp 18: int    Stack :: Number ( )
Stack1.cpp 19: {
Stack1.cpp 20: return nElements ;
Stack1.cpp 21: }
Stack1.cpp 22:
Stack1.cpp 23: int    Stack :: Empty ( )
Stack1.cpp 24: {
Stack1.cpp 25: return ( nElements == 0 ) ;
Stack1.cpp 26: }
...
```

```
sta1-use.cpp 10: void main ( )
sta1-use.cpp 11: {
sta1-use.cpp 12: Stack intStack ;
sta1-use.cpp 13:
sta1-use.cpp 14:
sta1-use.cpp 15:
sta1-use.cpp 16: intStack.Push ( 500 ) ;
sta1-use.cpp 17: intStack.Push ( 1992 ) ;
sta1-use.cpp 18: intStack.Push ( 33 ) ;
sta1-use.cpp 19: intStack.Push ( 1024 ) ;
sta1-use.cpp 20:
sta1-use.cpp 21:
sta1-use.cpp 22:
sta1-use.cpp 23: while ( ! intStack.Empty ( ) )
sta1-use.cpp 24: cout << intStack.Pop ( ) << endl ;
sta1-use.cpp 25: }
```

The advantage of this approach is the possibility of declaring a stack containing other elements just by modifying the *#define* directive. For example, to have a stack of characters, you can change the line to

```
#define TYPE char
```

and then include the files describing the generic class. However, you cannot have both those definitions in the same program, since the compiler and the linker can have serious problems distinguishing between the classes, which have the same name. This problem can be easily overcome using the template construct instead of the macro definition.

Emulating Genericity with Inheritance and Polymorphism

Another possible emulation of genericity can be obtained by using inheritance. If you define a container class (for example a stack) capable of handling pointers to a class of objects, it can be used to handle objects of any class derived from the original one. By combining the use of inheritance with polymorphism, you can obtain generic containers in C++. Unlike those based on macros, these generic containers can handle objects of different classes (that is, different data types) at the same time, yielding both a greater flexibility and also some additional risks. The risks result from the explicit type-casting that is needed to restore the original class of the objects retrieved from the container.

The following three listings contain the same example implemented in the previous section, but this time using inheritance and polymorphism instead of macros. The interface of the class also contains the definition of a class for generic objects.

```
// file STACK2.H                                        10/STACK2
// interface of a generic stack of objects of class GenericObject
// the stack is made of an array of 50 pointers
```

```
// defines the class for the generic objects

class GenericObject
{ } ;

class Stack
{
   GenericObject *  data [50];
   int              nElements;

public:
   Stack ( ) :
      nElements ( 0 )
      { }

      // adds an element to the stack

   void  Push ( GenericObject * elem ) ;

      // gets an element from the stack

   GenericObject * Pop ( ) ;

      // number of elements actually on the stack

   int    Number ( ) ;

      // is the stack empty?

   int    Empty ( ) ;
} ;
```

The second file contains the definition of the member functions, which corresponds exactly to those of the "macro" version:

```
// file STACK2.CPP                                        10/STACK2
// member function definition of a Stack of generic objects

#include "Stack2.h"

void Stack :: Push ( GenericObject * elem )
   {
      data [ nElements ] = elem ;
      nElements ++ ;
   }
```

```
GenericObject * Stack :: Pop ( )
    {
        nElements -- ;
        return data [ nElements ] ;
    }

int Stack :: Number ( )
    {
        return nElements ;
    }

int Stack :: Empty ( )
    {
        return ( nElements == 0 ) ;
    }
```

Also, the main function of this example resembles that of the previous one. Notice, however, the definition of a class derived from the class *GenericObject* used by the stack, and the type cast that is needed to access data once it has been retrieved.

```
// file STA2-USE.CPP                                          10/STACK2
// example of an instance of the Stack of generic objects

#include <iostream.h>

#include "Stack2.cpp"

// defines a class for integers, derived from the generic one

class IntObject : public GenericObject
{
public:
    int     data;

    IntObject ( int n ) :
        data ( n )
        { }
} ;


void main ( )
{
    // defines a generic stack

    Stack     genericStack;
```

```
// adds values to the stack

genericStack.Push ( new IntObject ( 500 ) ) ;
genericStack.Push ( new IntObject ( 1992 ) ) ;
genericStack.Push ( new IntObject ( 33 ) ) ;
genericStack.Push ( new IntObject ( 1024 ) ) ;

// prints the elements while emptying the stack: since the Pop function
// returns a pointer to a GenericObject, a type cast is needed to access it

while ( ! genericStack.Empty ( ) )
    cout << ( (IntObject *) genericStack.Pop () ) -> data << endl;
}
```

NOTE: The cast at the end of the previous program is dangerous, or *unsafe*. You can use RTT1 (see Chapter 12) to make a safe cast instead.

As we will return to the differences between inheritance and genericity, remember the example we have just seen, since we will compare it to the following one, that defines a generic class using the proper construct: templates.

Template Classes

The definition of a template class in C++ is quite simple. Before the class keyword you place a *template* clause, which usually has the following form:

```
template <class T>
```

The *class* keyword inside angle brackets indicates that *T* is a generic type: however, *T* is not limited to classes or user-defined data types, and can even take the value of arithmetic data types (integer, char, float, and so on). The class definition following a template clause can contain references to the generic type *T*, as in the following code in which the interface of the *Stack* class has been rewritten with templates:

```
// file STACK3.H                                    10/STACK3
// interface of a class template to define stacks
// ( the example is similar to the previous versions with macros and inheritance )

template <class T>
class Stack
{
    T     data [ 50 ] ;
    int   nElements ;
```

```
public:
    Stack ( ) :
        nElements ( 0 )
        { }

        // adds an element to the stack

    void   Push ( T elem ) ;

        // gets an element from the stack

    T      Pop ( ) ;

        // number of elements actually on the stack

    int    Number ( ) ;

        // is the stack empty?

    int    Empty ( ) ;
} ;
```

The external definition of the member functions of the class must be preceded by the same template clause of the class interface. Any reference to the class following the template clause can have the form *Stack <T>*.

```
// file STACK3.CPP                                              10/STACK3
// member function definition of template class Stack

#include "Stack3.h"

// note the peculiar syntax of the external member function definition for templates

template <class T>
void   Stack <T> :: Push ( T elem )
    {
        data [ nElements ] = elem ;
        nElements ++ ;
    }

template <class T>
T   Stack <T> :: Pop ( )
    {
        nElements -- ;
        return data [ nElements ] ;
    }
```

```
template <class T>
int Stack <T> :: Number ( )
    {
        return nElements ;
    }

template <class T>
int Stack <T> :: Empty ( )
    {
        return ( nElements == 0 ) ;
    }
```

To define objects of this class, you need to instantiate the class by providing values for the template parameters, as in the following examples that resemble the macro version:

```
// file STA3-USE.CPP                                      10/STACK3
// example of an instance of class Stack

#include <iostream.h>
#include "Stack3.cpp"

void main ( )
{
    // definition of a stack of integral numbers

    Stack <int> intStack ;

    // adds values to the stack

    intStack.Push ( 500 ) ;
    intStack.Push ( 1992 ) ;
    intStack.Push ( 33 ) ;
    intStack.Push ( 1024 ) ;

    // prints the elements while emptying the stack

    while ( ! intStack.Empty ( ) )
        cout << intStack.Pop ( ) << endl ;
}
```

So, what is the difference between this program and the first version that used macros? Almost nothing. In fact, "you can think of a template as a clever kind of macro that obeys the scope, naming, and type rules of C++." [Stroustrup 91A] This quote points out that templates effectively work in a way similar to macros: the compiler generates one copy of the code of the generic member functions for any different instance of the template class. On the other hand, templates provide a higher degree of security in type checking, code linkage, and so on.

It's also important to mention that when you create functions for the different template arguments, the resulting code does not need any run time mechanism to execute templates. The speed of the resulting code is the same as the speed of a corresponding code written by a programmer. At the same time, the size of the program is not always reduced by using templates in place of defining several classes, since every function using template parameters is actually duplicated once for every actual template class instance.

You can declare several different instances of a template class in a single source file. For example, you can use the template version of the stack in the following program (whereas the macro version cannot be used, and the polymorphic version could cause serious problems) to declare several stacks at the same time:

```
// file STA-MULT.CPP                                          10/STACK3
// example of three template instances of class Stack

#include <iostream.h>
// includes output manipulators:
#include <iomanip.h>
#include "Stack3.cpp"

void main ( )
{
    // defines a stack of integral numbers and two of floating
    // point numbers with different precision

    Stack <int>       intStack ;
    Stack <float>     floatStack ;
    Stack <double>  doubleStack ;

    // adds the same values to the three stacks

    intStack.Push ( 500.01 ) ;
    floatStack.Push ( 500.01 ) ;
    doubleStack.Push ( 500.01 ) ;

    intStack.Push ( 1992 ) ;
    floatStack.Push ( 1992 ) ;
    doubleStack.Push ( 1992 ) ;

    intStack.Push ( 33.333333333333333 ) ;
    floatStack.Push ( 33.333333333333333 ) ;
    doubleStack.Push ( 33.333333333333333 ) ;
```

```
intStack.Push ( 1024.1024 ) ;
floatStack.Push ( 1024.1024 ) ;
doubleStack.Push ( 1024.1024 ) ;

cout  << endl << "Contents of three stacks having a different data type"
       << endl << " ( the same values have been inserted ) " << endl ;

// prints the elements while emptying the stack

while ( ! intStack.Empty ( ) )
    cout  << "int: "          << setw ( 8 )      << intStack.Pop ( )
          << "\t float: "     << setw ( 12 )     << floatStack.Pop ( )
          << "\t double: "    << setw ( 12 )     << doubleStack.Pop ( )
          << endl ;
}
```

This program produces the following output:

```
Contents of three stacks having a different data type
(the same values have been inserted)
int:   1024     float: 1024.102417     double:  1024.1024
int:   33       float: 33.333332       double:  33.333333
int:   1992     float: 1992            double:  1992
int:   500      float: 500.01001       double:  500.01
```

It's easy to see that any object has its own operations, providing the proper type conversion. Inserting the same elements in the three stacks results in different stored values. If you had used a polymorphic stack, instead, you would have risked mixing the types of the different elements.

Type Compatibility Issues

After the previous example, you might have some doubts about the type compatibility rules between templates. Since an integer can be assigned to a float, could an *intStack* be assigned to a *floatStack*? Although it might seem strange, the answer is no.

In fact, there is not a proper way to automatically handle the conversion between the two classes, as would likewise be true if the classes had been defined separately. A template class doesn't define a type; the type depends on the different instances. Two instances have the same type only if they are defined with parameters having exactly the same values, as shown in the following code:

```
// file TEMPCOMP.CPP                                        10/TYPECOMP
// a program showing template compatibility rules

// definition of a simple template class containing a single element
```

```
template <class T> class Single
{
    T   data ;

public:
    Single ( )
        { }

    void  Set ( T el )
        {
            data = el ;
        }

    T  Get ( )
        {
            return data ;
        }
} ;

void main ( )
{
    // defines some "singles"

    Single <int>    oneInt ;
    oneInt.Set ( 5 ) ;

    Single <float> oneFloat ;
    oneFloat.Set ( 4.9 ) ;

    Single <int>    secondInt ;
    secondInt.Set ( 8 ) ;

    // assignment between instances of the template class are possible
    // only if they are type compatible

    oneInt = secondInt ; // CORRECT
    oneInt = oneFloat ;   // WRONG!!
}
```

If the code of the template class performs operations on the generic type, they must all be allowed on the actual type passed as a parameter. Before defining an instance of a template, the compiler checks that the actual type complies with this rule. Otherwise, it issues an error message and stops the compilation. But these error messages are somewhat misleading, since they refer to the use of the operation and not to the tentative instance with the wrong parameters.

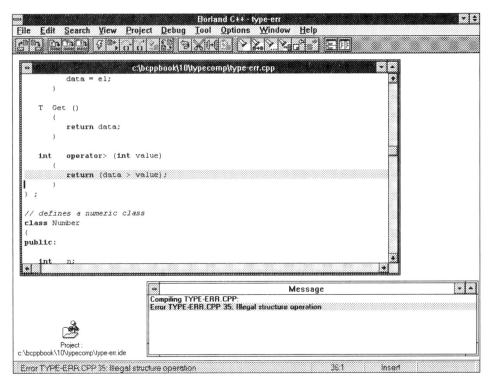

Figure 10.1 The misleading compilation error of program TYPE-ERR.CPP

For example, the following code produces the error warning "*Illegal structure operation,*" as shown in Figure 10.1. (As the figure shows, this example will also work with Turbo C++ for Windows.)

```
// file TYPE-ERR.CPP                                    10/TYPECOMP
// an example of how an error in the type parameter results
// in a misleading error message

// defines a class similar to that of the previous example ,
// having an ordering relationship defined

template <class T>
class OrdSingle
{
    T       data ;

public:
    OrdSingle ( )
        { }
```

```
void   Set ( T el )
   {
       data = el ;
   }

T      Get ( )
   {
       return data ;
   }

int    operator> ( int value )
   {
       return ( data > value ) ;
   }
} ;

// defines a numeric class

class Number
{
public:
   int    n ;
} ;

void main ( )
{
   // instantiates a couple of objects

   OrdSingle <int>   os1 ;
   OrdSingle <Number>   os2 ;
}
```

The actual error is in the second line of the main program, because the *Number* data type doesn't have a properly defined > operator. If you change its definition to the following one, the program will compile correctly:

```
// defines a numeric class ( with the > operator )

class Number
{
public:
   int    n ;
   int    operator> ( int i )
      {
          return ( n > i ) ;
      }
} ;
```

Template Arguments

Template arguments are not restricted to types, although this is their most common use. The parameters of a template can be character strings, function names, and constant expressions.

An interesting case is the use of an integer constant to define the "size" of a data structure of generic type. For example, the following code declares a generic vector of *n* elements:

```
template <class T , int n>
class Vector
{
   T  data [ n ] ;
   // ...
} ;
```

This constant argument might even have a default value, such as normal function arguments. The type compatibility rule between instances of template arguments remains almost the same: two instances are compatible if their type arguments are equal and their constant argument expressions have the same value. This rule means that the following declarations define two compatible objects:

```
Vector <float , 100>  v1 ;
Vector <float , 25 * 4>  v2 ;
```

These kinds of generic vectors, or arrays, are very useful. For example, we can rewrite the template class *Stack* without having to specify a fixed number of elements, as was the case in the previous version. Also, we can easily add a function to test if the stack is full. The interface of the class becomes the following:

```
// file STACK4.H                                          10/STACK4
// interface of a class template to define stacks
// with the number of elements defined on instantiation

template <class T , int nEl = 50> class Stack
{
   T      data [ nEl ] ;
   int    nElements ;

public:
   Stack ( ) :
      nElements ( 0 )
      { }

      // adds an element to the stack

   void  Push ( T elem ) ;
```

```
        // gets an element from the stack

    T    Pop ( ) ;

        // number of elements actually on the stack

    int    Number ( ) ;

        // is the stack empty?

    int    Empty ( ) ;

        // is the stack full?

    int    Full ( ) ;
} ;
```

The definition of the member functions uses a syntax even more complex than usual to specify the two template parameters, as shown below:

```
// file STACK4.CPP                                          10/STACK4
// member function definition of template class Stack
// with an undefined number of elements

#include "Stack4.h"

template <class T , int nEl>
void  Stack <T , nEl> :: Push ( T elem )
    {
        data [ nElements ] = elem ;
        nElements ++ ;
    }

template <class T , int nEl>
T     Stack <T , nEl> :: Pop ( )
    {
        nElements -- ;
        return data [ nElements ] ;
    }

template <class T , int nEl>
int    Stack <T , nEl> :: Number ( )
    {
        return nElements ;
    }
```

```
template <class T , int nEl>
int     Stack <T , nEl> :: Empty ( )
   {
       return ( nElements == 0 ) ;
   }

template <class T , int nEl>
int     Stack <T , nEl> :: Full ( )
   {
       return ( nElements == nEl ) ;
   }
```

An interesting property of this class is that it's "compatible" with the previous one, since the second parameter can be omitted using the default value as in the following example:

```
// portion of file STA4-USE.CPP                      10/STACK4
// example of an instance of template class Stack
// with a generic number of elements

#include "Stack4.cpp"

void main ( )
{
    // definition of a stack of integral numbers ( default size )

    Stack <int> intStack ;

    // defines a little stack of doubles

    Stack <double , 4>  miniStack ;
}
```

Template Functions

In addition to template classes, C++ allows you to define template functions in a very similar manner. A template function defines a family of functions, each operating with a particular data type. Unlike template classes, however, template functions do not need to be instantiated: the parameters of the function call determine which version of the function has to be executed. This can be seen as an extension of function overloading, the difference being that the various functions are generated automatically, as shown below:

```
// file TEMP-F1.CPP                                   10/TEMP-FUN
// example of template function declaration and use
```

```
# include <io stream.h>
template <class T> T min ( T a , T b )
{
    if ( a < b )
        return a ;
    else
        return b ;
}

void main ( )
{
    char   c1 = 'W' , c2 = 'h' ;
    int    n1 = 23 , n2 = 67 ;

    cout <<min ( c1 , c2 )<< end/ ;
    cout <<min ( n1 , n2 )<< end/ ;
}
```

However, problems can arise from this situation. Instead of operating type conversions on the parameters, the compiler generates different versions of a function even for compatible types. When you have more than one parameter, this can lead to type errors. If both versions are declared as type *T* parameters, they must match exactly. You can neither generate a *min (int, char)* instance of the template function nor convert *char* to *int* and use the *min (int, int)* version. The following code demonstrates this situation:

10/TEMP-FUN

```
// file TEMP-F2.CPP
// example of template function instantiation errors
# include <io stream.h>
template <class T> T min ( T a , T b )
{
    if ( a < b )
        return a ;
    else
        return b ;
}

void main ( )
{
    char   c1 = 'W' , c2 = 'h' ;
    int    n1 = 23 , n2 = 67 ;
    long   n3 = 10000 ;
    float  n4 = 34.23 , n5 = 7.77 ;

    cout <<min ( c1 , c2 )<< end/ ;
    cout <<min ( n1 , n2 )<< end/ ;
    cout <<min ( c1 , n1 )<< end/ ;  // ERROR
```

```
        cout <<min ( n2 , n3)<< end/ ;   // ERROR
        cout <<min ( n3 , n4 )<< end/ ;  // ERROR
        cout <<min ( n4 , n5 )<< end/ ;
    }
```

Compiling this program generates three errors, as shown in Figure 10.2.

Of course, template functions can also be used with classes. As usual, the class should define the operation performed on the object in the template function. In the following program, the *min* template function operates on the elements of a numeric class.

```
// file TEMP-F3.CPP                                          10/TEMP-FUN
// example of template function used with a class
# include <io stream.h>
template <class T> T min ( T a , T b )
{
    if ( a < b )
        return a ;
    else
        return b ;
}

class Number
{
    long   num ;
public:
    Number ( long n ) :
        num ( n )
        { }

    long   Value ( )
        {
            return num ;
        }

    operator < ( Number n2 )
        {
            return num < n2.Value ( ) ;
        }
} ;

void main ( )
{
    Number nn1 = 12 ;
    Number nn2 = 18 ;
    Number nn3 = min ( nn1 , nn2 ) ;
} cout <<nn3.Value ()<<end1;
```

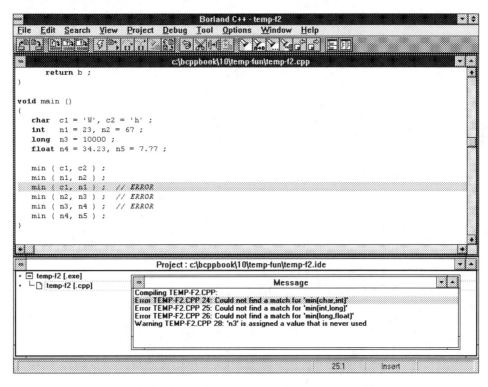

Figure 10.2 The compilation error of program TEMP-F2.CPP

Function RunSpeaking Revisited

In Chapter 8, we have already met a function operating on different data types. In fact, using polymorphism, we were able to pass the function a pointer to an object of a derived class (passing the pointer through a parameter). The function, *RunSpeaking,* had a "pointer to *Animal*" or "reference to *Animal*" parameter, but you could easily pass a pointer or a reference to one of the classes derived by *Animal*, such as those describing dogs and cows.

Now, you can use genericity to obtain a similar effect. The following program, which resembles the *Running.cpp* source file of Chapter 8, shows you how to do so.

// file RUNSPEAK.CPP   **10/RUNSPEAK**
// template version of RunSpeaking

```
#include <iostream.h>
#include <stdlib.h>
#include "animal.h"
#include "cow_dog.h"
```

```
template <class T>
void RunSpeaking (T t, int nSteps)
{
    randomize ( ) ;
    for (int i = 0; i < nSteps; ++i)
    {
        int x = random (5) - 2 ;
        int y = random (5) - 2 ;

        t.JumpBy (x, y) ;
        t.Speak ( ) ;
    }
}

void main ( )
{
    // the same main of the running.cpp
    // example of chapter 8
    Cow cow (Point (20, 10)) ;
    Dog dog (Point (10, 20)) ;

    RunSpeaking (cow, 5) ;
    RunSpeaking (dog, 28) ;
}
```

Again, to compile this program you need a project containing the above file, the *animal.cpp* and the *cow_dog.cpp* source files of Chapter 8. Three header files of that chapter are required, too: *point.h*, *animal.h*, and *cow_dog.h*.

The difference between this and the previous program is that the class for the dogs does not need to be derived from the one of the animals. You can pass as a parameter to the template function any class with the member functions *JumpBy* and *Speak*.

Another difference is that the first version of the program declared one *RunSpeaking* function, while this second actually defines two of them. However, the output of each program is exactly equivalent.

Templates vs. Polymorphism

After the previous example, you might wonder what the differences are between polymorphism and genericity. Can they be substituted for each other? And which one is better?

Adding to the ambiguity, while the two concepts are theoretically very different, in some situations they are practically interchangeable.

Let's look again at the definitions of the two concepts.

A function is polymorphic if one of its parameters can assume different data types, which must be derived from that of the formal parameter (the parameter present in the declaration). Any function having as a parameter a pointer to a class can be a polymorphic function and can be used with different data types. Polymorphic functions can be seen as a bonus for the type compatibility rules of the language.

A function is a template function only if it is preceded by a proper template clause. This definition means that these functions are designed, defined, and implemented with genericity in mind. Therefore, writing a template function implies a higher degree of attention in making it truly generic, avoiding any dependence on data types, numeric constants, and so on.

A template function is just a template—a pattern—and not a true function. Although it doesn't need to be instantiated, this process is done automatically by the compiler for any different call. As a result, you have a family of overloaded functions, having all the same name and different parameters. In other words, the template clause is an automatic generator of overloaded functions.

Polymorphic functions are functions that can be executed dynamically with parameters of different types. On the other hand, template functions are functions that can be compiled statically in different versions to comply with parameters of different data types.

If you look at the practical uses of the two constructs, you can see that:

- Template functions also work with arithmetic types.
- Polymorphic functions must use pointers or references.
- Polymorphic genericity is limited to hierarchies (and is thus constrained).
- Template genericity is unconstrained.
- Template functions require as a type a class that has defined all of the member functions used in the template function, while the constraints of polymorphism ensure that the member functions are present.
- Both check the correctness of the calls at compilation time.
- Templates tend to generate a bigger executable, since functions are duplicated.

Genericity vs. Inheritance

When we say that genericity and polymorphism can often be used interchangeably, we don't refer only to personal experience. A lot of theoretical discussion is going on about these two constructs and their relative properties and powers of expression. It has been shown that inheritance can be used to mimic genericity, while the opposite is often, but not always, true (see, among others, [Meyer 88]). This statement goes beyond the scope of this book, so we will not delve further into it. But remember that both inheritance and genericity can often be used to design and implement a group of classes.

One example is the definition of container classes. As you will see in Chapter 15, Borland used polymorphism for the first version of its Container Class Library, but now that templates are available has introduced a generic version of the library, which uses templates.

So the choice between the two constructs remains an open issue. Some programming languages support only one of the two ways to achieve genericity, and the supporters of those languages want to demonstrate that the other is almost useless. The best thing, instead, is to have both of them, and use the one that better suits the problem you are trying to solve. Often, the one that fits more easily into the design and can be easily implemented is the best choice.

POINTS TO CONSIDER

1. Implement a generic container class (different from a stack) using the three methods you have seen: macros, inheritance, and templates. Then, use this generic class in different situations, highlighting the pluses and minuses of the different methods.

2. Compare the definition of templates of C++ with the similar constructs of other programming languages you know.

3. In some cases, genericity can be used to replace inheritance. Find an example in this book in which derivation can be replaced by templates.

4. Template classes usually have a type parameter, but that is not a requirement. For example, you can define polygons with any number of sides by defining a class that contains the array of their vertexes. Implement a similar class.

5. Template functions are a very useful, often disregarded construct. Find some examples in which they are worthwhile.

11

Handling Exceptions and Errors

*An exception is an event caused by some abnormal condition
requiring special attention. [Coplien]*

Computers do not have unlimited resources and computer programs are not always
perfect, since programmers aren't perfect, either. Therefore, it's certainly better to work
with the idea in mind that the computer can run out of memory, that the hard disk might
fail, and that our programs might have bugs (the last problem being the most frequent).

To account for the possible erroneous behavior of an application, many programming languages have introduced an *exception handling* mechanism, which can add
robustness to program design and coding. Since the ANSI C++ committee has accepted this new language feature only recently, Borland C++ 4.0 is the first version of
this compiler including exception handling.

The Basics of Exceptions

There are alternative ways to cope with errors, as we will explore in some detail in the
second part of Chapter 14, including extensive testing of return values and various
kinds of *jumps* out of the misbehaving function. The C language includes in its standard libraries (see header assert.h) even an *assert* macro, which allows us to jump out
of the program when an abnormal condition is encountered.

As we will see, none of these approaches is completely satisfactory. If you make
lots of tests you just add new code, increasing the complexity of a program, slowing it
down, and introducing the possibility of new errors. If you jump out of a function the
stack remains *polluted*, and the destructors of the objects on the stack are not called.

Using the exception handling feature of C++, instead, a function can signal a
problem to its calling code; this can handle the problem or let the *message* reach its
calling code, and so on. Each block, however, is terminated properly, *cleaning* the
stack and calling the destructors of the object that go out of scope.

327

Eventually, if nobody handles the problem the program is terminated. Let's see the syntactical basis of exception handling in C++. There are three keywords:

- *Try* delimits a block of code that may raise exceptions.
- *Throw* raises the exception.
- *Catch* handles the exception of the preceding *try* block.

Here is a very short example. A function requires one of its parameters not to be zero, in order to avoid an error, and tests for this condition. If the condition is matched, it *throws* an exception, thus avoiding executing the rest of its code. In the main program the call of this function is inside a *try* block: If an exception is raised during the execution of one of the functions called inside the block, the *catch* statements at the end are searched for a parameter type matching the one used in the *throw* statement. If a match is found, then control is passed to the block following the corresponding *catch*.

```
// file BASIC.CPP                                        11/BASIC
// Basic exception handling example

#include <iostream.h>

// declares a function, requiring two integer values
// the second must be nonzero
int divide (int a, int b)
{
    if (b == 0)
        throw ("Divide by zero") ;
    return (a / b) ;
}

void main ( )
{
    int a, b ;

    cout << "Input two values to divide: " ;
    cin >> a >> b ;

    try
    {
        cout << a << " / " << b << " = " << divide (a, b) << endl ;
    }
    catch (const char * text)
    {
        cout << "ERROR: " << text << endl ;
    }
}
```

When you run the program with a nonzero value for *b*, its output might be:

```
Input two values to divide: 10 2
10 / 2 = 5
```

However, if you run the program using 0 as the second input value, the result is:

```
Input two values to divide: 10 0
ERROR: Divide by zero
```

On the other hand, if you remove or comment the *try* and *catch* statements in the main function, the exception is not trapped and the program stops, displaying a *system message box* with the text: *BASIC.EXE—Program Aborted.*

➤ *Note:* The Borland C++ 4.0 compiler allows you to enable or disable exception handling. Of course, to build and run the examples of this chapter, the exceptions must be on (as they are by default). You can also optionally turn off the stack unwinding mechanism, which should be done with extreme care.

This example is very simple: We could have made almost the same code without exceptions. The second version of the program, however, gives a better feeling for this mechanism. As you can see in the following source code, if an exception is handled inside a loop, the loop can continue to execute even when it is encountered.

```
// file BASIC2.CPP
// Basic exception handling - second example

#include <iostream.h>

// declares a function, requiring two integer values
// the second must be nonzero
int divide (int a, int b)
{
    if (b == 0)
        throw ("Divide by zero") ;
    return (a / b) ;
}

void main ( )
{
    int a, b ;

    cout << "This is an integer dividing machine!" << endl
```

11/BASIC

```
                << "(Input 0 as first value to end)" << endl << endl ;
    cout << "Input two values: " ;
    cin >> a >> b ;

    while (a != 0)
    {
        try
        {
            cout << a << " / " << b << " = " ;
            cout << divide (a, b) << endl ;
        }
        catch (const char * text)
        {
            cout << "ERROR: " << text << endl ;
        }

        // ask for new values
        cout << endl ;
        cout << "Input two values: " ;
        cin >> a >> b ;
    }
}
```

With this code you can obtain the output shown in Figure 11.1.

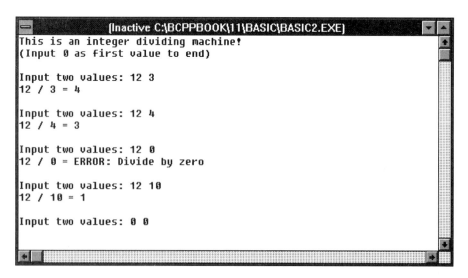

Figure 11.1 An example of the output of the BASIC2 program

Throwing Objects and Catching Types

"You throw an object and catch a type": This short description (heard from Pete Becker of Borland) describes most of the C++ implementation of exception handling. The *throw* expression, in fact, requires an object of a user-defined data type, a predefined arithmetic type, a string, a message and so forth. The corresponding *catch* statement requires a user-defined class, a parameter of an arithmetic type, a *const char **, an *xmsg* class and so forth.

➤ *Note:* The current C++ language standard *draft* defines a specific class for exceptions based on messages to be used instead of *char** or even strings. This class is called *xmsg* and encapsulates a string to describe its message.

The *xmsg* class has a couple of constructors, an assignment operator, and a *why* member function returning the message (a string). See the header file *except.h* and the compiler documentation for more details on this class.

Notice also that *xmsg* serves as a base class for the *xalloc* standard exception, which is raised when no memory is available. See the last section of this chapter for a discussion on memory exceptions.

The easiest way might be to throw an integer, perhaps defining some constant codes:

```
const int ZERODIVISION = 4;

int divide (int a, int b)
{
    if (b == 0) throw (ZERODIVISION);
    return (a/b);
}
...
catch (int err_number)
{
    if (err_number == ZERODIVISION )
        cout << "Error number " << err_number << ": Division by 0" << endl;
}
```

This is really much better than the previous version using strings, although it is somewhat similar. The problem lies in the fact that if you always use numbers (or strings) for each kind of error, the same *catch* is called each time, regardless of the error. Using switch statements to distinguish among the various cases is slow and error prone.

An advantage offered by the syntax of the exception handling construct is that if a *catch* statement is unable to handle a specific exception (one of the numbers), it can *reraise* it, propagating it to an outer *try* block and eventually propagate back to the system level.

The real power of C++ exceptions handling lies in another *exceptional* feature: Namely that in C++ exception handling is designed to be used with classes and objects.

With this in mind, our example can become:

```
// exception class:
class ZeroDivision { } ;

int divide (int a, int b)
{
    if (b == 0) throw ZeroDivision ( ) ;
    return (a / b) ;
}
...
catch (ZeroDivision)
{
    cout << "Error: Devide by zero" << endl ;
}
```

➤   *Note:* Exception class objects are often passed by copy from the *throw* statement to their handler (the corresponding *catch* statement). Therefore, if these classes are complex, they might require a proper copy constructor.

The **Throw** *Statement*

Let us now examine the syntax of exception handling with some detail, starting with the *throw* statement. After the definition of a class representing exceptions:

```
class ExceptClass
{
    // some data and/or functions
    // or nothing
};
```

you can raise an exception of this kind passing an object of that class:

```
void f ( )
{
    ExceptClass exeObject ;
    ...
    if (...)
        throw exeObject ;
}
```

This can also be done using a temporary object as in:

```
void f ( )
{
    ...
    if (...)
        throw ExceptClass ( ) ;
}
```

An alternative solution is to pass a pointer:

```
void f ( )
{
    ...
    if (...)
        throw new ExceptClass ;
}
```

In the first case a copy of the object is made and passed to the corresponding handler; in the second case the handler should remember to delete the object from the heap. In both cases, the program searches for a proper handler matching the exception that has been raised. If a handler is found in one of the *surrounding blocks* (one of the blocks or functions currently on the stack), then that handler is called; otherwise control is given to the *terminate* function, which by default ends the program.

The *throw* statement must always have a parameter indicating which object the exception refers to, with the exclusion of *reraise* statement. A *reraise* statement is a plain *throw* with no further exception object specified:

```
catch (ExceptClass exObj)
    {
    ...
    if (...)
        throw ;      // pass the exception to the next handler
    }
```

To *reraise* an exception it must currently exist (otherwise the *terminate* function is called). In practice the use of this construct is limited to *catch* blocks.

A second use of the *throw* keyword is to specify which exceptions a function can throw. The definition

```
void f ( ) throw (ExceptClass)
{
    ...
}
```

indicates that only the *ExceptClass* kind of exceptions can propagate out of the *f* function. This means that the function *f* itself or other functions called by *f* can raise any kind of exceptions, which must all be *catched* inside *f*. The interface specification of the exceptions a function can throw is a very important portion of the contract a function and its caller establish (see Chapter 14 for more details on this concept). A function can specify zero, one, or several type of exceptions:

```
void g ( ) throw ( )
{
    ...
}

void f ( ) throw (ExceptClass)
{
    ...
}

void h ( ) throw (Error, NoMemory, ExceptClass*)
{
    ...
}

void j ( )
{
    ...
}
```

The function *g* can propagate no exceptions, functions *f* and *h* should throw only objects (or pointers to objects) of the specified classes, and function *j* has no limit. If an exception of a kind different from the declared ones is raised and not handled inside of the function, the program calls a special function, unexpected. Of course, any kind of exception can be raised in each of these functions provided it is *catched* in the function itself.

➤   *Note:* Both the *terminate* and the *unexpected* functions can be modified by a program using the *set_terminate* and the *set_unexpected* functions, respectively.

The Catch *Statement*

The use of the *catch* statement is somewhat simpler. This statement can follow only a *try* block and can have one parameter or the ellipsis:

```
try
{
```

```
    // code
}
catch (ExceptClass exObj)
{
    // handler for the ExceptClass exception type
}

try
{
    // code
}
catch (...)
{
    // handler for any kind of exception
}
```

A try block can be followed by more than one catch statements. If a *try* block is followed by more than one exception handlers, they are evaluated in the order they are encountered. If two *catch* statements match with the thrown object only the first will be executed.

NOTE: If you think that the event of two matches is quite peculiar, think about it twice. Exception classes often form hierarchies, and there might be both a handler for the base class and one for a derived class. Since the handler for the base class can be used with the object of the derived class, their order is really very important.

Handling and Correcting Exceptions

Besides warning the programmer (not the user, who shall never see them), exceptions can be used to handle errors, and give a chance to correct the situation. Let us show a very simple but instructive example. Suppose that our *Divide* function (see the first section of this chapter) can work only with positive values: When a value is negative we can change its sign, and try again. Since this event can take place twice (i.e. once for each of the two operands), we need a way to run the *try* block over and over. A good choice is to include this piece of code inside a function which makes the division handling the negative values, *divideCheck*. The complexity of this examples depends on the parameters, which are all passed by reference to allow us to access to the original memory location when we want to change the sign of one of the two numbers. The resulting code is certainly not easy to grasp, but quite powerful.

```
// file BASIC3.CPP                                          11/BASIC
// Basic exception handling - third example: correct-and-retry
```

```cpp
#include <iostream.h>

class ZeroDivision { } ;
class Negative
{
public:
    int* pValue;
    Negative (int* pn) :
        pValue (pn)
        { }
} ;

int divide (int& a, int& b)
{
    if (b == 0)
        throw ZeroDivision ( ) ;
    if (a < 0)
        throw Negative (&a) ;
    if (b < 0)
        throw Negative (&b) ;

    return (a / b) ;
}

int divideCheck (int& a, int &b)
{
    int n ;

    try
    {
        n = divide (a, b) ;
    }
    catch (Negative neg)
    {
        // reverse the value...
        *neg.pValue = - *neg.pValue ;

        // warns the user
        cout << "A number was negative... reversing it to positive" << endl ;

        // tries again
        n = divideCheck (a, b) ;
    }
```

```
        return n ;
    }

void main ( )
{
    int a, b ;

    cout << "This is a dividing machine for positive integers!" << endl
            << "(Input 0 as first value to end)" << endl << endl ;
    cout << "Input two values: " ;
    cin >> a >> b ;

    while (a != 0)
    {
        try
        {
            int c = divideCheck (a, b) ;
            cout << a << " / " << b << " = " << c << endl ;
        }
        catch (ZeroDivision)
        {
            cout << "Error: Division by 0" << endl ;
        }
        catch (Negative neg)
        {
            // this code should never be reached
            cout << "Ouch!" << endl ;
            throw ;      // terminate!
        }

        // ask for new values
        cout << endl ;
        cout << "Input two values: " ;
        cin >> a >> b ;
    }
}
```

Although this example is quite interesting to understand how a *correct-and-retry* strategy can be used with exceptions (see the output in Figure 11.2), do not use it as a guideline. Exceptions have a specific role in programming, and they are not meant to be used as general *flow-control* statements, as in the above example, or to check for the input. Exceptions should be limited to handle *exeptional and uncommon* situations due to external factors or errors.

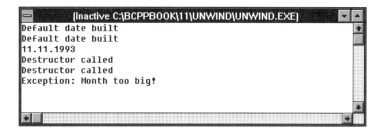

```
[Inactive C:\BCPPBOOK\11\BASIC\BASIC3.EXE]
This is a dividing machine for positive integers!
(Input 0 as first value to end)

Input two values: 24 6
24 / 6 = 4

Input two values: 24 -3
A number was negative... reversing it to positive
24 / 3 = 8

Input two values: -24 6
A number was negative... reversing it to positive
24 / 6 = 4

Input two values: -24 -2
A number was negative... reversing it to positive
A number was negative... reversing it to positive
24 / 2 = 12

Input two values: 12 0
Error: Division by 0

Input two values: 0 0
```

Figure 11.2   The output of the *BASIC3* program

```
[Inactive C:\BCPPBOOK\11\UNWIND\UNWIND.EXE]
Default date built
Default date built
11.11.1993
Destructor called
Destructor called
Exception: Month too big!
```

Figure 11.3 The output of the UNWIND program shows that destructors are called before the execution of the handler.

Unwinding the Stack

One of the most important aspects of exception handling in the C++ language is the so-called *stack unwinding*. When an exception is raised, it might be immediately *catched* or passed to a caller function. In the second case, if the *throw* statement is translated in a direct jump to the corresponding handler, the stack remains polluted and some *resources* may be lost. If you open a file or allocate memory in the constructor of an object, but forget to call the corresponding destructor, you run into a serious problem. On the other hand, calling the proper destructors (i.e., unwinding the stack) leaves the system in a stable state and the program can handle the situation and proceed.

The consequence of the use of exception handling in a program is that you must always request and release resources in constructors and destructors. This includes the use of *new* to allocate memory on the heap.

To verify that the stack unwinding really takes place, we can execute the following program, which produces the output of Figure 11.3:

```
// file UNWIND.CPP                                    11/UNWIND
// an example of stack-unwinding

#include <iostream.h>

class Date
{
private:
    int month ;
    int day ;
    int year ;

public:
    Date ( )
    {
        cout << "Default date built" << endl ;
    }

    ~Date ( )
    {
        cout << "Destructor called" << endl ;
    }

    void SetDate (int m, int d, int y)
    {
        if (m > 12)
            throw ("Month too big!") ;
        if (d > 31)
            throw ("Day too big!") ;

        month = m ;
        day = d ;
        year = y ;
    }

    void Print ( )
    {
        cout << month << '.' << day << '.' << year << endl ;
    }
} ;
```

```
void main ( )
{
    try
    {
        Date d1, d2 ;

        d1.SetDate (11, 11, 1993) ;
        d1.Print ( ) ;

        d2.SetDate (15, 11, 1993) ;
        d2.Print ( ) ;
    }
    catch (const char * description)
    {
        cout << "Exception: " << description << endl ;
    }
}
```

Notice the order of the execution: The destructors of the two objects are both called before the *catch* statement. In this example everything works fine, but the use of exceptions can become dangerous, particularly with existing programs.

Without using exceptions the code

```
Date d1, d2 ;

d1.SetDate (11, 11, 1993) ;
d1.Print ( ) ;

d2.SetDate (15, 11, 1993) ;
d2.Print ( ) ;
```

has the same effect as the code

```
Date *d1, *d2 ;

d1 = new Date;
d2 = new Date;

d1->SetDate (11, 11, 1993) ;
d1->Print ( ) ;

d2->SetDate (15, 11, 1993) ;
d2->Print ( ) ;

delete d1;
delete d2;
```

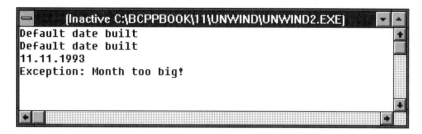

Figure 11.4 The output of the program UNWIND2 shows that the destructors are not properly called.

However if you place the second version in a *try* block, you disable the correct stack unwinding, which results in a memory error. Replacing the main function of the *unwind.cpp* program with the following code, the output of the program (see Figure 11.4) shows that destructors are not called (and memory is not properly deallocated).

```
// portion of the UNWIND2.CPP source code              11/UNWIND

void main ( )
{
   try
   {
      Date *d1, *d2 ;

      d1 = new Date;
      d2 = new Date;

      d1->SetDate (11, 11, 1993) ;
      d1->Print ( ) ;

      d2->SetDate (15, 11, 1993) ;
      d2->Print ( ) ;

      delete d1;
      delete d2;
   }
   catch (const char * description)
   {
      cout << "Exception: " << description << endl ;
   }
}
```

Again we want to stress that using exceptions requires a proper use of constructors and destructors, to avoid memory leaks and loosing resources. For example, if a program needs to open a file, the following code is dangerous when using exceptions.

```
{
    MyFile (...);
    file.openfile ( ) ;

    // various operations

    file.closefile ( ) ;
}
```

Consider the case in which the *various operations* raise an exception that is handled outside of the block. The file won't be closed, which might result in an unpredictable and potentially dangerous behavior of the program. Constructors and destructors must be properly declared and used instead:

```
class FileHandler
{
    MyFile;
public:
    FileHandler (...):
    File(...)
    {
        file.openfile ( ) ;
        // ...
    }

    ~FileHandler ( )
    {
        file.closefile ( ) ;
        // ...
    }

    // ...

} ;
```

the previous block becomes:

```
{
    FileHandler fh ;          // openfile

    // various operations

}   // destructor called      // closefile
```

With this code, in case an exception is raised, the stack unwinding mechanism grants that the file is properly closed, because the destructor of the *handler* class is always called.

As a final suggestion, consider rewriting all your code in a similar way if you want to use exceptions effectively.

Aborting a Constructor

A common problem of C++ programming is what to do when a constructor cannot properly build an object. Constructors cannot return an error code directly, because they have no return value, and using the typical C style methods (like using a pointer as parameter or a global variable to report the error) is not very elegant and error prone (you must remember to always check for error conditions).

Exceptions offer an interesting alternative. If a constructor meets some abnormal conditions (or cannot properly allocate memory or other resources) it can *throw* an exception and abort. Let us see how this works by rewriting the previous example.

```
// file CONSTRUC.CPP                                    11/CONSTRUC
// example of a constructor raising an exception

#include <iostream.h>

class Date
{
private:
    int month ;
    int day ;
    int year ;

public:
    Date (int m, int d, int y)
    {
        cout << "Entering the constructor... " << endl ;

        if (m > 12)
            throw ("Month too big!") ;
        if (d > 31)
            throw ("Day too big!") ;

        month = m ;
        day = d ;
        year = y ;

        cout << "Date object properly  built" << endl ;
    }
```

```
   ~Date ( )
   {
      cout << "Destructor called" << endl ;
   }

   void Print ( )
   {
      cout << month << '.' << day << '.' << year << endl ;
   }
} ;

void main ( )
{
   try
   {
      Date d1 (11, 11, 1993) ;
      d1.Print ( ) ;
      cout << endl ;

      Date d2 (8, 1992, 13) ;
      d2.Print ( ) ;
   }
   catch (const char * description)
   {
      cout << "Exception: " << description << endl ;
   }
}
```

Looking at the output of this program (shown in Figure 11.5) you can see that the constructor is called twice (*"Entering the constructor..."*), but only one destructor is executed when the exception is raised. This takes place because the second object was not properly built. The operations made by the constructor before the *throw* statement are *risky*, because their effect must be *un-done* manually:

```
A :: A ( )
{
   // allocate something

   if (...)
   {
      // dellocate what has already been allocated
      throw (...);
   }
}
```

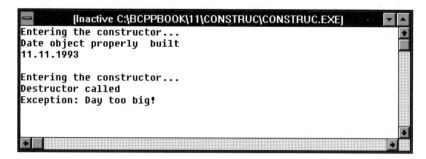

Figure 11.5 The output of the *construc* program, showing an exception raised by a constructor

This problem involves only the constructor of the class that is actually raising the exception. If this class inherits from a base class, the base class is properly destroyed, as the following program demonstrates.

```
// file CONSTR2.CPP                                    11/CONSTRUC
// example of a constructor of a derived class
// raising an exception

#include <iostream.h>

class ZeroError
{ } ;

class Base
{
protected:
    int value;

public:
    Base (int n) :
        value (n)
    {
        cout << "Base class constructor called for " << value << endl ;
    }

    ~Base ( )
    {
        cout << "Base class destructor called for " << value << endl ;
    }
} ;

class Derived : public Base
{
```

```cpp
public:
    Derived (int n) :
        Base (n)
    {
        cout << "Entering the derived class constructor for " << value << endl ;

        if (n == 0)
            throw (new ZeroError) ;

        cout << "Derived object properly  built for " << value << endl ;
    }

    ~Derived ( )
    {
        cout << "Derived class destructor called for " << value << endl ;
    }
} ;

void main ( )
{
    try
    {
        Derived  one (999) ;
        Derived  two (0) ;
        // ... operations on the objects
    }
    catch (ZeroError*)
    {
        cout << "Error: zero value!" << endl ;
    }
}
```

The output of the above example (see Figure 11.6) indicates that the *Base* class is always properly handled. Even when the constructor of its derived class throws an exception, its own destructor is properly called. As mentioned before, if you raise an exception in a constructor, you must bother to *roll-back* only the effects of the constructor itself. Since this affects only the portion that has been executed, it is quite obvious to suggest to test for error conditions and throw exceptions inside a constructor as soon as possible.

Hierarchies of Exception Classes

The use of classes to specify the *kind of* exception is very elegant, and powerful, too. Since these are user-defined data types, you can use any of the features of the C++ language to define them. These include templates, inheritance, virtual functions, and much more.

```
[Inactive C:\BCPPBOOK\11\CONSTRUC\CONSTR2.EXE]
Base class constructor called for 999
Entering the derived class constructor for 999
Derived object properly built for 999
Base class constructor called for 0
Entering the derived class constructor for 0
Base class destructor called for 0
Derived class destructor called for 999
Base class destructor called for 999
Error: zero value!
```

Figure 11.6 The output of the CONSTR2 program highlights the proper call of the destructors of a base class.

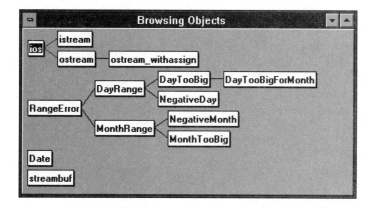

Figure 11.7 A hierarchy of RangeError classes for dates (as reported by the ObjectBrowser of the Borland C++ environment)

A very interesting example is the use of inheritance and virtual functions to define hierarchies of exception classes. For example, we can define some range error classes for the *date* class we have used in this chapter. Here is a simple example (illustrated in Figure 11.7):

```
// first part of HIERAR.CPP                          11/HIERAR

class RangeError { } ;

class MonthRange : public RangeError { } ;

class MonthTooBig : public MonthRange { } ;

class NegativeMonth : public MonthRange { } ;

class DayRange : public RangeError { } ;
```

```
class DayTooBig : public DayRange { } ;

class DayTooBigForMonth : public DayTooBig { } ;

class NegativeDay : public DayRange { } ;
```

This structure can be quite useful because if a functions throws a *DayTooBig* exception, its caller can handle it generically as a *DayRange* error. Libraries and application frameworks should make intensive use of hierarchies of exception classes, allowing the user to handle the exception with a lower or deeper detail. The following is an example (using the error classes we have just defined) of a class throwing specific exceptions and a caller looking at generic ones.

```
// second part of file HIERAR.CPP                              11/HIERAR

class Date
{
private:
    int month ;
    int day ;
    int year ;

public:
    void SetDate (int m, int d, int y)
    {
        if (m > 12)
            throw MonthTooBig ( ) ;
        if (m < 0)
            throw NegativeMonth ( ) ;
        if (d > 31)
            throw DayTooBig ( ) ;
        if (d < 0)
            throw NegativeDay ( ) ;

        month = m ;
        day = d ;
        year = y ;
    }

    void Print ( )
    {
        cout << month << '.' << day << '.' << year << endl ;
    }
} ;
```

```
void main ( )
{
   try
   {
      Date d1, d2 ;

      d1.SetDate (11, 3, 1993) ;
      d1.Print ( ) ;

      d2.SetDate (15, 11, 1993) ;
      d2.Print ( ) ;
   }
   catch (MonthRange) { cout << "Error in the month" << endl; }
   catch (DayRange) { cout << "Error in the day" << endl; }
}
```

Although this simple example should help you understand the use of exception class hierarchies, their full power comes from the possible use of virtual member functions. To make a significant example let us extend the previous one and use polymorphism for the sole purpose of choosing an output statement. This example can at least give an idea of what can be accomplished.

```
// file VIRT_EXC.CPP                                    11/HIERAR
// a hierarchy of exception classes with virtual functions

#include <iostream.h>

class RangeError
{
public:
   virtual void Print ( ) = 0;
} ;

class MonthRange : public RangeError
{
public:
   void Print ( )
   {
      cout << "Generic error in the range of the month" << endl ;
   }
} ;

class MonthTooBig : public MonthRange
{
public:
```

```cpp
    void Print ( )
      {
        cout << "Month is too big (december is the last)" << endl ;
      }
} ;

class NegativeMonth : public MonthRange
{
public:
    void Print ( )
      {
        cout << "Month is negative" << endl ;
      }
} ;

class DayRange : public RangeError
{
public:
    void Print ( )
      {
        cout << "Generic error in the value of the day" << endl ;
      }
} ;

class DayTooBig : public DayRange
{
public:
    void Print ( )
      {
        cout << "Day is too big" << endl ;
      }
} ;

class DayTooBigForMonth : public DayTooBig
{
public:
    void Print ( )
      {
        cout << "Day is too big for the specific month" << endl ;
      }
} ;

class NegativeDay : public DayRange
{
public:
```

```
        void Print ( )
        {
            cout << "Day is negative" << endl ;
        }
} ;


class Date
{
private:
    int month ;
    int day ;
    int year ;

public:
    void SetDate (int m, int d, int y)
    {
        if (m > 12)
            throw MonthTooBig ( ) ;
        if (m < 0)
            throw NegativeMonth ( ) ;
        if (m == 2 && d > 29)       // not too good
            throw DayTooBigForMonth ( ) ;
        if (d > 31)
            throw DayTooBig ( ) ;
        if (d < 0)
            throw NegativeDay ( ) ;

        month = m ;
        day = d ;
        year = y ;
    }

    void Print ( )
    {
        cout << month << '.' << day << '.' << year << endl ;
    }
} ;

void main ( )
{
    try
    {
        Date d1, d2 ;
```

```
        d1.SetDate (11, 3, 1993) ;
        d1.Print ( ) ;

        d2.SetDate (15, 11, 1993) ;
        d2.Print ( ) ;
    }
    catch (RangeError& error)
    {
        error.Print ( ) ;
    }
}
```

Allocating Memory with *new*

The role of exception handling in a programming language is particularly important when the underlying operating system (through the libraries of the compiler) is *exception-aware*: An operating system might raise an exception when there is no more memory available, or a file cannot be opened due to a disk error, and similar events.

Standard C libraries, of course, have no choice of raising exceptions. On the other hand, there are few C++ specific standard libraries (at least, for the moment), and only one of them is particularly important from our point of view: memory handling with *new* and *delete*. Before focusing on this problem, it is worthwhile to mention that version 2 of the ObjectWindows Library (included in the Borland C++ 4.0 compiler) makes an extensive use of exceptions when any of the possible Windows resources is exhausted.

The question we focus on in this section is: What happens when your program tries to allocate some memory (using *new*) and the computer hasn't got it?

In the past (before exceptions) the result of the *new* operator was a NULL (zero) pointer. Therefore if you wanted to check for an allocation, you had to write something similar to

```
pointer = new MyClass (...) ;

if (! pointer)
    // no more memory !!!
    // do not execute the following statements

// usual code
```

This approach worked fine only if you made such a check each time you allocated some memory. Of course, making all of these tests might be both tedious and error prone, since you have to figure out each time what to do if no memory is available. Worse than this, several memory allocations take place inside constructors, and it is not easy to determine how to report an error out of a constructor (without using exceptions), as we have already seen in a preceding section.

To provide a correct solution to these problems, the ANSI C++ commission has decided to add exception support to the *new* operator: This means that when no memory is available, *new* will raise an exception; to be precise, an *xalloc* exception.

This behavior is very interesting but has a defect: It breaks old code. In fact, if you run the previous code fragment, when the exception is generated the test on the return value of the pointer is skipped altogether, and if the *xalloc* exception is not handled the program will stop. To avoid having to change the old code, you can choose to use the older behavior of the *new* operator resetting the *new handler* function with:

```
set_new_handler (0)
```

The same function can be used to set a specific user-provided handler, which can try to free some memory instead of throwing the exception.

However, if you are writing new code, the advantage of exceptions over the test of the *new* return value is great, (although the following small program cannot really show it).

```
// file XALLOC.CPP                                     11/XALLOC
// First example of a failed memory allocation exception
// Compile this program with EasyWin target, using small memory model

// header file except.h defines the xalloc class
#include <except.h>
#include <iostream.h>

class BigClass
{
public:
    char bigText [5000] ;
    // 5KByte of text
} ;

void main ( )
{
    BigClass *      hugeArray [20] ;
    int i ;

    try
    {
        // try to allocate
        for (i = 0; i < 20; i++)
        {
            hugeArray [i] = new BigClass ;
            cout << "Memory allocated for element " << i << endl ;
        }
```

```
        // some code...
        cout << endl ;
        cout << "All requested memory allocated..." << endl ;
        cout << endl ;

        // free the memory
        for (i = 0; i < 20; i++)
        {
            delete hugeArray [i] ;
            cout << "Memory de-allocated for element " << i << endl ;
        }


    }
    catch (xalloc)
    {
        cout << "No more memory for element " << i << endl ;
        for (int j = 0; j < i; j++)
        {
            delete hugeArray [j] ;
            cout << "Memory de-allocated for element " << j << endl ;
        }
    }
}
```

Building this program (which has an *EasyWin* target) with the small memory model, all the memory allocations take place in the default data segment of the application, which has a maximum size of 64 KBytes, and where there is not enough space for 20 blocks of 5 Kbytes (i.e., for 100 KBytes). See Figure 11.8 for the output of this program, and try to change the size of the *BigClass* objects to see how the output changes (try, for example, with 1 KB and 30 KB object).

➤   *Note:* The behavior of this program (and the following one) depends on Windows memory handling capabilities and on the behavior of the Borland run-time library used for *EasyWin* applications. Basically, each Windows application has a default data segment of its own, having both a local stack and a local heap. When the application needs more memory, it can issue a request to the global heap handler. The on-line file of the Borland C++ 4.0 compiler WINMEM.DOC describes in some detail the use of the *new* operator under Windows.

The use of exceptions for memory errors is somewhat more interesting when the memory allocation scheme is more complex, perhaps involving constructors, as the following example demonstrates.

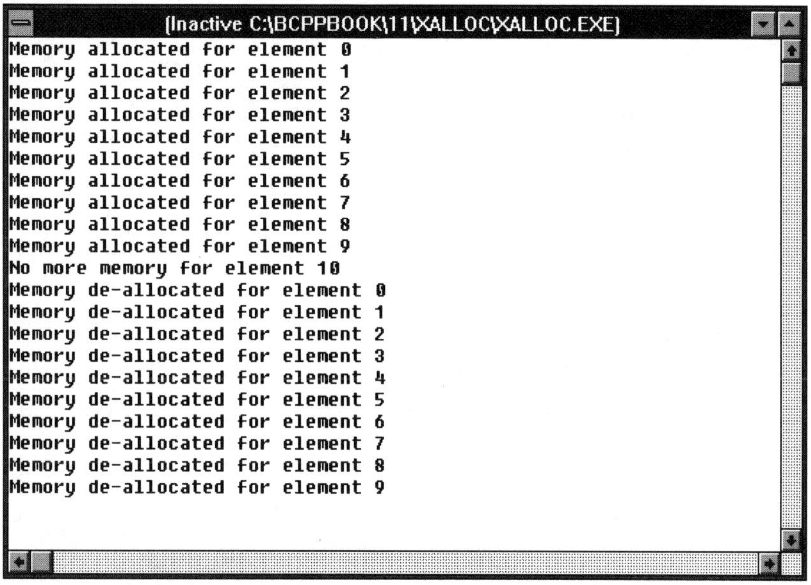

```
[Inactive C:\BCPPBOOK\11\XALLOC\XALLOC.EXE]
Memory allocated for element 0
Memory allocated for element 1
Memory allocated for element 2
Memory allocated for element 3
Memory allocated for element 4
Memory allocated for element 5
Memory allocated for element 6
Memory allocated for element 7
Memory allocated for element 8
Memory allocated for element 9
No more memory for element 10
Memory de-allocated for element 0
Memory de-allocated for element 1
Memory de-allocated for element 2
Memory de-allocated for element 3
Memory de-allocated for element 4
Memory de-allocated for element 5
Memory de-allocated for element 6
Memory de-allocated for element 7
Memory de-allocated for element 8
Memory de-allocated for element 9
```

Figure 11.8 The output of the *XALLOC.CPP* program

```
// file XALLOC2.CPP                                      11/XALLOC
// Second example of a failed memory allocation exception
// Compile this program with EasyWin target, using small memory model

// header file except.h defines the xalloc class
#include <except.h>
#include <iostream.h>
#include <cstring.h>

class BigClass
{
public:
    char bigText [10000] ;
    // 10KByte of text
} ;

// a class using BigClass (through a pointer)
class BigUser
{
private:
    BigClass *  pBig ;
    static long totalMemory ;

public:
```

```
    // default constructor
    BigUser ( )
    {
        cout << "Entering the default constructor..." << endl ;
        pBig = new BigClass ;
        totalMemory += sizeof (*pBig) ;
        cout << "Default constructor: " << sizeof (*pBig)
            << " bytes used for a total of " << totalMemory << endl ;
    }

    // copy constructor !!!
    BigUser (const BigUser & bu)
    {
        cout << "Entering the copy constructor..." << endl ;
        pBig = new BigClass ;
        totalMemory += sizeof (*pBig) ;
        // nothing to copy...
        cout << "Copy constructor executed: " << sizeof (*pBig)
            << " bytes used for a total of " << totalMemory << endl ;
    }

    // destructor
    ~BigUser ( )
    {
        totalMemory -= sizeof (*pBig) ;
        // optionally add this code:
        /*cout << "Destructor: " << sizeof (*pBig)
            << " bytes freed" << endl ;*/
        delete pBig ;
    }

    // do-nothig function
    void Fake ( )
    {
        cout << "Fake called" << endl ;
    }
};

long BigUser :: totalMemory = 0 ;

// a global function using and passing BigUser objects
BigUser GlobalUserFunction (BigUser bu)
{
    BigUser bu2 ;
    cout << "GlobalUserFunction called" << endl ;
```

```
    // uses the two BigUser objects
    bu.Fake ( ) ;
    bu2.Fake ( ) ;

    return bu2 ;
}


void main ( )
{
    try
    {
        // commenting and uncommenting the following line
        // the behaviour of the program changes
        BigUser bu, secondBu;
        BigUser bu1;
        BigUser bu2 = GlobalUserFunction ( bu1 );
        bu2.Fake ( ) ;
    }
    catch (xalloc exc)
    {
        cout << "Something went wrong: " << exc.why ( ) << endl ;
    }
}
```

If you run the program as it is, you should get the output of Figure 11.9. Removing one of the objects created in the *try* block, as object *bu*, the behavior changes considerably, because there is enough memory to run the program (see Figure 11.10 for the output of the same program without the *bu* and *secondBu* objects).

```
┌─────────────────────────────────────────────────────────────────┐
│ ─          (Inactive C:\BCPPBOOK\11\XALLOC\XALLOC2.EXE)      ▼ ▲ │
│ Entering the default constructor...                               │
│ Default constructor: 10000 bytes used for a total of 10000        │
│ Entering the default constructor...                               │
│ Default constructor: 10000 bytes used for a total of 20000        │
│ Entering the default constructor...                               │
│ Default constructor: 10000 bytes used for a total of 30000        │
│ Entering the copy constructor...                                  │
│ Copy constructor executed: 10000 bytes used for a total of 40000  │
│ Entering the default constructor...                               │
│ Default constructor: 10000 bytes used for a total of 50000        │
│ GlobalUserFunction called                                         │
│ Fake called                                                       │
│ Fake called                                                       │
│ Entering the copy constructor...                                  │
│ Something went wrong: Out of memory                               │
│                                                                   │
│ ◄ ▒                                                           ► │
└─────────────────────────────────────────────────────────────────┘
```

Figure 11.9 The output of the XALLOC2.CPP program, generating a memory exception

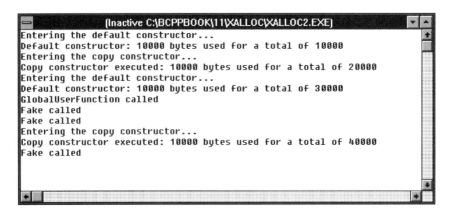

Figure 11.10 The output of the modified version of the XALLOC.CPP program, which has no memory problem

Exception handling is a very powerful C++ feature, which is new and will probably have a large impact on software development. Since this topic is very important, we will give it some more space in the second part of Chapter 14.

POINTS TO CONSIDER

1. Consider how you are used to handle errors. Look at old listings you have and evaluate how the use of exception handling can affect them.

2. Change one of the BASIC examples using the standard *xmsg* exception class.

3. Extend one of the programs of this chapter, trying to reraise an exception using *throw* without parameters.

4. Complete the examples *hierar.cpp* and *virt_exc.cpp* using the exception class hierarchy effectively.

5. The *xalloc* exception return by the *new* operator has the risk of breaking old code that tests the return value of *new*. Try to figure out a possible solution, besides disabling the exception with a call to *set_new_handler*.

PART THREE

Advanced Tools
and Methods

12

Run-Time Type Information

Not all checking can be done at compile time.
[Stroustrup]

Discussing object-oriented design, we have tried to stress that one of the central aspects of this approach is the idea of developing class hierarchies. Single classes might be useful if you focus on reusability and flexibility, but hierarchies offer a tremendous power for this purposes.

However, when you build the abstract base class at the head of a hierarchy, a question often arises: Should you place all the member functions of the derived classes in their common base, or limit its interface with the shared behaviors?

For example, if you have a hierarchy of animal classes, should you consider adding the *bark* function to the base *Animal* class? If you do not, then in the portions of the program using a generic pointer to animals, you cannot use the specific *bark* functions, except through the risk of a cast.

In this chapter we focus on this and similar problems, while we discover the features of the new *Run-Time Type Information (RTTI)* extension of the C++ language. This feature is new in Borland C++ 4.0, since it has been approved by the ANSI C++ committee only recently .

Getting Information on a Type

C++ used to be considered a static language, in which the notion of type is used by the compiler to perform a number of checks but has no meaning at run time. Now, although static checks are performed as before, a *dynamic* behavior has been added to the language.

Using the *typeid* operator, you can ask an object or an expression to report which its type is. The *typeid* operator returns an object of the standard *Type_info* class, which can be used to compare two types or to extract the name of a type. The following example demonstrates a basic (and silly) use of RTTI:

```
// file TYPENAME.CPP
// first example of the use of type_info class

// includes the definitions for RTTI
#include <typeinfo.h>
#include <iostream.h>

class AClass
{ } ;

void main ( )
{
      int number = 27 ;
      AClass anObject ;

      cout << "Variable: number, Value: " << number
         << ", DataType: " << (typeid (number)).name ( ) << endl ;

      cout << "Variable: anObject, DataType: "
         << (typeid (anObject)).name ( ) << endl ;
}
```

The output of this program is:

```
Variable: number, Value: 27, DataType: int
Variable: anObject, DataType: AClass
```

The expression *typeid (number)* returns an object of class *Type_info*, a standard class defined by the ANSI committee. This class is actually alloweed to be implementation dependent, although it should at least provide some standard member function. Here is a simplified version of the definition of this class that you can find in the *typeinfo.h* header file and that is fully documented in Borland C++ help.

```
class Type_info
{
public:
   tpid * tpp ;

private:  // private constructors
   Type_info (const Type_info _FAR &) ;
   Type_info & operator=(const Type_info _FAR &) ;

public:
   virtual    ~Type_info ( ) ;
   int operator== (const Type_info _FAR &) const ;
```

```
   int operator!= (const Type_info _FAR &) const ;
   int before (const Type_info _FAR &) const ;
   const char _FAR *__cdecl name ( ) const ;
} ;
```

Notice that, besides the *name* function, the *Type_info* class has two operators to test for equality. These operators, as well as the whole RTTI mechanism, are particularly worthy when you do not know the run-time type of an expression. For instance, when polymorphism is used among derived classes.

The Run-Time Type of an Animal

The next example can give an idea of the use of RTTI in a real case.

```
// file ANIMAL_T.CPP                                        12/TYPENAME
// using RTTI to determine the type of an animal

#include <typeinfo.h>
#include <cstring.h>
#include <iostream.h>

class Animal
{
private:
string name;

public:
   Animal (string n) :
      name (n)
   { }

   virtual void Speak ( )
   {
      cout << "Non-speaking animal" ;
   }

   string Name ( )
   {
      return name ;
   }
};

class Dog : public Animal
{
public:
```

```
    Dog (string n) :
       Animal (n)
    { }

    void Speak ( )
    {
       cout << "Arf, arf" ;
    }
} ;

void main ( )
{
    Animal * pAnimal = new Dog ("Snoopy");

    cout << "The animal is " << pAnimal->Name ( ) << endl;
    cout << "Here it speaks: " ;
    pAnimal -> Speak ( ) ;
    cout << endl ;
    cout << "Hey! It's a " << typeid (*pAnimal).name ( ) << endl ;
    cout << "but I'm accessing it with an " <<
       typeid (pAnimal).name ( ) << " pointer " << endl ;
    cout << endl ;

    delete pAnimal ;
}
```

As you can see from the output in Figure 12.1, the output highlights some interesting aspects of RTTI. Notice particularly the different output produced by the similar expressions:

```
typeid (*pAnimal).name ( )
typeid (pAnimal).name ( )
```

The first expression returns the name of the class of the object the pointer is currently referring to, while the second expression returns the *static* data type, determined by the pointer declaration.

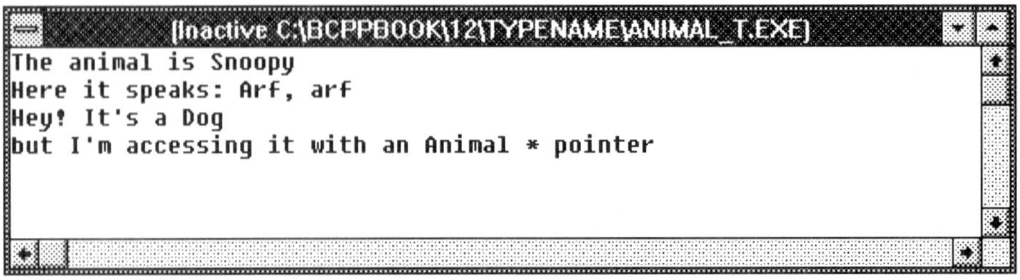

Figure 12.1 The output of the *animal_t* program, showing the use of RTTI

What Is This Pointer Pointing To?

This difference is particularly useful with run-time type checks. You can test if a pointer is referring to a particular class using the == operator among the *Type_info* objects returned by the *typeid* operator, as in the following program:

```
// file CHECK_T.CPP                                    12/TYPENAME
// using RTTI to check at run-time what a pointer is pointing to

#include <typeinfo.h>
#include <iostream.h>

class Base
{
public:
    virtual int function (int n)
    {   // nonsense code: we just need a virtual function
        return n*2 ;
    }
} ;

class Derived : public Base
{
    int function (int n)
    {
        return n*3 ;
    }
} ;

void main ( )
{
    Base* pBase = new Base ;
    Derived* pDerived = new Derived;

    cout << "Program starts..." << endl ;
    if (typeid(*pBase) == typeid(Derived))
        cout << "The base pointer is referencing a derived object" << endl ;
    else
        cout << "The base pointer really points to a base" << endl ;

    delete pBase ;
    pBase = pDerived ;
    cout << "Assignments..." << endl ;
    if (typeid(*pBase) == typeid(Derived))
        cout << "The base pointer is referencing a derived object" << endl ;
```

```
    else
        cout << "The base pointer really points to a base" << endl ;
    delete pDerived;
}
```

In the above program, the *typeid* operator is applied both to an object (the one *pBase* points to) and to a data type, testing if they correspond at the same type. The test fails the first time, because *pBase* is really referencing a *Base* class object. The second time, the test succeeds, since we have assigned to *pBase* a pointer to an object of the *Derived* class.

In a real example, we might use this kind of test to perform different operations on a pointer depending on its data type. Generally speaking, however, this is a terrible practice. We should use virtual functions and the typical C++ polymorphism to handle similar cases. It would be silly to use a number of nested if statements, similar to a *switch*, to replace properly used virtual functions, since object-oriented programming allows us to make exactly the opposite move!

At times, however, RTTI can be very useful, particularly to solve the problem we presented in the introduction of this chapter.

Making a Dynamic Cast

As we mentioned earlier, a problem using class hierarchies is that, at times, you might want to use a specific member function of a derived class, and you are accessing an object of the derived class via a pointer to its base. This problem is quite common and cannot always be solved using virtual functions (although most of the times it might be).

Here is a new version of the animals class hierarchy we already used in this chapter:

```
// file ANIM.H                                          12/DYNACAST
// animal and dog classes for the oldcast.cpp and dynacast.cpp programs

#include <cstring.h>
#include <iostream.h>

class Animal
{
private:
string name;

public:
    Animal (string n) :
        name (n)
    { }

    virtual void Speak ( )
    {
```

```
        cout << "Non-speaking animal" << endl ;
    }

    string Name ( )
    {
        return name ;
    }
};

class Dog : public Animal
{
public:
    Dog (string n) :
        Animal (n)
    { }

    void Speak ( )
    {
        cout << "Arf, arf" << endl ;
    }

    void Bark ( )
    {
        cout << "Bark, bark" << endl ;
    }
} ;
```

As you can see, beside a specific version of the *Speak* function, dogs can *Bark*. How can we call the latter member function while using a generic pointer to animal. The traditional *unsafe* way is the following: Cast the pointer to the derived class, and use it! But take care: If the cast is wrong, you're going to have problems.

Consider the following code:

```
// file oldcast.cpp                                    12/DYNACAST
// downcasting to a derived class in the old error-prone way

#include "anim.h"

void main ( )
{
    Animal * pa = new Dog ("Snoopy") ;

    pa->Speak ( ) ;
    // pa->Bark ( ) ;        // Compile error!
```

```
((Dog *) pa) -> Bark ( ) ;
delete pa ;
}
```

Since the *pa* pointer really refers to a dog, casting it to the derived class is correct. However, this approach is not safe, because if you use this same code in a bigger example, it might happen that you will use it even when the pointer really refers to an object of another class. This is particularly the case when this code is in a function, or when you process the return value of a function, trying to guess its real return value.

RTTI allows us to make a new kind of cast, called dynamic cast, which has a much safer approach. When you cast a pointer to a derived class using *dynamic_cast,* two different things might happen at run time:

1. If the pointer is really referencing an object of the derived class, the cast is performed as usual.

2. If the pointer is referencing an object of any other class (the base class, or another derived class), the result of the cast is a zero (NULL) pointer.

For a cast to be really safe, you have to test the pointer for a nonzero value before you perform any action on it. The following new version of the previous *main* functions shows the details of the dynamic cast syntax:

```
// file DYNACAST.CPP                                    12/DYNACAST
// downcasting to a derived class
// using dynamic cast (a new C++ feature based on RTTI)

#include "anim.h"

void main ( )
{
    Animal * pa = new Dog ("Snoopy") ;
    Dog* pdog ;
    pa->Speak ( ) ;
    if (pdog = dynamic_cast<Dog*>(pa))
        pdog -> Bark ( ) ;
    delete pa ;

    pa = new Animal ("Fish") ;
    pa->Speak ( ) ;
    if (pdog = dynamic_cast<Dog*>(pa))
        pdog -> Bark ( ) ;
    delete pa ;
}
```

In this program, the first time the *dynamic_cast* of *pa* toward the *Dog** type indicated between angle braces is executed it works; the second time it fails. So the *Bark* function is called only the first time, avoiding the risk of the second call, which would have been unsafe and risky.

Although we have applied the *dynamic_cast* construct to a very small example, it is really very powerful, and can be used at best in complex programs. An interesting example of the use of this cast is found in the code written with the *ObjectWindows Library*.

At times, in fact, there are functions returning a pointer to a generic window, which can be used to access an object of a specific derived class you have declared. To safely access a member function of your derived class using the pointer to the base window, a dynamic cast is much better and safer than an ordinary plain cast.

➤ *Note:* The C++ language has recently adopted a number of new casts, besides the old plain one and the *dynamic_cast* just explained. The Borland C++ compiler implements three other new forms of cast, which do not involve RTTI, but are statically resolved by the compiler:

- The *static_cast <T> (object)* is used to cast from a pointer or reference to a base class to a pointer or reference to derived class and vice versa, without the safety of a dynamic cast; it can also be used to cast from an integer to an enum.

- The *const_cast<T> (object)* is used to add or remove the const and volatile qualifiers from an object, without changing its type.

- The *reinterpret_cast <T> (object)* is a generic cast from a type to something completely different, used to pretend that an object is something else.

RTTI and Templates

The last example using RTTI we present here is quite strange; it was conceived of during a discussion with C++ programmers in Italy for a presentation of the Borland C++ 4.0 compiler.

When you use template classes, you can write flexible and reusable code, but you loose some control on the contents of your class. If you need run-time information to know which kind of template you are currently using, you are at a loss, unless you use RTTI!

```
// file TEMPRTTI.CPP                                        12/TEMPRTTI
// a small example of RTTI with tempaltes

#include <iostream.h>
#include <typeinfo.h>
#include <cstring.h>
```

```
template <class T>
class OneElement
{
   T  element;

public:
   OneElement (T t) :
   element (t)
   { }

   T Retrieve ( )
   {
      return element ;
   }

   void PrintAll ( )
   {
      cout << "Element <" << element
         << "> of type " << typeid (element).name ( ) << endl ;
   }
};

void main ( )
{
   OneElement<int> one (27);
   one.PrintAll ( ) ;

   OneElement<char> two ('x');
   two.PrintAll ( ) ;

   OneElement<int> three ('x');
   three.PrintAll ( ) ;

   OneElement<string> four ("Run-Time Type of a Template");
   four.PrintAll ( ) ;
}
```

In Figure 12.2 you can see in the output of the program the data type a template class is based on. The same output can be obtained using the following code for the *PrintAll* function. It uses T instead of the *element* member to get the data type, since the two match exactly.

```
cout << "Element <" << element
   << "> of type " << typeid (T).name ( ) << endl ;
```

```
[Inactive C:\BCPPBOOK\12\TEMPINFO\TEMPRTTI.EXE]
Element <27> of type int
Element <x> of type char
Element <120> of type int
Element <Run-Time Type of a Template> of type string
```

Figure 12.2 The output of the *temprtti* program, showing the data types a template is based on

Consider applying this kind of approach to the example of a template buffer class of Chapter 10. You could easily add a function to display the data type the buffer is working on and those of the actual objects inside the buffer. In fact, if the buffer contains pointers, these might refer to the object of a class or its derived classes.

POINTS TO CONSIDER

1. Consider the difference between the use of RTTI and the common method of inserting a virtual *Name* member function in a hierarchy returning the name of the actual class of an object.

2. Consider the dangers of traditional *casting* and the advantages of *dynamic_cast* in the development of a class hierarchy. Change one of the examples of hierarchies of the previous chapters of the book, where a cast was involved or might be added, to improve the code. If you don't find a very good example, do not bother too much. Dynamic casting is useful, but if you can avoid casts, it's still better.

3. Write a template buffer displaying run-time type information of the data type it is based on and of the objects which have been inserted in it, as suggested at the end of the chapter.

13

Software Reuse and Evolutionary Development

Reusability reduces software development costs, speeds up the development process, and reduces testing needs. It is to be expected that rising costs of software development will make software reusability increasingly important for many applications. [Ramamoorthy 84]

This chapter discusses two different aspects of software development: *reusability* and *evolution*. There are two starting points to consider for both elements: on one side there is the object-oriented design methodology, presented in Chapter 3; on the other side there are the object-oriented programming constructs available with C++, described in Chapters 5 to 10.

The problem of reusability, which is receiving a lot of attention from software developers, is quite complex. After introducing its main aspects, including an overview of the traditional programming methods to reuse source code, we will focus on the main object-oriented tool supporting reusability: inheritance.

The discussion of evolutionary applications, in contrast, is described theoretically, which is useful to grasp the fundamentals of this innovative method to build even large applications. However, some attention will also be given to practical aspects, such as the recompilations that are needed after a change in the source and the methods to handle them automatically.

In addition, this chapter also provides an introduction to the last part of this book, particularly the chapters regarding class libraries.

Different Forms of Reusability

Whenever you read about reusability, the starting point is always the same: software production is still mostly a craft, because every piece has to be thought, designed, and built almost from scratch. Through this process the craftsman programmer gains more experience, improves his or her technique, and is able to craft even better programs.

Two centuries ago, with the Industrial Revolution, there was a move from craftsmanship to the production of standard components, which could be used in many different products. This idea made possible mass production, which in turn led to more affordable products. The concept of interchangeable parts is still used today. For example, a car plant produces different vehicles with the same engine, and sometimes those engines are even sold to other factories. Other car parts are totally standard: batteries, for example, are all fairly similar; you can buy one in any auto parts store and feel pretty confident that it can be used with your own car. Today, few products are manufactured without interchangeable parts. Software production, however, is an exception.

The core of the problem is the need for standard software components and a standard way to assemble them: this method is already in use for computer hardware and has made possible its cost reduction during the past thirty years. On the other hand, the software situation is still uncertain: there still needs to be a strong effort to standardize software to make this idea feasible.

Although the whole issue will take a long time to settle, it's already possible to think in terms of planned code reuse, both with traditional tools such as function libraries and newer ones such as class libraries.

Reuse is possible at different levels: besides the code, you can reuse the analysis and design steps of the software development cycle. For example, if it's possible to reuse a class hierarchy in a different application, you save more than just the time needed for the implementation, but also the time spent to design the hierarchy as a whole, define the common interface, check the correctness of the whole hierarchy, and debug its code.

Before we examine the advantages of reusing classes, we will present a short view of the traditional methods to reuse code, which are still available in the Borland C++ programming environment.

Traditional Tools for Reusability

Several constructs of programming languages favor the reuse of parts of the code: it's important to remember that the attention to reusability is not new, and that even traditional programming languages (such as Pascal, FORTRAN, or C) let you reuse code.

During the evolution of programming languages, several methods of reuse have been developed. The first to be available were subprograms and macro expansions. Then came packages (or modules), generic modules, and inheritance among modules.

"The classical approach to reusability is to build libraries of routines [a synonym for subprogram, procedure, or function].... Each routine in such a library implements a well-defined operation. An area where this approach has been quite successful is scientific computation: excellent routine libraries are commonly used for solving problems in linear algebra, differential equations and other fields." [Meyer 88] Usually in these cases, we reuse object code already compiled and stored in a library, which can be linked to a program. Some languages, such as standard C and C++, also require the prototypes or declarations of the functions in the library, which are usually collected in one or more "header files."

Another method that has been available for a long time is the use of macro instructions, which can also take parameters. A macro definition can be thought of as a function definition, for which the valid set of parameters determines the value of a string; this string is the result of the macro expansion. With macros, it's possible to reuse parts of the source code, which can be duplicated, possibly with some changes through the value of the parameters present in the macro call. Usually, the macro substitution is made by a preprocessor, in a phase preceding the proper code compilation. Although some compilers, including Borland C++, perform the two operations at the same time, they remain two conceptually different phases of the compilation process.

As already noted [Wegner 68], the main difference between a macro and a function definition is that you can think of a macro as a physical substitution of source code that is performed when the macro is called (at preprocessing time); a function, on the other hand, is executed by transferring control to a closed subroutine (at runtime).

A further step has been made with packages, which group several procedures operating on the same data into one logical unit. Thanks to this construct, it's possible to reuse the data structure and its access functions at the same time, with great advantages in terms of abstraction and modularity, and also in terms of robustness and easiness of reuse by other programmers. Even greater reusability is offered by generic packages, which make possible the definition of parametric modules with regard to the data type of the variables used.

The C++ language offers all of these traditional tools supporting reusability. It's possible to use macro definitions and libraries of functions. A certain number of these libraries are already present in Borland C++, and several functions have also been used in this book.

Packages have been overtaken by the concept of class, which offers better protection of the data. C++ classes can also be generic, using the template construct to enhance the possibility of reusing the same class in a different context (and in a different application) without any runtime overhead.

Traditional Reusability in Borland C++

Borland C++ supports traditional C reusability with macros and function libraries.

C++ features (particularly constants and inline functions) are generally used in place of the old C style macros. Macros, however, are often present inside most C function libraries including the Windows API. Therefore, when discussing function libraries, we will also consider the macros stored in them.

Function libraries, the most common form of code reuse, have already been seen in several examples in this book. The most used libraries have been those concerning C++ input output (*iostream.h*), which is a class library. In some other examples, we have also used the standard C library to handle character strings (*string.h*), to access DOS (*dos.h*), and to handle the console directly (*conio.h*).

Some of these libraries really describe important features of the language, but are not part of the language itself probably because of C language influence. C was so terse that even input-output was left to libraries. C++ integrated heap management (*new* and *delete*) and exceptions handling into the language, but some other functionalities are still relegated to external libraries.

To use a function present in a library (that is, without having its source code available), you need:

- The declaration of the function—in standard C terminology, its "prototype"— usually contained in an *.H* file, called "header file" or "include file," which defines a set of related functions.

- The compiled code (object code) of the function, present inside a library (*.LIB*) file that is bound to the program by the linker.

In Borland C++, the files for the library that accompany the compiler are placed by default in the *INCLUDE* and *LIB* subdirectories. The list of the header files (including both the prototypes of the function libraries and the standard C++ class libraries) is available in the help system of the integrated environment. The standard library header files are shown in Table 13.1.

Table 13.1 The list of the header files for the "standard" libraries of the Borland C++ environment, as reported in the help system

---

alloc.h	Declares memory-management functions (allocation, deallocation, and so on).
assert.h	Defines the *assert* debugging macro.
bcd.h	Declares the C++ class *bcd* and the overloaded operators for *bcd* and *bcd* math functions.
bios.h	Declares various functions used in calling IBM-PC ROM BIOS routines.
bwcc.h	Defines the Borland Windows Custom Control interface.
checks.h	Defines the class diagnostic macros.
complex.h	Declares the C++ complex math functions.
conio.h	Declares various functions used in calling the operating system console I/O routines.
constrea.h	Defines the *conbuf* and *constream* classes.
cstring.h	Defines the *string* classes.
ctype.h	Contains information used by the character classification and character conversion macros.
date.h	Defines the *date* class.
_defs.h	Defines the calling conventions for different application types and memory models.
dir.h	Contains structures, macros, and functions for working with directories and path names.
direct.h	Defines structures, macros, and functions for dealing with directories and path names.
dirent.h	Declares functions and structures for POSIX directory operations.

Table 13.1 Continued

dos.h	Defines various constants and gives declarations needed for DOS and 8086-specific calls.
errno.h	Defines constant mnemonics for the error codes.
except.h	Declares the *exception-handling* classes and functions.
excpt.h	Declares C structured exception support.
fcntl.h	Defines symbolic constants used in connection with the library routine open.
file.h	Defines the *file* class.
float.h	Contains parameters for floating-point routines.
fstream.h	Declares the C++ stream classes that support file input and output.
generic.h	Contains macros for generic class declarations.
io.h	Contains structures and declarations for low-level input/output routines.
iomanip.h	Declares the C++ streams I/O manipulators and contains templates for creating parameterized manipulators.
iostream.h	Declares the basic C++ streams (I/O) routines.
limits.h	Contains environmental parameters, information about compile-time limitations, and ranges of integral quantities.
locale.h	Declares functions that provide country- and language-specific information.
malloc.h	Declares memory-management functions and variables.
math.h	Declares prototypes for the math functions and math error handlers.
mem.h	Declares the memory-manipulation functions.
memory.h	Contains memory-manipulation functions.
new.h	Access to *_new_handler*, and *set_new_handler*.
_nfile.h	Defines the maximum number of open files.
_null.h	Defines the value of *NULL*.
process.h	Contains structures and declarations for the *spawn...* and *exec...* functions.
search.h	Declares functions for searching and sorting.
setjmp.h	Declares the functions *longjmp* and *setjmp* and defines a type *jmp_buf* that these functions use.
share.h	Defines parameters used in functions that make use of file-sharing.
signal.h	Defines constants and declarations for use by the *signal* and *raise* functions.
stdarg.h	Defines macros used for reading the argument list in functions declared to accept a variable number of arguments.
stddef.h	Defines several common data types and macros.

Table 13.1 Continued

stdio.h	Defines types and macros needed for the standard I/O package defined in Kernighan and Ritchie and extended under UNIX System V. Defines the standard I/O predefined streams *stdin*, *stdout*, *stdprn*, and *stderr* and declares stream-level I/O routines.
stdiostr.h	Declares the C++ (version 2.0) *stream* classes for use with stdio FILE structures. You should use *iostream.h* for new code.
stdlib.h	Declares several commonly used routines such as conversion routines and search/sort routines.
string.h	Declares several string-manipulation and memory-manipulation routines.
strstrea.h	Declares the C++ stream classes for use with byte arrays in memory.
sys\locking.h	Contains definitions for mode parameter of locking function.
sys\stat.h	Defines symbolic constants used for opening and creating files.
sys\timeb.h	Declares the function ftime and the structure *timeb* that *ftime* returns.
sys\types.h	Declares the type *time_t* used with time functions.
thread.h	Defines the *thread* classes.
time.h	Defines a structure filled in by the time-conversion routines *asctime*, *localtime*, and *gmtime*, and a type used by the routines *ctime*, *difftime*, *gmtime*, *localtime*, and *stime*. It also provides prototypes for these routines.
typeinfo.h	Declares the *run-time type information* classes.
utime.h	Declares the *utime* function and the *utimbuf* struct that it returns.
values.h	Defines important constants, including machine dependencies; provided for UNIX System V compatibility.
varargs.h	Definitions for accessing parameters in functions that accept a variable number of arguments. Provided for UNIX compatibility; you should use *stdarg.h* for new code.

By selecting one of the libraries in the help system (clicking on its name with the mouse), it is possible to view a list of the functions declared (an example of such a list is in Table 13.2, which refers to the header file DOS.H)

Each of the functions of these lists is available (or even standard) under the different operating systems: Some will work both in DOS and in Windows, others are specific for one of these environments. Other functions have a broad coverage and are commonly available under OS/2 or UNIX, too. If you are concerned with writing portable code, use the *Portability* link of the Borland C++ help system for the specific functions to get the this kind of information (see Figure 13.1).

To use any library function, you need to include the corresponding header files in your programs. Once this operation has been made, the functions of the library can be used in the same was as those defined by the program. However, consider that most of

Table 13.2 The list of functions in *dos.h*

allocmem	bdos	bdosptr	_chain_intr
_chmod	country	ctrlbrk	delay
disable	_dos_allocmem	_dos_close	_dos_commit
_dos_creat	_dos_creatnew	dosexterr	_dos_findfirst
_dos_findnext	_dos_freemem	_dos_getdate	_dos_getdiskfree
_dos_getdrive	_dos_getfileattr	_dos_getftime	_dos_gettime
_dos_getvect	_dos_keep	_dos_open	_dos_read
_dos_setblock	_dos_setdate	_dos_setdrive	_dos_setfileattr
_dos_settime	_dos_setvect	dostounix	_dos_write
emit	enable	FP_OFF	FP_SEG
geninterrupt	getcbrk	getdate	getdfree
getdta	getfat	getfatd	getftime
getpsp	gettime	getvect	getverify
_harderr	_hardresume	_hardretn	inport
inportb	int86	int86x	intdos
intdosx	intr	keep	MK_FP
nosound	outport	outportb	parsfnm
peek	peekb	poke	pokeb
randbrd	randbwr	segread	setcbrk
setdate	setdta	settime	setvect
setverify	sleep	sound	unixtodos
unlink			

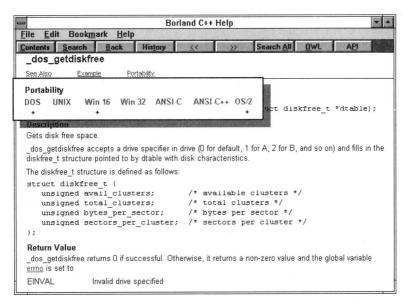

Figure 13.1 Help information about the *_dos_getdiskfree* function, with the portability hint open

the functions of the run-time library are global functions (since they are C language functions). If you want to use C++ to write object-oriented applications, you can consider writing *wrapper classes* around these functions and the corresponding data structures. This is one of the rare cases in which *private* inheritance is useful. Using it, we can derive well-behaved classes from the structures used in these libraries. The following example shows some interactions with DOS, but can run without problems under Windows, too.

```
// file WRAPPER.CPP                                      13/WRAPPER
// example of wrapper classes toaccess to library function

// includes input-output library (a class library)
// and the input-output manipulators (see chapter 15)
#include <iostream.h>
#include <iomanip.h>

// include exceptions support (and C++ strings used by xmsg class)
#include <except.h>
#include <cstring.h>

// includes operating system functions library (a C function library)
#include <dos.h>

// First wrapper class: DiskFree
class DiskFree : private diskfree_t
{
public:

    // constructor
    DiskFree ( )
    {
        // refers to current drive, filling the structure
        // returns 0 if everything is fine
        if (_dos_getdiskfree (0, this) != 0)
            throw (xmsg ("Disk Error")) ;
    }

    long KBytesFree ( )
    {
        long bytes = ((long) avail_clusters *
            (long) bytes_per_sector * (long) sectors_per_cluster) ;
        return (bytes / 1024) ;
    }
} ;
```

```
// Second wrapper: time and date in one
class TimeAndDate : private dostime_t, private dosdate_t
{
public:

    // constructor
    TimeAndDate ( )
    {
        // use the address of the first member of the base
        // structure as address of the structure
        _dos_getdate ((dosdate_t*) &day) ;
        _dos_gettime ((dostime_t*) &hour) ;
    }

    void PrintTime ( )
    {
        // setfill and setw are iostream manipulators
        // (see chapter 15 for details)
        cout << "The current time is: " << setfill ('0')
            << setw (2) << (int) hour << ':'
            << setw (2) << (int) minute << ':'
            << setw (2) << (int) second << endl ;
    }

    void PrintDate ( )
    {
        cout << "The current date is: " << setfill ('0')
            << setw (2) << (int) month << '.'
            << setw (2)  << setw (2) << (int) day << '.'
            << setw (4) << year << endl ;
    }

    // more functions to retrieve day, month, and so on
} ;


void main ( )
{
    DiskFree disk ;
    TimeAndDate now ;

    cout << "The current drive has "
        << disk.KBytesFree ( )
        << " Kbytes free" << endl ;
```

```
        now.PrintDate ( ) ;
        now.PrintTime ( ) ;
}
```

Borland C++ Libraries

The standard libraries of Borland C++ are worth further consideration. In fact, the list of the header files (see Table 13.1) is quite long. The files are present for different purposes. Some of them are there to comply with C and C++ standards, some to handle computer resources, some for compatibility with other C compilers or previous versions of Borland C, as shown in Table 13.3.

The purpose of most of these libraries is to provide functions to handle the different parts of the computer hardware: the memory, the keyboard input, the video output, the file system, and so on. Another important part of the headers is to define functions to handle some basic data types: chars, numbers, character strings, and so on.

You can classify the basic libraries provided with Borland C++ according to their source (as shown also in Table 13.3):

- Some of them are the standard ANSI C headers.
- Some are present in the almost standard AT&T C++ compiler (some of these are C++ class libraries).
- Others are Borland-specific, and some of them are also present in a second version, corresponding to that of the Microsoft C compiler.

Once the corresponding header has been included, all the functions contained in a library can be used anywhere in a program. If a program makes extensive use of some functions, it might be possible to encapsulate their calls in one or more classes, making the rest of the program independent. Examples of this method have been shown at the end of Chapter 5 within the class *Note* and in the last section with the *WRAPPER* example. The importance of this method lies in the possibility of making the program much more portable, since all the machine-dependent code is collected in a single location of the program (and hidden in a class). At the same time, the program becomes easier to modify and extend since it's possible to change the libraries used without recoding the whole application.

Borland C++ makes it possible to create, modify, and analyze libraries via the powerful TLIB utility. TLIB can be used to create, display, add functions to, and remove functions from a library file. You can also choose *static library* as the target of a project in the IDE. The advantage of defining and using a library instead of ordinary object files to store some of the functions of an application is that libraries are selectively linked, which means that if you use just one function of a library, the linker will add to the executable only the object code of that single function. On the other hand, with an object file, the linker will always add to the executable the object code of all the defined functions. With libraries, the executable can be reduced significantly.

Table 13.3 Compatibility header files of Borland C++

Header files for ANSI C compatibility:

assert.h	ctype.h	errno.h	float.h	limits.h
locale.h	math.h	setjmp.h	signal.h	stdarg.h
stddef.h	stdio.h	stdlib.h	string.h	time.h

Header files for ANSI C++ language "draft" compatibility:

constrea.h	cstring.h	except.h	fstream.h	generic.h
iomanip.h	iostream.h	new.h	stdiostr.h	strstrea.h
typeinfo.h				

Specific Borland headers for C++:

bcd.h	checks.h	complex.h	date.h	file.h
thread.h				

Header files for Windows programming

bwcc.h	excpt.h	windows.h

(and many more, from Windows SDK)

Borland C specific (memory, file system, graphics and so forth) including some functions similar to Microsoft C:

alloc.h	bios.h	conio.h	_defs.h	dir.h
dos.h	fcntl.h	io.h	mem.h	_nfile.h
_null.h	process.h	search.h	share.h	sys\locking.h
sys\stat.h	sys\timeb.h	sys\types.h	utime.h	

List of synonym header files for Microsoft C compatibility:

direct.h	malloc.h	memory.h

UNIX System V or POSIX compatibility headers:

dirent.h	values.h	varargs.h

➤ *Note:* The term "*object file*" has nothing to do with object-oriented programming. Object file denotes an intermediate representation of a program (as it is generated by the compiler, but before it is fed to the linker), whose origins date further back than object-oriented concepts. In the DOS environment, object files are usually denoted by the .OBJ extension.

TLIB's importance is in its ability to *change* the contents of a library, but it can also be used to *explore* the contents of the library. However, the cross-reference information in an object file can better be seen with the OBJXREF tool.

The use of *static import library* is particularly important in programming, but in the Windows environment there is another kind of library, *dynamic link library* (DLL). A dynamic library is the collection of compiled functions, but its code is not added to the programs during linking. Instead, at run time, when the programs need the code, the library is accessed directly. Therefore, linking takes place in a more *dynamic* and flexible way, with several advantages as the possibility of changing a *DLL* without having to recompile the application to use the new version of the library.

Notice that *dynamic linking* (as briefly described here) and *dynamic binding* (introduced in C++ with virtual functions) are two completely different concepts, although they offer some similar advantages and can be used together. Of course, this is not easy because DLLs have been invented for a C language binding, while virtual functions are specific to C++.

We end the section with an obvious but important consideration: the huge number of libraries available for the C language can be used also for C++. When possible, however, it's better to use class libraries. C++ class libraries are still quite rare, while C function libraries cover almost every aspect of programming. The use of libraries is notably suited for mathematics and any kind of computation, interfacing with special hardware devices, interfacing with the operating system, and interfacing with standard applications (for example, accessing their own data files).

The use of C libraries with C++ creates some problems due to the way C++ handles the names of the functions. This problem can be easily solved by adding an *extern "C"* clause to the header files (this turns off C++'s name mangling for those function calls).

Most of the header files included in the Borland environment can be compiled both under C and C++ because an *extern "C"* clause is added to each function whenever the code is compiled as C++. For example, in the *stdio.h* header file, you will notice the following lines of code:

```
#ifdef __cplusplus
extern "C" {
#endif

FILE far * far __getStream(int);

#ifdef __cplusplus
}
#endif
```

Reuse by Inheritance

A further step in source code reusability is offered by inheritance between classes. Inheritance provides a way to generalize or specialize the behavior of an abstraction, defining hierarchical connections between classes, and providing open classes that can be freely modified, extended, or reduced.

You have already seen several examples of class derivation, particularly about geometric shapes, showing the different properties of the construct. You have seen that it can be used to specialize classes, to generalize them, to define heterogeneous data structures, or to provide a common interface for a hierarchy.

However, one characteristic of inheritance in C++ is the possibility of using, modifying, and partially redefining classes produced by other programmers and stored in a library. All this takes place without you having access to the source code of the base class, but only to its interface (and a minimal technical description).

This aspect of object-oriented programming is a very important one and will be thoroughly examined in Chapters 15 to 17, which contain the description of Borland C++ class libraries, including the *Container Class Library* and the *ObjectWindows Library*.

Advantages of Reusability through Inheritance

Although the use of the class libraries included in the Borland C++ package will be discussed later on, you can compare them to the traditional function libraries. The following notes refer both to reusing code written by other programmers and stored in a library, and to reusing code in the development of one application, or a set of related applications, by a team of programmers.

The advantages of class libraries and code reuse through derivation are similar to those of the inheritance construct, and can be summarized in the following points:

1. The use of classes favors information hiding. Similarly, to reuse a class present in a library, you can ignore the internal data structures and focus on the available services or functionality of the class.

2. This method favors the modularity of the resulting application, and reduces the global dependency on the library, since all the exchanges of data take place through class interfaces.

3. Unlike functions, the reuse of classes is made easier by the possibility of changing some of the functionality or even adding new ones: the classes in libraries can be considered both as closed modules (well-defined and readily available) and as open modules (easily modifiable).

4. Inheritance opens up the opportunity of dynamic binding (see points 5, 6, and 7 for the consequences).

5. Using subclasses, you can avoid tag fields and heavy switch statements, which can be replaced using the dynamic binding feature.

6. Classes can be structured in hierarchies, delivering a family of standard interfaces and polymorphism, the capability of a common reference to all the classes and a way to call the specific functions of the proper class for any single object. The classes at the higher level of the hierarchy might be present in the library,

while the remaining ones could be added to meet the requirements of the application. This structure is typical, for example, of the user interface class libraries.

7. You can write, and place in a library, polymorphic functions; that is, functions able to comply with all of the classes of a hierarchy (and not a single data type). (This took place in the first version of Borland's Container Class Library, included in versions 2 and 3 of the compiler.)

8. A library can contain generic classes (template classes), which are independent of the data type of one or more members. It's therefore possible to reuse those classes in a wider range of situations, since they are more independent of their contents. (This takes place in the new version of Borland's containers, as you will see in Chapter 15.)

Even with these advantages, the programming process is not so straightforward as one might think. It's necessary to follow good object-oriented design principles and programming methodology (similar to the one described in Chapter 3) and use the C++ language features correctly (as we have tried to suggest in describing the main C++ concepts). The bibliography at the end of this book contains some suggestions for further reading on the subject: these books and articles can help you gain an even better understanding of correct object-oriented programming style with C++. (However, relatively few articles and books have been written on this specific subject.)

An important consequence of reusability through inheritance is the development of applications in an evolutionary manner, as discussed in the next section.

Maintenance and Evolutionary Development

Traditionally, there was a tendency to strictly and rigorously divide the different phases of software development: analysis, design, implementation, testing, and maintenance.

This scheme helps to develop huge applications, structure a project, and proceed with the right steps, but it can have serious drawbacks.

The quality of the design is evaluated during the implementation, when the programmer might come up with new ideas or discover new features that can be added easily. Particularly for an application covering a new field, it might be quite difficult to define *a priori* the most useful functionality, and the time required to code it.

Instead of designing the whole application in one monolithic step, you might consider starting with the most basic functionality, then adding new ones only later; this is what usually happens with subsequent versions of a software product. The modification required between subsequent releases of a program might even be quite considerable.

Structuring a project with the clear idea that it will evolve and change along its life span helps with an operation that is always required: maintaining the application. The work necessary after the release of a program can be divided into the following three areas:

- Corrective maintenance (usually covering about 20 percent of the total) is the effort of finding and eliminating errors, bugs, and unwanted features.

- Adaptive maintenance (about 20 percent) depends on hardware changes, new peripherals, and new releases of operating systems or windowing environments.
- "Perfective" maintenance (the remaining 60 percent) is the effort necessary to improve the programs, adding new functionality.

To document the basic ideas of the evolutionary approach, we will refer to a lengthy article by Peter Wegner about reusability. This article, while not very recent (it dates back to 1984), shows that there will probably always be a huge distance between the theoretical ideas on programming, the availability of the proper tools (languages, compilers, and programming environments), and a widespread use of the new techniques.

"Large software systems must be constructed so that modification and evolution can be accomplished in a time proportional to the magnitude of the changes rather than to the size of the system. Large systems that are easily maintained and enhanced have the property of local modularity and are constructible in an evolutionary manner from primitive components." [Wegner 84]

The feasibility of this approach requires that you be able to change the implementation and the structure of a part of the system without affecting the rest of it. In other words, it is important for you to have a highly modular structure, with very loosely coupled modules.

"Solving the maintenance problem requires an evolutionary life-cycle methodology that allows complex systems to evolve from a simple core by multiple independent extensions. Iterative enhancement is an example of an evolutionary life-cycle approach. It advocates using a skeletal implementation (rapid prototype) as a starting point for iterative redesign of what has already been produced and evolutionary addition of new features until the system is completed." [Wegner 84]

This kind of strategy can easily be joined with the object-oriented design principles described in Chapter 3, since they both stress the same basic idea: a system must be implemented with small modules (or classes) independent from each other (having private details and a small interface of public features) and be easily expandable (through inheritance).

Evolutionary Programming

Besides helping to solve the problems of maintenance, change, and extension of the applications, evolutionary programming might also help software development in other ways. The following advantages, although conceptually less important, might be quite interesting for applications of any size, and even for the casual programmer:

1. A first advantage in the development of a prototype—a rudimentary but working subset of an application—is the possibility of seeing the results of your work early. This is certainly an advantage (even psychologically) for the programmer, and even more for the client or user of the application, making it possible for you

to check that what is emerging from the development corresponds to the requirements. At the same time you might ask a chosen group of users to evaluate the prototype. Thus, it's possible to improve the application to better fit the needs of its users even before it's finished. Showing a working prototype is much better than communicating through a written description of what the program should be able to do.

This kind of evaluation is particularly useful for the development of the user interface. Following these criteria, you can start to build your Windows application—drawing menus, resources, and the graphic parts—before you write the effective code to handle them.

2. A second advantage lies in the opportunity of tackling implementation issues while the application is still almost in its design phase and can still be modified easily. Defining classes to describe the main abstractions used by the program, you might find that some of them are similar to classes already available in a library, and resort to using them, changing the original project.

The application should be built around some fixed classes or parts, which should be defined at the earliest possible stage and modified only if necessary. The initial development shouldn't produce a true prototype, but a "working nucleus," something that can be expanded into an application by adding new functionality yet remain stable through the process. Without some fixed points, the project could constantly be changing, indicating a programming method based on revolution and not evolution.

3. A third advantage of the method is its support of the programmer's creativity, instead of confining it to predefined steps. "A professional programming environment must capture a designer's momentary inspiration, much as a canvas captures even the most subtle brush strokes of an artist." [Urlocker 89]

Experimenting with the prototype, you might find elements that the written analysis didn't take into account. Sometimes the idea of an algorithm, or the classes already implemented, might stimulate new functionality or an extension in the use of the application.

4. This approach is particularly interesting for the solution of unstructured and poorly defined problems, to develop new kinds of applications, and to experiment with new software areas. If the domain of the problem is neither well understood nor clear, it's very difficult to design an application without writing some of its code and defining the main abstraction it's based upon.

5. Another advantage of evolutionary programming is its natural association to object-oriented programming, which offers some useful constructs for its implementation (notably inheritance and polymorphism).

"In an object-oriented program, classes are organized hierarchically, with subclasses automatically inheriting the data and functionality of higher classes. When proper encapsulation is used, no penalty is involved in changing the internal design of a class or creating a new subclass. Object-oriented languages make it easy for the programmer to evolve a program without breaking it." [Urlocker 89]

Mastering evolutionary programming requires some experience. However, the following rules of thumb derived from [Urlocker 89] show you the correct road to follow:

- Evolve the program from the initial prototype until its completion, and consider following the same road for further releases of the program.

- Experiments by themselves won't lead to a program. Just as in a traditional development cycle, beside changing the code, you still need to repeat the analysis and design steps over and over.

- Use tools that help creativity and experimentation, such as an object-oriented language and an integrated programming environment (Borland C++ might be a good choice).

- Follow a methodology that pays particular attention to flexibility and reusability (an object-oriented design methodology might serve the purpose).

- Try to make the program work in the shortest time without sacrificing its theoretical structure; then you will have time to worry about speed and patch things.

- Frequently check the correctness of the classes you build, perhaps writing small test applications for the classes or hierarchies.

- Base your application on few well-designed classes; avoid changing them radically along the way.

- Periodically, stop to rethink the whole problem and solution (the application) with an open mind, ready to change the errors made but also to find the good modules that should enter the "stable part" of the program.

An evolutionary project is like a "flexible vacation itinerary." [Urlocker 89] In it you must know the main cities and states you want to visit, the most common means of transportation, and have an idea of the route. In this kind of travel you don't plan all the trips and visits from the beginning, nor the number of days to spend in each town you will reach. As you discover new places, you change the projected itinerary. On the other hand, if all the hotels and restaurants were booked in advance, you would either have to follow the program, missing the interesting places you previously did not know of, or change the program, creating a bunch of problems for the rest of the trip. The same difference holds between evolutionary programming and the traditional approach to a software life cycle.

The Effect of Recompilations in C++

One of the features of C++ that eases the development of an evolutionary application is the ability to change some classes without having to recompile all the source code.

A program made up of different source files (.CPP) can generate several object files (.OBJ), independently compiled. Then, the linker builds the single executable program

(.EXE). When you change one source file, you only need to recompile that file and relink the program. The other source file need not be compiled, under some conditions that will be explained in this section.

Using an object-oriented methodology, each class can be divided into a header file containing its interface, and a file with the definition of the member functions (the body of the class).

After separating the interface and the body of any class in two files, the recompilations necessary for a change are summarized in Table 13.4.

- In case of a **client relationship** between two classes, a change in the interface implies the recompilation of the client, while a change in the body has no effect. If the class changed is among the data members of another class, the interface of this second class might be automatically changed (since it depends on the size of the first class). There is the risk of a chain propagation of this situation onto other classes. Therefore, it might be useful to make some classes totally independent from their implementation, using the *friend* construct and technique described in Chapter 5.

  Of course, a class using another class might be freely altered.

- In the case of **inheritance relationship**, the situation is more complex. The changes to the interface of a class always imply the recompilation of all the derived classes. The changes to the body don't require the recompilation of the subclasses, although the effect of their member functions might be altered.

  The changes to a derived class don't affect the base class. However, to change the binding of a member function you must modify the code of the base class that defines the function (adding or taking out the *virtual* keyword), then recompile the whole hierarchy.

Table 13.4 Recompilations to be done after a change

Relation between the classes A and B	Changes in the interface of class A	Changes in the body of class A
B uses A	Recompilation of A and B (after proper changes); even the interface of B might be altered	Recompilation of A only
A uses B	Recompilation of A only	Recompilation of A only
A derives from B	Recompilation of A, unless to change the binding of a member function	Recompilation of A only
B derives from A	Recompilation of A and B	Recompilation of A (even if the functions of B might change)

These rules give you an idea of the consequences of the recompilation process, which you might not always be aware of, since you only have to include in your source files the headers containing the interfaces of the classes you use or inherit from. Then the *project* and *make* tools can automatically decide which source files must be recompiled for any change you do.

Automatic Handling of Recompilations

Borland C++ includes two tools to automatically handle recompilation after a change in the source code. One is the traditional *make*, and the other is the easier-to-use *project*. We have already used the project tool to compile some applications with multiple source files. In this section, you will be given details and hints on using the project tool.

The most common tool used to handle the compilation of applications with multiple source files is *make*; this tool derives from the UNIX environment and is available in most programming environments, including Borland C++. You can get some information about *Make* in the Borland C++ documentation.

By using *make* you can write a special text file (called a *makefile*) that instructs the utility which source files make up the various parts of the program, which operation must be performed on them, and what their mutual dependencies are. You specify the compilers to be used and their parameters, the linker and its parameters, and so on. When make is executed after some changes in the source files, only the modules affected by the changes are recompiled. The check for changes takes place by examining the time stamps for each file. Whenever one of the source files that is part of a module has a later time stamp than the object file, it is recompiled. (Of course, the computer's internal clock must always be correct.) To recompile the whole project, you can alter the time stamp of the source files with the *touch* utility. A detailed description of the *make* tool can be found in Borland's documentation.

The *project* tool can be considered an extension to *make*; it offers all the features of the standard tool, but is much easier to use. Writing a makefile is not so intuitive, especially for beginners, and requires a lot of ongoing updates as the structure of the application changes. The project tool, instead, automatically looks for most information, checking all the file dependencies during the first compilation; *project* uses standard criteria, which can be changed easily by selecting the options offered in a dialog box.

A project lists all (and only) the source files that must be separately compiled, generating autonomous object code files. If a source code file (.CPP) is included in a second source file, only the last one must be inserted in the *project*.

Once you have compiled the *project*, you can select a file of the list to view the files included in the source. They are the files the object code depends on. The list of include files for an old project is shown in Figure 13.2. Any change in one of the files listed will cause the recompilation of the corresponding .*cpp* file.

A second important operation is to view, and modify, the operations to be performed on the different files. Clicking with the right mouse button on a item of the project list

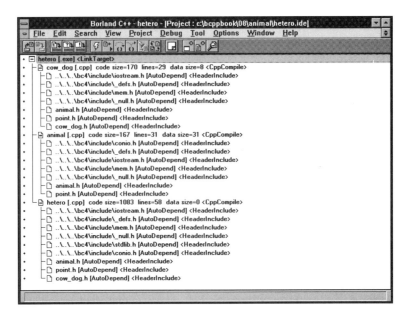

Figure 13.2 List of include files for one of the items listed in a project window

opens a local menu (see Figure 13.3), with the operations that can be performed on a file, such as compiling or preprocessing it, changing its compile options and so on. The actual operations depend on the kind of file (usually the extension of the file determines its kind).

Another advantage of the *project* tool is that it saves all the actual compiler and environment options. Every time you load a project the system restores all its options, letting you set different parameters for different projects (compiler options, the default *INCLUDE* and *LIB* directories, and so on).

POINTS TO CONSIDER

1. What "original" kinds of reusability are you already using in your work?

2. What kind of code reuse have you already used? (Macros? Function libraries?)

3. Find out in the examples of the previous chapters, or in other C or C++ programs, how many functions are used that come from libraries. Evaluate how much code is spared in the different occurrences. Check how many problems arise when the functions and the data you want to use with them don't match properly.

4. Evaluate the impact of modifications and the maintenance effort for applications you have developed in the past. Consider the time that was necessary to operate a small change, the number of places of the code to alter. Was it possible to change a part of the original assumptions of the application without rewriting most of its code?

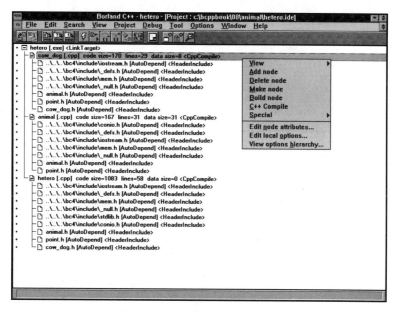

Figure 13.3 The local menu for a *.cpp* file

spared in the different occurrences. Check how many problems arise when the functions and the data you want to use with them don't match properly.

4. Evaluate the impact of modifications and the maintenance effort for applications you have developed in the past. Consider the time that was necessary to operate a small change, the number of places of the code to alter. Was it possible to change a part of the original assumptions of the application without rewriting most of its code?

5. Do you think that your programming style resembles more the traditional or the evolutionary model? Check yours against the ideas and the suggestions of the chapter. Do you feel that evolutionary and object-oriented programming have something in common? What are the differences?

6. Familiarize yourself with the *project* tool, changing some parameters of the shape project file or defining new ones. What happens if you alter the kind of compiler to be used or leave a module out of the linking process? What if you change the time stamp of a dependent file with *touch*?

14

Efficiency and Correctness of Code

It is great to have flexible software that is easy to build and easy to maintain, but we also need to be concerned that the software does what it is supposed to do. [Meyer 89]

Generally, the programs that you write—in addition to being "well designed"—must also have at least two other important features: they must be efficient and, most important, they must be correct. This chapter will introduce some of the support tools provided by the Borland environment (the integrated debugger, in particular) and some common programming techniques to achieve these two different aims.

We will try to analyze the execution speed of some basic constructs of the C++ language, as a means to explore the subject of efficiency of object-oriented programming languages. We will also examine the code optimizations that can be performed directly by the compiler. This topic is important in C++ because this language is a marriage of the low level efficiency of C with the higher-level abstractions of object-oriented programming languages.

The second part of this chapter is about the debugger, a traditional tool that is essential for analyzing an application and trying to solve its problems and correct its errors. You will then learn how to avoid errors or, failing that, how to correct them. Defensive programming (that is, adding a lot of checks in the code to ensure program correctness) is a legitimate approach, which in true object-oriented thinking is better replaced by contractual programming (that is, the responsibility of program correctness is subdivided precisely among the different modules). Finally, we explore the issue of assertion (stating the truth of an expression), or of a class "*invariant*" expression, as a way to debug a program.

This chapter provides only an overview of two main features (efficiency and correctness) and related tools (the debugger) from the point of view of object-oriented programming. Even though our descriptions of these two features will not be exhaustive, we feel it is important to cover them in relation to their basic relevance in the daily, routine effort of any programmer.

Efficiency in C++

One of the criticisms that is often addressed to object-oriented languages is that they generate executable code that is much less efficient than the code generated by traditional languages. This is unquestionably true for some object-oriented languages, especially those that are completely dynamic—like Smalltalk—but is far less apparent in the case of C++. In fact, efficiency is one of the goals stated by the inventor of the language, and some of his implementation decisions clearly reflect this. This is particularly evident with *inline* functions, the introduction of the *friend* construct, and the decision to allow both static as well as dynamic *binding*.

Inline Functions

One of the properties that can make an object-oriented program slower than a traditional program is the heavy use of data access functions, which is a direct consequence of the application of the information-hiding principle. For this reason, C++ lets you make *inline* substitutions of functions, which means that every function call is actually replaced by the function's executable code to avoid the overhead due to the actual calling of the function.

This problem of program speed has already been described in Chapter 4, where some criteria for deciding whether to use *inline* functions were exposed. Now instead, you will analyze this construct with the help of a *Timer* class, having a *start* and a *stop* function which read the system time, and a *difference* function returning the elapsed time. Here is the class that we will use in the next two examples.

```
// file TIMER.H                                          14/EFFICIEN
// definition of a timer class

#include <dos.h>

class Timer
{
    dostime_t   tStart, tStop;
    int         running;
    // running is a boolean indicating the timer status

public:
    Timer ( ) :
        running (0)      // FALSE
    { }

    void Start ( )
    {
        if (!running)
```

```
        {
            running = 1 ;      // TRUE
            _dos_gettime (&tStart) ;
        }
    }

    void Stop ( )
    {
        if (running)
        {
            running = 0 ;      // FALSE
            _dos_gettime (&tStop) ;
        }
    }

    // returns the difference in hundredths of seconds
    long Difference ( )
    {
        if (!running)
        {
            int sec = ( (tStop.hour - tStart.hour) * 60 +
                    tStop.minute - tStart.minute) * 60 +
                    tStop.second - tStart.second ;

            return ( sec * 100 + tStop.hsecond - tStart.hsecond) ;
        }
        else
            return 0;
    }
} ;
```

To make the first test, we have written a program that defines three similar classes. The difference between them is found in the different ways the single data items are accessed. In *ClassA*, the data item is *public* and can therefore be accessed directly with the *dot-notation* typical of traditional C structures. Instead, in *ClassB* and *ClassC* the data member is *private*, and can therefore be accessed only through a member function, which in the case of *ClassC* is an *inline* function (for the simple reason that it is defined inside the class itself).

➤   *Note:* Before you compile this example, if the two statements are to produce any different code at all, you must ensure that *inline* compilation is active by looking at the *Compiler, Debugging* options and making sure that the check box "*Out-of-line inline functions*" is *not* checked.

```
// file ACCESS.CPP                                    14/EFFICIEN
// efficienty test comparing different ways to access data:
// directly, using inline or ordinary member functions

#include <iostream.h>
#include "timer.h"

// class A: public data with direct access

class ClassA
{
public:

    int data;

    ClassA (int d) :
        data (d)
        { }
} ;

// class B: private data, normal access function

class ClassB
{
    int data;

public:

    ClassB (int d) :
        data (d)
        { }

    int Data ();
} ;

int ClassB :: Data ()
    {
        return data;
    }

// class C: private data, inline access function

class ClassC
{
    int data;
```

```
public:

    ClassC (int d) :
        data (d)
        { }

    int Data ()
        {
            return data;
        }
} ;

// example comparing the three different access methods

void main ( )
{
    int total ;
    long  i ;      // loop counter
    const long loop_times = 10000000L ;

    // three timers
    Timer t1, t2, t3;

    ClassA  a ( 10 ) ;
    ClassB  b ( 10 ) ;
    ClassC  c ( 10 ) ;

    t1.Start ( ) ;
    for ( i = 0; i < loop_times; i++ )
        total = a.data ;
    t1.Stop ( ) ;

    t2.Start ( ) ;
    for ( i = 0; i < loop_times; i++ )
        total = b.Data ( ) ;
    t2.Stop ( ) ;

    t3.Start ( ) ;
    for ( i = 0; i < loop_times; i++ )
        total = c.Data ( ) ;
    t3.Stop ( ) ;

    cout << "Direct access required " << t1.Difference ( )
        << " hundredths of seconds" << endl ;
    cout << "Normal function access required " << t2.Difference ( )
```

```
        << " hundredths of seconds" << endl ;
      cout << "Inline function access required " << t3.Difference ( )
        << " hundredths of seconds" << endl ;
  }
```

When you compile and run the program, its output will show you the time required for each of the three operations. The execution of this applications takes some time (about 25 seconds on a fast 486 machine) during which the system is completely blocked. If you have a slower machine you might consider reducing the value of the *long* constant indicating the number times the loop has to be repeated.

The reported times tend to vary a little each time you run the program. On the machine we have used they are (approximately): 483 for the direct access, 1214 for the normal function call, and 511 for the inline function.

From this data two significant conclusions can be drawn:

1. Direct access to data members is really much faster than the corresponding access through functions.

2. The access to data members with an *inline* function is comparable to that of direct access.

Therefore, if it is true that object-oriented programs with many data access functions are potentially a lot slower than traditional programs, then *inline* expansion of functions can completely overcome the problem.

Another advantage in this sense is the possibility of using the *friend* construct to directly access the private data members of another class, without having to rely on its data access functions. Sometimes, this construct can be useful, despite the fact that it is unmistakably in contrast with the rules of information hiding (that is, of encapsulation of data items).

A "purist" solution to this problem would be to never use the *friend* construct, except to make a key algorithm more efficient (provided there will be a significant performance gain in doing so). Any algorithm that is the main bottleneck of an entire application is a good candidate for an extreme optimization that takes advantage of all mechanisms available, even of this arguable construct.

Static and Dynamic Binding

Another option in C++ that favors efficiency is the choice of either static or dynamic binding between the call of a function and the code that gets executed in response to this call. The deficiencies of this approach, which requires you to make a decision at the design and implementation level of the topmost class in a hierarchy, have already been discussed.

However, we must stress that in order for the code generated by the compiler to resolve a dynamically bound call, it will at most have to execute a pair of indirect references to get to the address of the response function inside a table of virtual functions. On the contrary, some dynamic object-oriented languages (most notably, Smalltalk) deal with the search of a response function by means of a tree traversal, whose size (and thus the traversal time) is not limited.

Despite this, it is preferable for most of the functions, where dynamic binding is not strictly necessary, to use static binding simply because static binding is faster.

Let's try to check this out with the help of the *Timer* class we have used in the last example. This time we will look at the relative speed of the two types of binding. To do this, you can run the following program and look at its output.

```cpp
// file BIND.CPP                                          14/EFFICIEN
// testing the speed of functions with static and dynamic binding

#include <iostream.h>
#include "timer.h"

// Class1 definition
class Class1
{
    int value ;

public:
    Class1 (int n) :
        value (n)
    { }

    int Value ( ) ;
    void Value (int n) ;
} ;

// member functions of Class1
int Class1 :: Value ( )
{
    return value ;
}

void Class1 :: Value (int n)
{
    value = n ;
}

// Class2 definition,
// similar to the previous one, but with virtual functions
class Class2
{
    int value;
```

```
public:
   Class2 (int n) :
      value (n)
   { }

   virtual int Value ( ) ;
   virtual void Value (int n) ;
} ;

// Class2 member functions
int Class2 :: Value ( )
{
   return value ;
}

void Class2 :: Value (int n)
{
   value = n ;
}

// main, testing the relative speed
void main ( )
{
   // two timers and two objects of the two classes
   Timer t1, t2 ;
   Class1 *    pc1 = new Class1 (25) ;
   Class2 *   pc2 = new Class2 (25) ;

   long  i ;    // loop counter
   const long loop_times = 10000000L ;

   // the statement in the loop is *very* readable

   t1.Start ( ) ;
   for ( i = 0; i < loop_times; i++ )
      pc1->Value (pc1->Value ( )) ;
   t1.Stop ( ) ;

   t2.Start ( ) ;
   for ( i = 0; i < loop_times; i++ )
      pc2->Value (pc2->Value ( )) ;
   t2.Stop ( ) ;

   cout << "Static member functions required " << t1.Difference ( )
      << " hundredths of seconds" << endl ;
```

```
    cout << "Dynamic (virtual) functions required " << t2.Difference ( )
       << " hundredths of seconds" << endl ;
}
```

If you run this program, remember that it will require a lot of time, maybe around 40 seconds on a fast computer. As before, you can decrease the number of times the loop is repeated, but this will reduce the accuracy of the test. Another factor you should consider is that the Borland compiler supports different implementations of virtual functions. In the *Virtual Tables* section of the *C++ Options* you can choose among *Smart*, *Local*, *External*, and *Public*.

Approximate values for the output of the above program differ slightly in the different case, with values around 2040 for the static binding and around 2145 for the dynamic binding. This is a hint suggesting that there is just a little overhead involved in virtual function calls. The real disadvantage is that the static functions can be *inlined*; in this case the execution time for the first loops drops to 610.

More rigorous analyses have pointed out that the call overhead for dynamic binding is about 25%. This refers to the call by itself: The operations the function has to perform require some time, reducing drastically the overhead for any nontrivial function. You also have to consider that using polymorphism you spare some amount of code. A *switch* statement with many branches is certainly slower than the direct call of virtual function.

Borland's Optimizing Compiler

The Borland C++ compiler is an *optimizing compiler*, which means that it is capable of automatically performing many optimizing changes to your code.

A well-conceived algorithm can seldom be optimized any further by an optimizing compiler. So why use an optimizer? The answer is: to save time. Not execution time— in this case—but the programmer's time. It is not always easy to consistently come up with the "best" algorithm, but often the gain achievable with an optimizing compiler is more than adequate. In this way, the programmer can better concentrate on inventing an acceptable solution, rather then trying to squeeze out every bit of performance from the processor's cycles.

An optimizer can operate in two directions, making the code faster or more compact. In both cases, the compiler must ensure a perfect correspondence between the original code and the optimized one.

An optimizer can operate in several ways, both locally and globally. To understand how it can modify and improve the code, we will list the most important transformation made by a generic optimizing compiler (although not all of them are supported by Borland C++). It is necessary to note that usually real benefits come only if several of these transformations are applied to the same piece of code. The following list is derived from [Crespi 90]:

- *Copy propagation* is the substitution of a variable with its most recent value.

- *Constant folding* is the substitution of a constant expression with its value (this optimization is seldom directly applied to the original code, but might be used in conjunction with others).

- *Jump reduction* is the transformation of two consecutive jump expressions into a single one.

- *Dead code elimination* is the elimination of inaccessible code, which might result from other optimizations.

- *Redundant assignments elimination* statements, such as the first of two consecutive assignments to the same variable, or the assignment of a value to a variable that will not be used again, can be avoided.

- *Common subexpressions elimination;* if a subexpression is used several times without a change in the value of variables that appear in it, it could be computed only the first time, storing the value in a temporary location.

- *Loop invariants extraction;* an expression of a loop that does not change from one iteration to the following one is called loop invariant, and can be placed before the loop, where it will be computed only once.

- *Strength reduction* is the substitution of an operation with a simpler one, such as a sum for a multiplication; it's commonly used to reduce expressions within loops that operate on the induction variable of the loop.

- *Inline substitution*: an optimization we have already met and described, but that could be automatically performed by the compiler.

- *Loops unfolding*; a *for* loop executed a constant number of times might be replaced with several copies of its statements.

- *Stack pollution*; leaving useless information on the stack between two consecutive calls can reduce the number of operations to be performed to handle it.

- *Register allocation*; choosing the right variable to store in a register instead of in memory is a crucial point of any optimizer, since having the right values already at hand can save a huge amount of time.

- *Code hoisting*; if a subexpression will be encountered several times in different branches of a conditional statement, it might be interesting to compute it before the branch, storing its value in a temporary location (this might slow the program but can reduce its size).

- *Expression propagation* is the substitution of a variable with the expression used to compute it; this is a strange counter-optimizing operation, which can lead to other subsequent interesting optimizations that will actually improve the resulting code.

As we have already stated, not all of these operations can be performed by the Borland C++ compiler: its optimization features include register allocation, common subexpression elimination, loop invariants extraction, copy propagation, strength reduction, redundant assignments elimination, and inline substitution.

➤ *Note:* Some operations are described with different names, and they do not correspond exactly to those described above, although conceptually they are very similar.

Compiling the same piece of code with the optimization features enabled or disabled, you will see that the resulting code will probably be slightly different; however, unless you have a strong knowledge of assembly language, you will find it difficult to appreciate and understand the real effects of the differences.

The following is an interesting test that shows actual differences between optimized and nonoptimized code: if you compile a "silly" piece of code, such as the following one, enabling the optimizer, and then execute it step by step, you will notice that some statements will be completely disregarded, since they have been eliminated during the optimization process. On the other hand, if you repeat the same process, but this time disable the optimizer, the effect will be different since all the statements will be executed, even those that are ineffective.

```cpp
// file SILLY.CPP                                          14/SILLY
// example to show the effects of the optimizer on a "silly" piece of code

#include <iostream.h>

void main ( )
{
    int    x = 5 ;
    int    y = 8 ;

    x = 5 ;
    x = 4 ;
    x = 7 ;
    x = 25 * 8 ;

    y = 7 ;
    y = 89 ;
    y = 99 ;
    y = x ;

    cout  << x << " "
          << y << endl ;

    if ( 5 > 0 )
        x = y ;
```

```
    else
       x = 27 ;
    x = 8 ;

    cout  << x << " "
           << y << endl << endl ;
}
```

Another interesting test is the following: You can easily compile to assembler using the *Special* popup of the local menu for the source code, and look at the resulting code (just load the resulting *.asm* file). Even if you do not know much of the assembler language, you can compare two files produced with and without optimizations and see that in the optimized one some lines of the resulting code are omitted. The lines can be easily spotted because the C++ source text is included as a comment.

However, if you try to compile an already "hand-tuned" algorithm you will notice only a slight difference between the optimized and the nonoptimized versions. This happens because if an algorithm is already quite good, then the optimizer is certainly not so powerful as to improve the *code* in a way comparable to what one can do changing an algorithm in a suitable way. It is important to stress this difference: The optimizer works on the code generated by the compiler, while a mathematical enhancement pertains to the algorithm.

The following question might arise: How does optimization affect the object-oriented constructs of the language? Actually, optimization provides us with an important benefit, especially with inline member functions: "Once inlined, the code of a function becomes available to optimizers that would otherwise not optimize across a function call boundary." [Ellis 90]

This statement means that the optimizer is even more significant in a language like C++ —where the correct application of the principle of information hiding imposes the use of member data access functions—because it could nullify the (already minimal) differences between direct access to a data member and access through an (inlined) member function.

The Debugger

We will now describe a tool integrated with the Borland C++ programming environment: the debugger. This utility is necessary to test the code that you have written and to detect the errors that it might possibly have. In short, a debugger lets you execute a program step by step, analyzing what is actually happening both at the logical level (for instance, by inspecting the contents of a variable) as well as the machine level (for instance, by examining the machine code instructions that are executed and the values of the CPU registers).

Borland C++ actually comes with several debuggers, which can be used in different circumstances, although they all share the same kind of functionality: a basic debugger integrated in the IDE, and the standalone Turbo Debugger, having a only text-mode interface but different *flavors* for remote debugging (via a serial port from another computer or even through a Novell network link) and for debugging from a different virtual 386 machine.

Of course, we will not describe all the details of all of these tools in this book, but we will provide some general guidelines on the usage of the features of the standard debugger. In general, it is preferable to start by using the facilities of the integrated version, and load the standalone debugger only if necessary, because it is a lot more powerful but also a lot more complicated to use.

In this section, we give a brief overview of the type of information that can be obtained from the debugger in the most simple cases.

To show how the integrated debugger works, you can compile the following program, which looks simple but which actually conceals an error:

```
// file DEBUG.CPP                                                14/DEBUG
// program to demonstrate the use of the debugger

#include <iostream.h>

void main ( )
{
    int number = 1000 ;

    // computes 50 percent of the value and outputs it

    number = number * 50 / 100 ;
    cout << "50% of 1000 equals " << number << endl ;
}
```

If you try to run this program, you will get the output:

```
1000 * 50 / 100 = -155
```

Why is this? If you run the program step by step (clicking on the proper toolbar icon), you can examine (*inspect* or *watch*) the value of a variable at any point in the program, clicking on it with the right mouse button and selecting the corresponding action from the local menu. The effect of some of these operations on the previous DEBUG.CPP program is illustrated in Figures 14.1 and 14.2.

From Figure 14.2 you can infer that the evaluation of the expression *number * 50* is faulty (indeed it is an overflow error on the *int* type, which can represent a maximum value of 32767).

Once you understand the reason for the error, you can easily correct it: simply change the statement and execute the division before the multiplication, in order not to have partial results that overflow, like

```
number = number / 100 * 50;
```

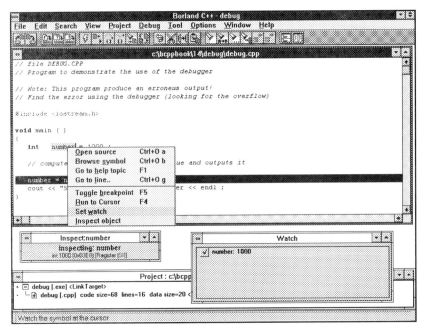

Figure 14.1 Watching and inspecting the *number* variable of the DEBUG program

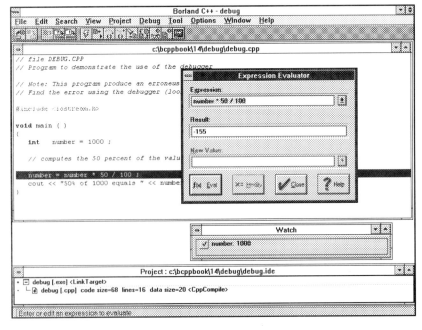

Figure 14.2 The evaluation of an expression in the IDE debugger

although the result of this expression is rounded (the last two digits are truncated), or converting the *int* into a different data type during the evaluation of the expression in one of the two following ways:

```
// conversion to float
number = number * 50.0 / 100;
```

```
// conversion to long
number = long (number) * 50 / 100;
```

➤   *Note:* The previous discussion becomes meaningless if you compile the program for a 32 bit environment. In this case the compiler will produce 32 bit code, using integer arithmetic at 32 bits instead of 16 bits. With a bigger representation, integers can treat numbers up to 2 billion (instead of up to 32 thousand).

In general, the debugger does not "find" an error; it just helps you to understand the "physical outcome" of the statements of your program. While the integrated debugger allows you to work at the logical level of the program (by inspecting variables and evaluating expressions at any point in the program, and maybe even changing them to see what happens), in general the standalone debugger gives a more complete and detailed vision of the physical machine (contents of memory segments, assembled code, values in CPU registers, and so on).

To continue with the preceding example, you can *step over* it once more opening the *register view* with the corresponding menu command. When you execute the multiplication the *carry* flag (*c*) will be set to one, indicating the error.

For now though, we will look at another program that behaves erratically: the DANGLE.CPP program that you saw in Chapter 6.

Once you have this program loaded and compiled, but before running it, set a *breakpoint* (that is, a position in which you want the program to stop) on the statement

```
delete ( a ) ;
```

by issuing a *Toggle breakpoint* command with the local menu after you position the cursor on the corresponding line in the editor. Now, running the program normally it will stop on the indicated breakpoint. By opening a *Watch* window with the variables *a* and *b* and the expressions **a* and **b* you can discover what happens during execution of this statement (which is the next *step*). You will, in this way, go from the correct situation shown in Figure 14.3 to the faulty one, shown in Figure 14.4, where the value of *b* becomes 12. You can thus verify for yourself what was already said on the issue of dangling references in Chapter 6.

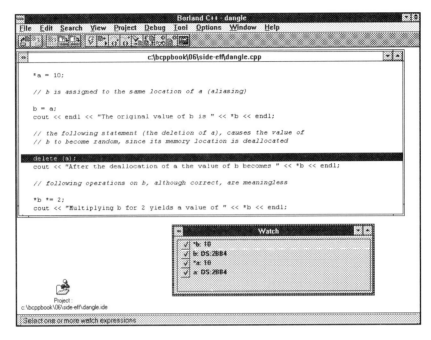

Figure 14.3   The variables *a* and *b* in the correct situation

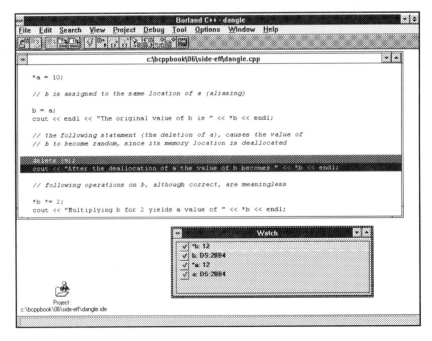

Figure 14.4   The situation of a dangling reference for the variable *b*

Strategies for Avoiding Errors

Certainly the best way to avoid errors is not to make them! But programming without errors is not easy. The methods and the strategies that can be used to avoid errors are numerous, so we will try to summarize some of the most interesting concepts.

First of all, it is necessary to note that some constructs introduced by C++, compared to those already available in C, are useful for avoiding errors. In particular, a big advantage for programmers is given by a more strict static type-checking on data and parameters passed to functions, which allows the compiler to detect some errors that can take place in parameter passing.

Another method that can help to reduce errors is the correct use of classes for applying the principle of information hiding. By eliminating global data and using mainly local data inside classes, you can lower the risk of errors when accessing and modifying data. Furthermore, possible errors pertaining to a certain data item are easier to identify (simply because they are local to the class that defines and uses that data item).

> "By designing classes with well-defined interfaces, you minimize the risk of system wide bugs. All bugs will be within some module and can be handled without messing up the rest of the program. Designing in small chunks also minimizes the chance of making mistakes and makes it easier to figure out what a module should do. In short, good design equals bug prevention." [Dlogosz 90]

All this does not eliminate the necessity of making run time checks in the program, to be sure that there are no abnormal conditions.

These abnormal conditions can be divided into two broad categories, boundary problems and programming errors, which must be tackled in different ways. With boundary conditions, the result of a function might be undefined, or the function might be unreliable due to some intrinsic limitation (such as round-off errors). In these cases, some run time errors might arise, which must be prevented by the programmer. For instance, a function could "hang" if it is presented a 0 parameter (because it performs a division by 0), an array could run out of space, or the program could try to access a data structure where no data has yet been written.

The second category involves the consequences of genuine programming errors, which cause wrong behavior by the program. Instead of waiting for these errors to become evident, then trying to get rid of them, it is theoretically more interesting and practically more comforting to have some kind of control mechanism. This control would allow you to be somewhat more confident in the correctness of an application. We will now examine these two situations in more detail.

Defensive Programming . . .

To avoid errors during run time in the critical conditions that the program might encounter, you should at least be careful with boundary conditions and check them out thoroughly.

You can use different strategies to identify potential problems, among which a very common approach is called *defensive programming*. However, there are also other alternatives such as *contractual programming*.

Before examining what all this is about, it is better to introduce a real example where it is necessary to have some kind of run time check. Assume that you need to describe a buffer to store numeric values (a buffer is a data structure that works like a FIFO queue) and to implement it as a circular buffer with a fixed sized array.

The code of the class and of an example of its usage—without making any kind of run time check—could be the following:

```
// file BUFFER.CPP                                          14/BUFFER
// Base class describing a FIFO buffer holding
// at most ten numbers of type long

#include <iostream.h>

const int elements = 10 ;

class Buffer
{
    long   data [elements] ;
    int nElements ;
    int nFirst ;
    int nLast ;

public:

    Buffer ( ) ;
    void Put (long n) ;
    long Get ( ) ;
    int NumEl ( ) ;
} ;

// member functions definition

Buffer :: Buffer ( ) :
    nElements (0) ,
    nFirst (0) ,
    nLast (0)
{ }

void Buffer :: Put (long n)
{
    data [nFirst] = n ;
    nFirst = (nFirst + 1) % elements ;
```

```
        nElements ++ ;
}

long Buffer :: Get ( )
{
    long n = data [nLast] ;
    nLast = (nLast + 1) % elements ;
    nElements — ;
    return n ;
}

int Buffer :: NumEl ( )
{
    return nElements ;
}


// example of Buffer use
void main ( )
{
    Buffer    buf ;
    char      command ;

    do
    {
        cout << "P)ut, G)et, Q)uit :" ;
        cin >> command ;
        switch (command)
        {
            case 'p':
            {
                long element ;
                cout << "Number to be added to buffer: " ;
                cin >> element ;
                buf.Put (element) ;
            }
                break;

            case 'g':
            {
                long element ;
                element = buf.Get ( ) ;
                cout << "Number retrived from buffer: "
                    << element << endl ;
            }
```

```
                break;
        }
    }
    while (command != 'q');
}
```

When running this program, you will notice that when you extract from the buffer more elements than those that have actually been inserted, or if you insert more than 10 elements at a time, its behavior becomes completely random, as shown in Figure 14.5. In fact, the program is not able to handle these boundary conditions; it continues to handle them with its ordinary operations.

Furthermore, if you input a character instead of a number, you will no longer be able to command the program (it will go on forever, printing its prompt on the screen). This error is caused by the user's input, on which it is always better to impose strict verification procedures.

To correct these problems, and particularly to avoid the extraction of data that is not available or the insertion of more data than can fit, let's try to create a "defensive" version of this buffer. This defensive approach means that you have to add checks inside the member functions that perform the insertion and the extraction of data elements of the class *Buffer*. You can then test the resulting program to see if it survives the preceding boundary conditions. The resulting program could be like this:

```
// file DEFENSIV.CPP                                       14/DEFENSIV
// Class describing a FIFO buffer holding ten numbers
// with a "defensive" strategy to avoid errors

#include <iostream.h>
#include <stdlib.h>
```

```
            C:\BCPPBOOK\14\BUFFER\BUFFER.EXE
P)ut, G)et, Q)uit :p
Number to be added to buffer: 111
P)ut, G)et, Q)uit :p
Number to be added to buffer: 222
P)ut, G)et, Q)uit :p
Number to be added to buffer: 333333
P)ut, G)et, Q)uit :g
Number retrieved from buffer: 111
P)ut, G)et, Q)uit :g
Number retrieved from buffer: 222
P)ut, G)et, Q)uit :g
Number retrieved from buffer: 333333
P)ut, G)et, Q)uit :g
Number retrieved from buffer: 69146
P)ut, G)et, Q)uit :g
Number retrieved from buffer: 171051624
P)ut, G)et, Q)uit :
```

Figure 14.5 Output of BUFFER.CPP at a boundary condition

```
const int elements = 10 ;

class Buffer
{
    long   data [elements] ;
    int nElements ;
    int nFirst ;
    int nLast ;

public:
    Buffer ( ) ;
    int Put (long n) ;
    int Get (long & n) ;
} ;

// member functions

Buffer :: Buffer () :
    nElements (0) ,
    nFirst (0) ,
    nLast (0)
{ }

int Buffer :: Put (long n)
{
    // returns 0 if OK, 1 if an error occurs
    if (nElements == elements)
        return 1 ;
    else
    {
        data [nFirst] = n ;
        nFirst = (nFirst + 1) % elements ;
        nElements ++ ;
        return 0 ;
    }
}

// the interface of the function changes!
// returns 0 if OK, 1 an error occurs
int Buffer :: Get (long & n)
{
    if (nElements)
    {
        n = data [nLast] ;
        nLast = (nLast + 1) % elements ;
```

```
            nElements — ;
            return 0 ;
        }
    else
        return 1 ;
}


// example of use of the defensive version of Buffer

void main ( )
{
    Buffer    buf ;
    char   command ;

    do
    {
        cout << "P)ut, G)et, Q)uit :" ;
        cin >> command ;

        switch (command)
        {

            case 'p':
            {
                long element ;
                do
                {

                    cout << "Number to be added to buffer: ";
                    // checks that a number is entered
                    char   string [10] ;
                    cin >> string ;
                    element = atol (string) ;
                    if (! element)
                        cout << "Error: it's not a number" << endl ;
                }
                while (! element) ;

                // checks that the value is properly added to the buffer
                if (buf.Put (element))
                    cout << "Error: too many values" << endl;
            }
                break;
```

```
        case 'g':
        {
            long element;
            if (buf.Get (element))
                cout << "Error: no value present!" << endl ;
            else
                cout << "Number retrived from buffer: " << element << endl ;
        }
            break;

    } // end switch
 } // end do-while
 while (command != 'q') ;
}
```

Now the program works well, with the only drawback being a slightly slower speed due to the execution of the check statements. Once this kind of check pervades an entire program, it should work flawlessly; at least, that is the opinion of many programmers. This type of program that takes into account extremes that the user may enter is known as a robust program.

. . . And Contractual Programming

Yet someone argues that even if "defensive programming is considered to be a programmer's best shot at reliability … [it] is a dangerous practice that defeats the very purpose it tries to achieve … one of the worst pieces of advice that can be given to a programmer … Reliability is not obtained by cowardly adding even more checks, but by precisely delineating whose responsibility it is to ensure each consistent requirement." [Meyer 89]

In fact, you could ask yourself if there exists any way to define a "safe" buffer, whose operations are defined in a clear and unique way, without the class itself having the burden to make checks on the data it receives, and the program check both the parameters it passes to functions as well as their results. This doesn't mean that the functions must work in *any* condition: it is sufficient to spell out clearly when the functions are meaningful, and when, instead, they are undefined. If the functions are always defined (that is, they are total functions), then it is certainly easier to deal with them; but if they are not defined for all values of the parameters (partial functions), then it is sufficient to know precisely which values are permitted and which are banned.

Once a class has established these rules for its member functions, the other classes that use it will know how to behave, and should simply avoid making erroneous calls.

This is, more or less, the starting point of the method known as *contractual programming*: every function has obligations and offers benefits, and every call to them incurs obligations and benefits, which can be summarized in a table.

In this case, the class *buffer* and its users could settle a contract as shown in Figure 14.6. You could note that even the previous version of the class, the "defensive" version, implied a kind of contract, though a lot less clear, as shown in Figure 14.7. Comparing the two contracts, in the case of *contractual programming*, the greater amount of obligation its users incur is far outweighed by the greater benefits that these users receive in exchange.

Following the ideas expressed in the first contract, which is well defined, you can rewrite the class and use it in this way:

Put routine	*Obligations*	*Benefits*
Clients	Call the function only if the buffer is not full.	The required element is always inserted; no need to test for the success of the operation.
Function	Insert the passed element.	No need to worry about whether the buffer is already full.
Get routine	*Obligations*	*Benefits*
Clients	Check that the buffer is not empty.	Always gets an element.
Function	Return the current first element.	No need to return anything meaningful if the buffer is empty.

Figure 14.6 Contracts referring to the class that describes the buffer in the "contractual" case

Put routine	*Obligations*	*Benefits*
Clients	None.	The element is inserted unless the buffer is full.
Function	Insert the element or return an error message if the buffer is full.	None.
Get routine	*Obligations*	*Benefits*
Clients	None.	Either gets an element or an error message.
Function	Return an element or an error message if the buffer is empty.	None.

Figure 14.7 Contracts referring to the "defensive" case

```
// file CONTRACT.CPP                                    14/CONTRACT
// Class describing a FIFO buffer of ten elements
// with error checking based on a "contract" between the class and its user

#include <iostream.h>
#include <stdlib.h>

const int elements = 10 ;

class Buffer
{
    long   data [elements] ;
    int nElements ;
    int nFirst ;
    int nLast ;

public:
    Buffer ( ) ;
    void Put (long n) ;
    long Get ( ) ;
    int Empty ( ) ;
    int Full ( ) ;
    int NumEl ( ) ;
} ;

// member functions

Buffer :: Buffer () :
    nElements (0) ,
    nFirst (0) ,
    nLast (0)
{ }

// insertion is defined only if the buffer is not full
void Buffer :: Put (long n)
{
    data [nFirst] = n ;
    nFirst = (nFirst + 1) % elements ;
    nElements ++ ;
}

// extraction is defined only if the buffer is not empty
long Buffer :: Get ( )
{
```

```
        long n = data [nLast] ;
        nLast = (nLast + 1) % elements ;
        nElements — ;
        return n ;
    }

    int Buffer :: NumEl ( )
    {
        return nElements ;
    }

    // returns 1 if the buffer is full, else 0
    int Buffer :: Full ( )
    {
        return (nElements == elements) ;
    }

    // returns 1 if the buffer is empty, else 0
    int Buffer :: Empty ( )
    {
        return (nElements == 0) ;
    }


    // example of the "contractual" use of the buffer
    void main ( )
    {
        Buffer    buf ;
        char   command ;

        do
        {
            cout << "P)ut, G)et, Q)uit :" ;
            cin >> command ;

            switch (command)
            {
                case 'p':
                {
                    long element ;
                    do
                    {
                        cout << "Number to be added to buffer: " ;

                        // checks that a number is entered
```

```
                char  string [10] ;
                cin >> string ;
                element = atol (string) ;
                if (! element)
                    cout << "Error: it's not a number" << endl ;
            }
            while (! element) ;

            // if the buffer is not full adds the element
            if (! buf.Full ( ))
                buf.Put (element) ;
            else
                cout << "The buffer is already full" << endl ;
        }
            break ;

        case 'g':
        {
            long element ;
            if (! buf.Empty ( ))
            {
                element = buf.Get ( ) ;
                cout  << "Number retrived from buffer: "
                    << element << endl ;
            }
            else
                cout << "The buffer is empty" << endl ;
        }
            break ;

    }   // end switch
    }   // end do-while
    while (command != 'q');
}
```

The functions of the *Buffer* class in this "contractual" version are simple, just like in the original version; in fact, a function that does not have to worry about its boundary conditions can concentrate on getting its job done and doing so in the most efficient way. Having a more limited task, it can also perform it more correctly. The more statements you insert, even if they serve the purpose of checking, the more probable it is that you will perpetrate errors; this is particularly true if the addition of statements makes the flow of control less linear.

You could object that, in case of errors, there is no longer any "safety net" like that delivered by the redundant checks of defensive programs; but we will see in the following section how you can alleviate this doubt.

Troubleshooting Through Exceptions

After seeing the problems that might arise with boundary conditions, you will now examine those that arise from actual programming errors. Obviously, these errors are less foreseeable than the previous ones, simply because there are many more causes that might produce them. Furthermore, although it might be relatively easy to check if a parameter is zero or if a data structure is full, it is much more difficult to check if at any given time a program is behaving *correctly*.

If it is impossible to reason at the program level, you can at least focus on the components into which a program is subdivided: more specifically on its objects. If you could check the "correctness" of every object and of its various functions, you could infer the correctness of the whole program. But what does it mean for a function or an object to be "correct?"

First of all, notice that we are now reasoning in terms of objects and not classes: in fact, this kind of correctness check can be performed during run time only, when the entities that the program handles are the real variables (the objects) and not the data types of those variables (the classes).

To make some run-time checks on a program, we can use the *exception handling* capability of the C++ language, already introduced in detail in Chapter 11. The use of the exceptions in the following examples is theoretically more sound than their use in several examples of Chapter 11.

> ➤ *Note:* Before exceptions became part of the C++ language, similar run-time checks could be made using *assertions*, based on the ANSI C *ASSERT* macro (defined in the *ASSERT.H* header file), used only for debugging purposes. Since exceptions have much more power, the following examples will be based on them.

Preconditions and Postconditions

During the description of the contractual programming method, one aspect of the problem has been left out: is it possible to ensure that the ensuing classes (and the code that uses them) will honor their contract? One possibility is to raise an exception if the checks before the execution of member functions (*preconditions*) and after their execution (*postconditions*) are not positive. These conditions are like normal checks, but they halt the program and do not try to remedy the problem, because they shall always be met. Thus, *preconditions* and *postconditions* are a tool to verify the correct implementation of the contract between a class and its client, and are not actually part of the program.

In the precondition, which will be checked before the execution of the function, you have to verify if the client has honored its obligations. In the postcondition, which will be checked before the function returns its value or the procedure terminates, you have to verify that the function has fulfilled its duties, as stated by the contract. You cannot always make these kinds of checks, because sometimes the situation is just too simple (like checking if a return value is actually a correct value) or too complicated (checking which data is present on screen, or the tone of a note already emitted by the computer). Although this use of exceptions is not always applicable, nonetheless they can be very useful, especially in certain types of classes, and for complex systems, when it is necessary to ensure a minimal amount of control on quality and integration of the various subsystems (or different classes).

Returning to the earlier example in this chapter, you can add to the class *Buffer* the preconditions of the main member functions, starting from the version presented in the file CONTRACT.CPP. The member functions will be modified in this way, throwing an exception if their preconditions are not met:

```
// insertion is defined only if the buffer is not full
void BUffer :: Put (long n)
{
    if (Full ( ))
        throw (xmsg ("Insertion in a full buffer")) ;
    data [nFirst] = n ;
    nFirst = (nFirst + 1) % elements ;
    nElements ++ ;
}


// extraction is defined only if the buffer is not empty
long Buffer :: Get ( )
{
    if (Empty ( ))
        throw (xmsg ("Extraction from an empy buffer")) ;
    long n = data [nLast] ;
    nLast = (nLast + 1) % elements ;
    nElements — ;
    return n ;
}
```

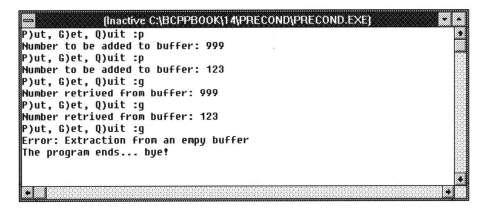

Figure 14.8 Run-time error in PRECOND.CPP

If you modify the class with the addition of these functions and you change the program (in the contractual version) by deliberately inserting an error, you will be able to see the effect of preconditions. Compiling and executing the following file, you will see the error reported by the screen shown in Figure 14.8.

```
// file PRECOND.CPP                                    14/PRECOND
// Class describing the LIFO buffer with a contract and some preconditions
// to ensure it (in fact, the main program doesn't comply to them)

#include <cstring.h>
#include <except.h>
#include <iostream.h>
#include <stdlib.h>

const int elements = 10 ;

class Buffer
{
    long   data [elements] ;
    int nElements ;
    int nFirst ;
    int nLast ;

public:
    Buffer ( ) ;
    void Put (long n) ;
    long Get ( ) ;
    int Empty ( ) ;
    int Full ( ) ;
    int NumEl ( ) ;
} ;

// member functions

Buffer :: Buffer () :
    nElements (0) ,
    nFirst (0) ,
    nLast (0)
{ }

// insertion is defined only if the buffer is not full
void Buffer :: Put (long n)
{
    if (Full ( ))
        throw (xmsg ("Insertion in a full buffer")) ;
```

```
        data [nFirst] = n ;
        nFirst = (nFirst + 1) % elements ;
        nElements ++ ;
}


// extraction is defined only if the buffer is not empty
long Buffer :: Get ( )
{
    if (Empty ( ))
        throw (xmsg ("Extraction from an empy buffer")) ;
    long n = data [nLast] ;
    nLast = (nLast + 1) % elements ;
    nElements — ;
    return n ;
}


int Buffer :: NumEl ( )
{
    return nElements ;
}


// returns 1 if the buffer is full, else 0
int Buffer :: Full ( )
{
    return (nElements == elements) ;
}


// returns 1 if the buffer is empty, else 0
int Buffer :: Empty ( )
{
    return (nElements == 0) ;
}



// example of buffer use, containing an error
void main ( )
{
    Buffer    buf ;
    char  command ;

    try
    {
        do
        {
            cout << "P)ut, G)et, Q)uit :";
            cin >> command;
```

```
                switch (command)
                {
                   case 'p':
                   {
                      long element ;
                      do
                      {
                         cout << "Number to be added to buffer: " ;

                         // checks that a number is entered
                         char  string [10] ;
                         cin >> string ;
                         element = atol (string) ;
                         if (! element)
                            cout << "Error: it's not a number" << endl ;
                      }
                      while (! element) ;

                      // if the buffer is not full adds the element
                      if (! buf.Full ( ))
                         buf.Put (element) ;
                      else
                         cout << "The buffer is already full" << endl ;
                   }
                      break ;

                   case 'g':
                   {
                      long element ;

                      // ERROR: there is no check
                      element = buf.Get ( ) ;
                      cout   << "Number retrived from buffer: "
                         << element << endl ;
                   }
                      break ;

                }   // end switch
             }   // end do-while
          while (command != 'q') ;

    }  // end try-block
    catch (xmsg message)
    {
       cout << "Error: " << message.why ( ) << endl ;
```

```
        cout << "The program ends... bye!" << endl ;
    }
}
```

Obviously, the error message and the subsequent execution halt will be displayed only if more elements get extracted from the buffer (with the *Get* command) than are actually present. This message is similar to the preceding example, but there is an important difference. When a programming error is met, the program stops gracefully (because an exception handler is provided), but you cannot go on to play with the program in an unstable state, as was possible in some previous examples. As already stated, this message is aimed to beta testers of the program, but should never be met by a real user.

Class Invariants

While the previous example using exceptions had the purpose of checking the correctness of the calls to member functions by the client code that uses the class, another possible usage is to verify the correctness of a class.

In this way, you can define *class invariants*, that is, conditions that must always be satisfied if the class is to maintain its semantic meaning.

> "A major concern of a class design is to get an object into a well-defined state (initialization), to maintain a well-defined state as operations are performed, and finally to destroy the object gracefully. The property that makes the state of an object well-defined is called an 'invariant.'" [Stroustrup 91]

You can check for these invariants every time that a member function is entered or exited, but not during its execution. In fact, an object of a class must be in a correct state only while it is not being operated upon (in other words, only *between* two consecutive member function calls).

For instance, for the class that describes the buffer of numbers, you can define the following conditions that must always be true:

- The number of elements must be greater or equal to zero and less than or equal to the maximum number of elements.

- The first element and the last element must fall within the same range.

- The difference between the first and last element must be equal to the number of elements that have been inserted into the buffer.

In other words, from these verbally formulated conditions, you can derive the following class invariant expressions:

```
nElements >= 0 && nElements <= elements
nFirst >= 0 && nFirst <= elements
nLast >= 0 && nLast <= elements
( nLast + nElements ) % elements == nFirst
```

We can test for these invariants, using the expressions above, or make the reverse check. In fact, if one of the conditions required by the class invariant is not true, we can throw an exception, as in:

```
if (nElements < 0 II nElements > elements)
    throw (xmsg ("Buffer error: nElements out of range")) ;
if (nFirst < 0 II nFirst > elements)
    throw (xmsg ("Buffer error: nFirst out of range")) ;
if (nLast < 0 II nLast > elements)
    throw (xmsg ("Buffer error: nLast out of range")) ;
if ((nLast + nElements) % elements != nFirst)
    throw (xmsg ("Buffer error: values out of sync")) ;
```

Instead of inserting this code at the beginning and at the end of each member function (when we want to check the class invariant), we can place it in a specific member function (*Invariant*), which is called in the proper cases. This way, you can implement the usual *Buffer* class as described in the following code. Notice that we have deliberately inserted an error, so that the invariant will not always be true.

```
// file INVARIA.CPP                                        14/INVARIA
// class describing a FIFO buffer having a class invariant

#include <iostream.h>
#include <stdlib.h>
#include <cstring.h>
#include <except.h>

const int elements = 10 ;

class Buffer
{
    long   data [elements] ;
    int nElements ;
    int nFirst ;
    int nLast ;

public:
    Buffer ( ) ;
    void Put (long n) ;
    long Get ( ) ;
    int Empty ( ) ;
    int Full ( ) ;
    int NumEl ( ) ;
```

```
      void Invariant ( ) ;
} ;

// member functions

Buffer :: Buffer ( ) :
   nElements (0) ,
   nFirst (0) ,
   nLast (0)
{
   Invariant ( ) ;
}

void Buffer :: Invariant ( )
{
   if (nElements < 0 ll nElements > elements)
      throw (xmsg ("Buffer error: nElements out of range")) ;
   if (nFirst < 0 ll nFirst > elements)
      throw (xmsg ("Buffer error: nFirst out of range")) ;
   if (nLast < 0 ll nLast > elements)
      throw (xmsg ("Buffer error: nLast out of range")) ;
   if ((nLast + nElements) % elements != nFirst)
      throw (xmsg ("Buffer error: values out of sync")) ;
}

// insertion is defined only if the buffer is not full
void Buffer :: Put (long n)
{
   Invariant ( ) ;
   data [nFirst] = n ;
   nFirst = (nFirst++) % elements ;      // ERROR !
   nElements ++ ;
   Invariant ( ) ;
}

// extraction is defined only if the buffer is not empty
long Buffer :: Get ( )
{
   Invariant ( ) ;
   long n = data [nLast] ;
   nLast = (nLast + 1) % elements ;
   nElements — ;
   Invariant ( ) ;
   return n ;
}
```

```cpp
int Buffer :: NumEl ( )
{
    return nElements ;
}

// returns 1 if the buffer is full, else 0
int Buffer :: Full ( )
{
    return (nElements == elements) ;
}

// returns 1 if the buffer is empty, else 0
int Buffer :: Empty ( )
{
    return (nElements == 0) ;
}


// example of buffer use
void main ( )
{
    Buffer       buf ;
    char         command ;

    try
    {
       do {
          cout << "P)ut, G)et, Q)uit :";
          cin >> command;

          switch (command)
          {
             case 'p':
             {
                long element ;
                do
                {
                   cout << "Number to be added to buffer: " ;

                   // checks that a number is entered
                   char        string [10] ;
                   cin >> string ;
                   element = atol (string) ;
                   if (! element)
                       cout << "Error: it's not a number" << endl ;
```

```
            }
            while (! element) ;

            // if the buffer is not full adds the element
            if (! buf.Full ( ))
                buf.Put (element) ;
            else
                cout << "The buffer is already full" << endl ;
        }
            break ;

        case 'g':
        {
            long element ;
            if (! buf.Empty ( ))
            {
                element = buf.Get ( ) ;
                cout  << "Number retrived from buffer: "
                    << element << endl ;
            }
            else
                cout << "The buffer is empty" << endl ;
        }
            break ;

        }   // end switch
    }   // end do-while
    while (command != 'q') ;

    } // end try-block
    catch (xmsg message)
    {
        cout << message.why ( ) << endl ;
        cout << "The program ends... bye!" << endl ;
    }
}
```

If you run this program and insert an element, the corresponding member function (*Put*) will generate an error during its final check on the invariant, throwing an *xmsg* (*"Buffer error: values out of sync"*) exception, as shown in Figure 14.9. This error is produced by the increment operator of *nFirst* in the *Put* member function, which should be a prefix increment instead of a postfix increment. (If this is not clear refer to the INCREMEN.CPP example in Chapter 4, describing the difference between the two forms of the increment operator.)

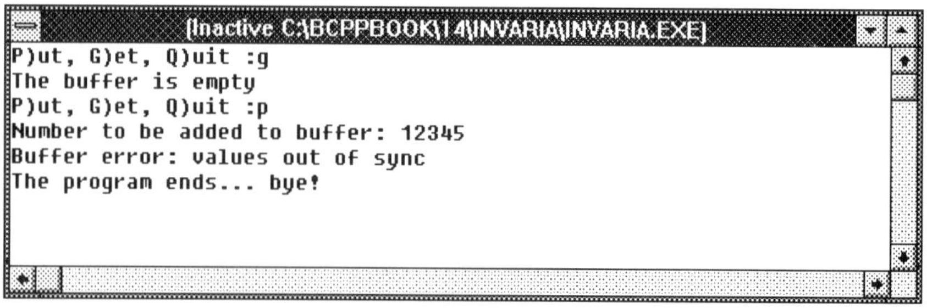

```
[Inactive C:\BCPPBOOK\14\INVARIA\INVARIA.EXE]
P)ut, G)et, Q)uit :g
The buffer is empty
P)ut, G)et, Q)uit :p
Number to be added to buffer: 12345
Buffer error: values out of sync
The program ends... bye!
```

Figure 14.9 The output of the *invaria.cpp* program, showing the exception

To complete the picture (which is only sketched here), note that generally you should include both invariants as well as preconditions and postconditions in all member functions. In fact, the integrity of the class invariant should be an integral part of the postcondition of every one of its member functions.

Invariants in Object-Oriented Languages

After having experimented with some of the constructs that are among the least used by programmers, such as invariants and pre- and post-conditions, you should now try to gain a deeper awareness of their meaning, especially in connection with object-oriented programming and the definition of classes.

First of all, it is important to stress that the importance of correctness and reliability of a class is amplified by the potentiality of its reuse. This is true to such a degree that it is certainly better to rewrite a class rather than reuse a class that doesn't work well enough. For this reason, the tasks and the operating conditions of every member function must be very well defined: this is the sense of programming by contracts. The "contract" must be a central piece of the documentation of a class.

From a theoretical point of view, the use of exceptions to express invariants, preconditions, and postconditions is a gigantic leap forward in programming techniques. These elements, when used with existing tools that favor the correctness of programs, still won't prove programs correct mathematically—but at least they make it far more likely.

The theory that is the foundation of invariants and conditions is associated with a precise mathematical notion: predicate calculus. Although it has been known for a long time, its most "convincing" introduction in programming is very recent. Eiffel is the first programming language that specifically supports this kind of construct, and even encourages a systematic use of it. A very detailed description of the subject—which here has just been touched upon in very simple terms—can be found in various books and articles by the inventor of this object-oriented language, and in particular in [Meyer 88] and [Meyer 89].

In these papers, another important issue—which has not been described here simply because the C++ language can handle it only with great difficulty—is dealt with: the relationship between the invariant of a class and those in any of its derived classes. In

C++, invariants and conditions are not handled directly by the language, but they must be related by the programmer to their classes, an operation that is rarely as simple as it was in the rudimentary examples examined in the previous sections. However, you should also be aware that this is true for almost all object-oriented languages, let alone traditional languages; so it can hardly be claimed as a deficiency of C++. Nonetheless, wishful thinking might strongly suggest an evolution of the language in this direction.

POINTS TO CONSIDER

1. Add some operations in functions *value* of the program BIND.CPP to slow down. This will give you an idea of how execution varies according to the complexity of the functions.

2. Another typical run-time error, which you can easily reproduce and then analyze with the debugger, refers to the range of definition of array indexes. Just define an array like

   ```
   int tenNumbers [ 10 ] ;
   ```

   and then access it with a loop like this:

   ```
   for ( int = 1 ; i <= 10 ; i++ ) ...
   ```

3. If you usually use a *defensive* programming style, critically evaluate its advantages and disadvantages. Then, compare it with the approach and ideas described in the sections toward the end of this chapter.

4. Practice defining invariants for some classes (that you might already have found in the text, or that you invent expressly).

5. Change the position of the *try* and *catch* statements in PRECOND.CPP and INVARIA.CPP examples so that if an error occurs the execution can continue. (Hint: Move these statements in the *case* branches.)

15

Class Libraries

The C of the eighties is C++, with a library of objects including visual objects and application objects. This means that huge portions of what you had to code before—the user interface pieces—are very easy to change... You don't have to program all the algorithms about how you do resource allocation, or what logic to use, or how to categorize things. [Gates 90]

In Chapter 13, we introduced the advantages of class libraries as compared to function libraries. We also described the "theory" behind class libraries. In this chapter (and the following one), we will see how to put into practice what you've learned about the libraries available within Borland C++.

Each of the libraries is described; then, there are a number of examples that illustrate the use of the classes, directly or through derivation of new ones.

The aim of the chapter is twofold: to show how to use the libraries and to explain the criteria and methods with which to reuse the classes present in the libraries. These criteria are more complex than those for the reusability of the code of function libraries.

First, we will describe the "standard" C++ language libraries, those defined by AT&T and found in any C++ compiler. Later in this chapter, we will discuss Borland C++'s *Container Class Library*, a collection of classes describing the most common data structures. Finally, in Chapters 16 and 17 we'll cover Windows programming and the *ObjectWindows Library* which is strictly a Borland class library that is connected with the Microsoft Windows operating environment.

Standard C++ Class Libraries

Among the class libraries accompanying Borland C++ are some that should be present in any C++ compiler—since they are almost part of the language—so that some libraries will probably be included in the ANSI definition of C++ (similar to what happened with Standard C). Since there is not yet an official C++ standard, these libraries usually match those defined by AT&T.

Most standard libraries concern input and output operations (in fact, you have already seen several examples of them in this book). The most common library is the one defined in the *iostream.h* header file, which contains the classes of the objects *cin* and *cout*.

Other important input-output classes are those used to handle files, defined in the header *fstream.h*. Besides the input-output libraries, there are some to handle BCD (binary-coded decimal) numbers, defined in the *bcd.h* header, and complex numbers, defined in *complex.h*. Other header files that are standard for C++ contain macro definitions and functions.

A recent addition to the standard ANSI C++ libraries is a class to handle strings, which is described in the *cstring.h* header file. Setting aside the classes describing BCD and complex numbers, which are very easy to use, we will focus on the libraries concerning input-output operations (with one section on the basic aspects and a second on file handling) and the string class.

Input-Output Library

Regarding input-output libraries, it's important to notice that they have changed from the first version of the language. The file *iostream.h* (the only one we consider in this book) describes the new libraries, while the file *stream.h*, which defines the old version, is still available for compatibility purposes only.

The hierarchy containing the main classes defined in the stream library (but not all of them) is shown in Figure 15.1.

In practice, it's not common to use all these classes directly: to handle keyboard input and video output the library defines two standard objects, *cin* and *cout*, that have already been used in several examples. Certainly it's possible to derive new classes from these to alter their behavior, but this isn't of much use. It's better, instead, to add your own classes to the data types handled by *cin* and *cout*: this is possible through the overloading of the operators << and >>, which was described in Chapter 6.

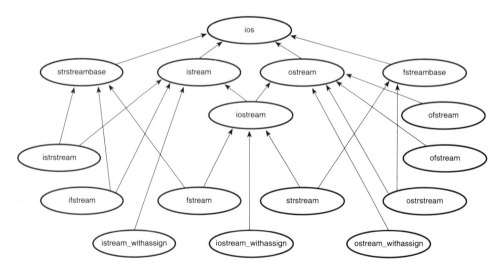

Figure 15.1 Hierarchy of classes of the stream library

The behavior of input and output streams can be altered using manipulators, which were used in a couple of examples (in Chapter 2 and Chapter 13) but not described in detail.

Input-Output Manipulators

Often, it's necessary to present output or ask for input in an elegant way, or at least a clear one. To show the output properly, it's usually necessary to format it. Luckily enough, the C++ stream classes already do a good job of formatting, deciding which representation to use for the different data types and values. Nonetheless, it's sometimes useful to change the way characters and numbers are shown on screen or paper. With C++ streams, you can display the output in two ways:

- Using the *ios* class member functions, you can set the field's width, fill character, and a number of format flags.

- Using manipulators, you can accomplish the same operations passing the proper parameters to *cin* and *cout*.

In the first case, you can issue statements such as

```
cout.width ( 5 ) ;
cout << number ;
```

while in the second you can use the corresponding form:

```
cout << setw ( 5 ) << number ;
```

It's clear that the second is easier to read, although the first better describes the operations performed. Whatever notation you use, some manipulators or functions affect only the operation that immediately follows.

C++ provides a number of manipulators, divided into two categories: those taking arguments and those without arguments. The main difference is that to use the manipulators taking arguments, you have to include in your program the header file *iomanip.h*.

The following list shows the standard manipulators:

- *oct, dec, hex,* and *setbase (int)* are used to determine the base of the numbers (octal, decimal, or hexadecimal).

- *setprecision (int)* determines the number of decimal digits.

- *setw (int)* and *setfill (int)* set the width of the field to be used and the fill character.

- *endl, ends,* and *flush* are used to force a stream flush (that is, to output the buffer), inserting respectively a new line (\n), a string terminator (\0), or nothing.

- *ws* is used to avoid the input of white spaces.

- *setiosflag (lon₀)* and *resetiosflag (long)* allow you to set or reset some or all of the format flags at the same time, and can take as parameters one or more defined values.

A similar effect can be obtained using some of the member functions of the class *ios*, a base class for both *ostream* and *istream*. The following list of these functions shows the strict correspondence with the manipulators. Notice also that there are two forms for every function: The first is used to set a new value (returning the previous one), and the second simply to retrieve the current one.

```
int    width (int w);
int    width ( ) const;
char   fill (char c);
char   fill () const;
long   flags (long f);
long   flags () const;
long   setf (long setbits, long field);
long   setf (long l);
long   unsetf (long l);
int    precision (int p);
int    precision () const;
```

The functions operating on flags, as with the *setiosflag* manipulator, are based on the some constant values defined in the *ios* class. They are:

skipws	skips white spaces in input
left	left aligned
right	right aligned
internal	inserts filling character between the sign and the number
dec	decimal base for integers
oct	octal base for integers
hex	hexadecimal base for integers
showbase	show the base for integers
showpoint	show trailing zeros after the comma
uppercase	uppercase (for hexadecimal characters and exponential)
showpos	shows the + for positive numbers
scientific	scientific notation for floating point numbers
fixed	fixed notation for floating point numbers
unitbuf	*flush* after each output operation
stdio	*flush* after each output character

These flags can be used in the following way:

```
cout.setf (ios::showpoint);
```

In the following example, the use of some of these manipulators is shown in the output of some numbers.

```
// MANIP.CPP                                          15/MANIP
// output stream manipulators

#include <iostream.h>
#include <iomanip.h>

void main ( )
{
    int    n = 1992 ;
    float  x = 123.456789 ;

    // outputs the number using several bases in an eight-character field

    cout  << setw ( 8 ) << n
          << setw ( 8 ) << oct << n
          << setw ( 8 ) << hex << n
          << endl ;

    // repeats setting some flags to show the base, the positive sign,
    // and using uppercase for hexadecimal digits

    cout  << setiosflags ( ios::showbase | ios::uppercase | ios:: showpos )
          << setw ( 8 ) << dec << n
          << setw ( 8 ) << oct << n
          << setw ( 8 ) << hex << n
          << endl ;

    // outputs the float normally, rounding it to the second decimal digit
    // and using scientific notation

    cout  << x << endl
          << setprecision ( 2 ) << x << endl
          << setiosflags ( ios::scientific ) << x << endl ;
}
```

The program produces the output shown in Figure 15.2.

Figure 15.2 Output produced by the program MANIP.CPP

File Input-Output

The classes of the stream hierarchy that operate on files have not yet been used, although file transfer is quite important in any serious application. As an example of a program using files, consider a common situation: filtering a file. When you filter a file, you transform a given input file into an output file by following a well-defined rule.

To begin, we define a simple filter that will eliminate from a file all the characters that are not alphanumeric, with the sole exception of the new line character. To find out if a *char* is alphanumeric, we can use the *isalnum* macro, defined in *ctype.h*, although it's not very good in handling the extended character set.

```
// file FILTER.H                                            15/FILTER
// simple example of a class describing the filter of a file

#include <iostream.h>
#include <fstream.h>
#include <ctype.h>

class Filter
{
protected:
    ifstream     filein ;
    ofstream     fileout ;
    int          error ;

public:
    Filter ( char * in , char * out ) :
        filein ( in ) ,
        fileout ( out )
        {
            // if the files cannot be opened, sets error to 1

            error = 0 ;
            if ( ! filein || ! fileout )
                error = 1 ;
        }

    ~Filter ( )
        {
            // closes the files
            filein.close ( ) ;
            fileout.close ( ) ;
        }
```

```
int Error ( )
    {
        return error ;
    }

void   Convert ( )
    {
        char   ch ;

    // scans the input file

    while ( filein.get ( ch ) )

        // if the element is alphanumeric or a new line, ...

        if ( isalnum ( ch ) || ch == '\n' )

            // then it is duplicated onto the output file

            fileout.put ( ch ) ;
    }
} ;
```

To test this class, we can compile and run the following file:

```
// file FILT-USE.CPP                                    15/FILTER
// example of a program using the class Filter

#include "filter.h"

main ( )
{
    char  in [ 126 ] ;   // note the space for long path names.
    char  out [ 126 ] ;

    cout << "Name of the input file: " ;
    cin >> in ;
    cout << "Name of the output file: " ;
    cin >> out ;

    Filter  ff ( in , out ) ;

    if ( ff.Error ( ) )
        cout << "Files cannot be opened!" << endl ;
    else {
```

```
        cout << "Conversion in progress ..." << endl ;
        ff.Convert ( ) ;
    }
}
```

This program will transform an input file such as

```
Test file for the program "FILTER.H"

punctuation: ,.-,.:_,.-*
UPPERCASE and lowercase
numbers: 985 2  9523 9756239171 987634
parentheses: () [] {}
symbols: _ $ % & ^ # @
and white              spaces!
```

into the file:

```
TestfiletheprogramFILTERH

punctuation
UPPERCASEandlowercase
numbers9852952397562391971987634
parentheses
symbols_
andwhitespaces
```

From the previous example, you get an idea of how easy it is to use the file stream classes (which offer much more power than what has been shown by these simple examples), although this book only minimally describes them.

To take the above example further, we introduce a second filter, which is an extension of the first one. In fact, the class *Small*, which performs a conversion from uppercase to lowercase characters, is derived from the class *Filter* in the previous example. Following this method, we are able to save much coding, reusing it from the class we have already defined.

Now, we just need to change the conversion: this operates on the characters, transforming them to lowercase unless they follow a period (or an exclamation or question mark). If the first alphanumeric character after a period is uppercase, it's not converted, while the rest of the word is treated as usual. The beginning of the text is considered to have a preceding period (with the initialization of *period* to 1).

```
// file SMALL.CPP                                      15/FILTER
// second example of filter class, derived from the previuos one,
// used to covert uppercase words to lowercase
```

```
#include "filter.h"

class Small : public Filter
{
    int nConvs ;    // number of conversions
    int nChars ;    // number of characters

public:

    Small (char * in, char * out) :
        nConvs (0),
        nChars (0),
        Filter (in , out)
        { }

    void  Convert ( ) ;

    void  PrintData ( )
    {
        cout  << "The filter has scanned " << nChars
            << " characters," << endl << "and has converted "
            << nConvs << " of them" << endl ;
    }
} ;


void Small :: Convert ( )
{
    char  chIn ;
    int period = 1 ;// period just encountered

    while (filein.get (chIn))
    {
        nChars ++ ;
        if (isupper (chIn))
        {
            if (period)
            {
                fileout.put (chIn) ;
                period = 0 ;
            }
            else
            {
                nConvs ++ ;
                fileout.put ((char) tolower (chIn)) ;
```

```
                  }
              }
          else
          {
              fileout.put (chln) ;
              if (chln == '.' || chln == '?' || chln == '!')
                  period = 1 ;
              if (islower (chln))
                  period = 0 ;
          }
      }   // end of the while loop
}


// the main program is similar to the previous example

void main ( )
{
    char  in [12] ;
    char  out [12] ;

    cout << "Name of the input file: " ;
    cin >> in ;
    cout << "Name of the output file: " ;
    cin >> out ;

    Small filt (in, out) ;

    if ( filt.Error ( ) )
        cout << "Files cannot be opened!" << endl ;
    else
    {
        cout << "Conversion in progress ..." << endl ;
        filt.Convert ( ) ;
        filt.PrintData ( ) ;
    }
}
```

This program can convert a file containing text such as

This text has been written to be FILTERED by the SMALL program!

There are several words in UPPERCASE that will be converted
to LOWERCASE characters during the processing. The FIRST uppercase
letter of a word following a PERIOD will be left unchanged.

IS SMALL A USEFUL PROGRAM? IT DEPENDS.
In fact it can easily be changed to address
similar problems...

HAVE YOU EVER HAD TO REWRITE INTO lowercase
THE UPPERCASE WORDS OF A TEXT?
It's an AWFUL experience! It is just like having to do a TOTAL REWRITE.

But not with SMALL! SMALL IS EASY TO USE!

into

This text has been written to be filtered by the small program!

There are several words in uppercase that will be converted
to lowercase characters during the processing. The first uppercase
letter of a word following a period will be left unchanged.

Is small a useful program? It depends.
In fact it can easily be changed to address
similar problems...

Have you ever had to rewrite into lowercase
the uppercase words of a text?
It's an awful experience! It is just like having to do a total rewrite.

But not with small! Small is easy to use!

The ANSI String Class

The use of character arrays, or strings, in the C language is very powerful but far from easy. The use of pointers, the functions of the *string.h* standard library, the problems with memory allocation have often been a nightmare for new C programmers. The C++ language, by itself, does nothing to approach this problem, since there isn't a predefined *string* data type. However, thanks to features of C++, it is quite easy to add new *abstract data types* to the language. This is the role of some standard class libraries: Instead of forcing each programmer or compiler vendor to implement a different version of the same class (leading to incompatibilities), the ANSI C++ committee has decided to add some common classes to the standard libraries of the language. One of them is the *string* class.

This standard string class is a very powerful one. There are a number of overloaded operators and member functions allowing different kinds of string extractions and compositions, searches, and all of the operations allowed by the corresponding C language library.

For a list of the operations see the on-line help or the header file *cstring.h* (notice the *c* in front of the name, used for this library in contrast to the ANSI C *string.h* header file). Some of the member functions resemble the typical C operations, but many of them are similar to BASIC, too. This last language, in fact, has a reputation for being one of the easiest at string manipulation.

We cannot browse through the list of these member functions (but you should do so, to get used to the capabilities of this class), but only provide a complex but interesting example of the use of the *string* class.

```
// file STRING.CPP                                         15/STRING
// Complex example of the use of the ANSI string class

// includes the header with the class definition and iostream
#include <cstring.h>
#include <iostream.h>

void main ( )
{
    string name1 = "Marco" ;
    string name2 = "Steve" ;

    // add some strings and characters
    string sum = name1 + '&' + name2 ;
    cout << sum << endl ;

    // adds some text at the beginnig or at the end
    sum.prepend ("We are ") ;
    sum.append (" and who are you?") ;
    cout << sum << endl ;

    // same but more involuted, applying the append function
    // to the result of the prepend function
    string stars ('*', 3) ;
    sum.prepend (stars + ' ').append (stars.prepend (' ')) ;
    cout << sum << endl ;

    // looks for & and replace it with "and"
    if (sum.contains ('&'))
    {
        int pos = sum.find ('&') ;
        sum.replace(pos, 1, " and ") ;
        // outputs the uppercase versione of the string
        cout << to_upper (sum) << endl ;
    }
```

```
// entangles the string producing a nonsense
int limit = 0 ;
while (sum.contains('e') && limit < sum.length ( ) / 6)
    {
    ++ limit ;
    sum.replace (sum.find_first_of('e'), 1,
        sum.substr (sum.find_last_of ('e')-limit%5), 5);
    }
cout << sum << endl ;
}
```

This example produces the output of Figure 15.3. Would you have guessed it?

The Container Class Library

Some data structures are very common in computer programming and have been extensively used in this book, including queues, stacks, lists, sets, and so on.

While the most common functions (such as those handling character strings) are almost always present in the libraries accompanying any programming language compiler, the absence of predefined and reusable data structures has always been a noteworthy deficiency. The reason for this absence is that traditional programming languages don't offer an easy way to define those data structures inside a library. Object-oriented programming languages offer, instead, a greater power in this area. And having on hand some ready-to-use fundamental data structures is certainly a great advantage.

While in some object-oriented languages the classes defining basic data structures are part of the system itself (such as in Smalltalk or Objective-C), in C++ this doesn't happen.

However, Borland—recognizing the importance of this matter—offers with its compiler a library of such classes: the *Container Class Library* (in short, *classlib*).

The idea of the "container" classes is borrowed from part of the huge hierarchy of system classes in the Smalltalk language programming environment. In Smalltalk, containers are called "collections." Most of the classes of the "collection" sub-hierarchy are shown in Figure 15.4. This set of classes has become very well known and is available for almost any object-oriented programming language. In fact, there are also

```
[Inactive C:\BCPPBOOK\15\STRING\STRING.EXE]
Marco&Steve
We are Marco&Steve and who are you?
*** We are Marco&Steve and who are you? ***
*** WE ARE MARCO AND STEVE AND WHO ARE YOU? ***
*** Wrar aro arrar aro arrar aro arrar aro arrare y yo you   y yo you   y yo you
y yo you   y yo are Marco and Steve and who are you? ***
```

Figure 15.3 The entangled output of the STRING.CPP example

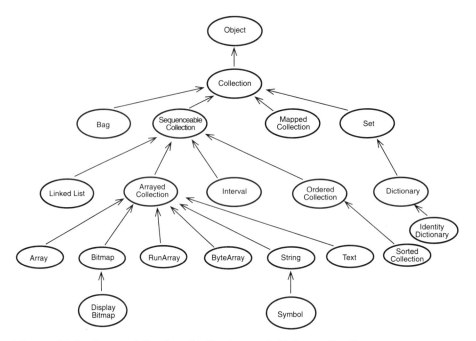

Figure 15.4   Some of the Smalltalk classes defining collections.

system classes in the Smalltalk language programming environment. In Smalltalk, containers are called "collections." Most of the classes of the "collection" sub-hierarchy are shown in Figure 15.4. This set of classes has become very well known and is available for almost any object-oriented programming language. In fact, there are also some C++ class libraries that closely match the whole Smalltalk hierarchy; among the best known is the NIH (National Institutes of Health) library developed by Keith Gorlen, a public domain class library for C++ under UNIX that is also available for several C++ compilers under DOS. Borland's containers, however, bear only a limited resemblance to Smalltalk collections.

Different from other object-oriented programming languages, C++ has a feature that makes container classes more powerful and flexible—templates— Therefore, Borland introduced a *template-based* version of the container class library in its 3.0 compiler, the first with template support. In the past the *template* version was smaller, being only a subset of the first *polymorphic version* (we call it polymorphic because it was based on a common base *Object* class, and used polymorphism to obtain genericity) which was still available. Now the older version has gone, having been relegated in a significantly named *obsolete* subdirectory for compatibility purposes.

The template version of the class library, which has been extended in Borland C++ 4.0 is much better than the previous one from a language perspective: It supports generic types using the template construct instead of using polymorphism and a single class hierarchy, therefore; it is also easier to use and less error prone.

The *Container Class Library* is defined in a series of header files (one for every class, plus another containing auxiliary functions or macros) and library files. By

a look at the implementation details, to alter them to suit their own needs (as you might expect with the source code of a traditional function library). Instead, the purpose is to make the library portable. If you want to transfer an application to a different kind of computer with a different operating system, you can recompile the library source code and the application code for that environment, as long as it has a C++ compiler. Therefore, you can use the library with a compiler that doesn't have a similar library.

Instead of changing the classes to meet one's own special needs, it's much better to change a class through inheritance rather than to change the original code.

An Overview of the Container Classes

The Container Class Library has a number of classes capable of storing your data. These classes describe a series of abstractions and can store either objects or pointers to objects with several strategies. Every *Abstract Data Type (ADT)* class can be implemented using one of several *Fundamental Data Structures (FDS)*. The exploration of the classes of the *Container Class Library* is quite complex, since there isn't a hierarchy of classes. Classes can actually be constructed from templates giving the proper parameters and following a particular naming convention.

The available abstract classes are:

- *Array*, similar to standard index-based arrays, but with a dynamic behavior, because their size can change at run time
- *Set*, container of objects with any particular order, which doesn't allow for duplicates
- *Bag*, container of objects similar to the *Set* but allowing multiple copies (instances) of the same element
- *Stack*, a list of objects stored in LIFO order (objects are stored and retrieved from the same end of the list)
- *Queue*, a list of objects stored in FIFO order (objects are stored at the tail and retrieved from the head of the list)
- *Deque*, a queue allowing operations (storing and retrieving) at both ends
- *Dictionary*, a list of objects with a key to access them

These *abstract classes* are built on some *low-level* containers, the fundamental data types. These data types, however, can also be used by themselves. Here is a list:

- *Vector*, a fixed-size index-based storage, like an array
- *List*, a common single-linked listed, which can be scanned only in one direction
- *DoubleList*, a double-linked list, allowing operations in both directions
- *BTree*, a complex structure for storing dynamically a large number of objects, allowing rapid searches
- *HashTable*, a list allowing speed access to the stored objects using a calculated *hash* value

How do you connect an *abstract data type* with its implementation? When you instantiate a class from the corresponding template, you have to ask for a specific version and to provide the data type of the objects the container is going to store.

The name of the specific template class can be built as follows: Start with the name of the ADT (for example, *Array*), add a prefix T indicating the template (*TArray*), optionally add an I for indirect, a V for virtual, an M for managed, an S for sorted (if allowed), and append to the name *As* and the name of an FDS class (for example, *AsVector*). For an array the result might be *TArrayAsVector*, *TMIArrayAsVector*, *TIArrayAsVector*, *TSArrayAsVector*, *TISArrayAsVector*, or *TMArrayAsVector*, since the only possible implementation is the use of a *Vector*.

As you have probably figured out, the situation is quite complex. On the other hand, you have the power to choose from a number of different versions the one that best suits your needs. Just to add some more confusion, most of the template classes describing a single abstraction are derived from each other.

In practice, once you have figured out the name of the template class you want to use, you need only to instantiate it, as in:

```
TSArrayAsVector <int> mySortedIntegerArray ;
```

The examples of the following sections, based on some of the container classes, might help you understand how to use this library in your programs. To compile and link properly each of these examples, you need to check the *Class library* box in the project *Target Expert* dialog box of the Borland IDE.

Stacks and Queues with the Container Library

To introduce you to the *Container Class Library*, you will see some examples of the most common classes, instead of a complete overview of the member functions of each class of the library, which is beyond the scope of this book and can be easily found in the *on-line* help files of the compiler.

We have already defined stacks and queues in some of the examples of the book. However; we could have avoided the effort using this library. Here is an example with two stacks and two queues; they have a different implementation but the same behavior, as shown in the output of Figure 15.5.

```
// file STACKQUE.CPP                                    15/STACKQUE
// Example of the use of some stack and queue classes of the container library

// to include the file you need to specify the proper directory
#include <classlib\queues.h>
#include <classlib\stacks.h>

#include <iostream.h>
```

```
void main ( )
{
    // defines two queues
    TQueueAsDoubleList <int>    que1 ;
    TQueueAsVector <int>        que2 ;

    // define two stacks
    TStackAsList <int>          stack1 ;
    TStackAsVector <int>        stack2 ;

    cout << "Input numbers into the data structures (0 to end)" << endl ;
    int value, counter = 1;
    do
    {
        cout << "Number " << counter << ": " ;
        cin >> value ;
        que1.Put (value) ;
        que2.Put (value) ;
        stack1.Push (value) ;
        stack2.Push (value) ;
        ++counter ;
    }
    while (value != 0) ;

    // prints the contents of the four containers
    // while emptying them
    cout << "Contents of the first queue: " ;
    while (que1.GetItemsInContainer ( ) > 0)
        cout << que1.Get ( ) << ' ' ;
    cout << endl ;

    cout << "Contents of the second queue: " ;
    while (que2.GetItemsInContainer ( ) > 0)
        cout << que2.Get ( ) << ' ' ;
    cout << endl ;

    cout << "Contents of the first stack: " ;
    while (stack1.GetItemsInContainer ( ) > 0)
        cout << stack1.Pop ( ) << ' ' ;
    cout << endl ;

    cout << "Contents of the second stack: " ;
    while (stack2.GetItemsInContainer ( ) > 0)
        cout << stack2.Pop ( ) << ' ' ;
    cout << endl ;
}
```

```
[Inactive C:\BCPPBOOK\15\STACKQUE\STACKQUE.EXE]
Input numbers into the data structures (0 to end)
Number 1: 123
Number 2: 999
Number 3: 345
Number 4: 333
Number 5: 555
Number 6: 888
Number 7: 0
Contents of the first queue: 123 999 345 333 555 888 0
Contents of the second queue: 123 999 345 333 555 888 0
Contents of the first stack: 0 888 555 333 345 999 123
Contents of the second stack: 0 888 555 333 345 999 123
```

Figure 15.5 The output of the program STACKQUE.CPP, showing the implementation doesn't affect the contents of a data structure.

An Overview of Sets

We have seen data structures defining stacks and queues, which are frequently used in programs. However, when you need more generic containers, the classes *Set* and *Bag* might be useful, too. The difference between these two classes is the possibility of having replicated copies offered by bags, while sets check for duplicate objects.

To test these containers we define a class for *Animals*, having a default constructor (required to initialize the objects of the underlying vector data structures) and the equality operator (==, to test if a set has a duplicate element). Since the arrays we use to fill the containers have some repeated values, the content of the *set* will be different from that of the *bag* (see Figure 15.6).

In the previous examples to print the elements of the stack and the queue, we retrieved each of their elements printing the corresponding value. This operation was quite easy, but had a serious drawback: To print the values of the objects in the containers we *destroyed* the container emptying them. The Container Class Library offers a better solution, although a little more complex. For each container class there is a *ForEach* member functions requiring a function as parameter. This function is applied to each of the objects stored in the container (this approach is similar to the *enumeration* functions of the Windows API). For example, with a *print* function we can see what's inside a set:

```
// definition of a function with a standard prototype: f (T&, void*)
void Print (Animal & ani, void*)
{
    cout << ani.Name ( ) ;
}


// execution of the function for each of the items of a set
set.ForEach (Print, &style) ;
```

```
┌──────────────────────────────────────────────────────────────┐
│ ═  {Inactive C:\BCPPBOOK\15\SET-BAG\SET-BAG.EXE}         ▼│▲│
├──────────────────────────────────────────────────────────────┤
│Bag (with duplicates):                                        ▲│
│monkey (age 2)                                                 │
│monkey (age 3)                                                 │
│hippopotamus (age 4)                                           │
│lion (age 5)                                                   │
│panda (age 3)                                                  │
│elephant (age 2)                                               │
│monkey (age 2)                                                 │
│hippopotamus (age 4)                                           │
│zebra (age 1)                                                  │
│zebra (age 2)                                                  │
│                                                               │
│Set (without duplicates):                                      │
│monkey: 2                                                      │
│monkey: 3                                                      │
│hippopotamus: 4                                                │
│lion: 5                                                        │
│panda: 3                                                       │
│elephant: 2                                                    │
│zebra: 1                                                      ▼│
│zebra: 2                                                       │
├──────────────────────────────────────────────────────────────┤
│◄│                                                          │►│
└──────────────────────────────────────────────────────────────┘
```

Figure 15.6 The output of the SET-BAG example, using the *ForEach* enumeration function

The second parameter of the *Print* function is a pointer to void that can be customized. In the example below we use it to pass a boolean flag to choose between two different styles of output, as you can see in the two portions of Figure 15.6.

```
// file SET-BAG.CPP                                    15/SET-BAG
// example of the use of classes Bag and Set,
// containing object of the Animal class

#include <conio.h>
#include <classlib\bags.h>
#include <classlib\sets.h>
#include <cstring.h>

// a class describing animals
class Animal
{
    string name ;
    int age;

public:
    Animal (string n, int a) ;
    // the default constructor is required by the library
    Animal ( ) ;
```

```
    string Name ( )
    {
        return name ;
    }

    int Age ( )
    {
        return age ;
    }

    // the == operator is required by the library
    int operator== (const Animal& a)
    {
        return (name == a.name && age == a.age) ;
    }
};

// definition of the constructors
Animal :: Animal (string n, int a) :
    name (n) ,
    age (a)
{ }

Animal :: Animal ( ) :
    name ("") ,
    age (0)
{ }



// global function operating on animals,
// following the standard prototype f (T&, void*)
void Print (Animal & ani, void* style)
{
    // convert the parameter to a proper data type
    int sty = *((int*) style) ;

    cout << ani.Name ( ) ;
    if (sty)
        cout << " (age " << ani.Age ( ) << ")" << endl ;
    else
        cout << ": " << ani.Age ( ) << endl ;
}

// defines a number of elements for the arrays
const int nElements = 10 ;
```

```
void main ( )
{
    string namesList [nElements] =
        { "monkey", "monkey", "hippopotamus", "lion", "panda",
        "elephant", "monkey", "hippopotamus", "zebra", "zebra" } ;

    int yearsList [nElements] =
        { 2, 3, 4, 5, 3, 2, 2, 4, 1, 2 } ;

    // a bag and a set storing animals
    TBagAsVector<Animal> bag ;
    TSetAsVector<Animal> set ;

    // insert the elements from the array
    for (int i = 0; i < nElements; i++)
    {
        bag.Add (* (new Animal (namesList [i], yearsList[i]))) ;
        set.Add (* (new Animal (namesList [i], yearsList[i]))) ;
    }

    // output the value of the objects of the two containers
    // applying a function to each of the elements
    // and apssing a different parameter to the Print function
    int style = 1 ;
    cout << "Bag (with duplicates):" << endl ;
    bag.ForEach (Print, &style) ;
    cout << endl ;

    style = 0 ;
    cout << "Set (without duplicates):" << endl ;
    set.ForEach (Print, &style) ;
}
```

Dynamic Arrays

Usually, the problem with arrays lies in the amount of space to allocate. If you define the array too big, you waste a lot of memory; if you define it too small, you can run out of space during program execution. The arrays defined in the *Container Class Library* overcome this problem because their size can vary according to the needs of the program.

Aside from that, these data structures work almost as ordinary arrays: You can add elements at a particular position (with the *AddAt* member function) or in the first free place (with *Add*), access the (via the usual [ ] operator), and destroy them (with the *Detach* function). Of course, there are several other member functions that can be quite useful.

Sorted Arrays

The behavior of the sorted version of the array container (which is obtained adding an S before the template class name) is really useful. It's like having a standard array you can access with an index between square braces, but the elements are automatically sorted. The order, maintained each time you add or detach an element from the array, is based on the >= operator. Therefore this operator is required for the class of the objects inserted in the container.

The following example shows the sorted version of the array template, showing two features. First, you can add an unlimited number (within memory constraints) of elements to the array. Second, the elements of the array are always in the proper order.

```
// file SORTED.CPP                                        15/SORTED
// Example of the SortedArray class using the template version
// of the Container Class Library

#include <classlib\arrays.h>
#include <iostream.h>
#include <iomanip.h>

void main ( )
{
    // the sorted array has five elements, the lower bound is set to 0
    // and the array can be resized, adding five elements each time
    TSArrayAsVector <short int>  numArray (5, 0, 5) ;

    // insert a random amount of random values in the array
    randomize ( ) ;
    int elements = random (300) ;
    for (int i = 0; i < elements; ++i)
    {
        int number = random (32000) ;
        numArray.Add (number) ;
    }

    // outputs the elements
    cout << "Contents of the sorted array:" << endl ;
    for (i = 0; i < numArray.GetItemsInContainer ( ); ++i)
        cout << setw (9) << numArray [i] << ' ' ;
}
```

Each time you run this program you should get a different output (an example is shown in Figure 15.7). Notice that beside the values, you can easily change the number of elements of the array, although it starts always as an array with five elements. If the number of elements grows too much, the program might crash.

```
┌──────────────────────────────────────────────────────────────────────┐
│                  [Inactive C:\BCPPBOOK\15\SORTED\SORTED.EXE]           │
│Contents of the sorted array:                                           │
│    333      865     1041     1179     1335     2220     2367     2705  │
│   2769     3378     3666     3677     4530     4571     4648     4975  │
│   5458     5802     6193     6347     6397     6529     6598     7190  │
│   7274     7380     7685     7781     7848     8203     8308     8332  │
│   8522     8867     8896     8915     9835    10024    10095    10610  │
│  10612    11666    11933    12030    12902    13306    13519    13614  │
│  14512    14568    14582    14766    14772    14982    15622    16054  │
│  16793    17018    17071    17586    18917    19682    19793    20040  │
│  20048    20408    21304    22224    22481    22482    22548    22561  │
│  22717    22727    23108    23435    24165    24489    24715    24832  │
│  25001    25184    25411    26392    26604    27166    27283    28175  │
│  28264    28445    28644    28707    28875    29599    29624    29701  │
│  30274    30773    31556    31703                                      │
└──────────────────────────────────────────────────────────────────────┘
```

Figure 15.7   An example of the *random* output of the SORTED program

POINTS TO CONSIDER

1. In this chapter, we haven't analyzed the class libraries handling complex and BCD format numbers, although they are part of the AT&T C++ standard. Looking at the header files of these classes and using the help system of the Borland's IDE, write a program using one of these classes.

2. The most common use of file input/output is the loading and storing of records (or structures) into a file. Using C++, you can define classes that are able to store or load themselves. You only need to add to the class a pair of functions to define the two operations.

3. In this book, there are several examples using queues and stacks. Rewrite one of them using the corresponding *Container Library* classes.

4. Write a program using one of the classes of the *Container Library* not used in this chapter. Although this might seem easy at first, the fact that the behavior of some classes is not well documented may create problems. Browsing the examples included with the compilers might help you to better understand how these classes work.

5. The output of the program SET-BAG.CPP example can be changed considerably if we modify the == operator of the *Animal* class. With a stricter test as

```
int operator== (const Animal& a)
{
    return (name == a.name) ;
}
```

the set will have fewer elements than in the previous version. Run this new program and try to make further changes.

16

Windows Programming

Windows provides a multitasking, graphical user interface, or GUI, that fosters the creation of interactive programs. Windows represents a relatively new type of operating environment that is optimized for interaction between human beings and computer programs. Windows programs have a different structure from programs in more traditional environments...Programs...are "event driven." That is to say, the structure and operations of these types of programs center around user-generated events (like keystrokes and mouse clicks). [Norton 91]

Having explored most of the aspects of the C++ language and its main available tools and libraries, we will now discuss a subject of huge interest today: programming for the Microsoft Windows environment. In fact, this user interface, since the release of its third version, has become the standard for the IBM-compatible personal computer industry.

The problem is that while a graphical user interface environment of this kind is convenient for the user, programming it requires much more work. Besides the new tools and a huge number of API functions, programmers face the new "logic" of event-driven programming.

Borland C++, starting from version 2.0, lets you develop applications for the Windows environment, including all the necessary tools and function libraries, freeing you from having to use the Microsoft software development toolkit (SDK).

Starting with version 3.0 of the Borland C++ environment, new advanced tools have been added to make Windows programming easier: the class library *ObjectWindows* and the *Resource Workshop*. Version 4.0 allows the programmer to develop applications both for the old 16-bit Windows and for the new 32-bit API of Windows NT and Win32s.

Besides the available classes, *ObjectWindows* represents the first true implementation of object-oriented programming for Windows, using the C++ language. The merit of this library is to merge event-driven and object-oriented programming.

This chapter introduces each of these features, describing the foundations of Windows programming along with some examples, and of course, it will give you a good idea of the problems involved in Windows programming and is a sort of Windows "road map," with an emphasis on object-oriented programming. Although there are two chapters about Windows programming, we cannot cover this topic entirely. Further reading might include both Windows programming books and books specifically about OWL. Notice, however, that with version 4.0 of its C++ compiler, Borland has introduced the second version of the ObjectWindows Library, which is the one we will focus on in these pages.

A Short History of GUIs

Graphical user interfaces (GUIs) are quite common today, particularly on personal computers. Although their popularity is fairly recent, their "invention" dates back almost twenty years.

The research that has led to the present generation of graphical user interfaces was conducted at the Xerox PARC (Palo Alto Research Center) in the 1970s. At the same time, the researchers at PARC developed the Smalltalk language and its accompanying development environment, which contains all the basic GUI concepts: windows, pop-up menus, icons, buttons, the use of the mouse as primary input device, and so on.

These features, which today seem quite obvious, were truly innovative, as you can see in the following description by their developers:

"A user and the Smalltalk-80 programming environment interact through a bitmap display screen, a keyboard, and a pointing device. The display is used to present graphical and textual views of information to the user. The keyboard is used to present textual information to the system. The pointing device is used to select information on the display screen. Smalltalk-80 uses an indirect pointing device called a mouse. A cursor on the screen shows the location currently being pointed to by the mouse. The cursor is moved by moving the mouse over a flat surface. The mouse has three buttons, which are used to make different kinds of selections." [Goldberg 83]

From the research that went on at PARC, Xerox produced the Star workstation. But almost at the same time, Apple Computer borrowed the concepts of the GUI and developed its Lisa computer (a commercial failure), followed shortly after (in 1984) by the Macintosh. This last computer was a great success, particularly among computer novices who could easily learn to use a powerful computer and its applications because of the friendly user interface.

The Macintosh success motivated the whole computer industry to adopt GUIs. Now we have *Windows* (for the DOS operating system), *Presentation Manager* (for OS/2), *Intuition* (for the Commodore Amiga), *X-Windows* and *Motif* (for UNIX), *NeWS* (for the Sun workstations), *NextStep* (for the NeXT computer), among others. All these GUIs differ in various aspects, but they all share the same concept of visual object manipulation and resemble each other in several ways.

The connection between GUIs and object-oriented programming languages has remained quite strong, to the point that many people look at object orientation only in the context of developing applications for graphical environments.

The Macintosh interface is a typical example of a GUI. It is based on object-oriented principles: an object-oriented extension of the Pascal language has been adopted to program for it. Another similar example is the NeXT computer, which supports an object-oriented environment. Certainly, windows interfaces can be better implemented with the data abstraction and information hiding offered by classes, which help to determine and program the behavior of the visual objects, simplifying the interaction with the user.

As a consequence, almost every product today defines its user interface as "object oriented." But that is not always true. With Windows, for example, this definition is misleading, since the GUI (Figure 16.1) does not have all the main object-oriented features. Based on the definition by Wegner presented in Chapter 4, Windows can be defined as "class based," since there is no notion of inheritance and polymorphism. One way to prove that Windows is not object oriented lies in the language used to program it: C. However, we will return to this later.

Basic Features of GUIs

All GUIs share some common basic features, although they might be implemented in different ways. Some of the functionalities depend on the underlying operating system. For example, Windows adds to DOS some new features, such as efficient handling of a larger amount of memory and the multitasking capability (that is, running several

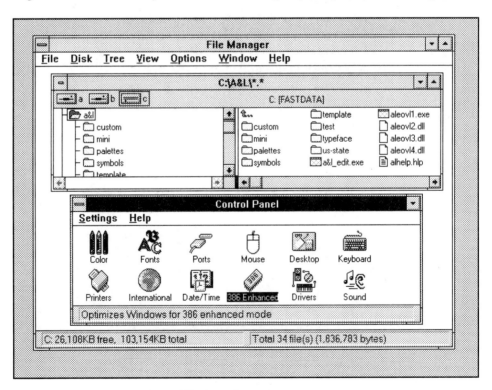

Figure 16.1 Example of the Windows interface

applications at the same time). Windows has many features, such as WYSIWYG (what you see is what you get) graphics, windows and dialog boxes, mice, icons, and menus, of GUIs. Its two main aspects are a consistent user interface—what the user sees—and an event-driven architecture—what the programmer uses.

A Consistent User Interface

One of the main features of GUIs is the consistency of their applications. All the programs for a GUI have several common properties and share a common "look and feel," a logical coherence. This way you can learn to use them in a shorter amount of time, since once you know how to interact with one application, you *almost* know how to use all of them; or, at least, you will have some familiar landmarks even when confronting a completely new program.

For example, in the Windows environment (as shown in Figure 16.2) you will find a label in the window with the name of the program and that of the file you are working

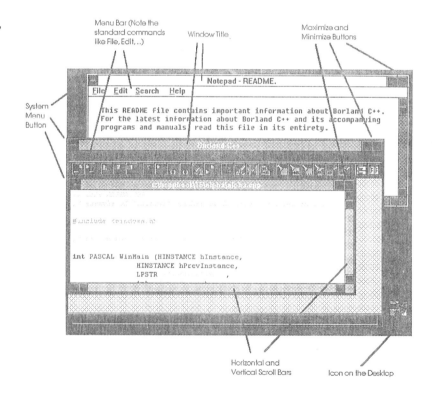

Figure 16.2 Common elements of Windows applications

on. At the same time, the scroll bars and the default buttons are shared by almost all the applications. When you select a scrollbar button, the contents of the windows should move in the desired direction, regardless of the program.

This logical coherence is true in other issues as well. For example, Windows menus tend to follow a standard: the first element of the menu bar is usually *File*, followed by *Edit*, while the last is usually *Help*. Also the items in the pulldown menus have some common defaults. For example, the *File* menu usually has items such as *New*, *Open*, *Save*, *Save as*, *Print*, and *Exit*.

However, it is important to notice that the consistency of the applications depends both on the interface and the programmer. The interface provides, through its API functions, most of the interface graphics and, through some written guidelines, indications on how to use them properly. It's up to the programmer to follow the indications and to use the API functions properly.

In Windows, the developers' standard guidelines are not enforced as much as in other windowing environments, which results in a slightly less consistent interface. The standard guidelines for Windows application development were previously those defined by IBM for OS/2 Presentation Manager and indicated by the acronym CUA (Common User Access referring to "IBM Systems Application Architecture Common User Access Advanced Interface Design Guide"). More recently, Microsoft has published slightly different guidelines, under the name of Windows Style Guide (WSG).

Event-Driven Architecture

From the programmer's point of view, the main feature of GUI environments is their event-driven or message-driven architecture.

Instead of having the program directly handle interactions with the user, it is the interface that drives the program. In a traditional application, the program waits for and responds to the input of the user, calling the proper function and possibly changing its internal state. The flow of the program can be illustrated by a diagram such as Figure 16.3.

In an event-driven application, however, the interface collects all the input from the user (such as a key press, an operation with the mouse, or the selection of a menu command) and with a message informs the application of what has happened (see Figure 16.4). Therefore, you can say that the application is driven by those messages (message-driven) or by the input operations or "events" (event-driven). These two terms are not completely synonymous, but are often used interchangeably.

It might seem that there is little difference from the traditional approach, but the overall architecture of the resulting program changes considerably (as Figures 16.3 and 16.4 suggest). For example, any of the windows present on the screem can handle its own input, and the system is able to deliver the user input to the proper window. The interface transforms the input into higher level commands (the messages); if the user moves the mouse and selects a menu command with it, the window receives a message concerning the menu item that was selected.

Note that the event-driven architecture and its principles can easily be associated with object-oriented programming. The fact that any window on the screen responds to

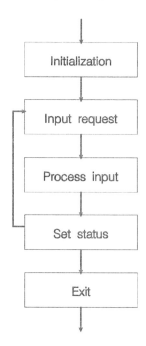

Figure 16.3 Flow diagram of a traditional application.

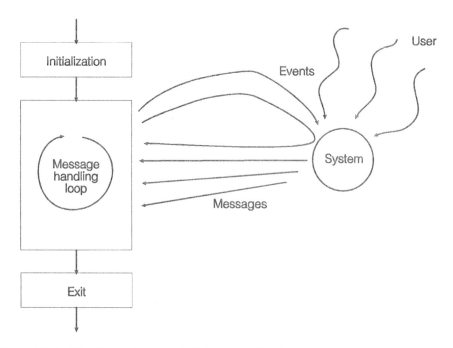

Figure 16.4   The flow of an event-driven application

its own messages without interacting with the rest of the system favors the definition of classes to describe these windows, and helps to divide the application in well-defined modules.

In short, we can describe event-driven programming as follows: any input action (or event) generates a message that the system dispatches properly; any window knows how to respond to the messages it receives.

In practice, traditional Windows programming consists of writing a huge *switch* statement with a *case* branch for every message that must be considered, leaving the rest of the messages to be processed by a default Windows procedure.

An important difference lies in the fact that the messages received by an application are generated by the interface on "user's request." It isn't the program that decides what should happen next—it's up to the user and the interface.

With Windows object-oriented programming using *ObjectWindows*, the interface can even directly call the proper member functions of the classes describing windows and other graphical objects.

Tools for Windows Programming

To build Windows applications, it's not enough to have a C (or C++) compiler and the proper library (including both a header file and a library file for the linker), although you need these two tools. Besides writing the program to handle the events, you must define some of the graphical items of the application (taking the name of *resources*), such as: dialog boxes, menus, icons, bitmaps, and so on.

➤ *Note:* The way Windows handles resources depends both on the fact that most of them are graphic elements, and that they are read-only data, which can be handled in memory in a particular way; in fact, they can be loaded from the *.EXE* file that contains them "on demand," saving some memory space. At the same time, they can be discarded to free up some memory, then reloaded when the application needs them again. Windows usually behaves in a similar way with the code of the application, but not with its data.

There are two different kind of resources: textual and bitmap. As the name implies, textual resources (dialog boxes, menus, accelerators, and string tables) can be described with a *textual* notation in a source file. On the other hand, bitmap resources (icons, cursors, bitmaps, and fonts) must be generated with a graphical editor (which usually generates files to be included in the global resource description). The main file (*.RC*) must then be compiled and linked to the program (both these operations are usually done by a *resource compiler*). Writing the source file describing the textual resources is a long and *tedious* operation. Therefore, several tools have been developed to generate the file in an interactive way; they are graphical programs that manipulate or directly paint dialogs, menus, and the other resources, and are themselves Windows applications.

The traditional Windows development environment, Microsoft's SDK, consists of the library, the resource compiler, a help compiler, several applications to generate the resources, the *Spy* application (to inspect Windows applications behavior), the *Heapwalk* application (to inspect how the memory is managed), and several other tools.

The Borland C++ programming environment includes the Windows header files. The Windows libraries are not included, because these dynamic libraries (or *DLLs*, such as the fundamental KERNEL.EXE, USER.EXE, and GDI.EXE, and many more) are part of Windows itself. To handle resources, the Borland environment includes the powerful *Resource Workshop* (see Figure 16.5). Besides generating any kind of resource, the *Workshop* can handle projects with one or more files describing the resources (even if there is always only one main file with the *RC* extension). It can easily handle the mapping of symbolic names to numbers and generate appropriate include files.

Therefore, *Resource Workshop* is the best tool to use to generate the resources that accompany a complex Windows application. It can directly generate a compiled resource file (with an *.res* extension), obviating the need to use the resource compiler.

To develop the examples in this chapter, we have used *Resource Workshop*. If we include the files describing resources, this is only for clarity. In fact, we have no other choice in describing resources, since it would require several screen shots of the *Workshop* to show all of the parameters for any single element, while we can describe the element fully with a few lines of text.

Another important element of a GUI application is its help system. Starting with Windows version 3.0, help is handled by a proper application and supports a kind of

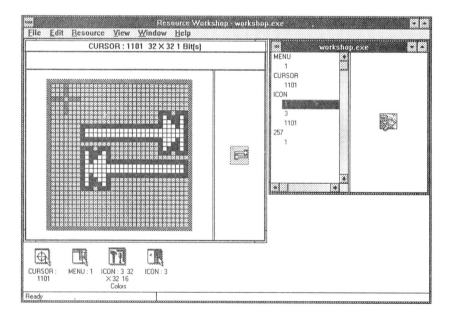

Figure 16.5 Borland's Resource Workshop

hypertextual linkage between different parts of the program description. To build a help system, you must define the help text and the internal links in a text file with a proper format. Using the help compiler, this text is transformed in a Windows internal format that the help application can easily interpret. The building of the help system is not covered in this book. However, Borland's manuals and a specific on-line "*Creating help*" help file give a detailed description of the subject.

"Standard" Windows Programming

Before describing the object-oriented approach, made possible by ObjectWindows, we want to introduce "standard" Windows programming. We will show a couple of "minimal" Windows applications, made in the usual way: with the Microsoft base libraries and the C language.

These applications serve as an introduction to the main aspects of Windows programming and as a base for comparing it with the "minimal" ObjectWindows application shown in the next section. The second part of this chapter will follow up with a comprehensive, and theoretical, description of Borland's object-oriented Windows programming library.

The application we want to start with is not much different from the usual "Hello, World" Windows program. The only unusual thing is its name: *alpha*. The first version of the application has only a dumb window, with no functionality beyond those shared by any window: movement, resize, zoom, and icon reduction. However, its size is not particularly small, since Windows requires a fair amount of overhead: several elements must be defined even if all you want is the default behavior.

The Smallest Windows Program

To generate any Windows application with the standard library, you must define all the basic properties of its main window (in a data structure named *class* in Windows terminology, although it is a normal *struct* of the C language). In the source file, which is followed by a detailed description, you will immediately notice something strange: the *main* function has disappeared, replaced by a *WinMain* function.

➤ *Note:* All the programs in this chapter have been written using the Windows 3.1 API. In the following source code, the only difference is in the parameters of the *WinMain* function: in Windows 3.0 (and in the previous versions), the first and the second parameters were of type *HANDLE*; now their type is *HINSTANCE*. The following program can be compiled starting with Borland C++ 3.1 but not with previous versions. However, to compile it with Borland C++ 3.0 you only need to change the data type of the first and second parameters of the WinMain function (or add a statement like *typedef HINSTANCE HANDLE*).

(Although seldom used in the examples of this book, Windows 3.1 introduces some new data types. To learn more about them, you can refer to any reference text on the Windows 3.1 API. If you are still using earlier versions of Windows, you will have to change or redefine these new data types in order to compile the sample programs.)

```
// file ALPHA.C                                            16/ALPHA
// example of "minimal" Windows application ( written in C )

#include <windows.h>

// window main function ( replaces "main" )

int PASCAL WinMain ( HINSTANCE hInstance , HINSTANCE hPrevInstance ,
        LPSTR lpszCmdLine , int nCmdShow )
{
WNDCLASS   wndClass ;                 // window "class"
HWND       hwnd ;                     // handle to the window
MSG        msg ;                      // message
char       name [ 6 ] = "alpha" ;     // application name

// if this is the first instance, defines and registers the "class"

if ( !hPrevInstance ) {
    wndClass.style = CS_HREDRAW I CS_VREDRAW ;          // window style
    wndClass.lpfnWndProc = DefWindowProc ;              // window procedure
    wndClass.cbClsExtra = 0 ;                           // class extra bytes
    wndClass.cbWndExtra = 0 ;                           // window extra bytes
    wndClass.hInstance = hInstance ;                    // instance handle
    wndClass.hIcon = LoadIcon ( NULL , IDI_APPLICATION ) ; // icon
    wndClass.hCursor = LoadCursor ( NULL , IDC_ARROW ) ; // cursor
    wndClass.hbrBackground = COLOR_WINDOW + 1 ;         // background color
    wndClass.lpszMenuName = NULL ;                      // menu
    wndClass.lpszClassName = name ;                     // class name

    // tries to register the window "class" with the values defined

    if ( !RegisterClass ( &wndClass ) )
        return FALSE ;
}

// creates the window ( based onto the registered "class" )

hwnd = CreateWindow
    ( name ,                          // class name
```

```
      "Alpha Application" ,          // caption
      WS_OVERLAPPEDWINDOW ,         // style
      CW_USEDEFAULT ,               // x position
      CW_USEDEFAULT ,               // y position
      CW_USEDEFAULT ,               // width
      CW_USEDEFAULT ,               // height
      NULL ,                        // parent window
      NULL ,                        // menu
      hInstance ,                   // instance handle
      NULL ) ;                      // pointer to a memory area

   // shows the window

   ShowWindow ( hwnd , SW_SHOWNORMAL ) ;

   // messages loop

   while ( GetMessage ( &msg , NULL , 0 , 0 ) ) {
      TranslateMessage ( &msg ) ;
      DispatchMessage ( &msg ) ;
   }

   return msg.wParam ;

} // end of WinMain
```

Although you don't need to understand every detail of this program at first glance, it's important to get acquainted with its main parts.

➤ *Note:* The previous program has been written following the so-called Hungarian notation. It is a naming convention used by many Windows programmers, because the Windows API adheres to it. This notation (introduced by Charles Simonyi) defines some type prefixes that should be used as the first part of the names of variables and parameters. This type prefix allows a programmer to identify the type of the variable without having to look at its definition. For example, any variable beginning with an *h* is of type *HANDLE*. The use of a similar notation makes the programs more readable, at least when you have gotten some practice with it.

All the examples of this chapter have been written following the Hungarian notation. ObjectWindows itself doesn't follow Hungarian notation. Since most books and tutorials on Windows programming use this naming convention, adopting it might help programmers who already have some experience in the Windows environment. However, since ObjectWindows introduces new non-Hungarian data types, it is not easy to adapt the notation to this library.

The following operations take place in the *WinMain* function.

- *The definition of the "class"* that describes the window (it's not a C++ *class*, but a normal C *struct*), with most of its parameters: the style, message handling procedure, icon, background color, menu, and "internal" name. Once the data structure has been filled, it must be registered.

- Having defined and registered the class, *the window can be created*, indicating the "internal" name (to get the corresponding class), a label or title, a style, the initial on screen position and size. Only at this point can the window be shown on the screen.

- The heart of the WinMain function is the *main message scanning loop*, which is almost always the same. It takes the incoming messages directed to the application (that is, those present in the application queue) and dispatches them to the window via its message handling procedure.

While you can create several instances of a window at the same time (usually executing several instances of the same application), the definition of the class and its registration should take place only once (in fact, this part of the code is executed only if the *hPrevInstance* parameter, indicating the previous instance of the same application, is null). The term *class* is used in Windows to indicate that a class can have several instances. Not having the other features of the C++ classes, this definition resembles those of the *class-based languages*, and not those of the *object-oriented languages*.

Although the application uses no particular Windows resources, to compile and run it you need a project including the C file, with *Application (.EXE)* as target and *Windows 3.x (16)* as platform. If you build the program with the source code file only, a linker warning will appear to indicate that there is no definition file. Borland C++ can work without one, using default values. If you want to provide it, your project should contain both the *ALPHA.C* source file and the following *ALPHA.DEF* file:

; file ALPHA.DEF   **16/ALPHA**

```
NAME          ALPHA
DESCRIPTION   'Alpha Application'
STUB          'WINSTUB.EXE'
EXETYPE       WINDOWS
DATA          PRELOAD MULTIPLE MOVEABLE
CODE          PRELOAD MOVEABLE DISCARDABLE
HEAPSIZE      2048
STACKSIZE     8192
```

➤ *Note:* The definition file of a Windows application contains a list of directives for the linker, concerning several memory options, the size of the stack, the minimal size of the heap, and other parameters of the resulting executable file. (These parameters differ from those needed by the usual DOS linker since Windows handles memory in a different way, and its executable files have a different format than DOS's.)

The application *alpha* can perform only default operations, and corresponds to the (almost) smallest Windows application that might be written. When you execute it (as long as the Windows environment has been loaded), the screen will contain a window, which has a title and the other visual properties that have been set (an example of *alpha* execution can be seen in Figure 16.6). The window (which has the default system menu) can be moved, zoomed, iconized and closed, using the usual mouse operations (or the system menu items).

Adding a Rectangle and a Message Box

The application we have just seen is not that interesting. To add functionalities to a window, a window procedure (or *winproc*) must be defined. This procedure determines the behavior of the program in response to the incoming messages. These messages are often generated by user "events," such as a key press or a mouse movement, and have a name and some identification parameters. When Windows receives input, it generates a message and places it in the application message queue. Therefore, any application must have a message scanning loop to check if there are messages (using the *GetMessage* function) and dispatch them to its own window procedure (with *DispatchMessage*), which defines the behavior of the window for each of the relevant messages.

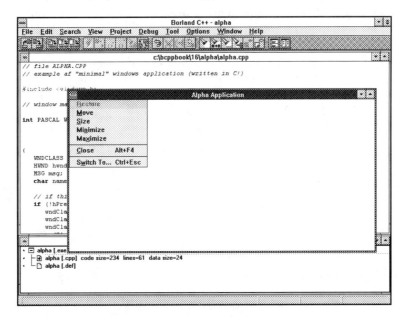

Figure 16.6 Executing alpha under Windows

➤ *Note:* Besides looking for a message in the application queue, the *GetMessage* function is the heart of Windows multitasking capabilities. In fact, if the message queue of the application is empty, a call to *GetMessage* (or the similar *PeekMessage* function) suspends the application and passes control of the system to one of the other applications that is running.

Windows cooperative multitasking is based on the principle that any application should perform frequent accesses to its own queue, allowing the other applications to be executed as well. However, if an application takes a long time to perform an operation, Windows has no way to halt it (in other words, it is a non-preemptive environment). You will see a very simple example of Windows multitasking in the next chapter.

In the following program, called *alpha2*, the window has a window procedure, the function *AlphaWinProc*.

➤ *Note:* As is true with the parameters of the *WinMain* function, those parameters in the window procedures have also changed in Windows 3.1. Until Windows 3.0, they were *HWND*, *WORD*, *WORD*, and *LONG*. Now, in Windows 3.1, they are *HWND*, *UINT*, *WPARAM*, and *LPARAM*. We have written the following *AlphaWinProc* with the new parameter types so that we can compile it starting with Borland C++ 3.1. However, this creates problems with earlier versions of the compiler. If you are using one of these earlier versions, you will need to replace the second and third parameter type with *WORD*, and the fourth with *LONG* (and replace the two *HINSTANCE* parameters of *WinMain* with the *HANDLE* data type).

In a Windows 3.1 program, it is better—but not required—to declare the functions as *WINAPI*, instead of as *FAR PASCAL* (although the two are equivalent, at least on 80x86 based computers), and return a value of type *LRESULT* instead of *LONG*. This doesn't make a big difference if you build for the 16-bit API (good old Windows), but leads to programs that are much more compatible with the 32-bit API (Windows NT, Win 32s, and the future 32-bit versions of Windows).

```
// file ALPHA2.C                                        16/ALPHA
// example of simple Windows application ( written in C )

#include <windows.h>
#include <string.h>

// window procedure

result winap AlphaWinProc ( HWND hwnd , UINT msg ,
          WPARAM wParam , LPARAM lParam )
{
```

```
        switch ( msg ) {

        // paints a rounded rectangle in the window

        case WM_PAINT:
            {
            HDC             hDC ;
            PAINTSTRUCT     pstruct ;
            HANDLE          hPen ;
            hDC = BeginPaint ( hwnd , &pstruct ) ;
            hPen = CreatePen ( PS_SOLID , 5 , RGB ( 255 , 0 , 0 ) ) ;
            SelectObject ( hDC , hPen ) ;
            RoundRect ( hDC , 20 , 20 , 200 , 280 , 20 , 20 ) ;
            EndPaint ( hwnd , &pstruct ) ;
            }
            break ;

        // pops a message box when the left mouse button is pressed

        case WM_LBUTTONDOWN:
            {
            MessageBox ( hwnd , "Mouse click" , "Message" , MB_OK ) ;
            }
            break ;

        // closes the window

        case WM_DESTROY:
            {
            PostQuitMessage ( 0 ) ;
            }
            break ;
        }

        // calls the default window procedure

        return DefWindowProc ( hwnd , msg , wParam , lParam ) ;
}

// window main

int PASCAL WinMain ( HINSTANCE hInstance , HINSTANCE hPrevInstance ,
        LPSTR lpszCmdLine , int nCmdShow )
{
WNDCLASS    wndClass ;                      // window "class"
```

```
HWND        hwnd ;                      // hwnd to window
MSG         msg ;                       // message
char        name [ 6 ] = "alpha" ;      // application name

// if this is the first instance, defines and registers the "class"

if ( !hPrevInstance ) {
    wndClass.style = CS_HREDRAW | CS_VREDRAW ;          // window style
    wndClass.lpfnWndProc = AlphaWinProc ;               // window procedure
    wndClass.cbClsExtra = 0 ;                           // class extra bytes
    wndClass.cbWndExtra = 0 ;                           // window extra bytes
    wndClass.hInstance = hInstance ;                    // instance hwnd
    wndClass.hIcon = LoadIcon ( NULL , IDI_APPLICATION ) ; // icon
    wndClass.hCursor = LoadCursor ( NULL , IDC_CROSS ) ;   // cursor
    wndClass.hbrBackground =
        CreateSolidBrush ( RGB ( 255 , 127 , 0 ) ) ;    // background color
    wndClass.lpszMenuName = NULL ;                      // menu
    wndClass.lpszClassName = name ;                     // class name

    // tries to register the window "class" with the values defined
    if ( !RegisterClass ( &wndClass ) )
        return FALSE ;
}

// creates the window ( based on the registered "class" )

hwnd = CreateWindow
    ( name ,                            // class name
    "Alpha Application ( 2nd version ) " ,  // caption
    WS_OVERLAPPEDWINDOW ,               // style
    CW_USEDEFAULT ,                     // x position
    CW_USEDEFAULT ,                     // y position
    CW_USEDEFAULT ,                     // width
    CW_USEDEFAULT ,                     // height
    NULL ,                              // parent window
    NULL ,                              // menu
    hInstance ,                         // instance hwnd
    NULL ) ;                            // pointer to a memory area

// shows the window

ShowWindow ( hwnd , SW_SHOWNORMAL ) ;

// messages loop
```

```
while ( GetMessage ( &msg , NULL , 0 , 0 ) ) {
   TranslateMessage ( &msg ) ;
   DispatchMessage ( &msg ) ;
}

return msg.wParam ;

} // end of window main
```

The function *WinMain* of *alpha2* is almost unchanged, besides the reference to *AlphaWinProc* and some minor changes, such as the selection of a different background color and the loading of another cursor. The only difference between the two versions of the program is the presence of a window procedure.

AlphaWinProc, defined in the first part of the listing, is made up of a big *switch* statement, which lets the program choose among different messages that can be received. Every *case* branch corresponds to a different message and is followed by the statements to be executed. At the end, any window procedure should call the default window procedure, which handles all the system messages (including those that resize, move, minimize, or zoom a window).

The first *case* branch of the *switch* statement in the example responds to the *WM_PAINT* message, which is "posted" by Windows to the application every time the windows must be repainted (for example, because of a change in the window size). This is a fundamental message, because if you paint the window area in other parts of the program, all the changes will be discarded the first time the system needs to repaint the window. The output of the operations executed in response to the *WM_PAINT* message defines the *constant contents* of the window. Therefore, almost any application performs its whole output operation in response to the paint message.

Within *alpha2*, the result of this message is the painting of a rectangle with rounded corners. This operation takes place in three steps, as does any other output: the request of a "*device context*" (*BeginPaint*), the actual paint functions (*RoundRect*), and the release of the "*device context*" (*EndPaint*). This so-called "*device context*" is a data structure handled by the *Graphics Device Interface* (GDI), the part of Windows that manages the output. To execute any output operation, an application needs to first request permission from Windows with *BeginPaint* (after a *WM_PAINT* message) or *GetDC* (in all the other cases). The return value of these functions is a handle to the device context, a data structure containing the description of the area that can be used for the output, and includes some parameters of the corresponding physical device (as indicated by the device driver), and the description of the tools that have been selected for painting (colors, pens, brushes, fonts, and so on). The device context is usually the first parameter of any other GDI function. As soon as it doesn't need it anymore, the application should release the device context (with the *EndPaint* or *ReleaseDC* functions) because they are limited in number.

In the example *alpha2*, we want to use the device context to paint a colored rectangle with rounded corners. Therefore, we need to select a pen with the proper kind of line, line width, and color. The color can be defined easily using the RGB macro, although there are several other ways to describe it. As the name implies, the RGB macro takes as parameters three integers (from 0 to 255) corresponding to the amount of red, green, and blue that make up the chosen color, and returns the definition of the color in Windows format.

➤ *Note:* As the RGB macro parameters suggest, Windows can handle 24-bit colors. Of course, if you have only a VGA or similar graphics adapter, you will not see all of them. In this case, Windows tries to mimic the chosen color by putting pixels of different colors side-by-side (this technique is known as *dithering*).

The second message of *AlphaWinProc* is *WM_LBUTTONDOWN*, sent to the application any time the left button of the mouse is pressed. When this occurs, the program displays a message inside a window (called *Message Box*) that has a caption, some standard buttons (in this case only the *OK* button), and the message itself (see Figure 16.7).

The last message handled by the window procedure is *WM_DESTROY*, which is issued when the window is closed, and must execute the standard statement to close the application queue, exit the message scanning loop, and terminate the application. In fact, when the corresponding *WM_QUIT* message is retrieved by the *GetMessage* function, it returns zero, thus terminating the *while* loop used to scan the messages.

With these three simple messages, we have defined the *alpha2* application. You can compile it in the same way as *alpha*, using the same definition file, ALPHA.DEF. The resulting window is shown in Figure 16.7. When you try to use it, you will see that the rectangle remains on the screen regardless of the operations you make on the window

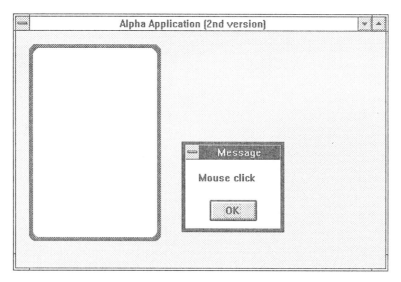

Figure 16.7 The alpha2 window with the message box shown

(moving, zooming, resizing, placing other windows above it, and so on). This is because Windows sends our application a *WM_PAINT* message whenever these other operations take place.

The Minimal ObjectWindows Application

Before presenting the *ObjectWindows Library* structure, we will develop a minimal application with this library, which will serve as a base to compare the traditional development of Windows applications with that supported by the library. This minimal Windows program resembles the first version of the *alpha* application, but its implementation is simpler and shorter. In fact, there is no need to define the class of the window, to register it, or to create the window with a lot of parameters. Since there are predefined classes describing the standard behavior of windows and applications, you can avoid declaring a lot of default values. Taking advantage of this fact, we obtain the following shorter code.

```
// file MINIMAL1.CPP                                    16/MINIMAL
// A minimal OWL 2.0 application

// inclusion of the library files
#include <owl\owlpch.h>
#include <owl\applicat.h>

int OwlMain (int /*argc*/, char* /*argv*/ [])
{
    TApplication   mini ("Minimal") ;
    return mini.Run ( ) ;
}
```

To generate a minimal application with OWL 2, you only need to create an object of the default *TApplication* class and *Run* it. The name you pass to the constructor of the application object is used for the caption of the frame window of the application, as shown in Figure 16.8. Notice another difference with the previous example: There is no *WinMain* function, but there is an *OwlMain* function instead, which takes parameters similar to those of a typical DOS *main*.

➤   *Note:* Although we have always seen a *main* function with no parameters, you can usually retrieve command line parameters in *main* with a notation similar to the one of the *OwlMain*. With *main* you can omit the parameters, while in *OwlMain* they are compulsory. You might ask yourself how *OwlMain* relates to *WinMain*. Simply, the OWL2 library provides a *WinMain* function for your application. This function initializes the library, then calls *OwlMain*.

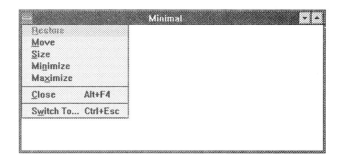

Figure 16.8 The output of the minimal application, made with two lines of code

Beside this "bare minimum" application, using a standard window and a standard application object, we can customize *ObjectWindows* code, deriving a class from *TApplication* and adding to it an initialization function in order to create the main window, *InitMainWindow*. In this function we create a frame window object dynamically, using the standard OWL class *TFrameWindow*, with a specific caption.

```
// file MINIMAL2.CPP                                    16/MINIMAL
// A minimal OWL 2.0 application

// inclusion of the library files
#include <owl\owlpch.h>
#include <owl\applicat.h>
#include <owl\framewin.h>

// class describing the application
class OwlApplication : public TApplication
{
public:

    // constructor:
    OwlApplication ( ) :
        TApplication ( )
    { }

    // main window initialization function
    void InitMainWindow ( )
    {
        // provide a value for the MainWindow data member of TApplication
        SetMainWindow (new TFrameWindow (0, "Minimal")) ;
    }
} ;

int OwlMain (int /*argc*/, char* /*argv*/ [])
{
```

```
    OwlApplication    mini ;
    return mini.Run ( ) ;
}
```

The output of this program is exactly the same as that of the previous one: We only wrote some code similar to the default one we used before.

The second step in customizing our OWL application is to define our own class for the window, deriving it from one of those in the library. Without changing the output, we can add some more *hidden* code to our example, as in the following listing:

```
// file MINIMAL3.CPP                                    16/MINIMAL
// A minimal OWL 2.0 application

// inclusion of the library files
#include <owl\owlpch.h>
#include <owl\applicat.h>
#include <owl\framewin.h>

// class describing the main window
class BaseWindow : public TWindow
{
public:
    BaseWindow ( ) ;

    DECLARE_RESPONSE_TABLE(BaseWindow) ;
} ;

DEFINE_RESPONSE_TABLE1(BaseWindow, TWindow)
END_RESPONSE_TABLE ;

BaseWindow :: BaseWindow ( ) :
    TWindow (0, 0, 0)
{ }

// class describing the application
class OwlApplication : public TApplication
{
public:
// constructor:
    OwlApplication ( ) :
        TApplication ( )
    { }

// main window initialization function
    void InitMainWindow ( )
    {
```

```
        // provides a value for the MainWindow data member of TApplication
        SetMainWindow (new TFrameWindow (0, "Minimal",
                new BaseWindow ));
    }
} ;

int OwlMain (int /*argc*/, char* /*argv*/ [])
{
    OwlApplication    mini ;
    return mini.Run ( ) ;
}
```

In this program we introduce a window class derived from *TWindow* to be used inside the frame class, with the statement:

```
SetMainWindow (new TFrameWindow (0, "Minimal", new BaseWindow ));
```

So we end up with two windows, a frame and our own window inside it. This might seems useless, but is really very powerfull. In fact, we might change the frame (using MDI or decorations) and the behavior of the program without modifying our *internal* window.

Notice that in the previous program there are a couple of macro calls (you can spot them, since they are capitalized) to define and declare a response table. More on this later.

All of these programs can be compiled using a simple project containing the source code and a standard *def* file, and they all produce the output of Figure 16.8. There are two basic ways to link them to the proper OWL library code. ObjectWindows, in fact, can use either static or dynamic libraries. Static libraries can be included within the executable code, so that when you distribute them, everything is contained in one *.exe* file. But that also means this file will grow larger. With the DLL (Dynamic Link Library) versions, you must distribute the DLL along with the executable code, but the *.exe* file is smaller. Thus, if several applications that use the same DLL are running, only one copy of the library needs to be loaded in memory. In contrast, with static linking you might have several copies of the same library in memory at once.

Once the program has been compiled, the linker will produce the executable code, as long as the libraries are properly selected. You can use the *Target Expert* of the Borland IDE to choose between the two link strategies. Selecting the proper option in this dialog box, the compiler will link either statically (see Figure 16.9) or dynamically (see Figure 16.10) the three main libraries (OWL, Containers, and Run-Time). As you select a choice in the *Target Expert* dialog box, the environment automatically sets the proper compiler options.

The main difference between the two resulting programs is in their size. Building with static libraries produces a bigger executable file, but as you run the program you might spare some memory, since only the required code of the library is linked to your application. Using a dynamic link, on the other hand, produces a much smaller execut-able; however to run this program you need to have loaded in memory the three DLLs

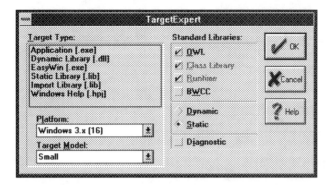

Figure 16.9 The Target Expert selections for a static link

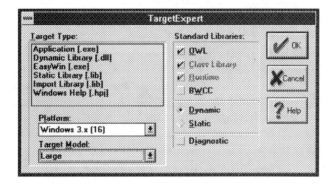

Figure 16.10 The Target Expert selections for a dynamic link

for OWL, the container library, and the run-time library. These three files should be present in the same directory as that of the program, in the *windows/system* directory, or in one of the directories of your *PATH*.

Although the MINIMAL.CCP program is easier to write and to understand than ALPHA.C, both programs are functionally useless. The full power of the ObjectWindows library will be more evident shortly, when we define full-blown classes derived from *TWindow*. But before we show you an example, it's useful to take a general overview of the features of the library.

ObjectWindows: Object-Oriented Programming for Windows

Traditionally, programming Windows applications required you to use the Microsoft SDK (Software Development Kit), and the Windows API, which is made up of several hundred function calls. ObjectWindows encapsulates the fundamental API calls within about twenty classes, which provide the basic elements of an application. Of course, these classes are not enough to write an application; you will still need to call some of the API functions.

The purpose of the library is to change the structure of the Windows applications, which can thus become truly object-oriented. One of the main features of the library is the elimination of the need for *switch* statements to handle messages by replacing these statements with member functions.

Windows and Objects

"The problem is this: Microsoft created windows to send a simple integral number to an application when an event occurs. How does Borland fix this to make Windows programming object-oriented?" [Eckel 91]

Windows messages should be assocaited to functions; so sending a message should result in a call to a function capable of handling it. To be able to obtain the *function-message* connection, in the past Borland chose a "risky" road: a language extension (supporting a mechanism known as *dynamic dispatching*). In the second version of the ObjectWindows Library, dynamic dispatching has been replaced by a "more standard" and more efficient mechanism, based on *message response tables*.

A message response table is a kind of map holding a list of the messages a window wants to handle, together with the names of the corresponding member functions of the class. Each time a message is sent to the window, the table is searched. In case of a match, the corresponding member function is called. If no match is found, the table of the base class is searched. In some cases, the message is sent to other related classes.

To define a *response table,* you need to add the macro

```
DECLARE_RESPONSE_TABLE(MyWin) ;
```

in the definition of your *MyWin* class (usually the end of the class, although the response table can appear in any other place you choosez); and you need to define this table outside of the class, indicating its first and last lines with:

```
DEFINE_RESPONSE_TABLE1(MyWin, TWindow)
```

```
END_RESPONSE_TABLE ;
```

In the *define* macro the first parameter is the name of the class, and the second is the name of its base class. It is possible to have more than one base class, but in this case you need to use a different version of the macro, replacing the final 1 with a 2, 3, and so on:

```
DEFINE_RESPONSE_TABLE2(MyWin, FirstBase, SecondBase)
```

Between these two macro calls you need to list the messages you want to process, as we'll see later. When this macro is expanded, some internal data structures and the corresponding access functions are defined. *Message response tables* simulate a dynamic interaction between the C++ object describing a window and the corresponding user-interface element. This interaction resembles the behavior of some object-oriented environments: even the Smalltalk system works in a similar way. Instead of sending numbers to the application, the Windows/ObjectWindows couple calls the functions of the classes describing the graphical objects. This is one of the main reasons to use ObjectWindows to write applications.

The advantages of this approach are great. Thanks to inheritance, it's possible to define a window by deriving it from an existing one, add functions to respond to new messages, or modify some of the functions already defined—inheriting all the other window functions and behavior. At run time, the system calls the functions of the proper class, regardless of the class that defines them. However, it's still possible to use the old-style switch statements, overriding the *WindowProc* function inherited from the *TWindows* class.

A similar extension of the capabilities of a window is possible using the traditional Windows approach, with an operation known as "subclassing." However, if you want to add just a new feature, you should always call the window procedure of the "super-class"; after a few "derivations," you end up calling several window procedures in cascade, traversing several *switch* statements. Even for a system with four or five derived classes, this can be quite costly in terms of performance and almost unmanageable by any programmer.

The use of *response tables* results in two other advantages, which were not available in the first version of the library. First, it is possible to use multiple inheritance, that is, to derive a class from two base classes describing windows, combining together their behavior. To make this possible, the base classes must be written with great care: Specific classes intended for this use often receive the name of *mix-in*.

If you look at the class hierarchy of *ObjectWindows,* you'll see a number of multiple derivations among the classes of the library itself.

➤   *Note:* To support multiple inheritance avoiding name clashes and ambiguous calls, the derivation from most of the base classes of the hierarchy is *virtual.* As you should remember from Chapter 7, in case of repeated inheritance from a virtual base class, only one object of that class is present in the derived class. In fact, although a class for a window might derive from two other classes defining windows, it is *one* window, having *TWindow* as virtual base, and not *two.*

As a side effect of the presence of virtual base classes, at times the constructor of derived classes might call the virtual base class constructor, even if this is not a direct base.

The second advantage of the use of *massage maps* is *message cracking.* Instead of using *wParam* and *lParam* for each message, and having to cast these parameters to their original types, the member functions called by the message maps have specific parameters, such as *TPoint* instead of *LPARAM* for the messages involving the mouse. This makes the program more readable and much more reliable, since casting is always a dangerous practice.

The Available Classes

Having stressed that the main aspect of the library is that it enables us to write object-oriented programs for Windows, we still have to show which classes ObjectWindows provides. Some of these classes are directly usable, while others serve as a base to derive one's own classes. A portion of the hierarchy with the most important classes of the library is shown in Figure 16.11.

You can find a more detailed hierarchy graph in the compiler's help file and documentation.

At the root of the hierarchy there are two classes, *TEventHandler* and *TStreamableBase*. From both these classes derive *TModule* (and hence, *TApplication*), *TWindow*, *TView*, *TDocManager*. The *TWindow* subhierarchy is the biggest one, and branches into:

- *TDialog* classes (including support for the Windows 3.1 common dialog boxes, such as *OpenSave*, *ChooseColor*, or *ChoooseFont*)

- *TControl* classes (including edit, button, listbox, static, visual basic control, scrollbar, slider, *gauge*, and other classes)

- *TFrameWindow*, Multiple Document Interface (*MDI*) classes, decorated frames, and other classes for main windows

- *TGadgetWindow* and the derived classes defining tool-bars, tool-boxes, and status-bars

- Other classes, including some mix-in (such as *TClipboardViewer* and *TKeyboardModeTracker*) and printer support classes

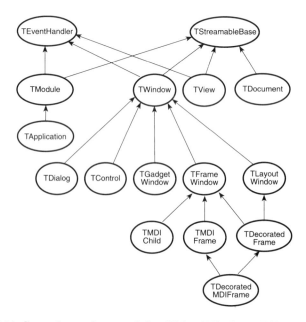

Figure 16.11 Some base classes of the ObjectWindows Library

Besides the main hierarchy, ObjectWindows has a number of other classes, some forming secondary hierarchies. For example, the graphic device interface (*GDI*) support is made with more than 20 classes derived from *TGdiBase*, and including *GDIObjects* support (bitmaps, fonts, regions, brushes, palettes, pens) and *device contexts* (for on-screen painting, related to a window, for the printer, in memory, and so on). Other hierarchies include menu support, clipboard support, scrollers, printers, validators, and exception handling classes. There are a number of *sparse* classes, some of which are derived from Windows data structures.

To show you how to use some of these classes, lets develop some examples. The first *minimal* application defined only a class derived by *TApplication* and one derived by *TWindow*, but used a number of other classes, too. In general you must derive from a class of the library to define windows and dialog boxes, while controls, GDI classes, and other support classes are used directly.

Some Further Considerations

ObjectWindows offers several advantages compared with the traditional development of Windows applications and even compared with several other application frameworks. However, there are still some noteworthy problems.

The most significant problem is that the existing separation between the code and the description of the resources reduces information hiding and code locality—that is, the possibility of having the full description of a graphical object inside a class, avoiding names with file scope. When changes are made, they affect at least two different places of the source and some global names. Also, the correspondence between resource names and identifiers used in the source code must be handled by the programmer. There is no check performed by the linker or the resource compiler: if you misspell a name, you get no warning, but the program won't run properly. In the case of a big application, this can cause serious problems.

In this context, Borland's Resource Workshop can help. Although it doesn't offer a "bridge" between resources and code, it greatly enhances the organization and handling of resource files, providing checks on the identifiers and the connection with a header file that contains their names.

Besides this typical Windows problem (the separation of the source code from the resource description), an annoying problem is that in using *response tables* you have to change the source code in three places just to add one function to respond to a message. In fact, you need to add the function declaration in the class definition, add an entry in the response table, and write the code of the function itself. This problem can be completely avoided using the *ClassExpert* tool of the Borland C++ environment. The only *drawback* is that you need to use the *AppExpert* to develop the structure of the application in the first place. However, this is really an advantage, since you can spare several hours of standard coding and start writing your program with an already working, although somewhat bare, application.

Since this is a book on the C++ language we decided not to cover the use of the *AppExpert* and the *ClassExpert*, although these are fundamental tools for Windows programming under Borland C++ 4.0. Instead, we want to focus on using C++ under OWL, to show the advantages of using of an object-oriented class library to program a user-interface.

The ObjectWindows Library is not the only library of classes available for Windows programming. There are really a number of class libraries for this environment and for several environments at the same time (i.e., portable to OS/2 PM or Motif). Borland has announced that in the future ObjectWindows application will be portable to OS/2, the Apple Macintosh, and other targets. One of the main competitors of OWL is the *Microsoft Foundation Class Library* (*MFC*), included in *Microsoft Visual C++* and other compilers.

The classes of MFC cover almost all of the elements and functions of the Windows API, as OWL does. However, the member functions of these classes are more similar to the original Windows' API, and thus allow experienced Windows programmers to move to MFC easily; however, MFC does not take advantage of some of the most useful features of C++, such as function overloading, default parameters, constructors, and destructors.

Besides being more interesting for newcomers to Windows programming (and for long-time OWL programmers), Borland's library tends to hide more details of Windows, and some dangerous behavior. For example the library will automatically check if a pen or a brush is no longer used and delete it automatically from Windows' reserved memory, avoiding wasting valuable resources. Particularly significant advantages of OWL are multiple inheritance and the use of exception handling.

A Simple Application Built Step by Step

Having presented a minimal application and a general description of the ObjectWindows Library, we now want to build an application step by step. It will be rather simple, but will have some drawing capability, an icon, a menu, and a dialog. Since this is our first full application, we will call it "*one*."

Our step-by-step approach should help convince those who have no confidence in Windows development, even using Microsoft's SDK and API calls. The starting point, step "zero," is the last version of the *minimal* program that we have already seen in the first part of this chapter. It had a class derived from *TApplication*, one derived from *TWindow,* and an *OwlMain* function. This structure won't change in the following steps.

In the new class for the window, called *OneWin*, we will place some code to draw some text in the center of the screen and redefine a couple of member functions (*GetWindowClass* and *GetClassName*) to change the behavior of the default *wndclass* structure used by OWL.

➤   *Note:* In fact, we want to add to the style of the class CS_HREDRAW and CS_VREDRAW, to receive a paint message each time the user changes the horizontal (H) or vertical (V) size of the window. Without this definition, changing the size will not result in repainting of the text in the middle of the window, and at times, in repainting only a part of it.

This depends on the fact that our output is not in a fixed position but is moved according to the size of the window (retrieved with the *GetClientRect* function).

Step 1: Drawing some text

The first version of the program is contained in the following listing.

```
// ONE1.CPP                                               16/ONE
// The first Object Windows program
// First version

// include some library header files
#include <owl\owlpch.h>
#include <owl\applicat.h>
#include <owl\framewin.h>
#include <owl\dc.h>

// define the class OneWin, derived from the standard TWindow
class OneWin : public TWindow
{
public:
    OneWin ( ) :
        TWindow (0, 0, 0)
    { }

    // function used to set the window attributes
    void GetWindowClass (WNDCLASS& wc)
    {
        // retrieve default values
        TWindow :: GetWindowClass (wc) ;

        // add automatic redraw on size change to the class style
        wc.style |= CS_HREDRAW | CS_VREDRAW ;
    }

    // define the name of the window-class
    char far * GetClassName ( )
```

```
    {
        return "OneWinClass" ;
    }

    void Paint (TDC& paintDC, BOOL, TRect&)
    {
        // define a rectangle and assigns to it the
        // size of the client area of the window
        TRect rect = GetClientRect ( ) ;

        // define centered alignment and outputs the text
        paintDC.SetTextAlign (TA_CENTER) ;

        // paint the text in the center
        paintDC.TextOut (rect.right / 2, rect.bottom / 2, "Hello! I'm application ONE") ;
    }

    void EvLButtonDown(UINT, TPoint&)
    {
        MessageBox ("Left button pressed", "ONE", MB_OK) ;
    }

    DECLARE_RESPONSE_TABLE (OneWin) ;
} ;

DEFINE_RESPONSE_TABLE1(OneWin, TWindow)
    EV_WM_LBUTTONDOWN ,
END_RESPONSE_TABLE ;


// define a class for the application
class OneApp : public TApplication
{
public:
    OneApp ( ) :
        TApplication ( )
    { }

    void InitMainWindow ( )
    {
        SetMainWindow (new TFrameWindow(0, "ONE (First version)", new OneWin)) ;
    }
} ;

// define OwlMain, replacing WinMain
```

```
int OwlMain (int, char* [])
{
    OneApp one ;
    return one.Run ( ) ;
}
```

The code of the program defines the main window of the application, *OneWin*, which derives from *TWindow*. In it, we redefine the function *Paint* (which is called automatically every time the window has to be repainted—such as when the *WM_PAINT* message is received). Inside the function, ObjectWindows already provides the handle for the proper device context. So the two API calls of the function can use the *PaintDC* parameter directly, avoiding calling the *BeginPaint* API function or declaring a *TPaintDC* object.

Inside the *Paint* function, there are the GDI functions to output some text at the center of the window. The size of the window is computed with a call to *GetClientRect*, which returns a rectangle, an object of class *TRect* (similar to a Windows *RECT* data structure). The *right* and the *bottom* members of this class indicate respectively, the width and height of the client area of the window.

➤ *Note:* The client area of a window is the area enclosed inside its frame (border and title bar). Usually, all the output is not performed in the entire area of the window, but only in its client portion. The painting of the non-client areas is usually Windows' responsibility.

Instead of using the call to the *GetClientRect* function, the size of the window could have been taken by accessing the *W* and *H* members of the *Attr* data structure (which is a member of the *TWindow* class). However, this indication refers to the size of the entire window, not just to its client area.

The call to *SetTextAlign* serves to center the text around the horizontal output position, indicated in the *TextOut* function as half the size and half the height of the window client area (i.e., its center). However, the string is not placed exactly in the middle, since the vertical output coordinate is aligned with the top of the string.

To compile the program, you need only select the proper libraries and issue a compilation. In terms of the dynamic and static link libraries used, the compilation is similar to that of the file *minimal.cpp*. Running this program results in a window similar to the one shown in Figure 16.12.

Step 2: Clicking Mouse Buttons

The next step in the application construction is to offer the user a basic way to interact with the window. The easiest way to obtain an interaction is to respond with a message when one of the two mouse buttons is pressed, in a way similar to application *alpha2* of the previous chapter.

Figure 16.12 The first version of the appplication *one*

In that same program, we defined the window "class." We have seen that, with ObjectWindows, there is no need to make this operation. But can we access this data structure and change some of its default parameters? Of course we can. The library provides for this in the member functions *GetWindowClass* and *GetClassName*, so that we can override making other changes (apart from the style, as we saw in *ONE1.CPP*), in the form of the cursor and the color of the background of the window.

```
// ONE2.CPP                                                    16/ONE
// The first Object Windows application
// Second version, with messages on mouse button clicks,
// and some other little additions

// include some library header files
#include <owl\owlpch.h>
#include <owl\applicat.h>
#include <owl\framewin.h>
#include <owl\dc.h>

// define the class OneWin, derived from the standard TWindow
class OneWin : public TWindow
{
public:
    OneWin ( ) :
        TWindow (0, 0, 0)
    { }

void   Paint (TDC& paintDC, BOOL, TRect&)
    {
        // define a rectangle and assigns to it the
        // size of the client area of the window
        TRect rect = GetClientRect ( ) ;
```

```
        // define centered alignment and outputs the text
        paintDC.SetTextAlign (TA_CENTER) ;
        paintDC.TextOut (rect.right / 2, rect.bottom / 2 - 20,
            "Hello! I'm application ONE (version 2)") ;
        paintDC.TextOut (rect.right / 2, rect.bottom / 2 + 10,
            "Try to press the mouse buttons") ;
    }


    // left mouse button down
    void EvLButtonDown(UINT, TPoint&)
    {
        MessageBox ("Left button pressed", "ONE", MB_OK) ;
    }

    // right mouse button down
    void EvRButtonDown(UINT, TPoint&)
    {
        MessageBox ("Right button pressed", "ONE", MB_OK) ;
    }

    // function used to set the window attributes
    void GetWindowClass (WNDCLASS& wc)
    {
        // retrieve default values
        TWindow :: GetWindowClass (wc) ;

        // set new value for some fields of the structure
        wc.style |= CS_HREDRAW | CS_VREDRAW ;
        wc.hCursor = ::LoadCursor (NULL, IDC_UPARROW) ;
        wc.hbrBackground = ::CreateSolidBrush (RGB (0, 255, 0)) ;
    }

    // definition of the name of the window-class
    char far * GetClassName ( )
    {
        return "OneWinClass" ;
    }

    DECLARE_RESPONSE_TABLE (OneWin) ;
} ;

DEFINE_RESPONSE_TABLE1(OneWin, TWindow)
    EV_WM_LBUTTONDOWN ,
    EV_WM_RBUTTONDOWN ,
END_RESPONSE_TABLE ;
```

```
// define a class for the application
class OneApp : public TApplication
{
public:
    OneApp ( ) :
        TApplication ( )
    { }

    void InitMainWindow ( )
    {
        SetMainWindow = (new TFrameWindow(0,
            "ONE (Version 2.0)", new OneWin)) ;
    }
} ;

// define OwlMain, replacing WinMain
int OwlMain (int, char* [])
{
    OneApp one ;
    return one.Run ( ) ;
}
```

When you run the *ONE2* program, which can be compiled together with a standard *module definition* file (.def), you get an output similar to the one of Figure 16.13.

Step 3: Adding Some Resources: A Menu and an Icon

In Windows, the interaction with the user, usually takes place through a menu, although in the preceding examples we used only the mouse. Windows uses pull-down menus: selecting one of the items in the menu bar usually causes a "vertical" submenu to appear.

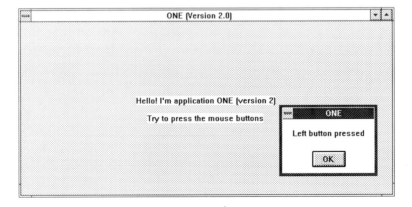

Figure 16.13 The output of the second version of the *ONE* program

To add a menu to application *one*, two different operations are required: the definition of the corresponding resource, and its loading and handling inside the program. To handle the menu command, we define a function for every menu item.

The definition of the resources can be done with the *Resource Workshop* or directly with a resource definition file. For the application *one* we want a menu with two submenus (*Information* and *Operations*) containing two items each (respectively *About* and *Hello*, and *Options* and *Draw*). Using the *Workshop*, we can define the submenus as shown in Figure 16.14.

➤   *Note:* The layout of a menu is a fundamental element of an application, since it is the most important "interface" with the user's requests. The Windows Style Guide contains several suggestions for the layout of menus. However, our very simple programs will not conform to these guidelines, since they have only a few menu items.

Having defined a menu, we can now use the *Workshop* to paint a proper icon for the application. For example, we can draw a big number 1, as shown in Figure 16.15. As we use the *Resource Workshop*, we can save the identifiers of the resources and of the menu items and in a specific header file, such as *one3.rh* below, which can be automatically generated on our request.

```
/************************************************

one3.rh                                              16/ONE

produced by Borland Resource Workshop
************************************************/
```

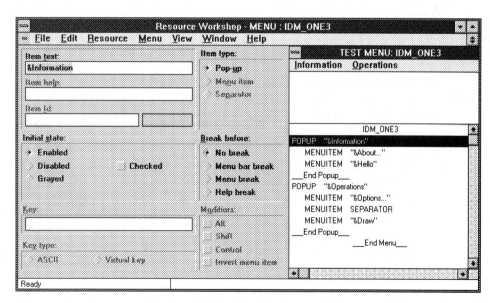

Figure 16.14 Definition of the menu of the application, using the *Resource Workshop*

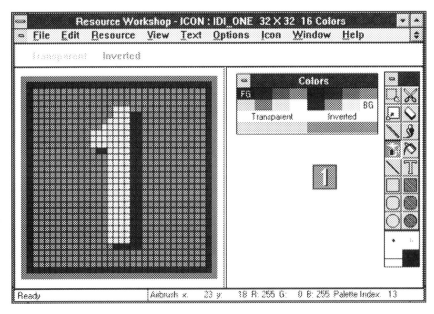

Figure 16.15 Drawing an icon with the *Resource Workshop*

```
#define CM_HELLO     101
#define CM_ABOUT     102
#define CM_OPTIONS  103
#define CM_DRAW      104
#define IDI_ONE      201
#define IDM_ONE3     200
```

Using the *Workshop*, we can save the resources already in compiled form, inside a file with an *.res* extension. Although that is the standard way of working, in the text we will report the resources in the textual description format (*.rc*), because this is the only possible way to print them. However, it's better to use the compiled form directly. Still better, it's possible to select (using the *File Preference* command) the multisave feature of the *Resource Workshop*—to save the resource project both as an *.rc* file and as a *.res* file simultaneously. In this way, you will have both a compiled version to link to the executable and a text version for documentation. (By the way, an *.rc* file must be loaded into the *Workshop* before the multisave feature can be activated.)

Here is the definition of the resources we have just built graphically (file *ONE3.rc*):

```
#include "one3.rh"
```
16/ONE

```
IDM_ONE3 MENU
{
  POPUP "&Information"
  {
```

```
        MENUITEM "&About...", CM_ABOUT
        MENUITEM "&Hello", CM_HELLO
    }

    POPUP "&Operations"
    {
        MENUITEM "&Options...", CM_OPTIONS
        MENUITEM SEPARATOR
        MENUITEM "&Draw", CM_DRAW
    }
}


IDI_ONE ICON "one.ico"
```

Now it's time to return to the application and change it, by using the resources we have just defined. We need to load the resources and add a member function for each menu command we have defined. These functions provide the operations that must be executed when the user selects one of the menu items, and are connected to the commands by using dynamic dispatching.

The full source code of application *one3* is:

```
// ONE3.CPP                                          16/ONE
// The first Object Windows application
// Third version, with a menu and its associated commands,
// an icon, and some other little changes

// include some library header files
#include <owl\owlpch.h>
#include <owl\applicat.h>
#include <owl\framewin.h>
#include <owl\dc.h>

// include definitions for resources
#include "one3.rh"

// define the class OneWin, derived from the standard TWindow
class OneWin : public TWindow
{
public:
    OneWin ( ) :
        TWindow (0, 0, 0)
    { }

void   Paint (TDC& paintDC, BOOL, TRect&)
    {
```

```
        // define a rectangle and assigns to it the
        // size of the client area of the window
        TRect rect = GetClientRect ( ) ;

        // define centered alignment and output the text
        paintDC.SetTextAlign (TA_CENTER) ;
        paintDC.TextOut (rect.right / 2, rect.bottom / 2 - 20,
                "Hello! I'm application ONE (v. 3)") ;
        paintDC.TextOut (rect.right / 2, rect.bottom / 2 + 10,
                "Beside mouse button messages, I've even got a menu") ;
    }

// left mouse button down
void EvLButtonDown(UINT, TPoint&)
{
    MessageBox ("Left button pressed", "ONE", MB_OK) ;
}

// right mouse button down
void EvRButtonDown(UINT, TPoint&)
{
    MessageBox ("Right button pressed", "ONE", MB_OK) ;
}

// function used to set the window attributes
void GetWindowClass (WNDCLASS& wc)
{
    // retrieve default values
    TWindow :: GetWindowClass (wc) ;

    // set new value for some fields of the struct
    wc.style |= CS_HREDRAW | CS_VREDRAW ;
    wc.hCursor = TCursor (NULL, IDC_UPARROW) ;
    wc.hbrBackground = (HBRUSH) (COLOR_WINDOW + 1) ;
}

// definition of the name of the window-class
char far * GetClassName ( )
{
    return "OneWinClass" ;
}

// command response functions
void CmAbout ( )
{
```

```
        MessageBox ("Application ONE: the first OWL program",
           "About ONE", MB_OK I MB_ICONINFORMATION ) ;
    }

    void CmHello ( )
    {
       TClientDC   dc (* this) ;
       dc.TextOut (10, 10,
          "Ciao to everybody from Marco and Steve") ;
    }

    void CmDraw ( )
    {
       TClientDC   dc (* this) ;
       dc.Rectangle (10, 200, 400, 280) ;
       dc.RoundRect (80, 30, 180, 130, 25, 25) ;
       dc.Ellipse (190, 120, 300, 180) ;
    }

    void CmOptions ( )
    {
       MessageBox ("Command still not implemented") ;
    }

    DECLARE_RESPONSE_TABLE (OneWin) ;
} ;

DEFINE_RESPONSE_TABLE1(OneWin, TWindow)
    EV_WM_LBUTTONDOWN ,
    EV_WM_RBUTTONDOWN ,
    EV_COMMAND (CM_ABOUT, CmAbout) ,
    EV_COMMAND (CM_HELLO, CmHello) ,
    EV_COMMAND (CM_DRAW, CmDraw) ,
    EV_COMMAND (CM_OPTIONS, CmOptions) ,
END_RESPONSE_TABLE ;


// define a class for the application
class OneApp : public TApplication
{
public:
   OneApp ( ) :
      TApplication ( )
   { }
```

```
        void InitMainWindow ( )
        {
            SetMainWindow (new TFrameWindow(0, "ONE (Version 3.0)", new OneWin)) ;
            GetMainWindow ()-> AssignMenu (IDM_ONE3) ;
            GetMainWindow ()-> SetIcon (this, IDI_ONE) ;
        }
    } ;


    // define OwlMain, replacing WinMain
    int OwlMain (int, char* [])
    {
        OneApp one ;
        return one.Run ( ) ;
    }
```

The new version of the class *OneWin* has four new member functions:

- *CmAbout* creates a message box containing some general information about the
  program. The message box even has an information icon, as shown in Figure 16.16.

- *CmHello* writes a phrase in the window's area. This text will disappear when the
  user resizes the window. In fact, in such a case, the window gets repainted,
  executing the *Paint* function.

- *CmDraw* paints two rectangles and an ellipse. As in the preceding function, this
  operation can be done only after having requested a device context and releasing
  it at the end.

- *CmOptions* outputs a message to indicate that it is still not working.

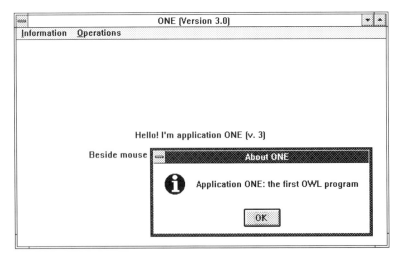

**Figure 16.16   The message box obtained selecting the menu item About. Notice
the icon of the application**

➤ *Note:* Windows application should generally avoid performing output operations outside of the Paint function (apart from a few special cases). In fact, the contents of the client area of a window should not change when the user changes its size or if other windows are overlapped on it. Painting the client area outside the Paint function might result in corrupted output.

For example, if you try to cover part of the window of the *one3* application with another window (see Figure 16.17), and move it away, only that part will be re-painted, leading to "nonsense" output (see Figure 16.18).

Usually, if an application has to perform some output, there are two choices: using a message dialog box or adding the output operations inside the Paint function. This second approach will be demonstrated in the next version of the *one* application.

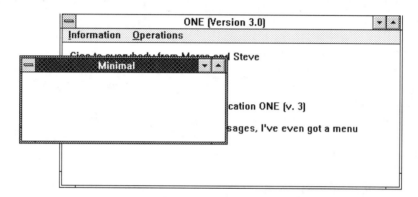

16.17

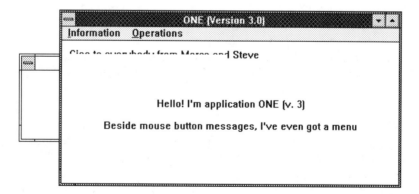

16.18

Figures 16.17 and 16.18 Painting to the window client area outside of the Paint function can lead to corrupted output: If a window is partially overlapped by a window from the *one3* application (16.17), only that part of the screen will be repainted (16.18).

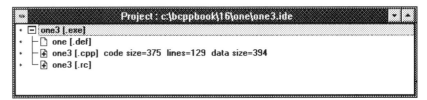

Figure 16.19 The project to compile the third version of the application *one*

Besides the new functions, which respond to menu selection messages, the menu should be initialized and shown in the first line of the window. To obtain this, the *InitMainWindow* function of the *OneApp* class calls the *AssignMenu* member function for the *MainWindow* object that has just been built. The parameter of this function is the identifier of the menu, as defined in the resources and in the *one3.rh* file. In the same function the program loads the icon of the application, too. The icon is attached with the *SetIcon* call to the main window, and not to the window we define (which is inside the main *frame* window).

Other minor differences between this and the previous version of the program are the definition of the background color (in the function *GetWindowClass*), which is based on the default color chosen by the user (via *Control Panel*) for the window surface.

To compile this program, you need to define a project containing the source code of the program, one of the resource definition files (ONE3.RC or ONE3.RES), and a module definition file, as in Figure 16.19.

Step 4: Adding a Dialog Box

The last step, a finishing touch to the menu and the end of this survey of the main elements of a Windows application, is to add a dialog box. The application will prompt (in this dialog box) for a selection from the *Options* menu, asking the user to select between two choices. This version of the application will also solve most of the problems connected with the output (as described in the previous section).

Also, in this case, we have to proceed using two different steps: the definition of the dialog with a graphical tool and its implementation in the program source code (deriving a class from *TDialog*). But first we must decide the functionalities of the dialog: in the case of application *one*, we want to determine whether the function *Paint* has to draw either a rectangle or an ellipse. Therefore, we need two radio buttons, to select one of the two exclusive choices, and two buttons to accept the selection (*OK*) or to exit (*Cancel*).

Using the *Resource Workshop*, we can actually draw a dialog, as shown in Figure 16.20, and generate the following dialog description file (ONE4.DLG):

```
#include <windows.h>                                          16/ONE

IDD_ONE DIALOG 18, 18, 180, 92
```

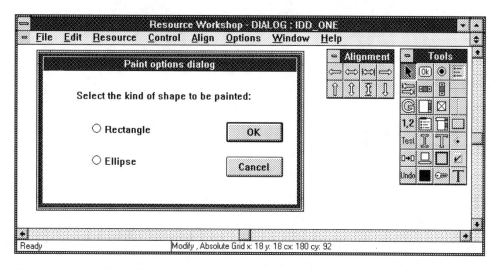

Figure 16.20 The definition of the dialog, using the *Resource Workshop*

```
STYLE DS_MODALFRAME I WS_POPUP I WS_CAPTION
CAPTION "Paint options dialog"
{
    CONTROL "Rectangle", IDB_RECTANGLE, "BUTTON",
        BS_AUTORADIOBUTTON I WS_TABSTOP, 35, 34, 50, 12
    CONTROL "Ellipse", IDB_ELLIPSE, "BUTTON",
        BS_AUTORADIOBUTTON, 35, 56, 49, 12
    LTEXT "Select the kind of shape to be painted:", -1, 24, 13, 129, 14,
        SS_LEFT I WS_CHILD I WS_VISIBLE
    DEFPUSHBUTTON "OK", 1, 130, 35, 40, 14
    PUSHBUTTON "Cancel", 2, 130, 59, 40, 14
}
```

Note that, while one can think of editing a menu directly, to define a dialog template you need a special tool: the few preceding lines are quite difficult to understand and modify directly. This file can be added to the ONE3.RC (or ONE3.RES) file, containing the resources for the previous version, resulting in the new ONE4.RC (or ONE4.RES). Then we can replace the file in the project and edit the source file to obtain a new program. A couple of identifiers have been added to *ONE3.RH,* which becomes *ONE4.RH.*

Once we have defined the resource corresponding to the dialog, we can use it in the source code to define the dialog window, as in the following listings, one with the definitions of the classes of the fourth version of the application, and the other with the definitions of their member functions.

```
// ONE4.H                                                          16/ONE
// Definition of the classes of the ONE4.CPP program
```

```
// define a dialog class, derived from TDialog
class DialogOne : public TDialog
{
public:
    static BOOL bRectSelected ;

    DialogOne (TWindow* parent) ;
    void SetupWindow ( ) ;
    void CmRectangle ( ) ;
    void CmEllipse ( ) ;

    DECLARE_RESPONSE_TABLE (DialogOne) ;
} ;

// define the class OneWin, derived from the standard TWindow
class OneWin : public TWindow
{
    BOOL      bRectSel;      // local boolean variable
    BOOL      bDrawEnabled, bHelloEnabled; // paint flags

public:
    // constructor
    OneWin ( ) ;

    // painting
    void   Paint (TDC& paintDC, BOOL, TRect&) ;

    // mouse buttons clicks
    void EvLButtonDown(UINT, TPoint&) ;
    void EvRButtonDown(UINT, TPoint&) ;

    // window-class definition
    void GetWindowClass (WNDCLASS& wc) ;
    char far * GetClassName ( ) ;

    // menu commands response functions
    void CmAbout ( ) ;
    void CmHello ( ) ;
    void CmDraw ( ) ;
    void CmOptions ( ) ;

    DECLARE_RESPONSE_TABLE (OneWin) ;
} ;

// define a class for the application
class OneApp : public TApplication
```

```
{
public:
   OneApp ( ) ;
   void InitMainWindow ( ) ;
} ;
```

```
// ONE4.CPP                                                      16/ONE
// The first Object Windows application
// Fourth version, with a dialog box
// to choose between a rectangle and an ellipse

// include some library header files
#include <owl\owlpch.h>
#include <owl\applicat.h>
#include <owl\framewin.h>
#include <owl\dc.h>

// include definitions for resources
#include "one4.rh"

// include definitions of the classes
#include "one4.h"

// member functions of the dialog class:

DialogOne :: DialogOne (TWindow* parent) :
   TDialog (parent, IDD_ONE)
{ }

void DialogOne :: SetupWindow ( )
{
   TDialog :: SetupWindow ( ) ;
   CheckRadioButton(IDB_RECTANGLE, IDB_ELLIPSE,
         bRectSelected ? IDB_RECTANGLE : IDB_ELLIPSE) ;
}

void DialogOne :: CmRectangle ( )
{
   bRectSelected = TRUE ;
}

void DialogOne :: CmEllipse ( )
{
   bRectSelected = FALSE ;
}
```

```
BOOL DialogOne :: bRectSelected ;

DEFINE_RESPONSE_TABLE1(DialogOne, TDialog)
    EV_BN_CLICKED (IDB_RECTANGLE, CmRectangle) ,
    EV_BN_CLICKED (IDB_ELLIPSE, CmEllipse) ,
END_RESPONSE_TABLE ;


// member functions of the window class:

OneWin :: OneWin ( ) :
    TWindow (0, 0, 0) ,
    bRectSel (TRUE) ,
    bDrawEnabled (FALSE) ,
    bHelloEnabled (FALSE)
{ }

void OneWin :: Paint (TDC& paintDC, BOOL, TRect&)
{
    // define a rectangle and assigns to it the
    // size of the client area of the window
    TRect rect = GetClientRect ( ) ;

    // define centered alignment and outputs the text
    paintDC.SetTextAlign (TA_CENTER) ;
    paintDC.TextOut (rect.right / 2, rect.bottom / 2 - 20,
        "Hello! I'm application ONE (v. 4)") ;
    paintDC.TextOut (rect.right / 2, rect.bottom / 2 + 10,
        "Now I've even got a dialog window") ;

    // if the hello message is enabled, output it
    if (bHelloEnabled)
    {
        paintDC.SetTextAlign (TA_LEFT) ;
        paintDC.TextOut (5, 5, "Ciao to everybody from Marco and Steve") ;
    }

    // if the drawing is enabled, draw the selected shape
    if (bDrawEnabled)
    {
        // merge the new drawing with the old one
        paintDC.SetROP2 (R2_XORPEN) ;
        if (bRectSel)
            paintDC.Rectangle (15, 60, 200, 180) ;
        else
```

```
            paintDC.Ellipse (200, 170, 300, 250) ;
        }
}


// left mouse button down
void OneWin :: EvLButtonDown(UINT, TPoint&)
{
    MessageBox ("Left button pressed", "ONE", MB_OK) ;
}


// right mouse button down
void OneWin :: EvRButtonDown(UINT, TPoint&)
{
    MessageBox ("Right button pressed", "ONE", MB_OK) ;
}


// function used to set the window attributes
void OneWin :: GetWindowClass (WNDCLASS& wc)
{
    // retrieve default values
    TWindow :: GetWindowClass (wc) ;

    // set new value for some fields of the struct
    wc.style |= CS_HREDRAW | CS_VREDRAW ;
    wc.hCursor = TCursor (NULL, IDC_UPARROW) ;
    wc.hbrBackground = (HBRUSH) (COLOR_WINDOW + 1) ;
}


// definition of the name of the window-class
char far* OneWin :: GetClassName ( )
{
    return "OneWinClass" ;
}


// command response functions
void OneWin :: CmAbout ( )
{
    MessageBox ("Application ONE: the first OWL program",
        "About ONE", MB_OK | MB_ICONINFORMATION ) ;
}


void OneWin :: CmHello ( )
{
    // change the value of the variable
    bHelloEnabled = (bHelloEnabled) ? FALSE : TRUE ;
```

```
    // invalidate the window client area
    // (this action adds WM_PAINT to the message queue)
    Invalidate ( ) ;
}

void OneWin :: CmDraw ( )
{
    // change the variable and repaint the window
    bDrawEnabled = !bDrawEnabled ;
    Invalidate ( ) ;
}

void OneWin :: CmOptions ( )
{
    // prompt the dialog box; if the user selects OK
    // the value is copied in the local variable
    DialogOne :: bRectSelected = bRectSel ;
    /DialogOne  dial(this);
    if (dial.Execute C)
    {
        bRectSel = dialogOne:: bRectSelected ;
        Invalidate ( ) ;
    }
}

DEFINE_RESPONSE_TABLE1(OneWin, TWindow)
    EV_WM_LBUTTONDOWN ,
    EV_WM_RBUTTONDOWN ,
    EV_COMMAND (CM_ABOUT, CmAbout) ,
    EV_COMMAND (CM_HELLO, CmHello) ,
    EV_COMMAND (CM_DRAW, CmDraw) ,
    EV_COMMAND (CM_OPTIONS, CmOptions) ,
END_RESPONSE_TABLE ;


// member functions of the application class:

OneApp :: OneApp ( ) :
    TApplication ( )
{ }

void OneApp :: InitMainWindow ( )
{
    SetMainWindow (new TFrameWindow(0, "ONE (Version 4.0)", new OneWin)) ;
```

```
      GetMainWindow() -> AssignMenu (IDM_ONE4) ;
      GetMainWindow() -> SetIcon (this, IDI_ONE) ;
}


// main function, OwlMain, replacing WinMain

int OwlMain (int, char* [])
{
   OneApp one ;
   return one.Run ( ) ;
}
```

Besides minor changes, the difference between this and the previous version of the application lies in the presence of the *DialogOne* class. This class is associated with its own resource inside the constructor. The class has two member functions, which get executed when one of the radio buttons is selected.

The *CmOptions* member function of *OneWin* creates and executes the dialog. The *bRectSel* member receives the value of the static dialog member *bRectSelected*, set by the dialog member functions called when one of the radio buttons is clicked. Notice also that before the dialog is created the static member receives a value, so that in the *SetupWindow* function of the dialog class the proper radio button (corresponding to the *current selection*) is checked.

Now the functions *Hello* and *Draw*, instead of executing output operations, set some Boolean values and issue a repaint message to the window (through the *InvalidateRect* function).

➤   *Note:* The execution of the *Invalidate* member function (which is really a call to the *InvalidateRect* API function) has the side effect of placing a *WM_PAINT* message in the message queue of the application. This message will be processed by the corresponding function as soon as possible, but not immediately. If we want to repaint the client area of the window on the spot, we can use the *UpdateWindow* function after the call to *Invalidate*.

The output of the Paint function depends on these Boolean values, so that the constant content of the screen can be changed by the selection of the menu items (by way of executing *CmHello* or *CmDraw,* toggle the output on or off, although they use two different expressions). In the last part of *Paint*, there is a call to the function *SetROP2*, which serves to select a particular way to merge the new drawing with the actual contents of the device context. Thanks to this call, the output of the application can be similar to that of Figure 16.21.

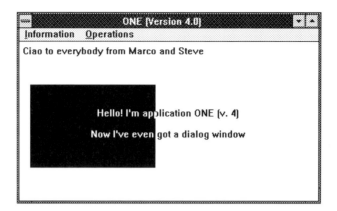

Figure 16.21 The output on the *one4* application

The fourth version of the application "one" is also the last. Of course, we could go on adding other interesting properties to the program, but we prefer to leave this work to you. Instead, we'll demonstrate a few applications. The first of them will be a program to paint strange graphs; then we will figure out what's behind Multiple Document Interface (MDI), and at the end, we will build a drawing application based on a hierarchy of shapes. All this will take place in the next chapter.

POINTS TO CONSIDER

1. It might be interesting to evaluate in detail the advantages and disadvantages of using a graphical user interface (GUI) both from the programmer's point of view and from the user's point of view.

2. If you already have some programming experience writing Windows applications, try to write a traditional application similar to one of those developed in this chapter with Object Windows, and compare them.

3. If you have used or know other advanced environments that produce Windows applications (such as CASE tools, Visual Basic, ObjectVision, and similar tools), compare them with Object Windows. In your analysis, consider which category of applications (graphical, scientific, data management, business) is best suited for each tool.

4. Extend the application "one" by adding new functionalities to its main window and new commands to the small menu. You can use the mouse to draw lines on the screen (adding some dragging capabilities), ask the user to input some text, in a dialog or directly on the main window, and so on.

17

Developing Object-Windows Applications

I've heard that a typical software system today (a Windows, graphical-user-interface kind of world) has 75 percent of the code tied up in the user interface, and only 25 percent doing number crunching. Most of the earlier methodologies provided no assistance—no guidance at all—for the user interface side of things, and it is such an obvious candidate for object-oriented design. [Yourdon 90]

After the presentation of the fundamentals of Windows programming and the ObjectWindows Library, we end this book by illustrating some complete object-oriented applications for Windows.

First of all we will provide a program to trace Connett's graphs, used to demonstrate some graphic capabilities of OWL, supporting Windows' GDI, to show how Windows multitasking works (or, better, does not work), and to introduce *Borland Windows Custom Controls*.

Then we will look at a very simple MDI (*Multiple Document Interface*) application, showing how the windows/frame paradigm supported by OWL helps moving an application to a different *target*.

The chapter ends with an application that paints shapes on the screen, allowing you to choose their color, position, and size. The program is based on a hierarchy of shape classes, probably the biggest hierarchy present in this book, which might be considered as the conclusion of Chapter 9 (we couldn't present this example in that chapter since we had no knowledge of Windows programming).

Connett's Graphs for Windows

The first full-blown Windows application we are going to present is an implementation of a program that draws "Connett's graphs". The algorithm that governs these graphs was invented by John E. Connett at the University of Minnesota and was described in an article by A. K. Dewdey in *Scientific American* [Dewdey 86].

509

The original algorithm

The idea is very simple and is based on the equation of the circle: $x^2 + y^2$. The original algorithm, as published in *Scientific American*, is this:

```
input anga, angb
input side
for i from 1 to 100
    for j from 1 to 100
        x = anga + ( side * i / 100 )
        y = angb + ( side * j / 100 )
        z = x² + y²
        c = int ( z )
        if c is even, then paint point ( i, j )
```

In other words, given that

- *x* and *y* are the "real" coordinates of the lower-left angle of the square area of the plane we want to explore
- *l* is the length of the side of the square we want to explore
- *r* is the resolution we want to use

we want to evaluate the *parity* of the *integer part* of the following expression:

$$(x + l * i / r)^2 + (y + l * j / r)^2$$

While, from a mathematical point of view, this image can be interesting, from a pure aesthetic point of view it becomes much more appealing if it is drawn in color. The algorithm varies a little: Instead of checking for the parity of the final result obtained from the computed expression, you only need to evaluate its modulus against the number of colors that you wish to use. The expression

```
fmod (value, numberOfColors)
```

will evaluate the number in the range from 0 to the numebr of colors indicated. This number can be chosen as you please, though it might be limited by the number of colors your video board can display. Using Windows this should not be a problem, since the interface has a virtual limit of 16 million colors, although your video driver has probably less, and therefore will use *dithering* and other techniques to simulate the *nearest* available color. In out program we choose to work with four basic colors (black, red, green, blue) using the following expression to determine the color of a point:

```
// map the value (0 to 3) into a color
TColor c = TColor (           // 0 = black
```

```
(value==1) ? 255 : 0,      // 1 = red
(value==2) ? 255 : 0,      // 2 = green
(value==3) ? 255 : 0) ;    // 3 = blue
```

An optimized version

Various optimizations of the original algorithm have been proposed in [Tendon 87] to improve the efficiency of the program. These optimizations are based on this principle: Move all possible computations outside of the two *for* loops. From the basic algorithm:

```
unsigned int   r = PointsNum ( ) ;
int         nColors = 4 ;
float         x1, y1, z ;

for (unsigned int i = 0; i <= r; i++)
{
   for (unsigned int j = 0; j <= r; j++)
   {
      x1 = x + l * float (i) / float (r) ;
      y1 = y + l * float (j) / float (r) ;
      z  = x1 * x1 + y1 * y1 ;
      PointValue (i, j, fmod (floor (z), nColors)) ;
   }
}
```

we can make a number of changes (some of which imply also slight approximations due to the low resolution of *float* numbers in C), and we can, in particular, use Hoerner's algorithm for the evaluation of integer polynomials (if you are interested, look at the formulas in Figure 17.1) and move every possible operation outside of the loop. We will not bother you too much with this optimization; here is the final result:

```
unsigned int   i, j ;
unsigned int   r = PointsNum ( ) ;
int            nColors = 4 ;
float          a, b, c, d, e, f, g ;

a = x * x + y * y ;
b = x + x ;
c = y + y ;
d = float (l) / float (r) ;
for (i = 0; i <= r; i++)
{
   e = d * i ;
   f = a + (b + e) * e ;
   for (j = 0; j <= r; j++)
```

```
      {
         g = d * j ;
         PointValue (i, j, fmod (floor (f + (c + g) * g), nColors)) ;
      }
  }
```

Simulating Multitasking in Windows

If we run a similar application under Windows, we are going to have some problems. In this operating environment, in fact, there is no real multitasking, so that our application will completely stop the whole system while it is computing the full graph. Windows multitasking is based on the assumption that each application makes a simple and short operation for each message it receives, then leads the control back to the system. The system will again pass control back to the application as soon as there is a message for one of its windows. So we need to divide our algorithm into smaller pieces, and run them one at a time. This is not particularly difficult, since it is based on a *for* loop: Our choice is to compute the inner loop each time (drawing a column of pixels).

However, we need a way to get control back from the system after a while, since it will be extremely tedious (and silly) to ask the user to give a menu command for each column of pixels in the graph. We can follow two different paths: Use a timer or get *background* processor cycles.

Following the first path, we can notice that Windows has a kind of input that doesn't depend on the user: the timer input. A timer is an "input device" that warns an application that a certain amount of time has elapsed. It sends a *WM_TIMER* message at fixed time intervals, determined by the application itself. When the application receives these messages, it can execute a part of the Connett's graph algorithm.

Let:	$a = x^2 + y^2$
	$b = 2 * x$
	$c = 2 * y$
	$d = 1 / r$
Compute:	$(x + 1 * i / r)^2 + (y + 1 * j / r)^2 =$
	$(x + d * i)^2 + (y + d * j)^2 =$
	$x^2 + 2 * x * d * i + d^2 * i^2 + y^2 + 2 * y * d * j + d^2 * j^2 =$
	$a + b * d * i + d^2 * i^2 + c * d * j + d^2 * j^2$
Now let:	$e = d * i$
	$f * a + (b + e) * e$ *Hoerner*
	$g = d * j$
Finally:	$a + b * d * i + d^2 * i^2 + c * d * j + d^2 * j^2 =$
	$f + (c + g) * g$ *Hoerner*

Figure 17.1 Mathematical substitutions that are the basis of the optimization

➤ *Note:* Although timer messages are sent at fixed time intervals, they are actually placed in the message queue. Therefore, the application processes each *WM_TIMER* message as soon as it becomes the first message in the queue, at almost *random* time intervals. If timer messages are very frequent, some of them might be destroyed, since there can be only one *WM_TIMER* message in any message queue.

To use a timer in an application, you need to create the timer with the *SetTimer* function, specifying a time interval between 1 millisecond and 65 seconds. The timer also receives a name, since any application can have more than one timer.

➤ *Note:* The total number of timers in Windows is limited to 31. Since they must be shared among all the applications, they should be used with great care, and released as soon as possible. Even if a single application can have several timers, this is quite uncommon, since they can be considered as a scarce resource, and thus must be used sparingly.

Following the second path, we can get background processor cycles for an application by modifying the main message loop. In ObjectWindows, this operation has already been done, and we can force background processing by redefining the *IdleAction* member function in any class derived from *TApplication* class. This function is invoked over and over when the application is idle, leaving control to other applications in the system, too.

In this example, we will use the timer approach, adding the following code

- We need to define a new identifier for the timer:

```
#define ID_TIMER        100
```

- The *CmDraw* function, executed in response to the selection of the corresponding menu command, sets the initial values of the algorithm and starts a timer:

```
void ConnettWin :: CmDraw ( )
{
    // set the values for the algorithm
    nColors = 4 ;
    a = x * x + y * y ;
    b = x + x ;
    c = y + y ;
    d = float (l) / float (r) ;
    i = 0 ;

    // start a timer
    SetTimer (ID_TIMER, 10) ;
}
```

- We need a function to respond to timer messages *(EvTimer)*. The function will execute one of the external loops of the algorithm each time it is called, painting a vertical line of pixels. The *for* loop on the *i* variable is replaced by a test and an increment. At the end, the timer is deleted (or killed).

```
void ConnettWin :: EvTimer (UINT)
    {
        e = d * i ;
        f = a + (b + e) * e ;
        for (j = 0; j <= r; j++)
        {
            g = d*j ;
            PointValue (pdcMem, i, j,
                    fmod (floor (f + (c + g) * g), nColors)) ;
        }

        // if the algorithm is not ended
        if (i <= r)
        {
            i++ ;
        }
        else
        {
            // stop the process
            KillTimer (ID_TIMER) ;
        }
    }
```

- The two functions *(CmDraw* and *EvTimer)* must share several variables; therefore they are moved to the class level:

```
class ConnettWin : public TWindow
{
    // data used to compute the Connett graph
    long x, y, l ;
    unsigned int i, j, r ;
    int nColors ;
    float a, b, c, d, e, f, g ;
    ...
```

Painting in Memory

The idea to divide the algorithm in small pieces favors multitasking but raises another issue: The window containing the graph might require repainting, which would restart the whole process from the begining even if the parameters have not changed! For the program to work correctly, we need to hold in memory the result of the algorithm, i.e., the graph. There are basically two ways to proceed: One is to store, in a huge array, all the values computed by the algorithm; the other is to store, in memory, a copy of the resulting bitmap representing the graph.

Although both techniques will work, the second is more "Windows compliant." In fact, the API of the environment includes several functions that operate on bitmaps: their main property is that they are very fast and efficient. These functions we supported by OWL 2, in the DC and GDI classes.

To define a bitmap in memory, one needs to proceed in three steps: create a memory device context compatible with the screen, create a bitmap compatible with the normal application device context (not the one in memory, because, by default, it is monochrome), and connect the two. These operations are performed by the following statements:

```
pdcMem = new TMemoryDC ( ) ;
TClientDC dc (HWindow) ;
r = PointsNum ( ) ;
TBitmap bitmap (dc, r, r) ;
pdcMem -> SelectObject (bitmap) ;
```

After this definition we can "paint" directly in the memory device context as we did on the screen. See, for example, the *PointValue* call in the *EvTimer* function above.

Once we have a bitmap in memory containing the graph, the only problem is to transfer the bitmap to the screen. To accomplish this operation, we can use the *BitBlt* function (*Bit Block Transfer*). To copy only the part of the graph we have already computed, we can use the following statement, indicating the destination and source device contexts, and the portion of the bitmap to be transferred (i by r pixels):

```
paintDC.BitBlt (0, 0, i, r, *pdcMem, 0, 0, SRCCOPY) ;
```

Inside the *Paint* function, we can call this operation or the one to paint the whole graph, depending on the current situation. And if we still haven't started to compute the graph, we must avoid making a copy because the memory bitmap contains random values. Therefore, we add to the window a status variable to determine which stage we have reached, and write the following *Paint* function:

```
void ConnettWin :: Paint (TDC& paintDC, BOOL, TRect&)
{
    // copy either a portion of the bitmap ...
    if (status == painting)
        paintDC.BitBlt (0, 0, i, r, *pdcMem, 0, 0, SRCCOPY) ;

    // ... or its whole surface
    if (status == painted)
        paintDC.BitBlt (0, 0, r, r, *pdcMem, 0, 0, SRCCOPY) ;
}
```

With this function, we can resize or zoom the window, overlap other windows, and essentially perform any operation (even iconize) without losing the graph.

We can even call the *Paint* function from the program—for example, at the end of the algorithm computing the graph. In fact, although we cannot call it directly, we can ask the window to deliver a *WM_PAINT* message, with the function:

```
Invalidate ( ) ;
```

A similar operation can be done after the computation of any single "column" of pixels of the graph. However, instead of invalidating the entire window, we invalidate only the portion we have just computed:

```
TRectrect (i-1, 0, i, r) ;
InvalidateRect (rect) ;
```

➤   *Note:* The effect of this operation is that the *Paint* function will operate only in the small portion of the window's client area defined by the *rect* rectangle, instead of its whole surface. As we will see later on, the device context of the *Paint* functions retains the "knowledge" of the invalidate area, and the GDI functions performed on it are executed only if their output falls in the invalid area.

Using Borland Custom Controls

The last step is the definition of the resources of the application, including a very simple menu, an icon and a dialog box to ask the user to input the basic values for the graph. Within the dialog, we need three line editors to input the starting *x* and *y* position, and the length of the graph. As we have already seen, designing a dialog is easy using the Workshop. But we would like to have a better-looking dialog— one having the feel of those that Borland uses in its applications. And we would like those nice "OK" and "Cancel" buttons with the corresponding "glyphs." In other words, we would like to use the Borland Windows Custom Controls in our application.

Using the *Resource Workshop,* we can design similar dialogs (this feature is technically documented in the files BWCCAPI.TXT and BWCCSTYL.TXT of the *doc* directory of the Borland compiler). You only need to create a new dialog box and select the proper option in the *Dialog Expert* (see Figure 17.2).

If you have an old existing dialog box, you can change it as follows. Double-click on the dialog box (while in the Resource Workshop, of course) and change the name of the class for the dialog box, choosing the *bordlg* option. With this operation the dialog surface changes and takes on the typical *chiseled steel* color, and you have a new column of tools in the Workshop toolbar that can be used to draw *Borland-like* buttons, lines, rectangles, and so on. When a push-button has a specific identifier (such as IDOK or IDCANCEL), it shows the corresponding bitmap automatically.

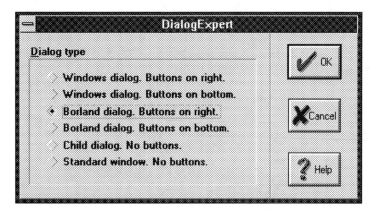

Figure 17.2 The Dialog Expert of the Resource Workshop

In this way we can define the dialog box for our program, shown in Figure 17.3. Remember, however, that to run this program properly, you need to link it to the *Borland Windows Custom Controls Library* (BWCC.DLL).

Figure 17.3 The resulting dialog box

If we want to be consistent with this *look-and-feel* in the rest of the program, we need to use the same style in message boxes, too. This can be achieved using the *BWCCMessageBox* function, defined in *BWCC.H*, which has the same parameters of the standard *MessageBox* API function.

Here is the textual description of the resources of the *connett* program, introduced by the corresponding definitions.

```
// file connett.rh
```
17/CONNETT

```
#define ID_EDITY 202
#define IDI_CONNETT  299
#define IDD_CONNETT 199
#define IDM_CONNETT 99
#define ID_EDITX 201
#define ID_EDITL 203
#define CM_OPTIONS   103
#define CM_DRAW   102
#define CM_ABOUT 101
```

```
// file connett.rc
```
17/CONNETT

```
#include "connett.rh"
#include <windows.h>

IDM_CONNETT MENU
{
   POPUP "&Graph"
   {
      MENUITEM "&Options...", CM_OPTIONS
      MENUITEM "&Draw", CM_DRAW
   }
   POPUP "&Help"
   {
      MENUITEM "&About...", CM_ABOUT
   }
}

IDI_CONNETT ICON "connet.ico"

IDD_CONNETT DIALOG 40, 33, 175, 108
STYLE WS_CAPTION I DS_MODALFRAME I WS_POPUP
CLASS "bordlg"
CAPTION "Basic values for the graph"
{
```

```
        CONTROL "Starting X:", 120, "static",
           SS_RIGHT I WS_CHILD, 19, 21, 35, 12
        CONTROL "", ID_EDITX, "edit",
           ES_LEFT I WS_BORDER I WS_TABSTOP I WS_CHILD, 69, 20, 40, 13
        CONTROL "Starting Y:", 121, "static",
           SS_RIGHT I WS_CHILD, 20, 47, 36, 12
        CONTROL "", ID_EDITY, "edit",
           ES_LEFT I WS_BORDER I WS_TABSTOP I WS_CHILD, 69, 45, 40, 13
        CONTROL "Lenght:", 122, "static",
           SS_RIGHT I WS_CHILD, 25, 72, 29, 12
        CONTROL "", ID_EDITL, "edit",
           ES_LEFT I WS_BORDER I WS_TABSTOP I WS_CHILD, 69, 70, 40, 13
        CONTROL "Button", IDOK, "BorBtn",
           BS_DEFPUSHBUTTON I WS_CHILD I WS_VISIBLE I WS_TABSTOP, 135, 25, 35, 25
        CONTROL "Button", IDCANCEL, "BorBtn",
           BS_PUSHBUTTON I WS_CHILD I WS_VISIBLE I WS_TABSTOP, 135, 60, 32, 26
        CONTROL "", 123, "BorShade",
           BSS_GROUP I WS_CHILD I WS_VISIBLE, 15, 11, 107, 86
    }
```

And Finally Comes the Program

After this long description of several portions of the connett application under Windows, here is its source code. There are three classes:

- A dialog box class, performing only a number of tests on the input value, avoiding terminating the dialog itself if they are not correct (this takes place in the function *CanClose*)

- The window class, which is in charge of calculating and showing the graph

- The usual application class

```
// CONNETT.H                                          17/CONNETT
// definition of the classes of the
// CONNETT.CPP program for Windows

// define a dialog class, derived from TDialog
class ConDialog : public TDialog
{
   // input data
   long  lx, ly, ll ;

public:
   ConDialog (TWindow* parent) ;
   BOOL CanClose ( ) ;
```

```
        void GetData (long& x, long& y, long& l) ;

        DECLARE_RESPONSE_TABLE (ConDialog) ;
} ;

// define a window to display the graph
class ConnettWin : public TWindow
{
    // status of the window (current operation)
    enum win_st {empty, painting, painted} ;
    win_st status ;

    // data used to compute the Connett graph
    long x, y, l ;
    unsigned int i, j, r ;
    int nColors ;
    float a, b, c, d, e, f, g ;

    // memory device centext holding the graph
    TMemoryDC* pdcMem ;

public:
    // constructor and destructor
    ConnettWin ( ) ;
    ~ConnettWin ( ) ;

    // painting
    void Paint (TDC& paintDC, BOOL, TRect&) ;

    // menu commands and events response functions
    void EvTimer (UINT) ;
    void CmAbout ( ) ;
    void CmDraw ( ) ;
    void CmOptions ( ) ;

private:
    // internal functions
    void PointValue (TDC* pdc, int x, int y,  int value) ;
    int PointsNum ( ) ;

    DECLARE_RESPONSE_TABLE (ConnettWin) ;
} ;

// define a class for the application
class ConnettApp : public TApplication
{
```

```
public:
    ConnettApp ( ) ;
    void InitMainWindow ( ) ;
} ;
```

```
// file CONNETT.CPP                                    17/CONNETT
// the Connett program with ObjectWindows

// include some OWL header files
#include <owl\owlpch.h>
#include <owl\applicat.h>
#include <owl\framewin.h>
#include <owl\dc.h>

// include Borland controls and math functions
#include <bwcc.h>
#include <math.h>

// include the definitions for resources
#include "connett.rh"
#define ID_TIMER    100

// include the definitions of the classes
#include "connett.h"


// definition of the member functions of the ConDialog class

ConDialog :: ConDialog (TWindow* parent) :
        TDialog (parent, IDD_CONNETT)
    { }

// the dialog can be closed only if the three input strings
// can be converted into proper numeric values
BOOL ConDialog :: CanClose ( )
{
    // retrieve the value of the three strings
    char  lpszX [8], lpszY [8], lpszL [8] ;
    GetDlgItemText (ID_EDITX, lpszX, 8) ;
    GetDlgItemText (ID_EDITY, lpszY, 8) ;
    GetDlgItemText (ID_EDITL, lpszL, 8) ;

    // try to convert them into long integers
    lx = atol (lpszX) ;
```

```
    ly = atol (lpszY) ;
    ll = atol (lpszL) ;

    // test the values (0 means "not a number")
    if ( (lx == 0) l (ly == 0) l (ll < 1) )
    {
        BWCCMessageBox (HWindow, "Input values are not correct",
            NULL, MB_ICONSTOP l MB_OK) ;
        return FALSE ;
    }
    else
        return TRUE ;
}


// retrive the input values
void ConDialog :: GetData (long& x, long& y, long& l)
{
    x = lx ;
    y = ly ;
    l = ll ;
}


// no specific handler
DEFINE_RESPONSE_TABLE1 (ConDialog, TDialog)
END_RESPONSE_TABLE ;



// definition of the member functions of class ConnettWin

ConnettWin :: ConnettWin ( ) :
    TWindow (0, 0, 0) ,
    x(12) ,         // default values
    y(15) ,
    l(20)
{
    pdcMem = new TMemoryDC ( ) ;
    status = empty ;
}

ConnettWin :: ~ConnettWin ()
{
    delete pdcMem ;
}

// map the value (0 to 3) into a color
void ConnettWin :: PointValue (TDC* pdc, int x, int y,  int value)
```

```
{
    TColor c = TColor (               // 0 = black
        (value==1) ? 255 : 0,// 1 = red
        (value==2) ? 255 : 0,// 2 = green
        (value==3) ? 255 : 0) ;  // 3 = blue
    pdc -> SetPixel (x, y, c) ;
}


// get the client rectangle and return the smallest size
int ConnettWin :: PointsNum ( )
{
    TRect rect = GetClientRect ( ) ;
    return (rect.bottom > rect.right) ? rect.right : rect.bottom ;
}


// display the about box
void ConnettWin :: CmAbout ( )
{
    BWCCMessageBox (HWindow,
        "Connett for Windows (from \"Borland C++ 4.0\" book by Cantu'-Tendon)",
        "About Connett",
        MB_OK I MB_ICONINFORMATION) ;
}


// start the drawing process
void ConnettWin :: CmDraw ( )
{
    // create a square bitmap based on the current DC
    // (display-compatible) and the size of the window
    TClientDC dc (HWindow) ;
    r = PointsNum ( ) ;
    TBitmap bitmap (dc, r, r) ;
    pdcMem -> SelectObject (bitmap) ;
    status = painting ;

    // set the values for the algorithm
    nColors = 4 ;
    a = x * x + y * y ;
    b = x + x ;
    c = y + y ;
    d = float (l) / float (r) ;
    i = 0 ;

    // start a timer and clear the window
    SetTimer (ID_TIMER, 10) ;
    Invalidate ( ) ;
```

```
        UpdateWindow ( ) ;
}

// compute a line of dots
void ConnettWin :: EvTimer (UINT)
{
    e = d * i ;
    f = a + (b + e) * e ;
    for (j = 0; j <= r; j++)
    {
        g = d*j ;
        PointValue (pdcMem, i, j,
                fmod (floor (f + (c + g) * g), nColors)) ;
    }

    // if the algorithm is not ended
    if (i <= r)
    {
        // repaint the new line of points
        TRectrect (i-1, 0, i, r) ;
        InvalidateRect (rect) ;
        i++ ;
    }
    else
    {
        // stop the process
        KillTimer (ID_TIMER) ;
        status = painted ;
        Invalidate ( ) ;
        UpdateWindow ( ) ;
    }
}

// display the dialog box used to input some values for the graph
void ConnettWin :: CmOptions ( )
{
    ConDialog  dialog (this) ;
    if (dialog.Execute ( ) == IDOK)
        // retrieve the input values
        dialog.GetData (x, y, l) ;
}

void ConnettWin :: Paint (TDC& paintDC, BOOL, TRect&)
{
    // copy either a portion of the bitmap ...
```

```
        if (status == painting)
            paintDC.BitBlt (0, 0, i, r, *pdcMem, 0, 0, SRCCOPY) ;

        // ... or its whole surface
        if (status == painted)
            paintDC.BitBlt (0, 0, r, r, *pdcMem, 0, 0, SRCCOPY) ;
    }


DEFINE_RESPONSE_TABLE1(ConnettWin, TWindow)
    EV_WM_TIMER ,
    EV_COMMAND (CM_ABOUT, CmAbout) ,
    EV_COMMAND (CM_DRAW, CmDraw) ,
    EV_COMMAND (CM_OPTIONS, CmOptions) ,
END_RESPONSE_TABLE ;


// member functions of the application class

ConnettApp :: ConnettApp ( ) :
        TApplication ( )
    { }

void ConnettApp :: InitMainWindow ( )
{
    SetMainWindow =( new TFrameWindow (NULL, "Connett for Windows", new
ConnettWin)) ;
    GetMainWindow ()-> SetIcon (this, IDI_CONNETT) ;
    GetMainWindow ()-> AssignMenu (IDM_CONNETT) ;
}


// main function
int OwlMain (int, char* [])
{
    ConnettApp app ;
    return app.Run ( ) ;
}
```

If you build this program with a program including the three files (*.ccp*, *.rc* and a standard *.def*) and run it, you can paint colorful graphs such as the one in Figure 17.4. The size of the graph depends on that of the window (naturally, the algorithm is faster when the graph is smaller). The program doesn't support a way to save the graphs to a file, but this can be accomplished simply, since under Windows you can capture the screen using the *PrintScreen* key or the contents of a single window with *Alt-PrintScreen*. Then you can copy the bitmap to any graphic editor (including *Paintbrush*) and save it to a file.

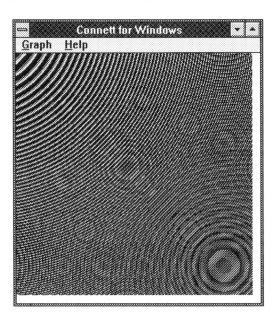

Figure 17.4 An example of the output of the connett application, showing a graph

A Multiple Document Interface Application

In the last couple of years, it has become common for Windows applications to have an MDI behavior. Multiple Document Interface is a specification of how applications should behave, but there is also some direct support in the Windows API. Of course, by using ObjectWindows the development of MDI applications becomes easier.

As examples of MDI applications, see the Borland environment, Resource Workshop, File Manager, or Program Manager (just to mention some applications you certainly have). There are some common traits: Generally each window corresponds to a file (or at least to a different document); you can maximize a window adding its title to that of the application, or reduce it to an icon (within the application window). At times when you change the current child window, the menu or even the toolbar changes accordingly. Here we assume you know how to use an MDI application; we want to show you how to build a simple one.

What's Behind MDI?

When you program through Windows' API, in order to build an MDI application you must place a special window in the client area of your main window (the frame). This is a window of a *preregistered WNDCLASS*, called *MDICLIENT*, which is part of Windows itself (it is registered by USER DLL, as are most of the Windows default *WNDCLASSes*).

An MDI application has the following windows:

- A main window, the frame, having a menu, an icon, and so on
- A *MDICLIENT* window, which is not distinguishable, since it covers the whole client area of the frame window
- Any number of child windows, which can move only inside the *MDICLIENT* window (i.e., inside the client area of the frame)

Using OWL you end up with the same structure:

- A frame window, of class *TMDIFrame*
- A *client* window, usually of a class derived from *TMDIClient*
- Any number of child windows, of any class derived by *TMDIChild*

A Basic MDI Example

The *TMDIClient* and the frame offer you the default behavior of an MDI application, including the most common operations: tile, cascade, arrange icons, close all, and a list of child windows in a pulldown menu. To enable this behavior, the menu should use default identifiers, as in the following resource file:

```
// file OWL_MDI1.RC                                                17/MDI

#include <owl\mdi.rh>

MENU_OWLMDI MENU
{
    POPUP "&Window"
    {
        MENUITEM "&New child",  CM_CREATECHILD
        MENUITEM "&Cascade", CM_CASCADECHILDREN
        MENUITEM "&Tile", CM_TILECHILDREN
        MENUITEM "Arrange &icons", CM_ARRANGEICONS
        MENUITEM "Close &all", CM_CLOSECHILDREN
    }
}
```

With this menu you can build a working (although bare) MDI application with the following code:

```
// file OWL_MDI1.CPP                                               17/MDI
// Minimal MDI application made with OWL 2.0

// files inclusion
#include <owl\mdi.h>
```

```
#include <owl\applicat.h>

// definition of a class for the MDI Client
class DemoMDIClient : public TMDIClient
{
private:
   WORD nChild;

public:
   DemoMDIClient ( ) :
      TMDIClient ( ) ,
      nChild (0)
   { }

   TMDIChild* InitChild ( )
   {
      char szChildName [14] ;
      wsprintf (szChildName, "Child #%d", ++nChild) ;
      return new TMDIChild (*this, szChildName) ;
   }

   DECLARE_RESPONSE_TABLE (DemoMDIClient) ;
} ;

DEFINE_RESPONSE_TABLE1(DemoMDIClient, TMDIClient)
END_RESPONSE_TABLE ;

// MDI application class
class DemoMDIApp : public TApplication
{
public:

   DemoMDIApp ( ) :
      TApplication ( )
   { }

   void InitMainWindow ( )
   {
      SetMainWindow (new TMDIFrame (
            "MDI Frame", "MENU_OWLMDI",
            *new DemoMDIClient)) ;
   }
} ;

// main function
```

```
int OwlMain (int, char* [ ])
{
    DemoMDIApp demo ;
    return demo.Run ( ) ;
}
```

The application resulting from this program (see Figure 17.5) is quite simple, because we have used as children plain *TMDIChild* windows. Deriving a new class from
this, you can implement more interesting programs. However, there is even another
choice. Instead of deriving a new class from *TMDIChild,* we can insert inside this child
window another one (using the child as a frame window). In this way you can add
"*MDI support*" to an existing application by using the *frame/client* approach (the one
we have always used in our programs).

An Input-Output Window

We want to follow this second alternative, because it is much more interesting. For
instance, you could decide, later on, to add decorations (like a toolbar and a status bar)
or other fancy support controls to the application without modifying the original code
of the window.

Let's start with a simple but significant example: a window capable of displaying a
rectangle, the position and size of which are determined by mouse clicks. By clicking
with each of the mouse buttons, the user sets the coordinates of the two extreme points
of the rectangle. The interesting point is that the window has to *remember* the mouse
position. This is really simple to do with OWL: You only need some data member in
the class. However, to accomplish the same thing in an MDI application using the

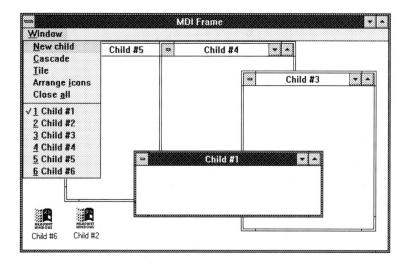

Figure 17.5 An example of the OWL_MDI1 application, with several child windows

Figure 17.6 The output of the TEST_WIN program, based on the *InoutWindow* class

Windows API, you have to use a very complex approach, such as the use of extra
bytes. In Windows, in fact, there is no easy way to attach data to a window, while with
OWL this is almost trivial.

The following is the source code of the input-output application we will later turn
into an MDI application. For this purpose we have divided it in two parts: the definition of the window and the definition of the application class. To build the program,
you need a project with both files (there are no resources). The resulting output of is
shown in Figure 17.6.

```
// file INOUT.H                                              17/MDI
// interface of a class describing a window
// with some input output support

class InoutWindow : public TWindow
{
private:
    TPoint pt1, pt2 ;       // points selected with the mouse
    TPen * ppen ;           // pen used to draw lines
    TBrush * pbrush ; // brush used to fill the frames

public:
    // constructor and destructor:
    InoutWindow ( ) ;
    ~InoutWindow ( ) ;

    // message response functions
    void EvLButtonDown (UINT, TPoint &) ;
    void EvRButtonDown (UINT, TPoint &) ;
    void EvMouseMove (UINT modKeys, TPoint &) ;
    void EvPaint ( ) ;
```

```
      DECLARE_RESPONSE_TABLE (InoutWindow) ;
};
```

```
// file INOUT.CPP                                                    17/MDI
// member functions of the InoutWindow class

#include <owl\window.h>
#include <owl\gdiobjec.h>

#include "inout.h"

// constructor: create pen and brush
InoutWindow :: InoutWindow ( ) :
    TWindow (0, 0, 0)
{
    ppen = new TPen (TColor::(TCyan)) ;
    pbrush = new TBrush (TColor::(TMagenta)) ;
}

// destructor: delete pen and brush
InoutWindow :: ~InoutWindow ( )
{
    delete ppen ;
    delete pbrush ;
}

// left mouse button down
void InoutWindow :: EvLButtonDown (UINT, TPoint &point)
{
    pt1 = point ;
    Invalidate ( ) ;
}

// right mouse button down
void InoutWindow :: EvRButtonDown (UINT, TPoint &point)
{
    pt2 = point ;
    Invalidate ( ) ;
}

// any mouse movement inside the client area
void InoutWindow :: EvMouseMove (UINT, TPoint &point)
{
    char szBuffer [50] ;
```

```
      wsprintf (szBuffer, "Cursor in (%d,%d)", point.x, point.y) ;
      Parent -> SetWindowText (szBuffer) ;
}

// window needs repaiting
void InoutWindow :: EvPaint ( )
{
      TPaintDC dc (HWindow) ;
      dc.SelectObject (*ppen) ;
      dc.SelectObject (*pbrush) ;
      dc.Rectangle (pt1, pt2) ;
}

// message map definition
DEFINE_RESPONSE_TABLE1(InoutWindow, TWindow)
      EV_WM_LBUTTONDOWN ,
      EV_WM_RBUTTONDOWN ,
      EV_WM_MOUSEMOVE ,
      EV_WM_PAINT ,
END_RESPONSE_TABLE ;
```

```
// file TEST_WIN.CPP                                              17/MDI
// application class and main function to test the InoutWindow class

#include <owl\applicat.h>
#include <owl\framewin.h>
#include <owl\gdiobjec.h>

#include "inout.h"

// class describing the application
class OwlApp : public TApplication
{
public:
      OwlApp ( ) :
        TApplication ( )
      { }

      void InitMainWindow ( ) ;
} ;

void OwlApp :: InitMainWindow ( )
{
      SetMainWindow =( new TFrameWindow (NULL,
```

```
            "Input/output", new InoutWindow)) ;
}

// main function
int OwlMain (int, char* [ ])
{
    OwlApp app ;
    return app.Run ( ) ;
}
```

From SDI to MDI

Now that we have a full working SDI (*Single Document Interface*) application, we want to turn it into an MDI application. This is simple: We only need a class derived from *TMDIClient* which will build a *TMDIChild* with an *InoutWindow* inside (the action takes place in the *InitChild* function which is invoked automatically in response to the *New* command).

In the previous test program, we built a main window calling the constructor:

```
TFrameWindow (NULL, "Input/output", new InoutWindow) ;
```

Now we create a child window with a similar statement:

```
TMDIChild (*this, szChildName, new InoutWindow) ;
```

The rest of the program is pretty simple.

```
// file OWL_MDI2.CPP                                        17/MDI
// Simple MDI application

// files inclusion
#include <owl\mdi.h>
#include <owl\applicat.h>
#include <owl\gdiobjec.h>

#include "inout.h"

// definition of a class for the MDI Client
class DemoMDIClient : public TMDIClient
{
private:
    WORD nChild ;

public:
    DemoMDIClient ( ) :
```

```
        TMDIClient ( ) ,
        nChild (0)
   { }

   TMDIChild* InitChild ( )
   {
       char   szChildName [14] ;
       wsprintf (szChildName, "Child #%d", ++nChild) ;
       return new TMDIChild (*this, szChildName, new InoutWindow) ;
   }

   DECLARE_RESPONSE_TABLE (DemoMDIClient) ;
} ;

DEFINE_RESPONSE_TABLE1(DemoMDIClient, TMDIClient)
END_RESPONSE_TABLE ;


// MDI application class
class DemoMDIApp : public TApplication
{
public:

   DemoMDIApp ( )  :
      TApplication ( )
   { }

   void InitMainWindow ( )
   {
      MainWindow = new TMDIFrame (
           "MDI Frame", "MENU_OWLMDI",
           *new DemoMDIClient) ;
   }
} ;

// main function
int OwlMain (int, char* [ ])
{
   DemoMDIApp demo ;
   return demo.Run ( ) ;
}
```

As you can see from the output in Figure 17.7 we have really mixed up the last two programs (see Figures 17.5 and 17.6) with a limited amount of code. This same technique can be used to solve much more complex situations. Remember, however,

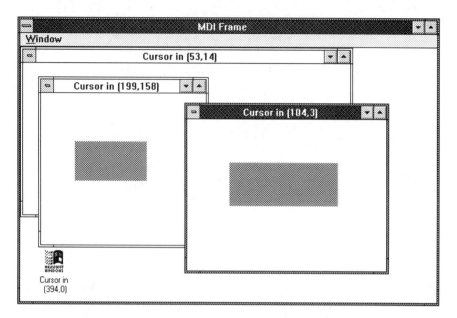

Figure 17.7 The OWL_MDI2 program is really a full working MDI application

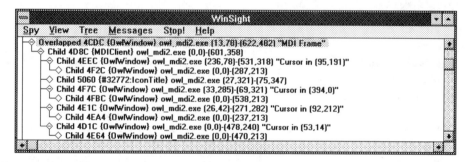

Figure 17.8 The structure of the windows of the OWL_MDI2 application as shown by *WinSight*

that if you want to make this kind of operation, you need to use the *frame/client* approach even when building standard (SDI) applications.

The application we have built has a huge number of windows: The frame has a *client* inside, and this has a number of child windows each having a window in it. To explore a similar situation, you can use the powerful *WinSight* application of the Borland environment, as in Figure 17.8.

Interactive Geometrical Shapes

At the end of this chapter, we want to build an application of a significant size. The basic idea is to develop a hierarchy of geometrical shape classes, and an interface to draw them

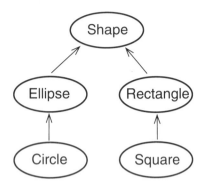

Figure 17.9 The hierarchy of classes describing geometrical shapes

in a window using the mouse. After a shape has been selected, the user should be able to press the left mouse button to determine the center of a shape, and drag the mouse to size it. During this actions, the user should see the effect directly on the screen.

The Hierarchy of Classes

First of all we need to develop a hierarchy of classes for the shapes including rect- angles, squares, ellipses, and circles. The hierarchy is shown in Figure 17.9. Notice, however, that to avoid name clashes between these classes and some global functions of the Windows API (such as *Rectangle*), the derived classes have a prefix "*S*" (which stand for Shape).

We need an abstract class, called *Shape*, at the top of the hierarchy, having all the member functions of the derived classes (the *common interface*, using the terms of Chapter 9). This class has a lot of virtual functions, overridden by the derived classes, with some other functions that perform specific tasks. In fact, *Shape* describes shapes having a center (*x* and *y* coordinates) and some attributes as the color of the border and its width, and the color used to fill the interior. Some other functions are directly related to Windows and the way we are going to show the new shape while the user drags the mouse pointer (for example, by using the function *BoundRec* to return the portion of the screen under the shape, and the function *SetCorner* to resize the shape). Here is the interface and the body of this class.

```
// file WSHAPE.H                                              17/WINSHAPE
// interface of the abstract class Shape

// a class describing shapes with a center
class Shape
{
protected:
```

```
    TColor      borderColor, fillColor ;
    int     borderWidth ;
    int     xCenter, yCenter ;

public:
    Shape (int x, int y, TColor bc, int w, TColor fc) ;

    // retrieve thhe position
    int GetX ( ) ;
    int GetY ( ) ;

    // change and read the color of the border
    // and its width and get the corresponding pen
    void BorderCol (TColor col) ;
    TColor BorderCol ( ) ;
    void Width (int w) ;
    int Width ( ) ;
protected:
    TPen GetPen ( ) ;

public:
    // change and read the color used to fill the
    // interior of the shape and the corresponding brush
    void FillCol (TColor col) ;
    TColor FillCol ( ) ;
protected:
    TBrush GetBrush ( ) ;

public:
    // return the description of the shape
    virtual char * Description ( ) = 0 ;

    // return the perimeter or the area
    virtual long Perimeter ( ) = 0 ;
    virtual long Area ( ) = 0 ;

    // move the shape to a new center
    void MoveTo  (int x, int y) ;

    // translate the shape by dx and dy
    void Move (int dX, int dY) ;

    // define a "corner" of the shape, indicating its extension
    // once the center is fixed
    virtual void SetCorner (int x, int y) = 0 ;
```

```
    // scale the size of the shape
    virtual void Scale (float s) = 0 ;

    // get the rectangle bounding the shape
    virtual TRect BoundRect ( ) = 0 ;

    // paint the shape on the device context
    virtual void Paint (TDC& dc) = 0 ;

    // test if two shapes are equal (needed to store
    // them in an TIArrayAsVector structure
    int operator == (const Shape& s) ;
} ;
```

```
// file WSHAPE.CPP
// member functions of the class Shape

#include <owl\dc.h>
#include <owl\gdiobjec.h>

#include "wshape.h"

Shape :: Shape (int x, int y, TColor bc, int w, TColor fc) :
    xCenter (x) ,
    yCenter (y) ,
    borderColor (bc) ,
    fillColor (fc) ,
    borderWidth (w)
{ }

int Shape :: GetX ( )
{
    return xCenter ;
}

int Shape :: GetY ( )
{
    return yCenter ;
}

void Shape :: BorderCol (TColor col)
{
    borderColor = col ;
}
```

```
TColor Shape :: BorderCol ( )
{
    return borderColor;
}

void Shape :: Width (int w)
{
    borderWidth = w ;
}

int Shape :: Width ( )
{
    return borderWidth ;
}

void Shape :: FillCol (TColor col)
{
    fillColor = col ;
}

TColor Shape :: FillCol ( )
{
    return fillColor ;
}

void Shape :: MoveTo (int x, int y)
{
    xCenter = x ;
    yCenter = y ;
}

void Shape :: Move (int dX, int dY)
{
    xCenter += dX ;
    yCenter += dY ;
}

TPen Shape :: GetPen ( )
{
    return TPen (borderColor, borderWidth, PS_INSIDEFRAME) ;
}

TBrush Shape :: GetBrush ( )
{
    return TBrush (fillColor) ;
}
```

```
int Shape :: operator == (const Shape& s)
{
    return (xCenter == s.xCenter && yCenter == s.yCenter) ;
}
```

As you can see, the above classes are not as trivial as the examples we have used up to now, but this additional complication is necessary if we want to build a fully working application. Consider that most of the member functions are related to Windows programming (and not to the *shape* abstraction itself). The following derived classes and the code of the program should help you understand how thess classes were put together.

Ellipses and Circles

Here come the four derived classes. Consider studying them carefully to grasp the example completely (and increase your consciousness of the importance of hierarchies in object-oriented programming).

```
// file WELLIPSE.H                                    17/WINSHAPE
// interface of class SEllipse
// the name of the class is prefixed with an S (for Shape)
// to avoid a name clash with the Windows API Ellipse function

class SEllipse : public Shape
{
protected:
    int xRadius, yRadius ;

public:
    SEllipse (int xc, int yc, int xr, int yr,
        TColor bc, int w, TColor fc) ;
    char* Description ( ) ;
    long Perimeter ( ) ;
    long Area ( ) ;
    void SetCorner (int x, int y) ;
    void Scale (float s) ;
    TRect BoundRect ( ) ;
    void Paint (TDC& dc) ;
} ;
```

```
// file WELLIPSE.CPP                                   17/WINSHAPE
// member functions of class SEllipse
```

```
#include <owl\dc.h>
#include <owl\gdiobjec.h>

#include "wshape.h"
#include "wellipse.h"
#include <math.h>

SEllipse :: SEllipse (int xc, int yc, int xr, int yr,
      TColor bc, int w, TColor fc) :
   xRadius (xr) ,
   yRadius (yr) ,
   Shape (xc, yc, bc, w, fc)
{ }

char* SEllipse :: Description ( )
{
   return "Ellipse" ;
}

long SEllipse :: Perimeter ( )
{
   // approximate formula
   return (3.14 * sqrt (2.0 * xRadius * xRadius
         + 2.0 * yRadius * yRadius)) ;
}

long SEllipse :: Area ()
{
   return ((long) xRadius * yRadius * 3.14) ;
}

void SEllipse :: SetCorner (int x, int y)
{
   xRadius = abs (x - xCenter) ;
   yRadius = abs (y - yCenter) ;
}

void SEllipse :: Scale (float s)
{
   xRadius *= s ;
   yRadius *= s ;
}

TRect SEllipse :: BoundRect ( )
{
```

```
        return TRect (xCenter - xRadius, yCenter - yRadius,
            xCenter + xRadius, yCenter + yRadius) ;
}

void SEllipse :: Paint (TDC& dc)
{
    TPen pen = GetPen ( ) ;
    dc.SelectObject (pen) ;

    TBrush brush = GetBrush ( ) ;
    dc.SelectObject (brush) ;

    dc.Ellipse (xCenter - xRadius, yCenter - yRadius,
            xCenter + xRadius, yCenter + yRadius) ;
}
```

```
// file WCIRCLE.H                                    17/WINSHAPE
// interface of class SCircle

class SCircle : public SEllipse
{
public:
    SCircle (int xc, int yc, int r, TColor bc, int w, TColor fc);
    char* Description ( ) ;
    long Perimeter ( ) ;
    void SetCorner (int x, int y) ;
} ;
```

```
// file WCIRCLE.CPP                                  17/WINSHAPE
// member functions of class SCircle

#include <owl\dc.h>
#include <owl\gdiobjec.h>

#include "wshape.h"
#include "wellipse.h"
#include "wcircle.h"
#include <stdlib.h>

SCircle :: SCircle (int xc, int yc, int r, TColor bc, int w, TColor fc) :
    SEllipse (xc, yc, r, r, bc, w, fc)
{ }
```

```
char* SCircle :: Description ( )
{
    return "Circle" ;
}

long SCircle :: Perimeter ( )
{
    return (2 * 3.14 * xRadius) ;
}

void SCircle :: SetCorner (int x, int y)
{
    // both radii are set to the lower of the two distances
    // from the corner to the center of the shape
    xRadius = (abs (x - xCenter) < abs (y - yCenter)) ?
        abs (x - xCenter) : abs (y - yCenter) ;
    yRadius = xRadius ;
}
```

Rectangles and Squares

After ellipses and circles, here come rectangles and squares, which are really very similar to the previous two classes:

```
// file WRECT.H                                          17/WINSHAPE
// interface of class SRectangle

class SRectangle : public Shape
{
protected:
    int base, height ;

public:
    SRectangle (int x, int y, int b, int h,
        TColor bc, int w, TColor fc) ;
    char* Description ( ) ;
    long Perimeter ( ) ;
    long Area ( ) ;
    void SetCorner (int x, int y) ;
    void Scale (float s) ;
    TRect BoundRect ( ) ;
    void Paint (TDC& dc) ;
} ;
```

```
// file WRECT.CPP
// member functions of class SRectangle

#include <owl\dc.h>
#include <owl\gdiobjec.h>

#include "wshape.h"
#include "wrect.h"
#include <stdlib.h>

SRectangle :: SRectangle (int x, int y, int b, int h,
       TColor bc, int w, TColor fc) :
   base (b) ,
   height (h) ,
   Shape (x, y, bc, w, fc)
{ }

char* SRectangle :: Description ( )
{
   return "Rectangle" ;
}

long SRectangle :: Perimeter ( )
{
   return ((base + height) * 2) ;
}

long SRectangle :: Area ( )
{
   return (long (base) * height) ;
}

void SRectangle :: SetCorner (int x, int y)
{
   base = abs (x - xCenter) * 2 ;
   height = abs (y - yCenter) * 2 ;
}

void SRectangle :: Scale (float s)
{
   base *= s ;
   height *= s ;
}

TRect SRectangle :: BoundRect ( )
{
```

```
        return TRect (xCenter - base/2, yCenter - height/2,
            xCenter + base/2, yCenter + height/2);
}

void SRectangle :: Paint (TDC& dc)
{
    TPen pen = GetPen ( ) ;
    dc.SelectObject (pen) ;

    TBrush brush = GetBrush ( ) ;
    dc.SelectObject (brush) ;

    dc.Rectangle (xCenter - base/2, yCenter - height/2,
        xCenter + base/2, yCenter + height/2) ;
}
```

```
// file WSQUARE.H                                           17/WINSHAPE
// interface of class SSquare

class SSquare : public SRectangle
{
// the side corresponds to both base and height of class SRectangle

public:
    SSquare (int x, int y, int side, TColor bc, int w, TColor fc) ;
    char* Description ( ) ;
    void SetCorner (int x, int y) ;
} ;
```

```
// file WSQUARE.CPP                                         17/WINSHAPE
// member functions of class SSquare

#include <owl\dc.h>
#include <owl\gdiobjec.h>

#include "wshape.h"
#include "wrect.h"
#include "wsquare.h"
#include <stdlib.h>

SSquare :: SSquare (int x, int y, int side, TColor bc, int w, TColor fc) :
    SRectangle (x, y, side, side, bc, w, fc)
{ }
```

```
char* SSquare :: Description ( )
{
    return "Square" ;
}

void  SSquare :: SetCorner (int x, int y)
{
    // similar to SCircle :: SetCorner
    base = (abs (x - xCenter) < abs (y - yCenter)) ?
        abs (x - xCenter) * 2 : abs (y - yCenter) * 2 ;
    height = base ;
}
```

Selecting and Dragging the Shape

Once we have the hierarchy of graphical classes, we can write a main window to create
and display them. We need four menu commands to select the shape to draw, and some
functions responding to mouse *dragging*. The four command response functions might
look like:

```
void ShapeWin :: CmSquare ( )
{
    pCurrentShape = new SSquare
        (10, 10, 0, crPenColor, nPenWidth, crFillColor) ;
    bShapeSel = TRUE ;
}
```

The functions creates a shape in a random position within the window using the
current pen and color attributes, then sets a flag to change the appearance of the mouse
pointer (this will take place when the mouse moves). To draw a shape, the user can
click the mouse button to define the center of a new shape, and hold it down while
moving the mouse to define the size of the shape. This operation of "moving the mouse
while holding down one of its buttons" is called *dragging*. To provide it in an application, you need to define three functions:

- *EvLButtonDown*, called as the left mouse button is pressed, should initialize the
  dragging—providing a device context and capturing the subsequent mouse input—
  and define the center of the shape. These operations are performed only if dragging
  is not already taking place and if a shape has been selected from the menu.

```
void ShapeWin :: EvLButtonDown (UINT, TPoint& point)
{
    // if a shape has been selected and the dragging
    // is not active, start the dragging phase
    if (!bMouseDown && bShapeSel)
    {
```

```
        // set the dragging flag
        bMouseDown = TRUE;

        // capture mouse input
        SetCapture ( ) ;

        // initialize the device context
        pdcDragging = new TClientDC (HWindow) ;

        // set the center and attributes of the shape
        pCurrentShape -> MoveTo (point.x, point.y) ;
        pCurrentShape -> BorderCol (crPenColor) ;
        pCurrentShape -> FillCol (crFillColor) ;
    }
}
```

- *EvMouseMove*, called when the mouse is moved, is used to erase the shape (repainting the part of the window corresponding to its bounding rectangle), and repaint it after it has been resized. This function is used also to select a different cursor when a shape has been selected using two, API functions (preceded by the scope operator):

```
void ShapeWin :: EvMouseMove (UINT, TPoint& point)
{
    // if a shape is selected changes the cursor to a cross
    if (bShapeSel)
        ::SetCursor (::LoadCursor (NULL, IDC_CROSS));

    // if the dragging flag is on
    if (bMouseDown)
    {
        // compute the bounding rectangle of the old
        // shape and repaint that area of the window
        TRect r = pCurrentShape -> BoundRect ( ) ;

        InvalidateRect (r) ;
        UpdateWindow ( ) ;

        // set the new parameters of the shape
        pCurrentShape -> SetCorner (point.x, point.y) ;

        // repaint the shape
        pCurrentShape -> Paint (*pdcDragging) ;
    }
}
```

- *EvLButtonUp*, called when the mouse button is released, ends the dragging, releasing the device context and the mouse input.

```
void ShapeWin :: EvLButtonUp (UINT, TPoint&)
{
    // if the dragging flag is on, end the dragging phase
    if (bMouseDown)
    {
        // unselect the dragging flag
        bMouseDown = FALSE ;

        // release the mouse capture
        ReleaseCapture ( ) ;

        // store the current shape in the array
        list.Add (pCurrentShape) ;
        nElements ++ ;

        // release the device context
        delete pdcDragging ;

        // no shape is selected
        bShapeSel = FALSE ;
    }
}
```

This code is not completely optimized, and when you have a number of shapes you'll see some *flickering* on the screen. However, in this code we use an interesting property of the device context. We can specify the area we want to repaint in the parameter of the *InvalidateRect* function. Then, if we want to repaint the window's client area immediately, we can call the *UpdateWindow* function.

➤ *Note:* When we call *InvalidateRect* we place a *WM_PAINT* message in the message queue of the window (together with the corresponding information about the invalidate area, also called *update region*). The window will process *WM_PAINT* only when its message queue is empty, since the paint is a "low priority" message. To force the immediate processing of the message, we can call the *UpdateWindow* function, which gets the *WM_PAINT* message from the queue and passes it to the window. Therefore, if no paint message is pending (i.e., no update region) the call to *UpdateWindow* has no effect.

The information about the invalid area is passed by OWL inside the third parameter of the *Paint* function. However, we seldom use this information directly. In fact, any GDI output function having as first parameter a "paint device context" (that is, a device

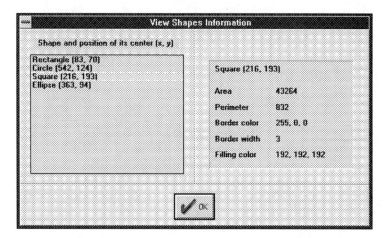

Figure 17.10 The dialog box of the application during its execution

context returned by the *BeginPaint* function, or passed to the *Paint* member function) operates only in the update region (which corresponds to the invalidate area). Any output outside of this area is completely ignored, even if the corresponding instructions are executed. Therefore, to repaint only the shapes that fall into the invalidate area, we can repaint all of them! In fact, the useless output operations will be completely ignored by Windows, which will lose no time in repainting outside of the update region.

Once we have created a new shape we store it in a *list*, which is based on the container class *TIArrayAsVector<Shape>* of the Borland Container Class library. Therefore, in order to paint all of the shapes (or the shapes in the current invalid area) we need only write:

```
void ShapeWin :: Paint(TDC& PaintDC, BOOL, TRect&)
{
    // repaint all the shapes of the list
    for (int i = 0; i < nElements; i++)
        list[i]->Paint (PaintDC) ;
}
```

If something goes wrong during the drawing process, the program allows you to remove the last shape using the *Undo* command (see the full source code later on) or restart with a brand new array (using *New*).

An Information Dialog with the List of Shapes

To get some information about the shapes, we will build a dialog box listing all the shapes of the array, and displaying data about any specific shape the user selects in the list. The dialog box has a listbox and some static control to display the data, as you can see in Figure 17.10. The dialog box template, from the resource file of the application, is the following:

```
IDD_VIEWINFO DIALOG 16, 41, 316, 187                    17/WINSHAPE
STYLE DS_MODALFRAME I WS_POPUP I WS_VISIBLE I WS_CAPTION I
WS_SYSMENU
CLASS "bordlg"
CAPTION "View Shapes Information"
FONT 8, "MS Sans Serif"
{
    CONTROL "", -1, "BorShade", BSS_HDIP I BSS_LEFT I
        WS_CHILD I WS_VISIBLE, -2, 147, 339, 4
    CONTROL "", IDOK, "BorBtn", BS_DEFPUSHBUTTON I
        WS_CHILD I WS_VISIBLE I WS_TABSTOP, 139, 156, 37, 25
    LISTBOX IDC_LISTBOX1, 10, 25, 137, 121, LBS_NOTIFY I
        WS_BORDER I WS_BORDER I WS_VSCROLL
    CONTROL "Area", -1, "BorStatic", SS_LEFT I
        WS_CHILD I WS_VISIBLE, 176, 55, 49, 10
    CONTROL "", IDC_AREA, "BorStatic", SS_LEFT I
        WS_CHILD I WS_VISIBLE, 230, 55, 66, 10
    CONTROL "Perimeter", -1, "BorStatic", SS_LEFT I
        WS_CHILD I WS_VISIBLE, 176, 70, 49, 10
    CONTROL "", IDC_PERIMETER, "BorStatic", SS_LEFT I
        WS_CHILD I WS_VISIBLE, 230, 70, 66, 10
    CONTROL "Border color", -1, "BorStatic", SS_LEFT I
        WS_CHILD I WS_VISIBLE, 176, 85, 49, 10
    CONTROL "", IDC_BORDERC, "BorStatic", SS_LEFT I
        WS_CHILD I WS_VISIBLE, 230, 85, 66, 10
    CONTROL "Border width", -1, "BorStatic", SS_LEFT I
        WS_CHILD I WS_VISIBLE, 176, 100, 49, 10
    CONTROL "", IDC_BORDERW, "BorStatic", SS_LEFT I
        WS_CHILD I WS_VISIBLE, 230, 100, 66, 10
    CONTROL "Filling color", -1, "BorStatic", SS_LEFT I
        WS_CHILD I WS_VISIBLE, 176, 115, 49, 10
    CONTROL "", IDC_FILLCOLOR, "BorStatic", SS_LEFT I
        WS_CHILD I WS_VISIBLE, 230, 115, 66, 10
    CONTROL "", -1, "BorShade", BSS_GROUP I BSS_CAPTION I BSS_LEFT I
        WS_CHILD I WS_VISIBLE, 171, 30, 131, 103
    CONTROL "", IDC_SHAPE, "BorStatic", SS_LEFT I
        WS_CHILD I WS_VISIBLE I WS_GROUP, 176, 34, 122, 14
    CONTROL "Shape and position of its center (x, y)", -1, "BorStatic", SS_CENTER I
        WS_CHILD I WS_VISIBLE I WS_GROUP, 12, 9, 132, 10
    CONTROL "", -1, "BorShade", BSS_VDIP I BSS_LEFT I
        WS_CHILD I WS_VISIBLE, 157, -4, 2, 152
}
```

The dialog box is somewhat complex, but the source code needed to make it work should be easier to understand. We only need to provide the proper startup values, filling the listbox with the data of the array, and update the static controls each time the user changes the selection in the listbox. Of course, we need to access only the static controls showing our data (and not the descriptive labels of the data).

```
// file VIDIALOG.H                                          17/WINSHAPE
// interface of class ViewInfoDial

typedef TIArrayAsVector<Shape> MyArray ;

#include <owl\listbox.h>
#include <owl\static.h>

class ViewInfoDial : public TDialog
{
    MyArray* pList ;
    TListBox* pLbox ;
    TStatic* pStatic [6] ;

    enum stat_names {ShapeName=0, Area, Perimeter, BorderC, BorderW, FillC} ;

public:
    // constructor and setup function
    ViewInfoDial (TWindow * parent, MyArray* pArray) ;
    void SetupWindow ( ) ;

    // control response functions
    void EvListSelChange ( ) ;
    void EvListDblClk ( ) ;
    void CmOK ( ) ;

    DECLARE_RESPONSE_TABLE (ViewInfoDial) ;
} ;



// file VIDIALOG.CPP                                         17/WINSHAPE
// member functions of class ViewInfoDial

#include <owl\owlpch.h>
#include <owl\listbox.h>
#include <owl\static.h>
#include <classlib\arrays.h>

#include "wshape.h"
#include "vidialog.h"
#include "winshape.rh"
```

```
ViewInfoDial :: ViewInfoDial (TWindow * parent, MyArray* pArray) :
    TDialog (parent, IDD_VIEWINFO)
{
    // copy the pointer to the array
    pList = pArray ;

    // create a new listbox
    pLbox = new TListBox (this, IDC_LISTBOX1) ;

    // create the new static controls for the data
    pStatic [ShapeName] = new TStatic (this, IDC_SHAPE) ;
    pStatic [Area] = new TStatic (this, IDC_AREA) ;
    pStatic [Perimeter] = new TStatic (this, IDC_PERIMETER) ;
    pStatic [BorderC] = new TStatic (this, IDC_BORDERC) ;
    pStatic [BorderW] = new TStatic (this, IDC_BORDERW) ;
    pStatic [FillC] = new TStatic (this, IDC_FILLCOLOR) ;

}

void ViewInfoDial :: SetupWindow ( )
{
    TDialog :: SetupWindow ( ) ;

    // for each item of the array create a descripion
    // with the kind of shape and the position of its center
    int nTotalEl = pList-> GetItemsInContainer ( ) ;
    for (int i = 0; i < nTotalEl; ++i)
    {
        char szBuffer [80] ;
        Shape* pShape = (*pList) [i] ;
        char szName [20] ;
        strcpy (szName, pShape -> Description ( )) ;
        wsprintf (szBuffer, "%s (%d, %d)", (LPSTR) szName,
            pShape -> GetX ( ), pShape -> GetY ( )) ;
        pLbox -> AddString (szBuffer) ;
    }
}

void ViewInfoDial :: EvListSelChange ( )
{
    char szBuffer [80] ;

    // retrieve the current selection
    int nItemSel = pLbox -> GetSelIndex ( ) ;
    Shape * pShape =  pList -> operator [](nItemSel) ;
```

```
    // copy the description of the shape
    pLbox -> GetSelString (szBuffer, sizeof szBuffer) ;
    pStatic [ShapeName] -> SetText (szBuffer) ;

    // retrive area and perimeter
    wsprintf (szBuffer, "%ld", pShape -> Area ( )) ;
    pStatic [Area] -> SetText (szBuffer) ;
    wsprintf (szBuffer, "%ld", pShape -> Perimeter ( )) ;
    pStatic [Perimeter] -> SetText (szBuffer) ;

    // retrive colors and border size
    TColor col = pShape -> BorderCol ( ) ;
    wsprintf (szBuffer, "%d, %d, %d",
        col.Red ( ), col.Green ( ), col.Blue ( )) ;
    pStatic [BorderC] -> SetText (szBuffer) ;
    wsprintf (szBuffer, "%d", pShape -> Width ( )) ;
    pStatic [BorderW] -> SetText (szBuffer) ;
    col = pShape -> FillCol ( ) ;
    wsprintf (szBuffer, "%d, %d, %d",
        col.Red ( ), col.Green ( ), col.Blue ( )) ;
    pStatic [FillC] -> SetText (szBuffer) ;
}

DEFINE_RESPONSE_TABLE1 (ViewInfoDial, TDialog)
    EV_LBN_SELCHANGE (IDC_LISTBOX1, EvListSelChange) ,
END_RESPONSE_TABLE ;
```

Using Common Dialog Boxes for the Color

We need some more dialog boxes to select the color of the shape and its border, to select the size of the border, and to display some help information to the user.

Instead of building a dialog box for the color, we can use one of the standard Windows common dialog boxes (defined in the *commdlg.dll*). This is very easy because OWL provides some support classes, for example, *TChooseColorDialog*. This class is based on a specific data structure you must properly fill with the current color and an array of colors defined by the user, declared in the class interface as:

```
    TColor      custColors [16] ;
```

This array is initialized with the following code:

```
    for (int i = 0; i < 16; ++i)
        custColors [i] = TColor (i*16, 255-i*16, 0) ;
```

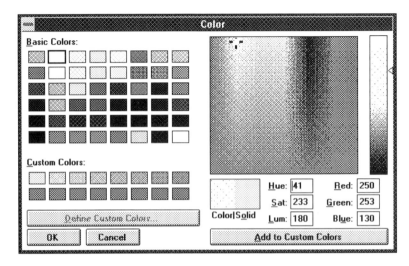

Figure 17.11 A common dialog box to display the color of the *shape* application

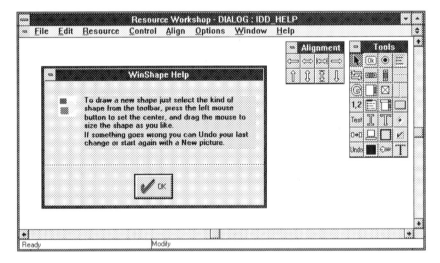

Figure 17.12 The definition of the help dialog box in the Workshop

The user can change these values from the *choose color* dialog box, clicking the "*Add to custom colors*" button.

Following is all the code you need to display the dialog box (Figure 17.11):

```
void ShapeWin :: CmBorderColor ( )
{
    // selects the color of the border of the shape
    TChooseColorDialog::TData ccData ;
```

```
ccData.Flags = CC_RGBINIT ;
ccData.Color = crPenColor ;
ccData.CustColors = custColors ;

if (new TChooseColorDialog (this, ccData)
      -> Execute ( ) == IDOK)
   crPenColor = ccData.Color ;
}
```

To select the size of the border of the shape, instead, we cannot use a common dialog box. However, there is a OWL class supporting an input line (*TInputDialog*), returning a string which must be converted to an integer:

```
void ShapeWin :: CmBorderWidth ( )
{
   // selects the width of the border, using a TInputDialog
   char  lpszText [5] = "" ;
   int nInputValue ;

   if (new TInputDialog (this, "Border of the shapes",
      "Input the new width:", lpszText,
      sizeof(lpszText)) -> Execute ( ) == IDOK )

      // tries to convert the input value
      if (nInputValue = atoi (lpszText))
         nPenWidth = nInputValue ;

      // if unseccessful shows a message
      else
         BWCCMessageBox (HWindow, "The input value is not valid",
            "Error", MB_OK I MB_ICONHAND) ;
}
```

The last dialog box we need, which will display some help, is completely defined in the resources of the application, with some static controls for the text (see Figure 17.12 for an example).

The Menu and the Code

Here is the menu of our application:

```
IDM_SHAPE MENU                                          17/WINSHAPE
{
   POPUP "&File"
   {
```

```
        MENUITEM "&New", CM_NEW
        MENUITEM SEPARATOR
        MENUITEM "&Exit", CM_EXIT
    }
    POPUP "&Edit"
    {
        MENUITEM "&Undo", CM_UNDO
        MENUITEM SEPARATOR
        MENUITEM "&View Info...", CM_VIEWINFO
    }
    POPUP "S&hape"
    {
        MENUITEM "&Square", CM_SQUARE
        MENUITEM "&Rectangle", CM_RECTANGLE
        MENUITEM "&Circle", CM_CIRCLE
        MENUITEM "&Ellipse", CM_ELLIPSE
    }
    POPUP "&Options"
    {
        MENUITEM "&Fill Color...", CM_FILLC
        MENUITEM "&Border Color...", CM_BORDERC
        MENUITEM SEPARATOR
        MENUITEM "Border &Width...", CM_WIDTH
    }
    POPUP "&Help"
    {
        MENUITEM "&About WinShape...", CM_ABOUT
        MENUITEM SEPARATOR
        MENUITEM "&Using WinShape...", CM_HELP
    }
}
```

Now that we have put all the pieces together, we can have a look at the full source code of the window this application is based on.

```
// file SHAPEWIN.H                                        17/WINSHAPE
// interface of the class ShapeWin,
// the main window of the Shape application

#include <owl\owlpch.h>

// include classes of the shape hierarchy
#include "wshape.h"
#include "wrect.h"
#include "wsquare.h"
#include "wellipse.h"
```

```
#include "wcircle.h"

#include <classlib\arrays.h>

// include resource identifiers
#include "winshape.rh"

class ShapeWin : public TWindow
{

    TIArrayAsVector <Shape> list ;

    Shape * pCurrentShape ;      // actual shape
    int     nElements ;          // total number of elements in the array
    TColor  crPenColor ,         // color of the shape border
            crFillColor ,        // color of the shape interior
            crBackgroundColor;   // color of the background
    int     nPenWidth ;          // width of the shape border
    BOOL    bMouseDown ;         // dragging phase (the mouse button is down)
    BOOL    bShapeSel ;          // a shape has been selected
    TDC *   pdcDragging ;        // device context for the dragging
    TColor  custColors [16] ;    // array of custom colors

public:
    ShapeWin ( ) ;
    Shape* GetShape (int nPos) ;

    void Paint(TDC&, BOOL, TRect&) ;
    void GetWindowClass (WNDCLASS& wc) ;
    char far * GetClassName ( ) ;

    void CmNew ( ) ;
    void CmUndo ( ) ;
    void CmViewInfo ( ) ;
    void CmSquare ( ) ;
    void CmRectangle ( ) ;
    void CmCircle ( ) ;
    void CmEllipse ( ) ;
    void CmFillColor ( ) ;
    void CmBorderColor ( ) ;
    void CmBorderWidth ( ) ;
    void CmAbout ( ) ;
    void CmHelp ( ) ;

    void EvLButtonDown (UINT modKeys, TPoint& point) ;
    void EvMouseMove (UINT modKeys, TPoint& point) ;
```

```
        void EvLButtonUp (UINT modKeys, TPoint& point) ;

        DECLARE_RESPONSE_TABLE (ShapeWin) ;
} ;
```

```
// file SHAPEWIN.CPP                                    17/WINSHAPE
// Member functions definition of class ShapeWin

// include class interface and dialog class
#include "winshape.h"
#include "vidialog.h"

// include specific portion of OWL
#include <owl\dialog.h>
#include <owl\inputdia.h>
#include <owl\chooseco.h>

// include Borland Windows Custom Controls
#include <bwcc.h>

ShapeWin :: ShapeWin ( ) :
    TWindow (0, 0, 0) ,
    list (10, 0, 5) ,                // 10 elements starting from 0
    nElements (0) ,                  // the array is empty
    bShapeSel (FALSE) ,
    bMouseDown (FALSE) ,
    crPenColor (TColor::Black),
    crFillColor (TColor::LtGreen),
    crBackgroundColor (TColor::LtCyan),
    nPenWidth (1)                    // 1 pixel
{
    // initialize the array of custom colors
    // used by the TChooseColorDialog
    for (int i = 0; i < 16; ++i)
        custColors [i] = TColor (i*16, 255-i*16, 0) ;
}

void ShapeWin :: Paint(TDC& PaintDC, BOOL, TRect&)
{
    // repaints all the shapes of the list
    for (int i = 0; i < nElements; i++)
        list[i]->Paint (PaintDC) ;
}

void ShapeWin :: GetWindowClass (WNDCLASS& wc)
{
```

```
   // load cursor, set background
   TWindow :: GetWindowClass (wc) ;
   wc.hCursor = LoadCursor (NULL, IDC_ARROW) ;
   wc.hbrBackground = CreateSolidBrush (crBackgroundColor) ;
}

char far * ShapeWin :: GetClassName ( )
{
   return "ShapeWinClass" ;
}

void ShapeWin :: CmNew ( )
{
   if (nElements > 0 &&  BWCCMessageBox (HWindow, "Delete ALL shapes?",
          "Attention", MB_YESNO I MB_ICONQUESTION) == IDYES)
   {
      list.Flush (TShouldDelete::Delete) ;
      nElements = 0 ;
      Invalidate ( ) ;
   }
}

void ShapeWin :: CmUndo ( )
{
   // delete the last element
   if (nElements > 0 && BWCCMessageBox (HWindow, "Delete last shape",
          "Attention", MB_YESNO I MB_ICONQUESTION) == IDYES)
   {
      list.Destroy (—nElements) ;
      Invalidate ( ) ;
   }
}

void ShapeWin :: CmViewInfo ( )
{
   if (nElements > 0)
   {
      ViewInfoDial dbox (this, &list) ;
      dbox.Execute ( ) ;
   }
   else
      BWCCMessageBox (HWindow, "There is no shape",
         "WinShape", MB_ICONSTOP I MB_OK) ;
}

void ShapeWin :: CmAbout ( )
{
```

```
       // show about message box using BWCC style
       BWCCMessageBox (HWindow, "WinShape by Cantu' and Tendon, \
    from our \"Borland C++ 4.0 Object-Oriented Programming\" Book",
          "About WinShape", MB_OK I MB_ICONINFORMATION ) ;
    }

    void ShapeWin :: CmHelp ( )
    {
       // show the help dialog box
       TDialog  dial  (this, IDD_HELP) ;
       dial.Execute ( ) ;
    }

    // functions to select the different shapes
    void ShapeWin :: CmSquare ( )
    {
       pCurrentShape = new SSquare
          (10, 10, 0, crPenColor, nPenWidth, crFillColor) ;
       bShapeSel = TRUE ;
    }

    void ShapeWin :: CmRectangle ( )
    {
       pCurrentShape = new SRectangle
          (10, 10, 0, 0, crPenColor, nPenWidth, crFillColor) ;
       bShapeSel = TRUE ;
    }

    void ShapeWin :: CmCircle ( )
    {
       pCurrentShape = new SCircle
          (10, 10, 0, crPenColor, nPenWidth, crFillColor) ;
       bShapeSel = TRUE ;
    }

    void ShapeWin :: CmEllipse ( )
    {
       pCurrentShape = new SEllipse
          (10, 10, 0, 0, crPenColor, nPenWidth, crFillColor) ;
       bShapeSel = TRUE ;
    }

    void ShapeWin :: CmFillColor ( )
    {
       // selects the color of the interior of the shape
       TChooseColorDialog::TData ccData ;
```

```
        ccData.Flags = CC_RGBINIT ;
        ccData.Color = crFillColor ;
        ccData.CustColors = custColors ;

        TChooseColorDialog dial (this, ccData) ;
        if (dial.Execute ( ) == IDOK)
            crFillColor = ccData.Color ;

    }

void ShapeWin :: CmBorderColor ( )
{
    // selects the color of the border of the shape
    TChooseColorDialog::TData ccData ;

    ccData.Flags = CC_RGBINIT ;
    ccData.Color = crPenColor ;
    ccData.CustColors = custColors ;

    if (TChooseColorDialog (this, ccData)
            .Execute ( ) == IDOK)
        crPenColor = ccData.Color ;
}

void ShapeWin :: CmBorderWidth ( )
{
    // selects the width of the border, using a TInputDialog
    char  lpszText [5] = "" ;
    int nInputValue ;

    if (TInputDialog (this, "Border of the shapes",
        "Input the new width:", lpszText,
        sizeof(lpszText)).Execute ( ) == IDOK )

        // tries to convert the input value
        if (nInputValue = atoi (lpszText))
            nPenWidth = nInputValue ;

        // if unseccessful shows a message
        else
            BWCCMessageBox (HWindow, "The input value is not valid",
                "Error", MB_OK | MB_ICONHAND) ;
}

void ShapeWin :: EvLButtonDown (UINT, TPoint& point)
{
```

```
        // if a shape has been selected and the dragging
        // is not active, start the dragging phase
        if (!bMouseDown && bShapeSel)
        {
            // set the dragging flag
            bMouseDown = TRUE ;

            // capture mouse input
            SetCapture ( ) ;

            // initialize the device context
            pdcDragging = new TClientDC (*this) ;

            // set the center and attributes of the shape
            pCurrentShape -> MoveTo (point.x, point.y) ;
            pCurrentShape -> BorderCol (crPenColor) ;
            pCurrentShape -> FillCol (crFillColor) ;
        }
    }

    void ShapeWin :: EvMouseMove (UINT, TPoint& point)
    {
        // if a shape is selected changes the cursor to a cross
        if (bShapeSel)
            ::SetCursor (::LoadCursor (NULL, IDC_CROSS));

        // if the dragging flag is on
        if (bMouseDown)
        {
            // compute the bounding rectangle of the old
            // shape and repaint that area of the window
            TRect r = pCurrentShape -> BoundRect ( ) ;

            InvalidateRect (r) ;
            UpdateWindow ( ) ;

            // set the new parameters of the shape
            pCurrentShape -> SetCorner (point.x, point.y) ;

            // repaint the shape
            pCurrentShape -> Paint (*pdcDragging) ;
        }
    }

    void ShapeWin :: EvLButtonUp (UINT, TPoint&)
    {
```

```
        // if the dragging flag is on, end the dragging phase
        if (bMouseDown)
        {
            // unselect the dragging flag
            bMouseDown = FALSE ;

            // release the mouse capture
            ReleaseCapture ( ) ;

            // store the current shape in the array
            list.Add (pCurrentShape) ;
            nElements ++ ;

            // release the device context
            delete pdcDragging ;

            // no shape is selected
            bShapeSel = FALSE ;
        }
    }

DEFINE_RESPONSE_TABLE1 (ShapeWin, TWindow)
    EV_COMMAND (CM_NEW, CmNew) ,
    EV_COMMAND (CM_UNDO, CmUndo) ,
    EV_COMMAND (CM_VIEWINFO, CmViewInfo) ,
    EV_COMMAND (CM_ABOUT, CmAbout) ,
    EV_COMMAND (CM_HELP, CmHelp) ,
    EV_COMMAND (CM_RECTANGLE, CmRectangle) ,
    EV_COMMAND (CM_SQUARE, CmSquare) ,
    EV_COMMAND (CM_CIRCLE, CmCircle) ,
    EV_COMMAND (CM_ELLIPSE, CmEllipse) ,
    EV_COMMAND (CM_FILLC, CmFillColor) ,
    EV_COMMAND (CM_BORDERC, CmBorderColor) ,
    EV_COMMAND (CM_WIDTH, CmBorderWidth) ,
    EV_WM_MOUSEMOVE ,
    EV_WM_LBUTTONDOWN ,
    EV_WM_LBUTTONUP ,
END_RESPONSE_TABLE ;
```

Decorating the Frame Window

We are almost finished with the application. Now we need only the *usual stuff*, a class for the application to create a window inside a frame and a main function. However, since this is our last example, we want to make it somewhat better looking than usual, adding a *toolbar* with a series of graphical buttons corresponding to some of the menu items of the application.

To add a toolbar to the application, we need to use a different kind of frame. Instead of the class *TFrameWindow*, we use *TDecoratedFrame*:

```
TDecoratedFrame* frame =
    new TDecoratedFrame (NULL, "WinShape", new ShapeWin) ;
```

After this step, we have to define a *TControlBar* object, add some *TButtonGadget* objects to it, and insert the toolbar in the frame:

```
TControlBar * cb = new TControlBar (frame) ;
cb -> Insert (*new TButtonGadget (IDB_NEW, CM_NEW)) ;
frame -> Insert (*cb) ;
```

Of course, we need to add not one but a number of gadgets, including some separators of class *TSeparatorGadget* (just for creating some space around the toolbar buttons). For each button gadget the resource file must include a corresponding bitmap definition such as:

```
IDB_NEW      BITMAP "new.bmp"
```

Using these new classes, the application class result is as follows:

```
// file SHAPEAPP.CPP                                    17/WINSHAPE
// Shape application and OwlMain function

#include <owl\applicat.h>
#include <owl\framewin.h>
#include <owl\decframe.h>
#include <owl\controlb.h>
#include <owl\buttonga.h>

#include "winshape.h"

// application class
class ShapeApp : public TApplication
{
public:
    ShapeApp ( ) :
        TApplication ( )
    { }

    virtual void InitMainWindow ( )
    {
```

```
        // define a frame window
        TDecoratedFrame* frame = new TDecoratedFrame
                (NULL, "WinShape", new ShapeWin) ;

        // define a toolbar
        TControlBar * cb = new TControlBar (frame) ;

        // add a number of controls to the toolbar
        cb -> Insert (*new TButtonGadget (IDB_NEW, CM_NEW)) ;
        cb -> Insert (*new TButtonGadget (IDB_UNDO, CM_UNDO)) ;
        cb -> Insert (*new TSeparatorGadget (8)) ;
        cb -> Insert (*new TButtonGadget (IDB_VIEWINFO, CM_VIEWINFO)) ;
        cb -> Insert (*new TSeparatorGadget (8)) ;
        cb -> Insert (*new TButtonGadget (IDB_RECTANGLE, CM_RECTANGLE)) ;
        cb -> Insert (*new TButtonGadget (IDB_SQUARE, CM_SQUARE)) ;
        cb -> Insert (*new TButtonGadget (IDB_ELLIPSE, CM_ELLIPSE)) ;
        cb -> Insert (*new TButtonGadget (IDB_CIRCLE, CM_CIRCLE)) ;
        cb -> Insert (*new TSeparatorGadget (8)) ;
        cb -> Insert (*new TButtonGadget (IDB_HELP, CM_HELP)) ;

        // insert the toolbar in the frame
        frame -> Insert (*cb) ;

        // set the main window adding menu and icon
        SetMainWindow (frame) ;
        GetMainWindow () AssignMenu (IDM_SHAPE) ;
        GetMainWindow () SetIcon (this, IDI_SHAPE) ;
    }
} ;

// main function
int OwlMain (int, char* [ ])
{
    ShapeApp  app ;
    return app.Run ( ) ;
}
```

To compile the whole application, you need a project similar to the one of Figure 17.13, having really a number of files. It is a big project (compared to the other ones in the book), but the final application you obtain (see Figure 17.14) is worth the effort: It (almost) has the look and feel of a a professional application. Consider, however, that you can produce an even better looking application (although with less capabilities) in just a few seconds by using the *AppExpert*. The difference is that we know what we have done.

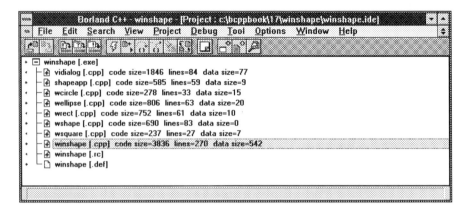

Figure 17.13 The project used to build the *winshape* application

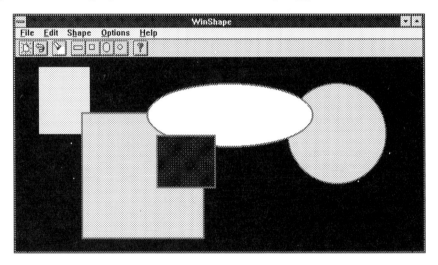

Figure 17.14 The professional-looking *winshape* application

POINTS TO CONSIDER

1. The timer, used in the program to draw Connett's graphs, is the basis for animations. Implement a program with something moving in its main window: a "walking line," a bouncing ball, a moving bitmap, and so on.

2. Rewrite the Connett Program or a similar one (see point 1) using the *Idle* member function of the application class instead of a timer. What are the differences?

3. Add new kinds of shapes, such as triangles or regular polygons.

4. Offer the possibility of changing the parameters of the shapes already stored in the array (their colors, size, position, and so on), adding also the corresponding menu items.

5. Add a real help system to the application using the help compiler. The *Creating Help* help file of the Borland environment has some good suggestions to offer.

Bibliography

Booch, Grady [1986] *Software Engineering with ADA.* (Second Edition) Menlo Park, CA: Benjamin/Cummings.

Booch, Grady [1991] *Object Oriented Design with Applications.* Menlo Park, CA: Benjamin/Cummings.

Brooks, Frederick P., Jr. [1986] "No Silver Bullet." *Computer,* (April), 10-19

Coplien, James [1992] "Advanced C++ Programming Styles and Idioms", Addison-Wesley, 385.

Cox, Brad J. [1987] "There Is a Silver Bullet." *BYTE* (October), 209-218.

Cox, Brad J. [1987] *Object Oriented Programming: An Evolutionary Approach.* Reading, MA: Addison-Wesley.

Crespi, Stefano Reghizzi [1990] "Sintassi, Semantica e Tecniche di compilazione," (Volume 3), *Masson.*

Deutsch, Peter L. and Goldberg, Adele [1991] "Smalltalk: Yesterday, Today, and Tomorrow." BYTE (August), 108.

Dlugosz, John M. [1990] "Debugging in C++." *Computer Language* (February), 33-41.

Duff, Chuck and Howard, Bob [1990] "Migration Patterns." *BYTE* (October), 223-232.

Eckel, Bruce [1989] *Using C++.* Berkeley, CA: McGraw-Hill.

Eckel, Bruce [1991] "Introduction to Windows Programming in Borland C++." A presentation for the second OOP World Tour, featuring C++ and Object Windows (May).

Gates, Bill [1990] "The BYTE Summit: Future Programming." *BYTE* (September), 335-340.

Ghezzi, Carlo, and Jazayeri, Mehdi [1987] *Programming Language Concepts.* (Second Edition) New York, NY: John Wiley & Sons.

Goldberg, Adele and Robson, David [1983] *Smalltalk-80: The Language and its Implementation.* Reading, MA: Addison-Wesley.

Hansen, Tony L. [1990] *The C++ Answer Book.* Reading, MA: Addison-Wesley.

Jossman, Paul R., Schiebel, Edward N., and Shank, Jere C. [1990] "Climbing the C++ Learning Curve." *Proceedings of USENIX C++ Conference*, San Francisco (April).

Lippman, Stanley B. [1989] *C++ Primer*. Reading, MA: Addison-Wesley.

Mansell, David [1992] "Designing Portable C++ Class Libraries." *BYTE* (March).

Meyer, Bertrand [1988] *Object-Oriented Software Construction*. Englewood Cliffs, NJ: Prentice-Hall.

Meyer, Bertrand [1989] "Writing Correct Software." *Dr. Dobb's Journal* (December).

Parnas, David [1972] "On the Criteria to Be Used in Decomposing Systems into Modules." *Communications of the ACM* (December), 1053-1058.

Ramamoorthy, C.V., et al. [1984] "Software Engineering: Problems and Perspectives," *IEE Computer*, (October), 191-209.

Schmidt, Heinz W. [1984] "Software Engineering: Problems and Perspectives." *IEE Computer*, (October).

Schmidt, Heinz W. and Stephen N. Omhofundro [1991] "CLOS, Eiffel and Sather: A Comparision." International Computer Science Institute, Berkeley, CA (September).

Stroustrup, Bjarne [1986] *The C++ Programming Language*. (First Edition) Reading, MA: Addison-Wesley.

Stroustrup, Bjarne [1988] "A Better C?" *BYTE* (August), 215-216.

Stroustrup, Bjarne, and Ellis, Margaret A. [1990] *The Annotated C++ Reference Manual*. Reading, MA: Addison-Wesley.

Stroustrup, Bjarne [1991] *The C++ Programming Language*. (Second Edition) Reading, MA: Addison-Wesley.

Stroustrup, Bjarne [1991] "Interview with Bjarne Stroustrup." *C++ Journal* (Volume I, Number 3), 16-25.

Stroustrup, Bjarne [1993] "Library Design Using C++." *C++ Report* (Volume V, Number 5), 18.

Urlocker, Zack [1989] "A Methodology for the Real World." *Computer Language*, (January), 47-58.

Wegner, Peter [1984] "Capital-Intensive Software Technology." *IEE Software* (July), 7-45.

Wegner, Peter [1987] "Dimensions of Object-Based Language Design." Special issue of *SIGPLAN Notices*.

Wirth, Niklaus [1976] *Algorithms + Data Structures = Programs*. Englewood Cliffs, NJ: Prentice-Hall.

Wulf, Yeh, R.T., et al. [1977] *Software Specification and Design* Volume I. *Current Trends in Programming Methodology*. Englewood Cliffs, NJ: Prentice-Hall.

Yourdon, Ed. [1990] "The BYTE Summit: Future Programming." *BYTE* (September).

Index

W